A CRITICAL INTRODUCTION TO
MODERN ARABIC POETRY

Also by M. M. Badawi

Coleridge: Critic of Shakespeare
An Anthology of Modern Arabic Verse
Yahya Haqqi's The Saint's Lamp and Other Stories: a translation with an Introduction
Rasā'il min London (Poems)
Coleridge fi Silsilat Nawābigh al-Fikr al-Gharbi
Dirāsāt fi'l Shi'r wa'l Masraḥ

A critical introduction to

MODERN ARABIC POETRY

M. M. BADAWI

Fellow of St Antony's College, Oxford

CAMBRIDGE UNIVERSITY PRESS

CAMBRIDGE

LONDON · NEW YORK · MELBOURNE

Published by the Syndics of the Cambridge University Press
The Pitt Building, Trumpington Street, Cambridge CB2 1RP
Bentley House, 200 Euston Road, London NW1 2DB
32 East 57th Street, New York, N.Y. 10022
296 Beaconsfield Parade, Middle Park, Melbourne 3206, Australia

Library of Congress Catalogue Card Number: 75-9279

ISBN: 0 521 20699 5 hard covers

ISBN: 0 521 29023 6 paperback

First published 1975

Photoset and printed in Malta by St. Paul's Press Ltd

For Mieke

CONTENTS

PREFACE

This survey of modern Arabic poetry is based on lectures delivered at different times at the University of Oxford. It is not a full history but a critical introduction to the study of the subject. In it I have not included every modern Arabic poet of note. To do so would require a book several times the size of this volume. Given the limitations of space, then, instead of providing an indiscriminate list of names, I have chosen to deal, in a relatively discursive manner, with the works of a few selected poets, who seem to me either to have intrinsic importance or to represent new departures to an extent that justifies separate treatment. Since the criteria of such a choice are, from the very nature of things, indissolubly bound up with personal judgment or subjective experience, I am aware that there must be a few names who, in the opinion of some, should have been included. This, however, is unavoidable. But, I repeat, if I have not discussed the work of a poet in this book it is no indication that I consider his or her work to be devoid of literary merit. The reader will soon realize that for lack of space I have not been able to discuss *all* the poets whom I regarded as sufficiently interesting to merit inclusion in my *Anthology of Modern Arabic Verse* (Oxford, 1970). And there are many more poets of all categories whose work I would wish to include in my Anthology if I was compiling it now.

I am also fully aware that my attempt to trace a pattern in modern Arabic poetry is fraught with dangers. All such attempts, of necessity, involve a certain degree of simplification, and, therefore, of distortion. My excuse is that the impulse to reduce the flux and multiplicity of phenomena to some sort of intelligible order seems to answer a basic need in the human mind. When Professor Gibb wrote in the late 1920s about modern Arabic literature (in his admirable articles, collected later in *Studies on the Civilization of Islam*, 1962) he seemed to find that two labels alone could serve his purpose:

'modernists' and 'classicists'. The situation has changed considerably since then, and under the heading 'modernists' a variety of brands appeared, that seemed to cry out for special designation – although I hardly need to remind the reader that labels are useful pointers only as long as we bear in mind that no living man can be reduced to a mere label.

St Antony's College, Oxford M. M. B.
June 1974

A note on transliteration and verse translations

For ease of reading and cost economy diacritical marks and marks indicating vowel lengthening are used on the first occurrence only of personal, place or technical names. On subsequent mentions the same spelling is used but the marks are simply omitted. The only exceptions to this rule are the *first* occurrence of a poet's name in the section devoted to a discussion of his work, the Notes and the Index in which will be given the fully transliterated forms of all names.

All verse translations used in this book are the author's own work.

Introductory

1

Not long after its appearance on the English stage in 1956, John Osborne's play *Look Back in Anger* was translated into Arabic and produced on the Egyptian radio. In Cairo during recent drama seasons the repertoire of the various local theatrical companies included Arabic translations of plays by authors ranging from Shakespeare, Chekhov, Sartre and Arthur Miller, to Dürrenmatt, Ionesco and Samuel Beckett. Arabic plays modelled on the theatre of the absurd have been attempted not only by the young *avant-garde*, but also by a veteran of the Arabic theatre like the Egyptian Taufīq al-Ḥakīm. In short, a cursory look at the modern Arabic theatre, as it is reflected in Cairo, is sufficient to show how open to foreign, and specifically western, influences modern Arabic culture is at present. This is clearly seen in other branches of literature as well. For instance, there is already at least one translation of Pasternak's novel *Dr Zhivago*. Most of the work of Sartre and Camus is available in Arabic. The Lebanese poetry quarterly *Shi'r* (1957–69) published together with its experimental original poetry, translations of works by established French and English poets, often side by side with original texts, even works (for instance, by John Wain) which had not yet appeared in their authors' native countries. One of the regular features of some Arabic literary reviews, like the Lebanese monthly *al-Ādāb* (1953–), was for a long time a letter from each of the main capitals of the western world, giving a summary of the main literary and cultural events there. The Cairo monthly *al-Majalla* (1957–71) devoted much space to full reviews of western publications, and it is not surprising to find on the pages of the Cairo newspaper *al-Ahrām* a discussion of the French anti-novel or a translation of a poem by Mayakovsky or Yevtushenko.

Of course, this contact with foreign culture has not always been a feature of the Arab world: in fact the present situation forms a glaring contrast to the state of Arabic culture just over a century ago. Today no serious Arabic author can afford to be unaware of what goes on in the literary and cultural scene in the West. (In fact the most significant authors in modern Arabic literature have, almost without exception, been directly or indirectly exposed to western cultural influences.) On the other hand, one can safely say that until the first third of the nineteenth century Arabic poets and prose writers and their reading public were alike utterly ignorant of what was happening outside the ever narrowing circle of Arabic letters. The healthy curiosity which marked the golden age of Arab culture and which rendered it susceptible to the enriching foreign influence of the Greeks and the Persians had long disappeared, and the Arab's pride in his cultural achievement had by the eighteenth century hardened into a sterile feeling of complacency and self-sufficiency. The vitality had given place to stagnation and isolationism. This was particularly noticeable in the case of poetry, because of the extraordinary degree to which Arabic poetry tended to adhere to conventions.

2

For the sake of convenience Arabic poetry is usually divided into the following stages: Pre-Islamic (500–622), Early Islamic and Umayyad, from the rise of Islam to the fall of the Umayyad dynasty (622–750), Abbasid (750–1258); the Age of the Mamluks (1258–1516) and of the Ottomans (1516–1798) and finally the Modern Period (1798–). If we follow the Greek formal classification of poetry we have to describe pre-Islamic poetry as lyrical as opposed to narrative or dramatic verse. But because in it the poet is almost constantly aware of the presence of an audience, chiefly his tribe, it is social rather than individualistic verse. Moreover, although it has no epic it possesses some epic qualities in both stylistic and thematic terms. It is the poetry of an heroic tribal society revealing an heroic scheme of values. Man in tribal grouping, faced with the stark realities of life and death in the inhospitable desert, has evolved the values necessary for survival: great physical courage and boundless hospitality. However, the keen awareness of death, of the fleeting and transitory nature of things, expressed in many an elegy and elegiac poem, is generally accompanied not so much by the somewhat constricting thought that 'ever the latter end of joy is woe' as by an equally keen impulse to pack into the short span of life allotted to man some earthly pleasures: love, wine, gambling, riding and hunting – provided that in the pursuit of such pleasures one's honour and the honour of the tribe remain untainted.

These themes are dealt with in poems written in a variety of highly complex and sophisticated metres, each poem adhering to one metre and one rhyme throughout – a clear evidence of the importance of sound patterns in Arabic poetry, which also explains why long Arabic poems are considerably shorter than long European ones. Each line of verse (roughly of the same length as an English couplet) is divided into two halves of equal metrical value, generally both rhyming only in the opening of the poem, especially in what is known as *qaṣīda*, which is translated as Ode. The *qasida*, unlike the fragment *qiṭ'a*, is a poem of some length and often of a particular structure. The general pattern, exemplified especially in many of those odes regarded as the finest achievements of pre-Islamic Arabia, *al-Mu'allaqāt*, once translated as the Golden Odes, is for a poet to start with an amatory preamble called *nasīb*, described aptly as an elegiac reminiscence of love in which the poet expresses his gloomy and nostalgic meditations over the ruins of the desert encampment of the beloved. In an attempt to forget her and his suffering he goes on a journey in the desert on the back of his she-camel, the excellence of which as well as various aspects of desert life he proceeds to describe in loving detail. The poet concludes his poem either by praising himself or his tribe, by satirizing a personal or tribal foe, or by eulogizing a patron.

In pre-Islamic Arabia the formal foundations of Arabic poetry were securely laid. From the points of view of prosody and versification practically everything goes back to that early time: the well-known sixteen metres with their elaborate structure, the absence of rhymeless verse, the use of monorhyme in the serious poem and of *rajaz* (a vaguely iambic kind of metre) with its rhyming couplets for less weighty themes. There were a few formal innovations later on, in particular the emergence in Muslim Spain in the eleventh century of a complex type of strophic or stanzaic poetry known as *muwashshaḥ*, but these were on the whole of a subsidiary character. Thematically too, the convention of the amatory prelude, together with the use of desert imagery, was followed by most poets, sometimes with a surprising degree of irrelevance, right down to the first decade of the twentieth century. The principal 'genres' or 'topics' (*aghrāḍ*) which Arab critics subsequently regarded as comprising the domain of Arabic poetry are all there in some form or another in the pre-Islamic period: they are self-praise (*fakhr*), panegyric (*madīḥ*), satire (*hijā'*), elegy (*rithā'*), description (*waṣf*) and amatory verse (*ghazal*). The only possible exception was religious or ascetic verse (*zuhd*), although there is plenty of moralization and gnomic verse in the work of the pre-Islamic Zuhair.

With the advent of Islam little change was immediately noticeable. Just as in early Christian Anglo-Saxon poetry Christ and his disciples were conceived of and described in terms of the pagan lord and his comitatus of thanes, so Muhammad, perhaps with lesser incongruity, was painted by his eulogists as a warrior in the old heroic manner. The main development after the establishment of the new religion is the appearance of a new type of love poetry which, however sensuous it might be, was not entirely free from a tendency towards idealization or emotionalism. A group of poets became associated with a type of love sentiment, in many ways a prototype of the medieval European courtly love known as *al-hawā al 'Udhrī* (after the tribe of Udhra). These were Kuthayyir, Jamīl, Ghailān and Majnūn (the Mad One) and their names became coupled in medieval literary accounts with the names of the women they loved, namely 'Azza, Buthaina, Mayya and Laila, respectively, and one of them, Majnun, became the subject of many attractive legends and in modern times, of verse drama. In their work the lovelorn poet is usually found complaining of his desperate passion for an idealized woman who is placed beyond his reach, but to whom he is eternally faithful. Out of this grew a powerful tradition of love poetry in which the poet presents a stock situation, with himself and his beloved in the foreground and in the background 'the confidant, the messenger, the spy, the slanderer, the reproacher'. As Professor Arberry points out, a body of conventional themes was developed particularly in Abbasid poetry.[1] For instance, the lovers weep tears of blood, the poet is confronted by the double perils of fire (from his burning heart) and flood (from his brimming tears); the flashing teeth of the beloved are compared with lightning, the beloved's glances with arrows or sword blades piercing the lover's heart; her lips intoxicating or healing the lover with their saliva; the lover is said to be wasted by grief to such a point that he vanishes. Similar themes and hyperboles will no doubt be recalled by readers familiar with Elizabethan conventional love poetry. In Muslim Spain, particularly in the poetry of Ibn Zaidūn in the eleventh century many of the elements of courtly love are most conspicuous and often blended with an exquisite feeling for nature.

But for purposes of what was considered serious poetry the *qasida* with its monorhyme, monometre, its amatory prelude and desert imagery remained the ideal which poets tried to emulate. For better or for worse, the early Umayyad poets set the example for later poets: they imitated the pre-Islamic models and were excessively concerned with the eulogy of their patrons. From now on panegyric occupied a disproportionately large place in the output of poets, and every ruler or governor of note saw to it there were one or more poets in his court whose main task it was to celebrate his achievement and immortalize his name. There were of course a few dissident voices who, with the spread of the empire and the vast increase in sophistication and civilized urban living under the Abbasids, saw the absurd irrelevances of pre-Islamic poetic conventions to modern life. For instance, the bucolic poet Abū Nuwās suggested a prelude in praise of wine instead of the practice of opening a poem with mourning over deserted encampments. But the reaction against the conventions was only half-hearted and Abu Nuwas himself followed the traditional practice in many of his works. Many reasons, literary, cultural and sociological, have been suggested for the dominance of these conventions, such as the general tendency in the Arab mind to revere the past, the tyrannical rule of conservative philologists in matters of taste and the unconscious association of the early poetry with the language of the Koran. Whatever be the real cause the underlying assumption was that the store of ideas or themes is limited, and the result was that poets became inordinately interested in style and form. In a tradition in which sound and rhythm already played an important part, to pay any more attention to form and style was inevitably a constricting factor; it also meant that the job of the translator from Arabic poetry is rendered doubly difficult. However, for many centuries to come, the guiding principle of the poet was to write 'what oft was thought, but ne'er so well expressed'. This had a positive result at least in the field of literary criticism, for in their analysis of style and the language of poetry, particularly metaphor and imagery, some of the medieval Arab critics reached conclusions of surprising subtlety and modernity in which the work of critics like I. A. Richards was fully anticipated eight or nine centuries ago. But in creative writing the poets' preoccupation with the minutiae of style manifested itself in the rise of the so-called *badī'* school of writing. The word *badi'* literally means 'new', but it was used to refer to a highly figurative and ornate poetic style in which modern poets tried to assert their individuality and originality in the face of the opposition of the upholders of the ancients. Another result is the dominance of the conception of the poet, not as a seer or a mouthpiece of the tribe, but as a craftsman, a jeweller whose medium is words. This, of course, lessened, but by no means destroyed, the scope of the poet's originality and self-expression. Nor did the good poets produce mechanical imitations of the old ode. Nevertheless the *qasida*, that impressive edifice of words relying on declamation and sonority of music, with or without the amatory prelude depending on the gravity of the occasion, was the ceremonious form of poetic expression. At the hands of giants like Abū Tammām (805–45) and Mutanabbī (915–65) the style of the *qasida* became the grand or heroic style *par excellence*. In their description of the military victories of their patrons over the leaders of Christendom they were celebrating not petty tribal quarrels or feuds, but themes of such magnitude that the grand manner seemed the only appropriate style that could be used. Strangely enough it was one of the most ardent admirers of Mutanabbi who managed to a large extent to break free from many of the conventions. The blind Syrian poet Abu'l 'Alā' al-Ma'arrī (973–1058) prided himself on not having written panegyrics for patrons, or 'sought to embellish my verse by means of fiction or fill my pages with love-idylls, battle-scenes, descriptions of wine-parties and the like. My aim is to speak the truth'.[2] Instead of the traditional ode he recorded his meditations on life, death, on human society and beliefs in poems of varying length, sometimes of as few as two or three lines. His rationalism and scepticism, his pessimistic cast of mind, his intellectual honesty and his metaphysical doubts and uncertainty no less than his rejection of many conventions have made him popular with many modern poets, as we shall see in the course of this book.

Of the other significant developments in Arabic poetry which came as a result of the spread of the Muslim Empire and the widening of the mental and geographical horizon of the Arabs, two ought to be mentioned: first, the descriptive genre, in particular the bucolic and the hunting verse of poets like Abu Nuwas, and the type of nature poetry which went beyond the confines of desert landscape and which appeared especially in Muslim Spain, Sicily and North Africa. The second development is the appearance of mystical verse which reached its zenith in the work of the Egyptian poet Ibn al-Fāriḍ (1182–1235) and the Andalusian Ibn al-ʿArabī (1165–1240). In the age of the Mamluks and the Ottomans the poets' preoccupation with form and expression, their passion for verbal ingenuity increased to the extent that poetry gradually descended to the level of mere artifice and verbal acrobatics, and ceased to have a bearing upon the serious business of life.

3

Literary historians are agreed that the Ottoman period of Arabic literature, the period, that is, which begins with the Ottoman conquest of Syria (1516) and Egypt (1517) and is conveniently thought to end with Napoleon's expedition to Egypt (in 1798), marks in fact the nadir of Arab culture. Of course it was not (not even in its latter part) a period of utter darkness as popular handbooks sometimes lead us to believe, and scholars like Gibb and Bowen are no doubt right when they insist that 'to deny all significance or value . . . to the Arabic literature of the eighteenth century is unjustifiable'. But even Gibb and Bowen admit that the literature 'confirms the general impression of a society which had exhausted its own resources'.[3] The recovery of Arabic letters, the movement generally known in Arabic as *al-Nahḍa* and sometimes *al-Inbiʿāth*, meaning Renaissance, began to be felt first in the Lebanon, Syria and Egypt and from there it spread gradually and in varying degrees to the rest of the Arab world.

In the eighteenth century these countries were still provinces of a declining Ottoman empire, that had lapsed into virtual isolation from intellectual movements in the west. The Arab provinces lived in a state of even greater cultural isolation. At the same time the political instability from which they suffered; the narrowness of the prevalent system of education which was chiefly theocentric in character and which did not encourage much initiative and originality; the lack of patronage as a result of the relegation of Arab lands to the position of provinces governed by Turks untutored in the Arabic tongue; the replacement of Arabic by Turkish as the official language; the scarcity and high cost of books owing to the absence of Arabic printing presses (for the purpose of printing Muslim and Arabic literature); the constant living on the cultural past, and not on what was best in that past, for that matter – all these factors resulted in the degeneration of the literature of the period, which remained basically medieval in outlook and tended to be slavishly imitative of the past.

Most of the Arabic poetry of the eighteenth century is bedevilled by the passion for verbal jugglery, the aim of the poets apparently being to impress their audience with their command of the language, with their ability to manipulate it with acrobatic effects. They vied with one another in imposing the most ludicrous limitations and constraints upon themselves, such as writing verses in which every word alliterates, or in which a word begins with the same letter as that with which the preceding one ends, or in which every word or every letter, or every other letter must be dotted. Sometimes poets would pride themselves on writing panegyrical verses which if read backwards would have a completely opposite, satirical significance.[4] The same essential lack of seriousness is found in the pursuit of *badi'*, empty figures of speech for their own sake, just as it is reflected in the preponderance of verse written on trivial social occasions in which greetings and compliments are exchanged by the poets or versifiers, and of which the theme is mutual admiration, and the phraseology is 'gaudy and inane', to borrow the famous epithets used by Wordsworth in his adverse criticism of the poetic diction of some of the bad English verse of the eighteenth century.

As a rule the subjects of the poems were traditional, limited largely to panegyric and *ghazal* (amatory verse), mystical, devotional and didactic verse, descriptive and bucolic verse, especially in the case of the circle of Amir Riḍwān (one of the few real patrons of literature in Egypt) which often wrote exaggerated descriptions of the sensuous pleasures available at his court, from wine-drinking to merry-making in the gardens of his richly decorated palaces. These descriptions were written by poets whose eyes were rarely fixed on their subject but, as in the case of the other themes, they abound in conventional images. For instance, the beloved always appeared like a gazelle, her figure swaying like a willow tree or branch, her face like a full moon, her eyes languid and sending forth fatal arrows which pierce through men's hearts, her lips like red beads, teeth like pearls, cheeks like roses and breasts like pomegranates. She is always coy and unwilling and the poet is desperately lovelorn and so on. From this generalization one may possibly except some of the work of the two mystics, the Egyptian Ḥasan Badrī al-Hijāzī (d. 1718), and the Syrian 'Abdul Ghanī al-Nabulsī (d. 1731). The former was capable of writing verse of biting social criticism best seen in his satirical poem on the ancient religious university of al-Azhar, which contains a vivid picture of the ways of some of the corrupt ulema and which deserves a better fate than to be buried in the pages of the historian al-Jabartī.[5] Likewise Nabulsi wrote some interesting poetry in which he managed to convey the warmth and the paradoxical nature of the mystical experience. His collection of verse *Dīwān al-Ḥaqā'iq* (Truths) was found sufficiently appealing to merit publication in Cairo in 1890.

4

Although it can safely be said that in the eighteenth century the Muslim Arabs lived in complete cultural isolation, a thin trickle of western thought of an exclusively religious nature had begun to work its way through a very small section of the non-Muslim Arabs. The graduates of the Maronite College (set up by Pope Gregory XIII in Rome in 1584) included many distinguished scholars who occupied academic posts in the West, but these belong properly to the history of Arabic scholarship and orientalism rather than to the history of the development of modern Arabic literature. Of more relevance is the career of Germānus Farḥāt (1670–1732), who besides being acquainted with western theological culture and Latin and Italian was passionately interested in creative Arabic literature. His collected poems were published in the form of a *Diwan* more than once in Beirut. As a poet, even in the opinion of an enthusiast like the eminent Lebanese critic Mārūn 'Abbūd, Farḥāt was easily excelled by many of his Muslim contemporaries, who were better masters of the Arabic language.[6] His verses tended to be rather turgid, he wrote poetry which was heavily moralistic and the devotional part of it, the poems written in praise of Christ and the Virgin Mary, betrays the strong influence of contemporary Muslim Sufi poetry. His real contribution consists in his bringing a serious concern for Arabic eloquence and good style into the religious circles of the Maronites who were not noted for their mastery of the Arabic language. Besides setting up relatively modern schools in the Lebanon the Maronite priests were also responsible for the introduction in the beginning of the eighteenth century of the first Arabic printing press in the Arab world, which was set up in Aleppo in 1706. Other presses followed in Syria and the Lebanon. However, because most, if not all the works printed in Syria were for a long time Christian texts, the Syrian Arabic press did not contribute directly to the development of Arabic literature until well into the nineteenth century. Egypt, the other country to play a decisive role in the *Nahda* movement, had to wait nearly a century for its first Arabic press, introduced by the Napoleonic expedition.

Historians generally regard the expedition as a turning point in the history of Egypt. The mere fact that Napoleon's troops were able to conquer the Muslim Mamluks, to say nothing of the ease with which the expedition was effected, and to which al-Jabarti drew attention more than once, was enough to shock the Muslims out of their complacency and groundless feeling of superiority. From now on the Arab world was denied the dubious luxury of living in isolation. This bloody and rude contact between the modern west and the Arabs had far-reaching consequences. Not the least of these is the appearance on the scene of Muḥammad Ali, the founder of the dynasty that ruled Egypt until the Egyptian Revolution in 1952. Muhammad Ali, the uneducated Albanian soldier who came with the Ottoman forces to help drive out the French, but remained behind and managed by opportunism and intrigue to become the sole ruler of Egypt, had direct experience of the efficiency and good organization of the French forces. He set out with single-minded determination to build up a large army modelled on the modern armies of the west. To achieve that he had to import western technicians, western scientists and western forms of education, and to send local Arabs to the west to learn and apply the secret of its military supremacy. While the members of these missions were pursuing their studies abroad Muhammad Ali experimented with new schools at home. From 1816 onwards he set up a large number of modern schools, both military and technological, in which European languages were taught, together with modern sciences, and where some of the teachers were Italian and French and later English. In so doing he superimposed upon the country a whole educational system which was western in character and which had very little in common with the traditional religious Azhar system.[7]

Yet despite their many serious drawbacks the educational innovations of Muhammad Ali proved to be of crucial importance in the development of modern Arabic culture. Without them many later developments would not have been possible. It is in this period that the most dramatic break with the past began to take place, a break which Muhammad Ali himself did not intend and could not forsee. It was not easy to keep interest in western technology entirely separate from interest in some of the cultural values connected with that technology. At the same time the setting up of a new and different system of education which soon produced men destined to occupy important posts in the government could only lead in the long run to the weakening of the authority of traditional values. Arab Muslim society ceased to be the 'closed' culture it had been for so long and western culture and western languages were to play an ever-increasing role in the cultural make-up of the Arab world. Moreover, because secular education did not grow by a process of natural development out of the indigenous traditional system of al-Azhar, but was rather imposed upon it from above, a dichotomy or polarity of education ensued with grave psychological consequences still visible even today.

Among the innovations of Muhammad Ali in the sphere of education there are two items which deserve to be singled out because of their direct relevance to this study. These are the use of the Arabic printing press (originally in order to provide the necessary text books for his new schools) and the establishment of the Cairo School of Languages (where French, English and Italian were taught), and the movement of translation to which this school gave rise. At the beginning of the movement translators were not very well versed in the subjects they were translating, nor was their command of Arabic very great. Hence arose the need for editing and correction.[8] The importance of the part played by these translators, editors and correctors in the development of the language cannot be exaggerated. It is the translation of scientific works, together with journalism, that in the course of time helped to rid modern Arabic prose (and ultimately poetry) of the excessive preoccupation with *badīʿ* and other forms of verbal ingenuity. Under the enlightened direction of Rifāʿa al-Ṭahṭāwī, whom Muhammad Ali appointed as director of the School of Languages in 1836, the School produced a large number of distinguished translators and writers.

Whatever we may think of his intentions, in encouraging Arabic translation Muhammad Ali started a process which, in fact, is still gathering momentum to this day. In importance and in size the modern Arabic movement of translation is no less impressive than its famous counterpart in the ninth century under the Abbasids. Although in the beginning the books translated were of an almost exclusively technological and military nature, in the course of time we notice an appreciable increase in the percentage of literary works. Under Ismaʿil the number of literary and historical books rose to one fourth of the total works translated, and during the last two decades of the nineteenth century literary works alone formed no less than one third of the total output of translations.[9] As the century drew to its close the realization of the vital importance of translation was so keen that some of the best minds in Egypt and the Lebanon were engaged in it. This marked the beginning of a conscious movement that aimed at providing reliable and accurate Arabic versions of literary and cultural works, a movement in which most of the great Arabic authors of the twentieth century took an active part. The effect of Arabic translations of western poetry on the development of modern Arabic poetry from the rise of romanticism to the present day has been enormous. This can be seen not only in the choice of themes and attitudes but also in the diction and the very language used.[10]

Another important factor in the process of westernization which helped to shape the course of modern Arabic literature and thought is the increase in the number of Europeans residing in Egypt (as a result of Muhammad Ali's encouragement) and consequently the increase of missionary activity and the spread of European schools. Even more significant in the subsequent development of Arabic culture was the role played by European schools in Syria. In this respect, because of Muhammad Ali's liberal policy towards the Europeans, the decade of Egyptian occupation of Syria (1831–40) was of major importance and has been described by one historian as 'epoch making in the cultural history of that land'.[11] Missionary activities by the Jesuits and the British and American Protestants were suddenly intensified and various educational institutions were established which determined the course of Arabic culture in Syria and the Lebanon. There was strong competition between the Jesuits and the American Protestants in this area. After the Lebanon achieved independence in 1860 as a result of the influence of western governments, European (and Russian) educational institutions were set up on a wider scale still, and these included schools for girls. The Americans, who had started a college in 1847, founded the American College in 1866 in Beirut, to which the Jesuit College was transferred in 1874. The graduates of these institutions played a formative role in the movement of westernization in Arabic literature. The Lebanese and Syrian cultural revival revealed itself in a number of ways. The first attempts at writing Arabic drama and the Arabic novel were made in Beirut, the former by Mārūn al-Naqqāsh in 1847 and the latter by Salīm al-Bustāni in 1870. Literary societies began to appear in Beirut in 1847, the first being the Syrian Society which, inspired by the American missionaries, aimed at promoting the cause of arts and sciences among Arabic-speaking people, and included among its members distinguished men like the American missionary, physician and scientist-orientalist Dr Van Dyck, and authors like Buṭrus al-Bustāni and Nāṣīf al-Yāzijī. Periodicals appeared in rapid succession and some of them published translations and adaptations of works of fiction (together with original works). The well-known cultural review *al-Muqtaṭaf* which gave the Arab reader much information about the intellectual life of the West[12] was brought out in Beirut by Ya'qūb Ṣarrūf and Fāris Nimr in 1876, and it transferred to Egypt only in 1885, where it continued to appear until 1952. When religious and political disturbances broke out in Syria after the forced departure of Muhammad Ali's Egyptian forces, a process which culminated in the massacres of 1860, many Syrians later emigrated to Egypt, either for fear of future massacres or attracted by prospects of material gain during the British occupation. The result was that they played an active part in the Arabic cultural renaissance, especially through their activities in the field of journalism.[13] Still later generations emigrated to America and were to contribute one of the most interesting chapters in modern Arabic poetry.

The coming of Syrian immigrants to Egypt coincided with the various cultural and educational schemes launched by Khedive Isma'il. The age of Isma'il is in many ways of crucial importance in the history of Arabic culture in Egypt. Towards the end of his life Muhammad Ali lost interest in education, which was also neglected by his successors 'Abbas Pasha (1849–54) and Sa'id Pasha (1854–63). But Isma'il (1863–79), who was educated in France, promoted the cause of modern Arabic learning and culture, and particularly the cause of popular education. He may have been a vain man and a foolish administrator, but whatever were his motives his policy in the field of education was enlightened, even though in other fields it eventually led the country to financial ruin and ultimately to political disaster. During his reign the direction which Arabic culture was to take was defined once and for all, and westernization was assured. Over a hundred European schools were opened in Egypt, and the number of Europeans residing in the country grew larger than ever before.

One of the contributions of Isma'il in the field of culture was the establishment in 1872 of the first Teachers' Training College, the syllabus of which combined traditional Arabic culture with western learning (taught in Arabic). The College was to play a significant role in the revival of the serious study of Arabic literature. Its establishment coincided with the appearance of the influential religious leader, Jamāl al-Dīn al-Afghānī (1839–97) on the Egyptian cultural scene, and the growing importance of his disciple, the Azhar reformer Muḥammad 'Abduh, who together with his followers tried not only to liberate Islam from the stranglehold of centuries of traditions and to reconcile it with modernism but also to reform the Arabic language by making it a fit instrument for expressing modern needs. It was also at that time that Egyptian journalism took a major step forward – it was in newspapers and periodicals that poets published their work and reached society at large. Another significant development in the reign of Isma'il was the growing importance of the position of the Arabic language, which ousted Turkish as the official language of the country. Isma'il ordered that all Ottoman laws passed since Muhammad Ali should be translated into Arabic. He also gave financial help to Butrus al-Bustani to produce the first modern encyclopaedia in Arabic.

As a result of the spread of modern education in Egypt various literary and scientific societies began to appear (for instance, *Jam'iyyat al-Ma'ārif*, which was established in 1868 for the purpose of facilitating the publication of literary and cultural works, especially ancient Arabic texts). Furthermore in 1870, apparently in response to Isma'il's wishes, 'Ali Mubārak set up the Khedivial library, later to be known as *Dār al-Kutub*, the present national library, where most of the holdings of the various mosques and *madrasas* were transferred. He also encouraged, for a while, the nascent Arabic theatre and allowed productions of some Arabic plays (for example, by the Egyptian dramatist Ya'qūb Ṣannū' whom he called the Molière of Egypt) in the Cairo Opera House, which he had built (in 1869) as part of the celebrations of the opening of the Suez Canal. Isma'il was indeed intent on impressing the West by seeking to make Egypt look as much as possible like a western state.

Very often, of course, westernization was only skin-deep and did not touch the very roots of cultural life. But as we have seen in the sphere of education (and this was paralleled in legal, political and social spheres), many institutions were drastically changed in an attempt to make them follow western patterns. Furthermore, the political influence of the West was growing very fast indeed, culminating in the British occupation of Egypt not long after Isma'il's reign and resulting in the speedy emergence of nationalism. The cultural penetration of the West in certain areas of life was felt to be so deep and alarming that those who were seriously concerned about the native cultural heritage reacted in one of two ways: they either endeavoured to combat it fiercely, using every possible means at their command, or else they tried, sometimes ingeniously, to reconcile it with that heritage. At any rate they felt they could no longer view it with indifference. The ignorance of the West and western cultural values which reigned supreme in the Arab world of the eighteenth century had now given place both in Egypt and in Syria to an almost obsessional preoccupation with these values. On the whole, it can be said that during Isma'il's reign Arabic culture in Egypt reached a stage at which it became involved in a conscious and dynamic conflict with the culture of the West. Out of this conflict between East and West modern Arabic literature was born.

2

Neoclassicism

Arabic literature was slow to react to the changes that were taking place in the Arab world in the nineteenth century. The adoption of western literary modes came much later than that of western technology or even of western thought. And although contemporary Arabic poetry betrays a high degree of westernization, bearing little relation to the traditional Arabic ode or *qasida*, of all the branches of Arabic literature poetry was the last to come under western influence. This is not at all surprising. Poetry is the subtlest and most complex form of literature, and its appreciation therefore presents peculiar problems to the foreign reader. It requires not only an intimate and living knowledge of the language, but also a complete readjustment or re-education of the reader's sensibility. Moreover, the Arabs have always prided themselves on their poetry, which they regarded as their greatest and most congenial mode of literary expression. For a long time they could not conceive of any terms in which to express their experiences other than those supplied by their own poetic tradition. Until the end of the nineteenth century we find even those writers who were familiar with western literature expressing their firm conviction that Arabic poetry was superior to western poetry in all respects and can therefore learn nothing from it. It is on these grounds that al-Muwailiḥī, who himself was not averse to experimenting in imaginative prose, berated the young poet Shauqī for daring to suggest in the preface to his first volume of verse, *al-Shauqiyyāt*, which appeared in 1898, that he could benefit from his reading in French poetry.[1]

For many decades after the Arabs' cultural contact with the West had been firmly established, Arabic poetry, therefore, continued to pursue the same path as in the eighteenth century. The works of these poets who were popular throughout the first half of the nineteenth century do not materially differ from those of their immediate predecessors. We encounter the same imitativeness and lack of originality, the same addiction to hyperbole and verbal tricks, the same fundamental lack of seriousness in the writings of the Egyptians Sheikh Ḥasan al-ʻAṭṭār (1766–1834) – who incidentally rose to the position of Head of al-Azhar during Muhammad Ali's reign – his friend Ismaʻīl al-Khashshāb (d. 1815), or al-Sayyid ʻAlī Darwīsh (d. 1853), just as much as in those of the Syrians Buṭrụs Karāma (1774–1851) or Sheikh Amīn al-Jundī (d.1841). Butrus Karama, for instance, chose to write a poem of twenty-five lines all ending with the same word, used in a different sense in each line.[2] Similarly the Lebanese Hāj ʻUmar al-Unsī wrote a panegyric to Prince Amīn Arslān in a multiplicity of metres and rhymes, arranged in such an intricate way that at least nineteen different poems of different metres, each having a different rhyme repeated throughout, can be extracted from it if certain parts of it are taken together and read in a certain order.[3] This sort of verbal jugglery could in no way be described as poetry in any meaningful sense of the word, and yet such acrobatic exercises met with much approbation at the time. The subject matter of these poems was confined to the narrow range of conventional empty panegyric addressed to local rulers and officials, commemoration of events in poems ending in chronograms, trivial social occasions like congratulations on a wedding or greetings to a friend. These were often treated in inflated and high-falutin terms, the Arabic being poor and stilted, the style generally turgid and the imagery merely conventional and lacking in original perception. This tradition continues well into the second half of the nineteenth century in the works of poets like the Egyptians al-Sayyid ʻAlī Abu'l Naṣr (d. 1880) and Sheikh ʻAlī al-Laithī (1830–96).

The true precursor of the modern poetic revival was in fact the Egyptian al-Bārūdī, in whose work is abundantly clear the conscious return to the classicism of early medieval Arabic poetry, especially the poetry of the Abbasid period. This neoclassicism, or return to the Arab heritage of the past, marks the first stage in the modern literary revival – a stage in which the modern Arabs asserted their own cultural identity in a world threatened by alien forces. Barudi's appearance, however, might have been retarded had it not been for certain factors, not the least important of which was the growing realization of the excellence and relevance of the ancient Arabic poetic heritage, which was being continually rediscovered and edited throughout the nineteenth century, thanks to the indefatigable efforts of scholars, particularly orientalists. This can easily be detected in the work of many writers like Aḥmad Fāris al-Shidyāq (1804–87), Maḥmūd Ṣafwat al-Sāʻātī (1825–80) and especially Nāṣīf al-Yāzijī (1800–71).

Al-Yaziji's poetry, which appeared in three volumes under picturesque titles between 1864 and 1883, is not particularly remarkable for its originality or its author's creative imagination.[4] Yet Yaziji's contribution was by no means negligible. He managed to purify the language of poetry of much of the artificiality and absurd or hyperbolical accretions of the past centuries of decadence. At his hands the language of poetry recaptured something of the classic simplicity, tautness and the forceful rhetoric of Abbasid poetry, especially the poetry of Mutanabbi, the poet he admired most. But there is nothing in Yaziji's work that suggests even remotely that it was written in the nineteenth century. In spite of his competence and verbal skill Yaziji must be regarded as basically an imitative poet, drawing upon the traditional imagery of the desert. There are one or two poems, like his elegy on his dead son,[5] which do express some personal emotion, but by far the main bulk of his work is far too literary or bookish, relying too much upon the work of the past and is fatally divorced from whatever concrete, living experiences the poet may have had. He still tends to indulge in too many verbal tricks and chronograms and much of his poetry deals with trivial social occasions.[6] The historian of modern Arabic literature must, therefore, give more space to his prose than to his poetry, and even in the former, as in his collection of *maqāmāt* (*Majma' al-Baḥrain*), his contribution is also more negative than positive, when compared with a remarkable creative prose writer like al-Shidyaq.

Barudi

Unlike Yaziji, Maḥmūd Sāmī al-Bārūdī (1839–1904) managed to combine a return to the purity of diction, the forceful expression and the classicism of the Abbasids with the ability to express his own individual experience often, though by no means always, in terms of the environment in which he actually lived. Likewise, he differs considerably from his Egyptian contemporaries or immediate predecessors in that at his best he produced works which are free from artificiality, and in which there is a direct expression of an earnest mind and an impressive personality. That is why Arab critics and historians of literature are generally agreed that it is with al-Barudi that the renaissance of modern Arabic poetry truly begins.

Barudi is often referred to in Arabic as *rabbu'l saif wa'l qalam* (master of the sword and the pen) because he distinguished himself both as a soldier and as a poet. In the imagination of the Egyptian reader a certain glamour surrounds his person; he is the Sir Philip Sidney of the modern Arabic renaissance, the all-round figure who is a soldier, courtier and scholar in one. Descended of an old Circassian family, he was educated first privately at home, then in one of the modern military schools first introduced by Muhammad Ali.[7] On his graduation as an army officer in 1855 he left for

Constantinople, where he occupied a post in the Ministry of Foreign Affairs, and perfected his Turkish and learnt Persian. When Isma'il became viceroy in 1863 Barudi was one of his favourites: in 1865 he sent him to help suppress the revolt in Crete and also to the Russo-Turkish wars in 1877, where he did well and was rewarded with the title of Major-General. Isma'il appointed him governor of the Sharqiyya province, then of Cairo. Under Taufiq he reached the high position of Minister of Education and *waqf* in 1879, and in 1882 he headed the 'Urābī revolutionary cabinet from which he resigned in protest against the Khedive's interference in government shortly before the British occupation of Egypt. Because of his involvement with the unsuccessful 'Urabi rebellion he was tried and exiled to Ceylon, where he spent seventeen years. During his exile both his daughter and his wife died, and he nearly lost his eyesight. He was allowed to return to Egypt only in 1900, when he was already a wreck, four years before his death.

This very brief account of the main happenings in Barudi's very eventful life is of some importance in the study of his poetry, for he used events of his life as material for his poems to a remarkable degree. He was an exceedingly ambitious man, to the extent that some people think he secretly aspired to the throne of Egypt.[8] He was also very proud: he knew his own worth and never tired of making a point of displaying his own merits. His poems are full of descriptions of the various battles in which he fought and of the different landscapes in the countries he visited in the course of his wide travels. Likewise, many of his poems deal with the great vicissitudes of his life, with the extreme changes of fortune he underwent from the pleasures of great power and authority to the humiliation of defeat. Much of his poetry is inspired by the sorrows of exile, the homesickness and the longing for scenes and places in an idealized Egypt.

Barudi's works, his *Dīwān*, not all of which, unfortunately, have so far been published, appeared posthumously in 1915. Before his death, however, he had written a preface to his *Diwan*, which is a critical document of great importance. It sheds much light on his poetry and helps explain why he occupies a crucial position in the development of modern Arabic poetry. What strikes us in the preface is, in the first place, the serious view of poetry which Barudi expresses in it. Far from being a frivolous entertainment or a mere intellectual exercise, poetry is regarded as a serious art with a serious aim. His definition of it is diametrically opposed to the purely formal definition, which had been current for so long, namely that it is 'rhyming metrical speech'. For the first time in modern Arabic we have a poet who is fully aware of the engagement of the whole personality in the creative process and of the living effect poetry has upon the reader. Poetry, he says, is

> an imaginative spark that radiates in the mind, sending forth its rays to the heart, which then overflows with a light that reaches the tip of the tongue. The tongue then utters all manner of wisdom which dissipates darkness and guides the wayfarer.[9]

Poetry satisfied a real need in man, for the love of poetry is 'imprinted in the hearts of men'. Whoever is endowed with the gift of good poetry and happens 'to be virtuous and pure of soul will have control over the hearts of men'. In Barudi's view of poetry morality is, therefore, an essential ingredient: he has no doubt that the end of poetry, as well as its effect, is moral. If poetry does no more than 'educate the soul, train the understanding and awaken the mind to noble virtue' it will have achieved its ultimate purpose.

But it is not enough to be virtuous and to have a lesson to preach, for poetry is primarily an art, and as such it has to be learned and mastered. Barudi is aware of the enormity of the task, partly because he is fully conscious of the whole of the Arabic poetic tradition and of his place in it. There is no poet in the history of modern Arabic poetry to whom Eliot's thesis in the celebrated essay on Tradition and Individual Talent applies more aptly. Barudi writes 'not only with his own generation in his bones', in Eliot's words, but with a feeling that the whole corpus of Arabic poetry of the past 'has a simultaneous existence and composes a simultaneous order'.[10] This is abundantly clear not only from his poetry,' or the vast anthology of Abbasid poetry which he compiled,[11] but also from the preface, which, short as it is, reveals his knowledge of the Arabic poetic heritage. Understandably, this acute awareness of the tradition places a heavy responsibility upon the poet which at times he finds somewhat daunting. The theme of *ars longa vita brevis* is conspicuous in the preface: he quotes the famous lines by an ancient Arab poet:

> Poetry is difficult and its uphill path is long.
> Whoever tries to ascend it, not being familiar with it,
> Will stumble and fall into the abyss.

Because of his keen awareness of the difficulty of the *métier* Barudi admits that at one point he decided to give up writing verse. But, he says, like the Umayyad poet 'Umar ibn Abī Rabī'a, he failed to carry out his resolution because he could not 'go against his own nature'. In other words Barudi wrote poetry simply because he could not do otherwise.

This brings us to the last important issue raised in the preface, namely the poet's sincerity:

> I did not use poetry as a means for an ulterior end, nor did I hope to achieve any worldly gain by it. Instead, I was moved by certain impulses, overwhelmed by a spirit of magnanimity and a feeling of love that flowed in

> my heart, which drove me to raise my voice with poetry or to chant it in order to obtain solace for my soul.

Here Barudi expresses a principle which sets him apart from his immediate predecessors and which proved to be an all important principle in modern Arabic poetry: namely, that a poet should write only in obedience to an inner urge, and not in order to attain worldly gain. Indeed, the history of Arabic poetry since the Abbasids is not devoid of poets who did not prostitute their talents. But this should not belittle the significance of Barudi's revolutionary stand. For here is an implied condemnation of the long tradition of the 'genre' of panegyric, in which the poet does not give expression to his true feelings. And in fact, despite his traditionalism, Barudi wrote no more than a handful of panegyrics, and even these do not entirely conceal the poet's own convictions and attitudes. Likewise, despite his deep awareness of the importance of mastering the technique and craft of poetry,[12] Barudi emphasizes, as a corollary to his insistence on the principle of inner compulsion, the element of spontaneity. Here again we find a feature of his work which distinguishes it from the bookish and artificial creations of the philologically-trained Yaziji, although, of course, we do not find in Barudi the degree of the 'spontaneous overflow of powerful feeling' which we shall later encounter in the work of the romantics. Time and time again in the preface we find him drawing the reader's attention to the need for sincerity, truth, nature and spontaneity. The best poetry, he says, is that which is not only marked by 'the harmony of words' and 'brilliance of ideas', or which is at once clear and profound, but which is also 'free from the taint of artificiality'. He quotes approvingly that 'poetry is the quintessence of a man's mind' and that 'the best verse you can utter is that of which, when you recite it, people will say "how true".'

The preface in fact gives a clear indication of the middle position Barudi holds between the old and the new. Despite the essential modernity of some of the principles enunciated – the need for sincerity, spontaneity and the engagement of the whole of the poet's personality in the creative process – the terms in which they are formulated, indeed the very language of the whole preface, are traditional in the extreme. Significantly enough, he opens it with a long passage expressing his religious piety, the traditional pious preamble to medieval works.

The traditional aspect of Barudi's work, his conscious return to the classicism of the past literary heritage of the Arabs, reveals itself in a number of ways. Mention has already been made of the anthology he compiled from the works of thirty poets beginning with the Abbasid Bashshār, which was published posthumously in four large volumes under the title *Mukhtārāt al-Bārūdī* in 1909. In his own poems he deals with the main themes of classical

Arabic poetry such as boastfulness, satire and elegies, together with bucolic, amatory, hunting and war themes and descriptive, gnomic, moralistic, didactic and traditionally pious subjects, including the praise of the Prophet. He imitated well-known ancient Arab poets, for example al-Nābigha al-Dhubyānī (I,73), Abu Nuwas (I,129), al-Sharīf al-Raḍiyy (I,22), al-Ṭughrā'ī (II,207), Abu Firās al-Ḥamdānī (I,134), al-Mutanabbī (I,9,70), Ibn al-Nabīh (I,61), among others, using the same metre and monorhyme as in his models. Like the ancients, he sometimes meditated over ruins and old encampments (II,445), described desert life and used traditional ideas, images, similes and metaphors in his *nasib* or amatory verse: the beloved is like a gazelle, her eyes are like those of a wild cow and so on. (I,41,257) He could write a love poem which was strongly reminiscent of the Umayyad tradition of love poetry, where Arab tribal honour is a source of fear for the woman lest the identity of the man who sings her praises is discovered by her male relatives (I,40). Even his language is at times very similar to that of the ancients, especially the Abbasids. He had a predilection for the old and archaic word, and even for 'poetic diction': the pigeon is called *ibn al-aik* (the child of the grove), the cock *al-a'raf* (the crested one) (I,124), and sea-birds *banāt al-mā'* (daughters of the water) (I,142).

Barudi's intense desire to relate himself to the tradition produced at times unfortunate results, when the poet's individuality is utterly crushed by the weight of the tradition. Not content with introducing into his poetry, perhaps not always consciously, echoes from or allusions to well-known poems of the past[13] he wrote some poems which, however interesting they may be in revealing the poet's complete assimilation of the tradition, must be dismissed by the impartial critic as mere literary exercises. For instance, in a poem which by its combination of metre and rhyme is meant to evoke the poetry of the pre-Islamic al-Nabigha al-Dhubyani, we find Barudi writing in the manner of pre-Islamic poets about love and war and desert life in a tribal or heroic society (I,73). He opens his poem with his gloomy meditations on the eve of his departure from his beloved, then moves abruptly from thoughts of love to an account of his heroic achievements in war, gives a detailed description of his horse, followed by a description of his wine-drinking and merry-making with his boon companions, and finally he relates his amorous and sexual exploits: his stealing into women's tents under cover of darkness and his leaving them in disguise brandishing his gleaming sword in his hand, and so on. Such poetry can be no more than a literary curiosity, for the ancient Arabic poetic conventions are used in it as an end in themselves; they do not point beyond themselves in the sense that the poet does not use them as a convenient medium or a set of pregnant symbols to express his own genuine experiences.

When Barudi imitates *creatively*, as indeed he does quite often, he ceases to be a mere echo of the great poets of the past, and the effect of his poetry then becomes a subtle one. By introducing details from modern life or elements from his own concrete situation into the conventional structure, the poet manages to do two things at once: he expresses a real personal experience and he places his work within the context of the larger Arabic poetic tradition. For instance, he opens a poem (I,79) with the traditional preparation for a journey – but the journey is an Ottoman expedition to fight the Greeks, and it is the hooting of a train that announces the imminent departure of the poet and his companions, and their parting with their loved ones, and the poet makes a point of emphasizing the absence of camels. This juxtaposition of the conventional and the new, the traditional and modern is often cunningly used. In his love poetry the occasional introduction of an almost colloquial and homely expression or a local name or setting[14] suddenly breathes life into what otherwise might have remained a dead convention, thereby making it relevant to the poet's time and place.

Related to this is the occurrence of a lively description, an accurate observation or an original perception in his bucolic and nature poetry, even at its most traditional and imitative. A graphic description of palm-trees, laden with red dates and soaring in the sky like beacons of fire (I,153), or a cock at dawn, for example,

> Standing on the wall, unawares, intent on dispelling the
>   sleepers' dreams,
> Strutting in a brilliantly decorated gown, ample at the
>   waist and with pendulous sleeves,
> Looking disdainfully with a proud air about him, like a
>   crowned monarch. (I,124)

Even his gnomic and moralistic verse is not entirely devoid of this feature. In a poem, the main theme of which is the mysterious wisdom of the Creator (II,6–64), there is a description of a hawk, a lion and an adder rendered in vivid detail. The account of the hawk swooping over its prey, in particular, is rendered with much feeling and pity for the hapless victim.

Barudi's forceful personality and energetic mind continue to break through the conventional phraseology. The language may be traditionally rhetorical, and the idiom that of classical Arabic poetry of *fakhr* (boasting), yet these by no means obscure the intensity and vehemence of the poet's feelings.[15] This ability to express his personality and his emotions despite the use of traditional idiom is abundantly clear in most of his poetry, especially his poems of nostalgia, which he wrote in exile, and his elegies on friends or relatives. For instance, the depth of emotion in his elegy on his wife is unmistakable (I,89–90):

Never again shall my heart rest from sorrow, now that you have gone,
Never again shall my bed be soft.
When I awake you are the first thought in my mind, and when
I retire to sleep you are my last nourishment.

His elegy on his friend 'Abdullah Fikrī, to mention another example (a short poem of nine lines), is no less sincere, although the feeling expressed in it is of a different nature: the poet's affection for his friend and his reverence for his memory reveal themselves in the dominant image of light which is sustained throughout the whole poem.[16]

Barudi's originality is shown in his readiness to write about new themes, which do not form part of the traditional subjects or 'kinds' of poetry, to record a personal memory or a mood as in the following charming poem:

A strange little sound I heard. It released my eyes from a
slumber, which was a trap for a vision that visited me at dawn.
I asked my eyes to explore what my ears had heard. My eyes
replied, 'Perchance we shall see.'
Searching, they found a bird perched on a bough, furtively
looking around and cautiously listening,
Ready to take wing above the bush, fluttering like a heart on
remembering a dear one who has been absent so long,
Ever restless on its legs, no sooner did it settle than it
would turn away again,
Now and then the branch swaying with it, throwing it up in
the air, like a stick hitting a ball on the field,
What ails it that, safe and sound as it is, it should always
be looking with caution and fear?
It it should go up it would be amidst the soft green, and should it
fall down it would drink of the brooks or pick up food with its beak.

O Bird, you have driven away the vision of my beloved which
granted me joy when it visited me at night,
White of complexion she is, with the eyes of a gazelle and
fair as the moon when it shines bright.
Now that her image has departed from me, I am stricken with
longing, grief and sleeplessness.
Would that slumber return to me that I might in her absence
satisfy my longing with her image! (I,166–8).

This is, of course, both a love poem and a nature poem. As a love poem it is based on a novel and original situation, and as a nature poem it reveals a new attitude of sympathy towards the bird which makes the poet observe lovingly and record the details of its little furtive movements. We can see here the germ of what will later become the dominant sympathetic attitude to nature in the work of some of the 'romantic' Arab poets.

Nature, in fact, constitutes one of the dominant themes of Barudi's poetry. He devoted whole poems to describing, generally from personal experience, its various aspects: tempestuous nights, starlit skies, raging seas, mountains and forests. He wrote many a poem on the pleasures of spring, on autumn, on clouds, dawn, palm-trees, brooks and birds.[17] There is much local Egyptian colour in his *Diwan*: we find the Egyptian countryside, cottonfields, the Nile with its busy traffic of sailing ships.[18] He often found in nature, in the idyllic life of the countryside, a refuge from the turbulent and dangerous world of politics (I,157). His descriptive poetry is, of course, by no means confined to nature and the countryside. He described some of the antiquities of Pharaonic Egypt like the Pyramids (I,149). In this he may have been inspired by the patriotic verse of Rifāʿa al-Ṭahṭāwī, but he certainly set the example for succeeding neoclassical poets like Shauqi.

Because with Barudi poetry ceased to be a mere artificial display of linguistic ability, and became of direct relevance to the poet's serious business of life, it is not surprising to find him dealing, directly or indirectly, with political themes. His poems contain much political criticism, diverse attacks on the tyranny of Ismaʿil and especially Taufiq, earnest calls to the people to revolt in order to realize a more democratic or representative system of government.[19] His anger and alarm at the deteriorating political situation are often expressed in outspoken terms.[20] In the single panegyric on Taufiq, which he wrote on the occasion of his accession to the throne, he emphasizes the need for the people to have a say in their own government, which is rather an odd thing to say in what is meant to be an eulogy (I,69). He has no soft words to say for tyranny:

The most fatal disease is for the eye to see
A tyrant doing wrong,
Yet having his praises sung
At public gatherings. (I,73)

He makes a desperate attempt to rouse the nation to take action against tyranny and persecution (I,316–17).

Barudi's arrest and exile on account of the role he played in the Urabi rebellion resulted in much of his best poetry. He expressed in many moving poems the sufferings he endured, his homesickness, his nostalgia for past happy times in an idealized Egypt, grief over the death of his relatives and friends during his absence, although the cumulative effect tends to be perilously close to self-pity. Here is an example, a short poem in which he registers his feelings when he was in prison:

Wasted by grief, worn out by lack of sleep,
I am blinded by curtains of care.
Neither will the darkness of night pass,
Nor is the bright morning to be expected.
There is no companion to listen to my complaint,
No news to come, no figure to pass my way.
(Here I am) between the walls and behind a door securely bolted,
Which creaked as soon as the jailer began to open it,
Pacing up and down he is outside,
But at the slightest sound I make he halts.
Whenever I turn to do a thing darkness says to me:
Hold it, do not move.
I grope my way, looking for what I want,
But neither do I find the object of my search,
Nor does my soul find its repose.
Darkness without a single star,
Broken only by the fire of my breath.

So be patient, my soul, till you attain your desire,
For good patience is the key to success.
We are indeed no more than breaths which are spent,
And man is a prisoner of Fate, wherever he may be. (I,192–3)

This poem, in fact, is an admirable illustration of Barudi's poetic powers, of his ability to bring about a true marriage between the new and the old. The feelings of grief, anxiety, isolation and loneliness, the seemingly endless night in the darkness of the prison cell are all there. The poet's concrete situation is very well realized, partly by the mention of some realistic details: the jailor pacing up and down outside; the creaking door of the cell. The feeling of utter disappointment as the result of the failure of the poet's hopes and aspirations did not preclude his anger and even rage expressed in the image of the fiery breath. Here are no clichés, no facile conventional phraseology; on the contrary, there is much originality in the imagery, of being blinded by curtains of care, or of darkness without a single star being broken only by the fire of the poet's breath. Yet, towards the end of the poem, when he exhorts himself to be patient, the poet resorts to typical traditional generalizations, and he concludes his poem with pious thoughts, the kind of sentiments one associates with classical Arabic gnomic and moralistic verse. At first sight there seems to be some discordance between the individuality and concreteness of the experience as expressed in the main body of the poem and the easy generalizations of the conclusion. But on closer examination one realizes that far from being independent aphorisms loosely strung on to the poem the following thoughts:

We are indeed no more than breaths which are spent,
And man is a prisoner of Fate, wherever he may be

arise naturally and organically from the individual experience itself. Breaths are related to the poet's breath, already mentioned in the poem, and the idea that man is a prisoner of Fate is suggested by the poet being actually a prisoner himself at the time. By generalizing his own personal situation, by making his own individual fate the fate of all mankind, the poet is in fact fortifying himself to face his situation, thus becoming better able to be patient and endure his predicament. Barudi's use of what is, at one level, a purely literary convention, a mere stylistic feature of classical Arabic poetry, in reality turns out to be a source of comfort, of psychological security and sustenance. I cannot think of a better example of the functional use of the ancient poetic idiom in modern neoclassical Arabic poetry. Here there is no clash between the old and the new; on the contrary, the old is a source of strength for the new.

Barudi was a conscious innovator, who even experimented with verse forms.[21] But in his attempt to break new ground he sometimes employed naive and unsuccessful methods. His search for novelty drove him to use, sometimes with childish effect, imagery derived from the field of modern scientific inventions or discoveries, like electricity (I,123), photographic apparatus (I,28,134), or the railway train (I,21). Here again, although he was preceded by al-Tahtawi[22], he exercised an influence on succeeding neo-classical poets desirous of being regarded as 'modern', like his great admirer Ḥāfiẓ Ibrāhīm. But the mention of scientific discoveries or modern inventions does not, in fact, confer the quality of modernity upon Barudi's poetry, nor does it form any really valuable contribution on his part. What makes Barudi the first poet of the modern Arabic renaissance, or the first modern Arabic poet, is his ability to express vividly his powerful and earnest personality through the old idioms, and indeed at times in spite of them. He himself was aware of the fact, for in one of his poems he wrote:

> Look at my words, therein you will find my soul depicted. (II,414)

Furthermore, by raising poetry above the level of mere verbal jugglery and intellectual frivolity, by concerning himself in his poems with his own immediate experiences, Barudi was a substantial innovator in Arabic poetry. At last, after centuries of decadence during which it suffered from a fundamental lack of seriousness, Arabic poetry was once more brought to bear upon the serious business of life.

Barudi's neoclassical manner of writing was soon followed by a large number of poets who until the past two decades were the best-known modern poets in the Arab world: Isma'īl Ṣabrī, Aḥmad Shauqī, Ḥāfiẓ Ibrāhīm, Waliyy al-Dīn Yakan, 'Alī al-Ghāyātī, Aḥmad Muḥarram, Muḥammad 'Abd al-Muṭṭalib, 'Alī al-Jārim, Jamīl Ṣidqī al-Zahāwī, 'Abd al-Muḥsin al-Kāẓimi, Ma'rūf al-Ruṣāfī, Muḥammad Riḍā al-Shabībī, and later Badawī al-Jabal, Aḥmad Ṣafī al-Najafī and Muḥammad Mahdī al-Jawāhirī. This is only a random selection of a few of the many names of poets who wrote in a neoclassical vein. The most important of these are perhaps the Egyptians Shauqi and Hāfiz Ibrahim, and the Iraqis al-Zahawi, al-Rusafi and al-Jawahiri. As these poets are described here as neoclassical it might be useful at this stage to pause briefly and try to explain in some detail what we mean by this term.

Before we proceed any further, however, a word of warning is necessary. In our attempt to describe the development of modern Arabic poetry, particularly in its earliest phases, we have to be very much on our guard when using European critical terminology. For all their vagueness, when used to describe western literary phenomena, terms like 'neoclassicism' or 'romanticism' still denote, in a general way, a cluster of meanings. When we apply these terms to Arabic poetry (as indeed for the sake of convenience we must) we sometimes have to impose a drastic limitation on these meanings – otherwise we run the risk of reading one culture exclusively in terms of another, of viewing Arabic literature, in other words, with too western eyes. This is particularly true of neoclassicism, the earliest of the stages in the development of modern Arabic poetry. The fact that this risk grows noticeably less with the succeeding stages, that the western critical terms do in fact become increasingly relevant to Arabic poetry, the most traditional form of Arabic literature, shows beyond any doubt the full measure of cultural westernization that in the meantime has taken place.

Unlike western neoclassicism, the neoclassicism of Barudi and his followers has no philosophical foundations, is not based upon a conscious and elaborate theory as regards the respective roles of reason and the imagination, and is not a philosophically sophisticated humanist movement which assumes that man's ethical reason is, or should be, his guiding principle in life. In a sense nothing can be further from Arabic poetry with its wealth of descriptive details than the western neoclassical belief in 'generality': the belief best expressed by Samuel Johnson in a famous statement in chapter x of *Rasselas*:

> The business of the poet is to examine, not the individual, but the species; to remark general properties and large appearances.

Nevertheless in the classical Arabic poetic tradition the part played by imagination and inventiveness was, as has already been pointed out, very severely curtailed, and conventions predominated to an extraordinary degree. This resulted in the early development and prevalence of 'types', particularly noticeable in the poetry of eulogy in which it is exceedingly difficult to distinguish between the subjects of encomium in different poems, since they are all made to display the same or closely similar virtues such as great courage, martial valour, munificence and hospitality. Furthermore, the neoclassicism of the poetry of Barudi and of his followers shares with western neoclassicism the tacit or explicit belief that, first, there are absolute rules and standards of judgment; secondly, although these rules and standards are valid for all time they are to be found in the works of a glorious period of the past; and thirdly, it is the duty of the poet to imitate creatively these works which are regarded as exemplars of good poetry. To these authors the equivalent of the Greek and Latin norms are the norms derived from a study of the works of the medieval Arabic poets, especially those of the Abbasid period, and foremost among them is Mutanabbi. The *qasida*, the old Arabic ode, with its monorhyme and monometre, or rather the Abbasid version of it, remained the ideal poetic form, an imposing verbal edifice which relied for its effect upon sheer rhetoric, oratory and resounding music. In place of the embroidery of preceding poets Barudi and his followers tried to achieve on the whole the verbal economy, the pithiness, tautness and simplicity of the medieval Arabs and to breathe new life into much of the old vocabulary. They took great trouble to polish their language: like the western neoclassicists they believed in the value of, and need for, what Horace described as *labor limae*, to the extent that their conscious artistry was always in danger of becoming mere skill and cold craftsmanship, and indeed at times it was no more than that, particularly where a poem is choked with archaisms.

However, for all the attention they paid to form the neoclassicists were on the whole earnest moralists whose work is sometimes marred by too much solemnity and didacticism. These poets, especially the younger generation among them, set themselves up as teachers and reformers of their community and attacked its social and political ills. Within the formal and stylistic limitations of the *qasida* the neoclassical poets managed to give adequate expression to their modern problems and preoccupations. At their hands the role of the poet was considerably changed. The poet as the craftsman who was prepared to sell his wares to the highest bidder, or who vied with his fellow craftsmen in verbal acrobatics and display of stylistic ingenuities, was gradually but unmistakably replaced by the poet as the spokesman of his community. It is true, of course, that in the history of Arabic poetry this was by no means a new function: but it was a function long lost, and by recovering it Arabic poetry was once more (after centuries of intellectual frivolity) made relevant to life. And since the problems and preoccupations of twentieth-century Arab society were obviously not the same as those of, say, a pre-Islamic tribe, it cannot be said that the most successful of 'committed' neoclassical poems are in any meaningful sense a mere copy or pale reflection of classical poems. The distinguished Egyptian writer Yaḥya Ḥaqqī clearly realized this when, in his interesting essay on Shauqi's elegies he recently wrote: 'Shauqi is a modern extension of the tribal poet in his golden age'.[23] This role of spokesman of the community was, of course, not confined to Shauqi, although because of his greater poetic gifts he obviously excelled in it and took great pride in it: he said, for instance:

> My poetry was the song in the joys of the east,
> And the comfort in its sorrows.[24]

All the neoclassicists, in one way or another, played this role with such frequency and seriousness that they had a lasting effect upon the later development of Arabic poetry: in a sense modern Arabic poetry has never been entirely free from social or political commitment. But the resounding phrase, the oratorical tone, the rhetorical magniloquence and grand style, the pronounced and almost incantatory rhythm, and the clinching rhyme of the *qasida* style rendered it a perfect form for this 'public' type of poetry. Poems of this type have once been likened to leading articles: they may indeed have fulfilled similar functions for a while, but they do much more besides, and at its best this is journalism of the very highest order – the order of Dean Swift's *A Modest Proposal* or similar tracts. And because it is poetry that relies heavily upon the peculiar formal features of the language, unlike journalism (and, of course, unlike much later poetry) it is bound to lose a great deal in translation. Moreover, because the neoclassical poets used the language of statement at its highest potency, and were masters of rhetoric and the art of persuasion, they were on the whole more successful in their political and social poetry which took the form of direct address to the reader than in their short narrative poems (favoured by Zahawi and Rusafi) which related stories designed to point an obvious moral connected with a political or social problem. Finally, although the neoclassical form and style were eminently suited for public themes, where the poet was constantly aware of the presence of an audience to exhort or instruct, or to derive comfort and reassurance from – and it is no accident that neoclassical poetry was recited or declaimed at public gatherings and that its effect was greatest when read aloud – the figure of the poet in communion with his own thoughts has not been entirely absent from neoclassicism. Poets like Barudi and Shauqi were able to express something of their inner thoughts and feelings within the framework of convention, in fact by putting the conventions themselves to their own personal use.[25] Yet, despite the fact that in a man like Zahawi self-preoccupation can sometimes turn into an irritating feeling of self-pity, on the whole neoclassical poetry, as is to be expected, is characterized by its impersonality.[26]

Shauqi

Perhaps the best-known of the neoclassicists, if not the best-known of all modern Arabic poets, is the Egyptian Aḥmad Shauqī (1868–1932). An Iraqi scholar once called him the Arab Shakespeare.[27] This, of course, is a gross exaggeration, but in the opinion of many Arabs, although he may not compare with Mutanabbi or Ma'arri, Shauqi is without doubt the greatest of modern Arabic poets.

Shauqi was born of well-to-do parents of mixed origin, Arab, Circassian, Turkish and Greek – a fact of which he often boasted. Like Barudi, he was brought up in the modern secular schools of Egypt. After completing his secondary education he studied law and translation at the Law School, and in 1887 he was sent by Khedive Taufiq to France in order to study law at the University of Montpellier. On his return to Egypt in 1891 he was appointed to a high office in the court and soon became the favourite poet of Khedive Abbas, a virtual poet laureate. He composed panegyrical poems on official occasions such as the anniversary of Abbas's accession to the throne and expressed the Khedive's official policy in his poems praising the Ottoman Caliph or criticizing British policy in Egypt. Much of his time was consumed by his office at the court, which he occupied for over twenty years, and which, although it conferred prestige and power upon him, also cost him some of his freedom. However, Shauqi managed at the time to compose much poetry which was not of an official nature. When the First World War broke out Shauqi's patron, Khedive Abbas, who happened to be abroad, was prevented by the British authorities from entering the country because of his sympathy for the Ottoman government and was deposed in his absence. In his place was appointed Sultan Husain Kamil, and Egypt was declared a British Protectorate. Shauqi, who was known for his attachment to Abbas and his loyalty to the Ottomans as well as for his virulent attacks on the British, was exiled to Spain in 1915, where he spent all the war years. He returned towards the end of 1919. During his exile he developed his interest in Spanish Arabic poets, especially Ibn Zaidun, wrote poems commemorating the glories of the past Arab civilization of Spain and describing its remains, and like his predecessor Barudi expressed his deep nostalgia for Egypt in a more subjective and meditative type of poetry.

Once the war was over Shauqi returned to Egypt, but not to resume his office in the court. Being by now a man of independent means, he devoted his time to his literary activities and to giving expression to the mood of the people with whom he came into closer contact than he had done before in his life. No longer the mouthpiece of the official policy of the court, he tended to identify himself with the cause of the Egyptian people, whose nationalistic feelings and aspirations took a more active and violent form, especially in the 1919 rebellion. Shauqi's poems became more clearly concerned with nationalist and social subjects. It was also during this period that he wrote all his poetic dramas (except for his *'Alī Bayk al-Kabīr*, composed in 1893). Shauqi remained active until his death in 1932 which occurred when he was, as one scholar put it, 'at the height of his great poetic gifts'.[28]

Shauqi published his first volume of verse, entitled *al-Shauqiyyāt*, in 1898. His poems, like the compositions of his contemporaries, generally appeared first in the newspapers and periodicals of the time, such as *al-Ahrām*, *al-Mu'ayyad*, *al-Liwā*, *al-Majalla al-Miṣriyya* and *al-Zuhūr*. Later on his collected works were published, also under the title *al-Shauqiyyat*, in four large volumes, the first two in 1926 and 1930 respectively, while the third and fourth appeared posthumously in 1936 and in 1943. The first volume contains the poems on political, historical and social themes, the second the descriptive, amatory and miscellaneous poems, the third volume is devoted to elegies and the last is a mixed collection including, together with poems belonging to the preceding categories, juvenilia, fables and poems for children as well as some humorous verse. This edition, however, does not include all of Shauqi's poems. In 1961 Muḥammad Ṣabrī published two further volumes entitled *al-Shauqiyyāt al-Majhūla*, although the authorship of some of the works in them has not been established beyond all doubt.

Besides his poetry Shauqi also published a number of short prose romances of an indifferent quality: *'Adhra' al-Hind* (The Maid of India, 1897), *Lādiyas* (1899), *Dall wa Taimān* (1899), *Shaiṭān Bintā'ur* (published in *al-Majalla al-Misriyya*, 1901–2), and *Waraqat al-Ās* (1904); a work of euphuistic and rhyming prose, *Aswāq al-Dhahab*, which appeared belatedly in 1932; and, of course, his poetic dramas: *'Alī Bayk au mā hiya Daulat al-Mamālīk* (1893, revised version published as *'Alī Bayk al-Kabīr*, Ali Bey the Great, 1932), *Maṣra' Kīlūbaṭra* (The Fall of Cleopatra, 1929), *Qambīz* (Cambyses, 1931), based on the romance *Dall wa Taimān*, *Majnūn Lailā* (1931) a dramatization of the well-known desert romance of Qais narrated in *Kitāb al-Aghānī* and translated by A. J. Arberry (1933) – who described Shauqi's 'lyrical drama', not without exaggeration, as 'a contribution of unique and immortal value'[29] – *'Antar* (1932), which dealt with the medieval Arabic romance of love and chivalry; one verse comedy about a contemporary Egyptian equivalent of Chaucer's Wife of Bath, *al-Sitt Hudā*, published long after Shauqi's death, and finally one prose historical play *Amīrat al-Andalus* (The Princess of Andalusia, 1932).

Although he was more directly exposed to western influences than many poets of the romantic school were to be later on, Shauqi was essentially a neoclassicist. It is true that during his sojourn in France he became acquainted with French poetry, but his reading was not confined to the romantics, for beside Hugo, de Musset and Lamartine he also read La Fontaine who inspired him to write a number of fables of his own. Shauqi also translated Lamartine's *Le Lac* into Arabic verse, though the translation is lost. What is even more significant for the development of modern Arabic literature is that, while he was in France his interest in the theatre was born and he wrote the first serious modern Arabic poetic drama, which is directly indebted to French example. Yet, in spite of this formal indebtedness to the west, Shauqi remained profoundly a neoclassicist; he may have borrowed the external form of western literature, but for his language and for his inspiration he was an Arab revivalist, turning back to the past poetic achievements of the Arabs. No doubt, in the last analysis, the felicity of his memorable phrases, the sonority of his music and his use of language at its highest potency were the product of his great poetic gift, which rendered his handling of the Arabic language so sensitive and masterly, but at the same time these would not have been possible without a thorough education and training in the Arabic classics. One of the main sources where he could read numerous specimens of the best in the old Arabic poetic tradition, together with the best of Barudi, was the philological-cum-rhetorical-cum-critical study called *al-Wasīla al-Adabiyya* (The Literary Apparatus) written by the celebrated Sheikh Ḥusain al-Marṣafī towards the end of the nineteenth century. And when he was a student in France Mutanabbi's poems were apparently his constant companion.[30] Some of Shauqi's best-known poems are deliberate imitations of works by Arabic poets of the past – in the way Pope, for instance, imitated Horace or Johnson imitated Juvenal. He imitated al-Buḥturī (II,54)[31], Abū Tammām (I,61) al-Mutanabbi (III,146), al-Ma'arri (III,55,103), al-Buṣīrī (I,36) and al-Ḥuṣrī (II,152), among others. He also wrote a variation on Avicenna's *Ode on the Soul*, thereby setting an example which was to be followed by other succeeding poets (II,71). After his exile in Spain he fell under the spell of Spanish Arabic poetry, which is clearly reflected in his felicitous creative imitations of Ibn Zaidun (II,127,162) and Ibn Sahl (II,214).[32]

Shauqi's traditionalism shows in other ways. In a poem on al-Azhar (I,177) he writes:

> Do not follow a bewitched band,
> Who find hateful all things old.

Not only does Shauqi liken himself to Abu Tammam, eulogizing al-Mu'taṣim in his panegyric on the Khedive of Egypt (II,94), but he often resorts to the idiom and imagery of traditional Arabic poetry. For instance, in his poem entitled 'The Chief Events in the History of the Nile Valley' which he composed on the occasion of the Conference of Orientalists held in Geneva in 1894 (I,17) we find that the boat on a rough sea is described (albeit effectively and vividly) in terms of Arabic desert poetry: hope attending on the boat in the manner of a camel driver singing to his camel. The clamour of the sea is likened to that of 'horses' in the thick of battle, waves surging and piling upon one another resemble 'rocks' in a desert; the movement of ships rising and falling on the crest of waves is likened to that of camels in a caravan. In a poem dealing, among other things, with the problem of food shortage after the First World War (I,66), he begins with an apostrophe to the ruins of encampment, much after the manner of a pre-Islamic poet. He is also capable of opening a political poem dealing with an issue affecting the future independence of the country, entitled 'The Milner Plan' (I,74), with a *nasib*, an amatory prelude of no less than seventeen lines couched in purely conventional phraseology in which women are referred to as wild cows and gazelles, their slim figures as willow branches, their heavy buttocks as sand hillocks, their eyes as narcissi, and so forth. Shauqi shares the medieval Arabic view that Arabic is the most beautiful language in the world (I,130) and explains, in a poem addressed to the eminent Syro-American author Amīn Rīḥānī (I,135), that America has produced no good poetry to match her technological achievements. In fact Shauqi's traditionalism and his tendency to follow the classical models of the past are so pronounced that Ṭāhā Ḥusain at one point described him and the rest of the neoclassicists as mere revivalists, and al-'Aqqād accused him of being no more than an accomplished craftsman.[33] While this is certainly true of some of Shauqi's slavishly imitative poetry, such statements are far from the truth if they are regarded as considered judgments on the entire work of the poet.

Shauqi used the old idiom to express strictly modern and contemporary social, cultural and political concerns. The subjects he tackled in his poetry cover almost every aspect of public life in Egypt, and much of what was happening to the Arab and Ottoman worlds. Of the four volumes comprising his collected works, *al-Shauqiyyat*, the whole of volume I is, as we have seen, devoted to political, social and historical themes, while volume III is taken up by the elegies composed mainly on public figures, and much of the posthumous volume IV is also about social and political current issues. He wrote to welcome Cromer's departure from Egypt (I,206), to rejoice at Ottoman military victory (I,61;330), to lament the waning of Ottoman glory and military defeat (I,277), to note the ending of the Caliphate by Mustafa Kamal (I,114), to commemorate the patriotism of Muḥammad Farīd

(IV,63) and celebrate the nationalist struggle, as in his powerful poems: *al-Ḥurriyya al-hamrā'* (Red Freedom) (II,235) and *'Īd al-Jihād* (Anniversary of the Struggle) (IV,29), to underline the need for Egyptian political parties to sink their differences (II,205), to support Syria's nationalist struggle against French imperialism (II,88), and in memory of its 'martyrs' (II,227). Shauqi also composed poems on the occasion of the safe arrival of the first Egyptian pilot from Berlin in 1930 (II,194), on disasters like the fire in the town of Mait Ghamr in 1905 (IV,45), the golden anniversary of the Teachers' Training College (Dār al-'Ulūm) (IV,21), the establishment of the National University (I,182) and on the Egyptian University (IV,10), on the foundation of Misr Bank in 1925 (IV,14; I,223), the opening of a new building of Misr Bank in 1927 (IV,17), and of a branch of it in Alexandria in 1929 (IV,24), the foundation of the Oriental Music Club in 1929 (IV,49), and on the Red Crescent (the Islamic branch of the Red Cross) (I,175,340). He addressed the country's workers in verse (I,95) and members of educational missions before their departure for Europe (IV,69). He greeted journalism (I,190), supported fund-raising efforts for social welfare purposes (IV,26), welcomed al-Azhar reforms (I,177), and defended women's education (I,110) and their freedom (II,208), expressed alarm at the growing incidence of suicide among students on account of failure in examinations (I,151), and exposed social scandals like the tendency in aged married men to marry young girls whom they virtually bought from their greedy parents (I,155).

Of course, much of this work is closer to verse journalism than to what an *avant-garde* Arab poet of today would be prepared to regard as poetry. This, however, is not the point, although it has been argued that in this Shauqi represents the last stage in the development of Arabic poetry which seemed to revolve mostly round 'occasions'.[34] What Shauqi managed to do, which is no mean service, was to make the traditional Abbasid idiom so relevant to the problems and concerns of modern life that poetry became a force to be reckoned with in the political life of modern Egypt. The banishment of Shauqi by the British authorities is in fact an eloquent testimony to the extent and significance of this force. Unlike Barudi, Shauqi was exiled not because of his political activity, but simply because of his *poetry*.[35] Moreover, in Shauqi's poetry the conventions of the old Arabic *qasida*, the desert imagery and the amatory prelude perform a function not altogether different from that of Greek and Roman mythology in the poetry of modern Christian Europe, a point which has already been noted by an eminent scholar, Shauqī Ḍaif, who in his study of the poet argues that Shauqi uses these things as conscious symbols to bestow beauty and dignity upon his poetry. Like classical mythology in modern western poetry the Arab desert imagery in Shauqi's verse 'helps to create a beautiful poetic atmosphere in which the old and the new, the past and present meet'. Furthermore, the cultural significance of the persistence of the ancient Arabic poetic conventions, and the *nasib* or amatory prelude in particular, has also been noticed by Professor Gibb who claims that these conventions have a real cultural and psychological function[36] – a function, one may add, the importance of which was greatly enhanced at the turn of the century, when Arabs felt that their cultural identity, among other things, was being threatened by powerful alien forces. This, in fact, may help to explain, at least in part, the secret of the unparalleled popularity which Shauqi enjoyed throughout the Arab world. For Shauqi managed to manipulate skilfully the ancient poetic conventions, breathing life into them and releasing their still powerful latent energies. In many ways he was the modern Arab poet of cultural (and probably personal) nostalgia *par excellence*. And because of his spectacular success Shauqi made it extremely difficult for modern Arabic poetry to change its idiom as quickly as it might otherwise have done if he had not appeared on the literary scene.

There are, however, points worth mentioning in this connection. First, some of Shauqi's poems on public themes (like his panegyrics) are constructed in such a way that the amatory prelude is easily detachable and in these cases it fulfils a function, interestingly enough similar to that which the medieval critic Ibn Qutaiba had assigned to it in the pre-Islamic Ode: it creates the right atmosphere by establishing a relationship of kinship with the reader, by evoking stock emotional responses it puts him in a receptive mood, preparing him for the poet's political or social message on the important issue of the moment. Secondly, not all the poems of course begin with the customary prelude. When the issue is a truly burning one the poet's earnestness and involvement are such that he dispenses with the prelude and plunges directly into the subject, in an overwhelmingly angry or jubilant mood, as for instance in his poem on Lord Cromer's departure (I,206), or *al-Mu'tamar* (The conference) (II,190) in which he celebrates the occasion of the all-party conference convened by the Egyptian leader Sa'd Zaghlūl in 1927 in order to save the constitution.

Shauqi's poems then are varied in subject, ranging from the traditional panegyric, elegiac, amatory, bucolic, descriptive, didactic and devotional verse to poems on social and political themes as well as poems of a more subjective and lyrical nature. Shauqi's heart was not in the panegyrical type of poem which he wrote to the Khedives, Taufiq, Abbas, Husain and Fuad. Significantly enough he felt panegyric to be at least an outmoded subject, if not beneath the poet's dignity, and he wished modern Arabic poetry to be rid of it altogether. In the introduction to the first edition of his *Shauqiyyat* (1898) he wrote that 'poetry is too noble to be brought down to the level of a profession that relies upon panegyric and nothing else'. Shauqi, however, was too weak a man to resist the temptation of worldly glory. Because he had an eye on his social prospects and advancement he was obliged to compromise his principles about which his feelings could not have run very deep. By virtue of his office at court he was expected to turn out panegyric poems whenever the occasion demanded them. It was a great pity, since so much of his time and effort were relatively wasted on what in some cases amounted to mere exercises in which he borrowed extensively and indulged in hyperbole, exaggerating the merits of the subject of his praise, sometimes to the degree of absurdity, although he often covered up the lack of originality in his ideas by the musical powers of his verse and his easy-flowing rhythms, which seem never to have forsaken him at any period of his poetic career. After his return from exile, it must be pointed out, Shauqi's panegyrics grew noticeably less until they virtually disappeared.

Shauqi's elegies are much less forced than his panegyrics. He wrote a large number of elegies, some on the death of near relations like his parents or his grandmother, and others more public or even official in nature, like the one on the death of Khedive Taufiq, or on the death of political leaders or social reformers like Muṣṭafā Kāmil, Sa'd Zaghlul or Qāsim Amīn. A further category of elegies consists of those written on the death of celebrated authors, whether Arab or western. This was a new type of elegy at the time, addressed to the reading public at large and strongly linked to the rise of journalism, since not only did the newspapers place such personalities before the public, but they also provided space in their columns for the publication of such poetic efforts, which, when the subject of the poem was not personally known to the author, generally served as occasion for his meditations on life and death. Shauqi, by no means the only poet of the time to compose such elegies, wrote on the occasions of the deaths of Hafiz Ibrahim, the journalist Yaqub Sarruf, the prose writer al-Manfalūṭī, the polymath Jurjī Zaidān, and also on the deaths of Victor Hugo, Tolstoy and Verdi. Partly because of the impassioned tone of the writing, his elegy on his fellow poet Hafiz Ibrahim is one of the best known among his works.

Shauqi's amatory and bucolic poetry bears the mark of the sophisticated society in which he lived. His imitations of Arabic poets in these fields are not usually so impressive as his description and analysis of his own actual experiences, in for instance the poems describing palace balls or his reminiscences of Parisian life. Much of his *nasib* is full of purely conventional imagery: the beloved is like a gazelle (II,150), her figure like the branch of the willow tree (II,146,171) and her teeth like pearls (II,153). The situation is conventional, with the figure of the jealous spy or stern counsellor ever present (II,148). The language may at times attain great simplicity (II,174), and a poem (such as II,143) may in fluent and musical verse attempt to depict the pains and tribulations of love, but despite the general pleasant effect there is no depth of feeling. Here the poet's remarkable ease of writing can sometimes be a defect. Yet because of their fluency and musicality and their simplicity of language many of Shauqi's poems in this genre were successfully set to music by the popular composer and singer 'Abd al-Wahhāb who became the poet's close friend and companion.

It would be wrong, however, to think as 'Aqqad and others have done that in Shauqi's poetry the subjective element is completely absent. Paradoxically enough there is more lyricism and passion in some of the speeches of lovers in his dramas, especially, as is to be expected, in his *Majnun Laila*, than in many of Shauqi's own love poems. But the personal element is there nonetheless, although often combined with nostalgia and a looking back upon the past. Because it is nearly always recollected in tranquillity the emotion naturally loses something of its sharp edge and poignancy. A typical example is his poem 'Bois de Boulogne' (II,30). A similar mixture of love and nostalgia with even more pronounced echoes from Abbasid poetry is to be found in his well-known poem *Zahla* (II,224), part of which has been set to music. The poem opens with these lines:

> With a weeping heart I bade farewell to my dreams;
> From the way of fair maidens I gathered my nets,
> Tracing my steps back from youth and its rosy path.
> And now I walk upon thorns . . .

He goes on to lament his lost youth and recall an old love. A purer note of nostalgia is struck in his Andalusian poem *Andalusiyya* (II,127), which by its combination of metre and rhyme is deliberately designed to recall Ibn Zaidun's famous poem of courtly love, the Nūn poem. The subjective element in Shauqi's poetry is not to be found only in his poems of nostalgia. There are many poems of his which arise from personal experience, if we care to look for them; poems like *al-Hilāl* (The Crescent Moon) (II,34) which was inspired by the poet's thirtieth birthday. Here the poet's sense of boredom and monotony of life, his disappointed hopes and aspirations, his awareness of the insignificance of individual man measured against the endless expanse of all human history as well as the transience of man compared with the permanence of planets, are all subtly blended together while the poet is contemplating a moonlit sky.[37] Or, to take another example, his simple and charming poem *Ukht Amīna* (Amina's sister) (II,126), which describes how the sight of a little Greek girl, whom he encounters on the boat on his way back home and who resembles his daughter, fills the poet with longing for his own child. In fact in one of his poems Shauqi says explicitly that

> If verse has neither recollection nor passion
> Nor wise sentiment it is no more than numbers.

Shauqi's pronouncements on the nature and effect of poetry are very scarce indeed, and are to be found mainly in the introduction to his first edition of *Shauqiyyat* and in an even briefer word in the preface to one of his poems (On Rome, I,292). Nevertheless, and despite what Taha Husain once said,[38] it is not difficult to arrive at Shauqi's conception of poetry. Clearly, as we have just seen, he did not believe that poetry was simply rhyming metrical speech. Besides passion (*'āṭifah*) poetry should also have what he called 'wisdom' (*ḥikmah*). Like Barudi, Shauqi believed in the moral function of poetry. He often poses as a moralist and teacher and that too at times in a crudely direct way; for instance, he calls his countrymen and the whole of the Muslim world to study their past glory and learn how to compete in the modern world, how to acquire science, technology and military strength to meet the challenge of the West.[39] In a poem addressed to the workers (I,95) he urges them to work hard and emulate the example of ancient Egyptian craftsmen, to possess civic virtues and generally lead a virtuous life. Shauqi's didacticism is in fact a very pronounced element in his work: in a poem on the Bee Kingdom (I,171) he looks for the relevant moral lesson which we can learn from nature. On the moral effect of poetry he writes:

> God has ordained that truth and wisdom should
> Coil around the sceptre of Poesy.
> No nation has been roused to what is right
> Except when guided by Poesy.
> No brass band can so affect the hearts
> Of the brave and the cowardly alike. (II,241)

At other times he feels that the moral effect of poetry and of art in general is less crude, and in a poem written on the occasion of the opening of an Oriental Music Club (IV,50) he clearly conceives of art as a source of consolation for the soul. Nature herself, he says, resorts to some kind of art when in the midst of the desert she creates an oasis 'to which the soul turns, seeking refuge from the searching heat of the desert, finding therein shade or water'.

In the preface to his poem on Rome Shauqi writes that the main springs of poetry are two: history and nature (I,292). Of Shauqi's preoccupation with history more will be said later. It might be more useful here to try first to define Shauqi's attitude to nature, which he regards as one of the main sources of poetic inspiration. As is clear from the poem *al-Rabīʿ wa wādi'l Nīl* (Spring and the Nile Valley) Shauqi views nature from outside and in terms of civilized society. His description is very detailed, and the overall impression is not altogether dissimilar from that of mosaic or tapestry, although now and again an observation in the form of an image, a simile or a metaphor reveals deep feeling or pathos. Underlying the whole poem, as indeed is the case with much of Shauqi's poetry, including his nature poetry, is an attitude to life which views it and its pleasures as a fleeting moment in time. We constantly find Shauqi likening nature to human beings in a *civilized* context: in this, of course, Shauqi is writing within the classical Arabic poetic tradition. In one poem (describing a Swiss landscape) the fields are seen as 'green garments' (II,39), and in another shrubs are viewed as women or female slaves wearing bracelets and ankle bands (II,43); palm trees also are likened to women with plaited hair (II,56), and when their tops are hidden in the clouds they are seen as brides wearing white mantles (II,154). The brook running in the green fields is likened to a mirror inside an ornamental frame (II,44). The grove is seen 'wearing a necklace and ear-rings made of the golden rays of the setting sun' (II,63). Once more we read about trees like women 'with bare legs' (II,123), and Spring is likened to a prince (II,240). This 'civilized' view of nature – so different from the romantic vision which far from man civilizing nature sees a bond of spiritual significance between nature and man – can be seen in Shauqi's poetry often coupled with hard, clear and sharply defined imagery, reminiscent of Imagist poetry as, for example in the lines on a scene of 'Palm Trees Between Muntaza and Abū Kīr':

> I see trees now hidden in the sky, now breaking through
> the horizon – a wondrous sight.
> Minarets rising here and there,
> with branches for their topmost stairs,
> From which no muezzin calls out for prayers, but
> only crows sing.
> Amongst them one tall tree sprung from
> the sand, growing in the shade of the hillock.
> Like a ship's mast, an obelisk or a lighthouse
> beyond the billows.
> Growing now longer, now shorter behind the
> hillock as the wind bends it to and fro.

When it is ablaze in the morning or when sunset
 envelops it in its flame
And when the rays of the sun go round it on a clear
 day or through the folds of clouds
You would think it was Pharaoh's maid,
 standing, waiting, in the palace courtyard,
Wearing round her head a diadem of agates intercalated with beads
 of gold,
On her bosom necklaces of coral, her sash made of brocade,
And round her body a mantle tightly wrapped. (IV,64)

In the poem 'The Bee Kingdom' (I,171), the bees, like other aspects of non-human nature, such as trees and birds, are seen as human beings, not in their basic elemental nature, their passions and instincts, but as living in a civilized context, wearing clothes, living in luxury and in organized communities.

No wonder then that Shauqi, in whose work descriptive poetry occupies a large and important part, was fascinated particularly by artefacts and the interior of buildings. He wrote poems on mosques and churches (II,27,60), on the Roman remains in Syria (II,123), and on Islamic architecture in Spain (II,60). One of his favourite subjects was ancient Egyptian antiquities, and he wrote on the temples at Philae (II,68), Tutankhamon (II,116) and the Sphinx (I,158). In such poems we get more than a mere graphic description: they often express the poet's attitude to life, to the past and present and to his own country. A magnificent example of this is to be found in the poem on the Sphinx (*Abu'l Haul*, I,158), which perhaps illustrates the poet's creative imagination at its best. Here the complexity of the poet's attitude is clear: we notice his irony and his time-weariness, his awareness of the past, of the transitory nature of life, his sense of the great vista of time against which he sees every human endeavour. Together with this there is the poet's sense of evil and of man's sinfulness. Furthermore, despite the poet's moral and philosophical meditations this is a deeply patriotic poem (as the last seven lines clearly show). All this is conveyed through a series of impressive images and ideas: such as the image of sand stretching before the Sphinx and on both sides like 'the sins of men' (I,162), or men wondering at the strange form of the Sphinx as half man, half beast, while if their own outward form were to be a faithful expression of their true nature they should all have the shapes of beasts of prey (160), or the image of the Sphinx 'mounting the sand' and journeying endlessly through days and nights (158), or crouching there from time immemorial and witnessing the birth and death of one world after another and the endless procession of empires.

Shauqi's interest in history is evident throughout his career. We have seen how early in life he wrote both historical narrative and historical drama.

With one exception, all the plays which he wrote towards the end of his career were historical. In the foreword to the poem on Rome (I,293) he tells us that history and nature are the main sources of poetic inspiration. As is clear from this poem and his other historical poems, to Shauqi history provided examples of the paradoxes and contradictions of human nature, and it therefore became the source of the poet's irony. It also became the source of his moralizing on the human condition. To his interest in history we must relate Shauqi's realistic view of human nature, for the poem on Napoleon's Tomb (I,301), among others, reveals that Shauqi had no illusions about men. He was fully aware that man does not change and that evil is a permanent part of his nature; there will always be wolves ready to devour the sheep and right prevails only when it can be backed up by might. Moreover, Shauqi's interest in history and historical remains must be related to the influence of the Arabic poetic tradition, particularly the pre-Islamic preoccupation with ruins. It is also another manifestation of Shauqi's cultural nostalgia which has already been discussed. Finally, Shauqi went to the glorious past of the Arabs or ancient Egyptians for the obvious reason of providing effective and instructive contrasts with the sad present and deriving from it an impetus for reform, improvement and progress. The contrast between the past glory of the Egyptians and their present backwardness is a theme which is repeated *ad nauseam* in the work of Shauqi and indeed of many others. It is sometimes expressed with great irony, as in his *rajaz* poem on Tutankhamon and Parliament (II, 197), where Shauqi imagines the Pharaoh rising from the tomb only to be shocked by the lowly state of his country under foreign domination.

Probably because of his high birth and his wide travels Shauqi's range of experience was much wider than that of many of his contemporaries. His extensive travels may have resulted in his religious tolerance, which shows itself in his respectful and even affectionate reference to religions other than Islam, all the more remarkable since, for all his obvious lack of puritanism or even of strict adherence to the outward forms of religion (shown, for instance, in his love of wine), Shauqi was, in fact, a firm believer in Islam about which he wrote many an impressive poem. The widening of his interests which followed his return from exile was reflected in his championing the political and social causes of the nation, such as the cause of independence or constitutional democratic government, or the feminist movement or popular education, with the result that his poetry became an impressive record of the political, social and intellectual happenings in modern Egypt. Some of his political comments in particular are expressed in brilliant political satires in which the mock heroic style is effectively used.[40] His sympathy was not confined to Egypt, however, and he was a staunch believer in Ottoman Caliphate and, especially later, he derived subjects for his poems from other Arab countries, taking the entire Arab world for his province: it was partly because of this broad sympathy for all the Arabs, in Syria and the Lebanon, in Iraq no less than in Egypt, that he was named the 'prince of poets'.

It may be useful to conclude this account of Shauqi's poetry with an attempt to list the main characteristics of his style. Although basically a revivalist, profoundly influenced by the great poets of the past, Shauqi evolved a style of writing which, for all its classical character, is entirely his own. And perhaps the most striking feature of this style is his cunning use of the musical potentialities of the Arabic language. Shauqi is essentially a great craftsman, a fact which is soon borne out by any close analysis of the structure of sounds in his successful poems. But he is more than a mere conscious craftsman: he was, in fact, greatly endowed with what Coleridge called 'the sense of musical delight'. This explains not only the haunting, incantatory effect of some of his lines, but also their untranslatability: few poets are more difficult to translate, or at least lose more in translation, than Shauqi.[41] It may also help to explain why much of his poetry has been set to music.

Secondly, Shauqi's descriptive power has already been mentioned, his ability to convey the effect of rapid movement or to breathe life into an inanimate object. Related to that is his power of thinking in terms of images. At his best his creative imagination is so active that one image follows another in quick succession. Sometimes, it is true, the images are borrowed or even commonplace, but the sheer force of rhetoric and the music of the verse manage to hide the lack of originality. A typical example is to be found in the way he celebrates Sa'd Zaghlul's narrow escape from assassination, through an elaborate and extensive use of the images of Noah's ark and the Ship of the State (I,309).

Thirdly, Shauqi has epigrammatic power to a very high degree, the power, that is, of embodying a commonplace in a condensed, pithy form. That, together with their smooth flowing rhythm, explains why so many of Shauqi's lines are eminently quotable and memorable.

Fourthly, although Shauqi's poetry is free from the turbulence or violence of passion, through it often runs a certain feeling or undercurrent of tenderness, and of nostalgia.

Lastly, at its best Shauqi's poetry has the impersonality of great classical art. This is seen particularly in a poem which deserves much more praise than most of the better known poetry of Shauqi – a poem called 'The Destiny of Days', *maṣā'ir al-ayyām* (II,182–6), in which, with great irony, calm contemplation and detachment the poet describes, in alternate moods of humour and deep seriousness, a class of school children and meditates upon their diverse individual futures, both pitiful and great, tracing it until they are all lost in the wastes of time.

Hafiz Ibrahim

Shauqi's name is often linked in the minds of most Arabs with that of Ḥāfiẓ Ibrāhīm (1871–1932), the two Egyptian poets being among the best-known neoclassicists in the Arab world. In spite of much resemblance between them in style and general attitudes they form a contrasting pair, for whereas Shauqi was for a large part of his life the poet of the court, Hafiz Ibrahim was more related to the common people. He was often described as 'the people's poet', and that was not simply because he was born in a lower middle class family and grew up in poverty, but because he wrote much of his poetry about the suffering of the people and about nationalistic themes – although lately he has come under severe criticism on the grounds of not being nationalistic enough.[42]

Hafiz was of mixed origin: his father was an Egyptian engineer and his mother Turkish. He lost his father at the early age of four, and from that time on his uncle, also an engineer living in Cairo, took charge of his upbringing. Hafiz was sent to a modern secular school, but his schooling was interrupted when his uncle took him to Tanta to which he had been transferred. After a period of irregular attendance at the Azhar type of *madrasa* at Tanta Hafiz felt he was not particularly welcome at his uncle's, and so he moved to Cairo where he first tried unsuccessfully to take up the profession of law, then joined the military academy and graduated as army officer in 1891. In 1896 he was posted in the Sudan which he regarded as exile. He was accused of taking part in an abortive army rebellion and was court-martialled. In 1900 he was cashiered and given the meagre monthly salary of £4.

After an unsuccessful attempt to get a post in the newspaper *al-Ahram* Hafiz sought the help of the well-known religious reformer Muhammad 'Abduh, who soon became his patron and introduced him to the leading figures in the intellectual and political life of the time, like Sa'd Zaghlul, Qasim Amin, Mustafa Kamil and Lutfī al-Sayyid. Hafiz Ibrahim's wit and sense of humour soon made his company welcome to the leading personalities of the day, to whom he addressed panegyrics, or poems on various social or political themes of particular interest to them. During this period of his life he wrote his prose work *Lyālī Saṭīḥ* (1907), in which he dealt with the problems of contemporary Arab society in a manner showing the influence of his master Sheikh Muhammad Abduh, and of al-Muwailihi, the author of *Ḥadīth 'Isā Ibn Hishām*. He also tried to learn French from which, in spite of his lack of proficiency, he attempted a free translation of Hugo's *Les Misérables* (1903). In 1911 he was appointed to a post in the National Library and this put an end to his financial troubles – although the fear lest he should lose his job and once more find himself impecunious limited the scope of his published political utterances. We are told that he wrote much political poetry of a revolutionary nature, which he recited to friends but did not dare to publish, with the result that some of his poetry which contained forceful political criticism has failed to reach us.[43]

The main inspiration for Hafiz Ibrahim the poet was Barudi, whom he regarded as an exemplar even in his life. Like his master, he joined the military academy, and like him too as an army officer he became involved in a rebellion which only spelled disaster for him. He also turned to the ancient Arabic heritage for his inspiration, endeavouring to model his style on the rhetoric and the pregnant phrase of the Abbasid poets. But, although there are times when it is even more rhetorical than Barudi's, on the whole Hafiz Ibrahim's poetry is much simpler, and that, in part, may be explained by the fact that his themes were more popular and his poems designed for declamation at large gatherings or for publication in newspapers and were, therefore, addressed to a wider audience. Furthermore, Hafiz Ibrahim lacked the forceful personality of his militant, ambitious and aristocratic master; his was a gentler and more humorous spirit, in many ways typical of the lower orders of Egyptian society who came of peasant stock. When it is not vitiated by forced conceits, his poetry is melancholic, even to the point of sentimentality. Yet in the midst of his earnest political utterances one often comes upon lines of poetry which are moving by their irony and deep humanity.

As in the case of Shauqi, Hafiz Ibrahim's favourite reading as a youth was al-Marsafi's book, *al-Wasila al-Adabiyya*, where he could read some of Barudi's poetry, together with much Abbasid verse.[44] His main reading, however, was largely confined to the several volumes of the well-known medieval compendium of poetry and biographical information on poets, *Kitāb al-Aghānī* (Book of Songs), by Abu'l Faraj al-Iṣfahānī, which according to his friend and biographer Aḥmed Maḥfūẓ he had read several times over.[45] To that, together with his extraordinarily powerful retentive memory, Hafiz owed the solid grounding in the Arabic tradition which might otherwise have been denied him on account of his lack of regular schooling. The extent of his indebtedness to the classical Arabic heritage was fully realized early in the century and was commented on a little too harshly perhaps by his younger contemporary al-Māzinī.[46] Like Shauqi, Hafiz was provincially Arabocentric in his outlook: he believed Arabic poetry to be the greatest and most eloquent in any language. The highest praise he could think of to confer on Victor Hugo was to say that he nearly surpassed Arabic poets (I,33).[47] His conception of poetry revealed in the preface he wrote to his *Diwan* is traditional in the extreme, and that is despite his famous poem in which he laments the stranglehold of conventions on Arabic poetry and calls for its liberation (I,225).

Hafiz Ibrahim composed poems of the traditional type such as panegyric, elegy and description and treated traditional themes like love and wine. But with the exception of his elegies these poems tend to be cold, artificial and purely imitative. This is particularly true of the very few love poems he wrote. His elegies, on the other hand, are seldom regarded by critics as mere literary exercises devoid of feeling. Taha Husain, who can never be accused of critical partiality for either Shauqi or Hafiz, commented on the excellence of Hafiz's elegies which he attributed to the poet's keen sensibility and great loyalty to his friends.[48] Similarly, Aḥmad Amīn expressed his admiration for his elegies in the introduction he wrote to the poet's *Diwan*. Another critic remarked that 'in two genres Hafiz excelled Shauqi, namely elegy and description of natural disasters'.[49] The poet himself is reported to have said, 'I enjoy composing poetry only when I am in a sad mood',[50] and wrote that 'whoever peruses my *Diwan* will find that half of it consists of elegies' (I,130). Hafiz's elegies therefore seem to agree with his melancholy temperament. It is surprising that in his poetry there is very little trace of his celebrated sense of humour which was apparently such a marked feature of his conversation. On the contrary, he was prone to complain of his ill-fortune and the way he was treated by the world. Most of the poetry he wrote during his sojourn in the Sudan expresses his unhappiness and his longing to be united with his friends and nostalgia for familiar scenes and haunts in Cairo. The fact that he had to spend many years in poverty and without employment did not help to make his poetry less gloomy. In a poem in which he bids farewell to this world he describes himself as one who finds more 'solace and profit in the darkness of a tomb'. (II,114ff.)

Hafiz wrote some of the best-known of the elegies produced on the deaths of public figures such as Muhammad 'Abduh, Mustafa Kamil and Sa'd Zaghlul. These are obviously not purely personal statements, in spite of the strong element of personal emotion which some of them contain; because of the public career of the persons whose death he laments the poems are full of social and political commentary. However, Hafiz was not a profound thinker, and his sentiments and reflections were little more than what the average Egyptian of the time felt and thought on current issues. Critics are agreed that his imaginative power was not of the highest and that he dealt with a narrow range of subjects.[51] His poems are free from any deep philosophical or moral reflections and his more subjective pieces are limited to complaints. Much of the effect he had upon his contemporaries – which according to enthusiastic reporters was at times overwhelming – was due to the skilful way he intoned and declaimed his verse at public gatherings. In this respect he was a master of so-called 'platform poetry'.[52] His was oratorical poetry *par excellence*,[53] and in it what matters most is less what is said than the manner in which it is said, a manner calculated to affect the listener at first hearing. Thought is often sacrificed for the sake of immediate emotional effect. Consequently, even more than Shauqi, Hafiz Ibrahim generally comes across in translation very badly.

As is to be expected, the bulk of Hafiz Ibrahim's poetry is public poetry written on social or political occasions, ranging from the fall of the Ottoman Caliphate or the Anglo-French *entente cordiale* of 1904, or the injustice of the occupying power, to the establishment of ophanages and educational institutions. He also wrote on natural disasters like fires and earthquakes, important events in the Orient like the Japanese victory over the Russians (II,7ff.), whose significance was understandably inflated, as well as Islamic themes, as in his long poem on the life and achievement of the second Caliph 'Umar Ibn al-Khaṭṭāb (I,71–90). Throughout these poems Hafiz Ibrahim gives expression to his sympathy for the cause of Islam and the Arabs, his belief in the political aspirations of his nation, his tortured awareness of the social problems of the time: poverty, ignorance and disease. He particularly emphasised the subject of the sufferings of the poor and the victims of natural disasters, the lurid details of which he described with so much gusto that it seems to betray what is perhaps at bottom a rather crude and blunted sensibility in the poet.[54] What is perhaps of lasting value in Hafiz Ibrahim's poetry is not the mawkish emotionalism and the near hysteria which some critics mistake for sensibility, but its irony which, although it shows the depth of the poet's feelings towards his subject, acts as a brake against blind emotionalism and therefore helps him maintain his clarity of vision. A typical example of this irony is to be found in the poem he wrote on Danshaway. The Danshaway incident, which became symbolic of the injustice of the imperialist and has been the theme of many a poem and popular ballad for decades after,[55] occurred in 1906 under Lord Cromer. A fight broke out between three British officers, who were shooting birds, and the villagers of Danshaway in Upper Egypt, during which one officer lost his life. Two days later the government retaliated by sentencing four villagers to death, two to life imprisonment and three to one-year imprisonment and fifteen lashes, and the sentence was that the hanging and flogging should be carried out publicly in the village. Naturally the harshness of the sentence only helped to inflame nationalist feeling. Addressing the British government in his poem, Hafiz Ibrahim says:

> O you, who manage our affairs, have you forgotten our loyalty and affection?
> Reduce your armies, sleep soundly, search for your game in every corner of the land.
> Should the ringdoves be lacking on the hill, surely there are men enough for you to shoot.
> We and the woodpigeons are one, for the rings have not yet parted from our necks (II.20).

Equally ironic is his poem 'Women's Demonstration' in which he describes in mock heroic terms the unequal battle between the British troops and a procession of women peacefully demonstrating in protest against the arrest and exile of the nationalist leader Sa'd Zaghlul to Malta in 1919 (II,87ff.):

> The ladies came out in protest: I watched their rally.
> They assumed their black garments as their banner,
> Looking like stars shining bright in the midst of darkness,
> They marched down the road, making for Sa'd's house
> Making clear their feelings, in a dignified procession,
> When lo, an army approached, with galloping horses
> And soldiers pointed their swords at the women's necks,
> Guns and rifles, swords and points, horses and horsemen formed a circle round them.
> While roses and sweet basil were the women's arms that day.
> The two armies clashed for hours that turned the baby's hair grey,
> Then the women faltered, for women have not much stamina.
> Defeated, they scattered in disarray towards their homes.
> So, let the proud army rejoice in its victory and gloat over their defeat.
> Could it be perhaps that among the women there were German soldiers wearing veils,
> A host led by Hindenberg in disguise,
> So the army feared their strength and were alarmed at their cunning?

Or consider how he addresses Lord Cromer in a poem commenting on the difference between the era of British occupation and earlier periods in Egyptian history (II,25):

> In the past our injustice was untidy, but now its loose ends have been trimmed off: injustice is orderly everywhere.

Of direct western influence there are some traces, though not many, in Hafiz Ibrahim's poetry. His knowledge of European languages was very limited, compared, for instance, with Shauqi's. He wrote poems on foreign authors like Tolstoy, but it is clear from the poem itself that he never read any Tolstoy, although he did read some western literature, and as we have already said, he produced a free translation of Victor Hugo's *Les Misérables*.

He also claimed to have translated into verse Macbeth's well-known speech on the air-drawn dagger, but the resultant translation (I,222) is really more of an adaptation, in fact almost a new poem inspired by the original. Moreover, he attempted to write a short one-act poetic drama on the subject of the bombardment of Beirut by the Italian navy (1912) which shows a total ignorance of the basic rules of dramatic art: it is no more than a long passage (in no way a dramatic dialogue) which is divided between four speakers – a wounded man, his wife, a doctor and a fellow Arab (II,69ff.). Hafiz Ibrahim's desire to be regarded as a modernist, manifested in his naive introduction of modern inventions like the aeroplane or train, led in some cases to very amusing results. For instance, in a well-known poem which he wrote on the occasion of the opening of an orphanage, he begins with a lengthy description of the railway train, very much in the same way as in the opening part of his work the pre-Islamic poet provided a description of his camel (I,271ff.). And it is revealing to see how the internal combustion engine is conceived of in terms of a beast of burden, how the industrial aspect of modern life is felt and described in terms of life in the Arabian desert – a classic example of the unresolved tension between the old and the new, between traditional Arab culture and modern western civilization.

Zahawi

Just as in the case of the Egyptians Shauqi and Hafiz Ibrahim, the names of the Iraqi poets al-Zahawi and al-Rusafi became linked in the minds of their readers, partly because of the keen and at times bitter rivalry between them.[56] Both poets published their first volumes of verse in Beirut at roughly the same time: Zahawi in 1908 and Rusafi in 1910.

Jamīl Ṣidqī al-Zahāwī (1863–1936) was born to parents of Kurdish origin, and his father was a learned scholar who occupied the post of Mufti (official expounder of Islamic law) of Baghdad. He did not receive a modern schooling, his early formal education being confined to the traditional religious upbringing, but he developed, largely through translations, both Turkish and Arabic, an interest in liberal ideas and modern scientific thought which he maintained throughout his life. In an autobiographical note he acknowledges his debt to the scientific material popularized in the articles that appeared in the early numbers of the Syro-Egyptian periodical *al-Muqtataf*, and such Arabic works on modern astronomy, physiology and anatomy as those which the famous orientalist Van Dyck published in Beirut.[57] In 1910 he published a pseudo-scientific treatise *On Gravity*. Although Zahawi knew no European language, he mastered Turkish and Persian from which he translated al-Khayyam's *Quatrains* into Arabic (1928). He occupied many posts, in the fields of education, publishing, journalism and law, and was successively member of the Baghdad Education Council (1886), head of the Baghdad Press, editor of the official Gazette, known as *al-Zaurā'* (1888), and member of the Baghdad Court of Appeal (1890). His fame soon spread throughout the Arab world, and in 1896 he was invited to Istanbul. On his way there he passed through Egypt where he was well received by distinguished authors like Ya'qub Sarruf, editor of *al-Muqtataf*, and Jurji Zaidan, founder of the periodical *al-Hilāl*. In 1897 the Sultan ordered him to accompany (in the capacity of preacher), an official mission sent out to reform Yemen. A year later he returned to Istanbul, but as he felt he was being watched by the Sultan's men he is said to have composed a poem attacking the Sultan which resulted in his imprisonment and his subsequent exile to Iraq. In Iraq he incurred the enmity of a leader of the Wahhabis, the Muslim puritan fundamentalists, who accused him of heresy and informed the Ottoman Government that he had been attacking the Sultan's policies. In response to the charge Zahawi published his refutation of the Wahhabi doctrines in his book *al-Fajr al-Ṣādiq* (The True Dawn) (published in Cairo in 1905) and to avoid the Sultan's wrath he had to preface it with an eulogy of his person.

After the Revolution of the Young Turks of 1908 Zahawi left for Istanbul where he was appointed lecturer in the philosophy of Islamic jurisprudence, then lecturer in the Law School of Baghdad. In 1908, as a result of an outspoken article he published in the Egyptian newspaper *al-Mu'ayyad*, entitled 'In Defence of Woman', in which he championed the cause of woman, he incurred the enmity and indignation of many of his compatriots. We are told that a demonstration of angry reactionaries, believing that he had attacked *al-Sharī'a* (the sacred law) marched to the governor of Iraq, Nazim Pacha, demanding his dismissal from his office as teacher in the law school. The governor apparently gave in to the angry masses, although Zahawi was later reinstated by Jamal Pacha. During the British occupation he was appointed head of a committee to translate Ottoman laws, and finally in independent Iraq he was a member in the House of Senators for four years (1925–9). According to an autobiographical note he declined an offer from King Faisal to become the poet laureate with a handsome salary because he did not wish to sink to the level of a paid eulogizer.[58]

From this brief account of the main events in Zahawi's life the picture that emerges is that of a man who led a full and active life, as poet, thinker, politician and social reformer. He was a prolific poet who published several volumes: *Poetic Utterances* (1908), *Zahawi's Quatrains* (1924), *Diwan* (Collected Works) (1924), *The Essence* (1928), *Revolt in Hell*, a long narrative poem first published in a Beirut periodical (1931), but in 1934 included in *Trickles*. Two further volumes appeared posthumously, *Last Drops*, published by his widow in 1939, and finally the daring and revolutionary *Evil Promptings* which was rescued from oblivion and published by Hilāl ʿNājī in 1963 in his painstaking study of the poet.[59] Zahawi was fond of revising his own poetry and republishing it in subsequent collections with the result that, as in the case of the contemporary American poet Robert Lowell, editing the canon is a task which presents formidable problems.

Zahawi reacted very strongly against the artificiality and affectation of much of previous Iraqi poetry, its mental sterility and its blind imitation of past models. His revolutionary views on poetry and society shocked his contemporaries in Iraq, yet he was later hailed as the father of modern Iraqi poetry. In 1922, when Zahawi was in his late forties, we find an Iraqi critic like Buṭṭī claiming that he was still regarded by the rising generation as their supreme poet. Zahawi's fame, however, seems to have suffered something of an eclipse in his own country after his death.[60]

Like Barudi, Zahawi managed to rid the Arabic poetry of his country of the associations of frivolous verbal tricks which had clustered round it in the past. Perhaps more than any other poet of his generation Zahawi wrote about the importance of poetry and the seriousness of the poet's function. In his *Diwan* (1924) he devotes a whole section (pp. 240–62) to his compositions on poetry and poets. One manifestation of his belief in the seriousness of poetry is his attempt to eschew all forms of *badi'*, the false conceits and exaggerated figures of speech in which many of his predecessors indulged, and his systematic adherence to what he calls the principle of the simplicity of language, which he claims in one of his poems he was the first to declare.[61] 'The best poetry', he says in one poem, 'is that which interprets the heart and its sorrows' (p. 247). In another he writes, 'in poetry lying is not sweet and deceit is not permissible' (p. 250), thereby rejecting by implication the popular medieval Arabic view that 'the sweetest poetry is that which feigns most'. Like Barudi, too, but with a much greater freedom, he brought Arabic poetry to bear upon modern life. He turned away from the mechanical imitations of the ancient poetry of the Arabs – the weeping over ruins, the deserted encampments of the beloved, the description of desert life – in favour of his own immediate experiences, whether social, political or intellectual. Furthermore he had a feeling for nature and wrote many poems describing in loving detail various aspects of spring and autumn, sunrise and sunset, birds and particularly the night sky. Of all the neoclassical poets Zahawi was perhaps the most desirous of change, and was not averse to experimenting in new forms; yet he cannot really be called a pre-romantic, let alone a romantic, because, in spite of his so-called 'modernism', his roots were firmly fixed in the literary past. His intellectualism bears in fact a close affinity to that of a poet like al-Ma'arri whose influence on him was deep and of whom he regarded himself as a disciple.[62] Zahawi's poetry contains echoes from well-known works by classical poets such as Mutanabbi, Ma'arri and others.[63] One still encounters conventional imagery and forced conceits in his work, particularly in his elegies.[64] His 'imitations' of classical Arabic poets have been amply illustrated by at least one scholar[65] and the essentially classical character of his language has been pointed out by another.[66] When, under the influence of some of his contemporaries outside Iraq, he tried to revolutionize his forms by doing without rhyme altogether, the result was a complete failure.[67] Besides, in most of his poetry, and especially in his many narrative poems, he always took care to point a moral. As for his numerous quatrains, which add up to more than one thousand written professedly in imitation of 'Umar al-Khayyam,[68] and in which he wrote on almost every topic under the sun, from scientific fact to philosophic speculation, Zahawi's didacticism is only too palpable. That his successful poems are limited to those cast in the traditional mould, and that there is in his poetry a hard core of morality and didacticism, and that his language is that of explicit statement in which the power of suggestion is reduced to a minimum – all these factors point to a sensibility which is basically neoclassical. And it is significant that in his most successful long poem, the so-called epic *Revolt in Hell* which runs into 434 lines and which represents one of the peaks of his creative activity, he chose the traditional form which observes one metre and one single rhyme throughout.

The case of Zahawi, however, is complicated by some of his critical utterances which may suggest that in his actual poetry he advocated complete poetic freedom or that he believed in relative and not absolute standards. For instance, in his introduction to the 1924 Cairo edition of his *Diwan*, he says, 'I cannot see that there are any rules for poetry, since poetry is above all rules... A poet is allowed to write in any metre he likes, irrespective of whether or not it is one of the metres codified by al-Khalīl.' Again, in the preface to his selection of his own poetry, *The Essence* (1928), he wrote that 'the "New" in poetry is that which is soaked in modern consciousness'. Yet, as we have already indicated, when we look at Zahawi's own poetry we find that he wrote nothing which from the point of view of versification, al-Khalil would have found objectionable, let alone revolutionary, and the poetry which Zahawi calls *al-shi'r al-mursal* in which he dispenses with rhyme seems to cry out for rhyme. Towards the advocates of western poetic values Zahawi's attitude is rather reactionary and traditional. Likewise, his words about the different means of excellence in ancient and modern poetry may suggest that

Zahawi believed in relative criteria of judgment, but here again that is not quite true. For where, in his opinion, does modernity lie? The emphasis throughout is on the so-called modern consciousness, on the notion that poetry is primarily an expression of a state of consciousness which (in spite of Zahawi's almost irritating egoism and arrogance) is not so much the poet's own individual consciousness as the consciousness of the age. And what distinguishes the present age from other times, in Zahawi's opinion, is its complexity of knowledge, the vast increase in facts which are now available and of which the ancient Arabic poet was ignorant. These important points are clearly reflected in his own poetry, namely in its excessive intellectuality, its tendency not only to parade facts and scientific knowledge (from astronomical data to Darwin's evolutionism and Nietzsche's superman),[69] but also to be discursive and argumentative, to proceed from premise to conclusion in the manner of a syllogism, to the extent that his language gives the impression of being nearer to scientific than to literary language – his poetry is sometimes thought of (for instance, by the Egyptian poet and critic al-'Aqqad) more as versified philosophy or science. It is true that Zahawi's poems dealing with scientific data are frequently not merely attempts to versify scientific commonplaces. For instance, in his poem 'A View of the Stars' the night sky is clearly both a scientific phenomenon and an object of aesthetic feeling. Likewise in his long poem 'The Skyscape' there is a tendency to view the planets, stars and constellations poetically, somewhat in the manner characters from Greek mythology are treated in western poetry. Yet in this last poem he writes boastfully: 'I have come to sing of truth, leaving imagination to poets'.[70] And it is a fact that his almost scientific desire to treat a subject exhaustively, to view it from all possible angles, has led him to write much that was too prosaic, too facile by poetic standards, and in which the poet simply ceases to be a craftsman or artist whose medium is language. Furthermore, Zahawi's assumption that the duty of the modern is to express modern consciousness reveals itself in his writing countless poems on political and social issues of the day.

In the field of political verse Zahawi started off by writing panegyrics to the Ottoman Caliph, much in the same way as his Egyptian contemporaries Hafiz and Shauqi, and the Iraqi Rusafi. But when the inhumanity and injustice of Abdul Hamid grew worse, he soon joined the ranks of those who, again like Rusafi, attacked the Caliphate and the tyrant Ottoman rulers of Iraq as, for instance, in his poem 'The Tyrant of Baghdad'. Zahawi wrote many poems, some of which are deeply moving, dealing with the suffering of the subjects who in various ways had fallen victim to the injustice of the Caliph's henchmen, the tortures of those who were hunted down or reported by his spies

('To Fazzān'), the miseries of widows whose husbands had been pressed into the army by the Ottoman viceregents and lost their lives fighting in Ottoman wars, in Greece, or Russia ('The Soldier's Widow'). He welcomed in many optimistic poems the declaration of the Constitution in 1908, and later recorded his disappointment on account of the Turkish ill-treatment of the free Arabs: some of his best political poetry, in fact, occurs in a long poem in which he mourns the death of a number of free Syrians who were beheaded by Jamal Pacha because of their political activities.[71] Zahawi's attitude to British occupation was not unequivocal. He even wrote poetry in praise of the British, even after the Iraqi revolt in 1920. This was rather unfortunate since it laid him open to the charge of lack of patriotism or nationalist sympathy. Recently the motives behind his political criticism have become the subject of great controversy among scholars.[72] But it can be maintained that later in his life Zahawi's interest in political themes gave place to a preoccupation with philosophic and metaphysical meditations, although it cannot be said that he ever entirely lost his interest in the social questions of his community.

Zahawi's poetry dealing with social themes is not all of one kind. There is the type of poem in which the poet directly preaches, arraigning in general terms the shortcomings of Arab or oriental society compared with that of the West, its ignorance and superstition, its stifling and meaningless conventions, its outworn habits and customs and its grossly unequal distribution of wealth. More interestingly he sometimes resorts to the form of verse narrative, of which he grew fond early in his career and which was not altogether new in Arabic poetry, but had been largely confined to the context of amatory verse. The use of narrative verse with social themes is, in fact, one of the new literary phenomena of the *Nahda* period, although Zahawi was by no means the first or the only poet to employ it: other Arabic poets, including Iraqis like Rusafi, also used it to express their views on social matters. But it must be noted that Zahawi resorted to verse narrative so often that it can be regarded as one of the peculiarities of his style. His method is simply to narrate a story with a sad end, giving in broad outline a situation which underlines a particular social disease or a problem, for instance, the injustice of the government and its inhuman treatment of the innocents ('To Fazzan'), or lack of security, peace and order ('The Murder of Lailā and Rabīʻ'), or the lack of respect for women's rights as shown in men marrying women for their wealth and divorcing them after squandering their money ('Salma, the Divorced Woman') or in forcing young women to marry old men, thereby driving some of them in desperation to commit suicide ('Asmāʼ'),[73] and so on. Although the style of the narrative is often racy and the situation is created with a few bold strokes, the characters generally remain wooden puppets, lifeless symbols embodying the author's message. On the whole Zahawi's most effective social poems deal with the subject of women's rights: in them he championed the cause of women, called for their education and their taking a full and active part, with men, in the life of the community, and for their casting off the veil. He also attacked polygamy. His sympathy for women enabled him to write a moving dramatic monologue in which a bereft mother laments the death of her daughter.[74]

In the more personal type of his poetry Zahawi often betrays an arrogance and egoism which is sometimes irritating. He also indulges in self-pity[75] and seems to suffer from persecution mania, which drove him to flee Iraq, thinking that his life was in danger, and emigrate to Syria and Egypt, from which he soon returned, embittered and disappointed. His sense of being persecuted is amply expressed in the preface to the last collection of his verse published in his lifetime (*Trickles*, 1934). Nevertheless his passionate belief in truth, in spite of the martyrdom of those who uphold it, as well as his belief in the value and nobility of the poetic ideal, resulted in some interesting personal poems, in which the strain of allegory is particularly strong, such as 'We are Both Strangers Here' in which one can detect a possible allusion to the Sufi martyr al-Ḥallāj.[76] This tendency to write allegorically is revealed in the many poems addressed to Laila, which at first sight seem to read like love poems, but on closer examination show that for Zahawi the figure of Laila was often more than the young woman he is supposed to have known and loved in Istanbul; Laila was at times a symbol of his ideal and of justice, and at others it stood for Iraq, much in the same way as the Rose symbolized Ireland for the younger W. B. Yeats.

In his last volume of verse (which was recently unearthed and published by his editor Hilal Naji (1963)) Zahawi gives expression to his metaphysical doubts in outspoken language. For instance, in a poem entitled 'I Paused' he writes:

> I paused before the facts, not knowing
> Whether it is I who have created God
> Or He created me.

Another poem of Darwinian conviction, 'As He Came So He Left', opens with the words describing the condition of man:

> He came to the world not knowing why,
> And as he came so he left.

In the very last poem in the collection, entitled 'To Hell', Zahawi asserts that he is 'a child of reason alone' and therefore dismisses as illusions and superstitions all belief in resurrection, the Day of Judgment and Hell.[77]

The most striking poem of the more personal and meditative type which Zahawi wrote was, however, his so-called epic 'Revolt in Hell'. One of the longest poems, if not the longest, in Arabic (comprising 434 lines), it was composed in 1929 and first published in Beirut in the periodical *al-Duhūr* in 1931. 'Revolt in Hell' was regarded as Zahawi's best work alike by the poet himself and by many critics and orientalists such as Amin Rihani, Ismā'īl Adham, Kratschowsky and Widmer, the last of whom translated it into German.[78] The poem shows signs of the influence of al-Ma'arri's *Epistle on Forgiveness*, and the possible indirect influences of Dante, Milton and Victor Hugo have been claimed by scholars.[79] It is cast in the medieval framework of a dream: the poet dreams he is dead and buried. While he is in the grave two angels appear before him to judge him: they ask him many questions regarding the intricate details of the Muslim faith and all the accretions of superstition that have gathered round it. When, in impatience, the poet demands that they should rather ask him questions about things of more value to mankind, like his ceaseless struggle to promote a recognition of human rights, his championing the cause of women and his defence of Truth, they only insist upon testing his knowledge of superstition. Finding him wanting on that score, they torture him and take him to paradise to give him a glimpse of the bliss that has been denied him before sending him finally to hell. He describes heaven and hell in terms derived from the Koran but not devoid of irony and sarcasm, as in his description of the houri in paradise. In hell he finds his beloved Laila once more – and here one can detect a faint echo from the *Divine Comedy* – as well as the greatest poets, philosophers and thinkers of all time: poets like Dante and Shakespeare, Imru' al-Qais, 'Umar al-Khayyam, Abu Nuwas, Mutanabbi and Ma'arri, philosophers like Socrates, Plato, Aristotle, al-Kindī, Ibn Sīnā (Avicenna), Ibn Rushd (Averroes), thinkers and scientists like Copernicus, Newton, Voltaire and Rousseau, Darwin and Spencer. Clearly it is only the intelligent and the gifted among the human species who inhabit hell, and, dissatisfied with their lot, they stage a revolt against the angels. With the help of the devils, the inhabitants of hell are led to victory by Zahawi's favourite poet, Abu'l 'Ala' al-Ma'arri, despite his blindness. Just as they are celebrating their victory over the host of the angels the poet wakes up from his dream. The influence of Ma'arri's *Epistle on Forgiveness* is clear throughout and especially in details such as the need to produce a permit to be admitted into paradise, the miraculous manner in which live birds are promptly served cooked as soon as the faithful desire to eat them, and how in hell the poet meets great literary figures who, he thinks, deserve a better fate, with the result that he questions the justice of his Creator. Apart from its remarkably vivid descriptions of war in hell, the poem is most impressive by the tone of irony that runs through it. Here the poet has managed to express in a concise and forceful style his whole philosophy of life, his passionate belief in the ideal of reason, and the dignity of man, his bitter and angry rejection of all superstition. The overall irony of the poem becomes apparent at the very end, which is a deliberately designed anti-climax. We are told unexpectedly that the poet wakes up in the morning to find that the sun is high in the sky, and that in truth the whole thing was no more than a dream – a bad dream, the cause of which was nothing greater than the poet's having eaten too much watercress before he went to sleep.

It is strange, however, how many Arab critics and scholars seem to have missed the poet's *ironic* intentions, although some have seen even a political significance in the poem, regarding it as an allegory embodying a rallying cry for revolution against the contemporary feudal system.[80] The one scholar who devoted a monograph to the study of the poem, Jamil Sa'īd, was not sufficiently aware that it is part of the satiric intention of the poet to introduce comically absurd elements, like the description of certain aspects of life in paradise, with the ennumeration of the items of food provided, ranging from fried fish and roast chicken to the honey puddings of which the ground was made; he also glosses the overt sexuality of the account of the faithful making love in public to the houri of heaven causing the beds to shake underneath them, and fails to notice the deliberate and perhaps slightly sacrilegious borrowing of Koranic images and the verbal allusions to the descriptions of heaven and hell given in the Holy Book. The result is that although the critic points out quite rightly the poet's happy choice of mono-rhyme and metre which allows him an abundance of rhyme words, relatively few forced rhymes and a rhythm which is close to that of prose, an important requirement in a work of this length, the same author complains that the picture of hell in Zahawi's poem is paler or less vivid than that in the Koran and in Ma'arri's *Epistle on Forgiveness*. Because of his inability to see the ironic significance of the whole poem he regards it as an artistic failure. Similarly the irony of the poem seems to have eluded other scholars.[81] This is unfortunate, because it is this particular feature of the poem, and not its striking verbal felicities, no more common here than in the rest of Zahawi's poetry, which renders the poem a worthy tribute.

Rusafi

Of Zahawi's compatriot and contemporary, Ma'rūf al-Ruṣāfī (1875–1945), one Arab critic has said, perhaps with slight exaggeration, 'Had his share of modern education been commensurate with his poetic gifts, the whole course of modern Arabic poetry would have been different'.[82] Rusafi was of humble origins: his father was a policeman whose duties necessitated his frequent absence from home, with the result that the boy was brought up virtually by his mother to whom he remained strongly attached all his life. After receiving his early education in a Baghdad Koranic school Rusafi joined the military school which he left after only three years without completing his training. He subsequently attended religious schools in Baghdad, studying Arabic and traditional Islamic sciences, mainly under the scholar Maḥmūd Shukrī al-Alūsī, of whom he was a pupil for many years. Later he worked as teacher of Arabic in a government school in Baghdad, where he remained until 1908, the year of the declaration of the Ottoman Constitution, that significant event which many Arab intellectuals regarded as a symbol of political freedom. In 1908 he was invited to Istanbul to work as editor in the newspaper *Sabīl al-Rashād*. In Istanbul he was also appointed as teacher of Arabic, then (in 1912) as an Iraqi representative in the Ottoman Parliament. His sojourn in Istanbul, which he loved dearly, was probably the happiest period of his life: there he received recognition, lived in comparative ease, and married a Turkish woman. During the First World War he worked as a teacher, and when the war ended he left Istanbul but did not return immediately to Baghdad. He first spent some months in Damascus which he left, a bitterly disappointed man: his well-known Pan-Islamism and his attack on al-Sharif Husain for the latter's declaration of war on the Ottomans in the name of the Arabs, had not endeared him to Husain's son, King Faisal.[83] Rusafi then moved to Jerusalem to teach Arabic literature in the Teachers' Training College. In 1921 he returned to Baghdad at the invitation of the Iraqi Government and from then on held a number of posts in the fields of education, politics and journalism. Rusafi lost all hope of ever attaining senior office in the government when Faisal became King of Iraq. He resigned his last job as teacher as early as 1928 and consequently had to live for many years on a meagre pension which he supplemented for a while by keeping a small tobacconist shop. He withdrew from Baghdad, and chose to lead a solitary life. He died a poor man.

Rusafi's fame, like Zahawi's, soon spread throughout the Arab world, because of his powerful poems which were full of outspoken social and political criticism, especially of the tyranny of Sultan Abdul Hamid (and later of British imperialism). Like Zahawi, he too used to send his poems to be published in Egypt, in reviews and newspapers like *al-Muqtataf* and *al-Mu'ayyad*. It is perhaps interesting to mention that he published his first *Diwan* or collection of poems in Beirut in 1910 while he was on his way home from Istanbul, in order to raise enough money to pay for the journey. A second and much enlarged edition of the *Diwan* came out also in Beirut in 1932 and was republished several times (although the best edition is the sixth which appeared in Cairo in 1958). The *Diwan* however, does not include all of

Rusafi's poetry: Rusafi did not take sufficient care to preserve all his work: more than 600 lines, we are told, were lost in a fire.[84] Some of his poetry was suppressed on political, religious or moral grounds. Together with his *Diwan* Rusafi published a collection of children's songs for use in schools (Jerusalem, 1920), his lectures on Arabic literature, some literary criticism (mainly on al-Ma'arri) and a number of philological studies. Other prose works of his are still unpublished: these are chiefly philological and religious in content but they include a social and political commentary on Iraq with revolutionary implications, entitled *al-Risāla al-'Irāqiyya* (The Epistle on Iraq) and written in 1940.[85] While he was in Turkey Rusafi improved his knowledge of the Turkish language from which he translated into Arabic a work by the Turkish author Namiq Kemal.

Rusafi's personality did not have the complexity of Zahawi's. He was a relatively simple, passionate and impulsive person whose frankness often caused him much trouble. In his younger days he was inclined to lead a Bohemian kind of life, clearly reflected in some of his poems which have been saved from oblivion. In many ways Rusafi's poetry forms an interesting contrast to Zahawi's. Even when both poets wrote on similar social and political subjects, which happened fairly often, Rusafi's poems were freer from the dry, cerebral approach of Zahawi; they were on the whole more direct and impassioned. Because of this and also because of the music of his verse Rusafi attained a greater degree of popularity. Nearly all who wrote on him emphasized the poet's sincerity and candour.[86] In a poem he wrote for the reception held in honour of the Egyptian poet Shauqi, he did not refrain from attacking the Egyptian government for her suppression of the freedom of thought reflected in the way writers like Taha Husain and 'Alī 'Abdul-Rāziq were maltreated on account of their unorthodox views.[87] Rusafi's view of poetry is directly emotional. 'Poetry', he writes in one of his poems, is 'my comforter in my loneliness', adding that 'my soul is melancholy, and inclined to melancholy verse' (p. 196). Unlike Zahawi, Rusafi tends to be conservative in the few pronouncements he makes on modern poetry. He believes that metre and rhyme are essential in poetry and he therefore emphasizes the need to adhere to traditional forms.[88] In his actual poetry he never abandons metre and rhyme and when he seeks a change from the monorhyme form he resorts to the stanzaic structure of the traditional *muwashshah*. Rusafi's range is also wider than that of Zahawi who on the whole tends to be solemn and whose humour is somewhat heavy. Rusafi, in contrast, is just as capable of levity as of high seriousness. Some of his erotic poetry which has been preserved for us possesses considerable charm: he can write well about his feelings as he watches a woman dancer in an Istanbul night club, he can paint a highly erotic picture of a nude courtesan and give an amusing vivid description of a game of billiards which reveals his unabashed homosexual feelings (pp. 201ff; 283ff; 509). Such things were beyond the ability of Zahawi, and Rusafi has been severely chided for them by respectable Arab critics and scholars, although it is fair to point out that he did not altogether lack advocates, albeit embarrassed ones.

But the two poets had much in common. Like Zahawi, Rusafi was generally troubled by doubt as regards man's fate and the truth of revealed religion. Both poets have been accused of heresy and described as infidels (a charge which both denied in many poems, but in terms not altogether convincing).[90] This was the result partly of their reading of popular scientific literature, partly of the deep influence upon them of one aspect of the Abbasid poet al-Ma'arri. In a poem entitled 'My Negative Truth' Rusafi asserts that he is not one of those who 'believe that religions are founded on revelation sent down to prophets, and not man-made creations', or who 'wrongly imagine that the soul goes up to Heaven, For the Earth floats in space and Heaven is nought but this space' (p. 189). Like Zahawi, and probably under his influence, Rusafi sometimes inserts in his poems allusions to scientific theories, to electricity, gravity and astronomy, and he even writes whole poems based on ill-digested modern scientific information. For instance, a poem like 'The Earth' (pp. 27ff.) is really no more than versified scientific commonplaces. This didacticism is shown in many works, like his 'The Arab Galen' (pp. 359–66), which merely summarizes the life and achievement of the medieval Arab thinker and scientist Abu Bakr al-Rāzī. Moreover, Rusafi's desire to be regarded as a modern poet is sometimes expressed in the same naive form as that which we have seen in the poetry of the Egyptians Barudi and later Hafiz Ibrahim. He even wrote complete poems on modern inventions like the railway train, the motor car and the telegraph (see pp. 204ff.; 211ff.; 250).

However, these poems like others in which he attempted to describe aspects of modern living, such as a school game of football (p. 222), are by no means among Rusafi's best or most serious works. Of far greater significance are his poems dealing with political and social themes, for Rusafi was a committed poet whose attack on Iraqi feudalism reveals the full extent of his revolutionary ideas.[91] In Iraq Rusafi is regarded as the poet *par excellence* of freedom, for his poems contain many violent attacks on the tyranny of Abdul Hamid and his men and many moving exhortations to the people to rise and demand their political rights – although it is also fair to point out that part of his popularity as the poet of freedom is probably due to the large number of patriotic children's songs he wrote. Rusafi identified himself completely with the liberal forces in Ottoman Turkey. He first welcomed the declaration of the Constitution of 1908, and then in powerful language expressed his bitter disappointment and fiery anger at the way in which it had been subsequently flouted and liberties denied to the people, as can be seen in 'Complaint to the Constitution' (p. 397). In a poem written to celebrate the deposition of Abdul Hamid (p. 385ff.), he boasts 'If a tyrant goes too far we rise and hurl him down' and adds the threatening comment, 'Abdul Hamid was not unique: many are those who resemble him.' With the fall of the Ottoman empire Rusafi was fully aware of the danger posed by the presence of the British, whom he never trusted, but rather regarded as the most cunning nation in the world (p. 467). He was the most vociferous foe of the British mandate and he bitterly attacked the sham independence granted to Iraq by Britain:

> A Flag, a Constitution and a National Assembly!
> All these have been distorted here.
> They have become names, words only, their meaning
> Not known to us (p. 461).

The mock cabinet formed of collaborators with the imperialists came under the merciless fire of his tongue: ministers, he once said, occupy 'seats which from excess of shame have nearly collapsed under them' (p. 463). On another occasion he wrote:

> Many are those in government who look like masters, but are in truth slaves,
> Dogs owned by foreigners, yet towards their own people they act like lions (p. 460).

The sight of Iraqi ministers who gave themselves the airs of governors but were in fact themselves governed behind the scenes by the British always filled him with scorn and anger, best expressed in his excellent poem 'The Guilty Cabinet' (pp. 464ff.). Among the remarkable poems in which he attacked imperialism is a short piece entitled 'Freedom under Imperialist Policy' (p. 448), in which he comments on the intention of the western powers to divide up the Arab world after the First World War. In this poem he complains that under tyranny, because of the threat of force, all values are completely reversed: the only people who prosper are those who willingly forgo their reason, understanding, speech and the sense of hearing, to say nothing of the desire for happiness or justice, in short those who willingly give up their humanity. Full of bitter sarcasm, barely-suppressed anger and self-laceration, and gathering force until it rises to a powerful crescendo, this seething political poem definitely gains from the monorhyme and monometre of the *qasida* form, which helps create a feeling of inevitability, of mechanical and almost imbecile repetition to accord with the idea of the completely dehumanized automaton to which the individual is reduced under a system that robs him of all dignity. In this manner we are prepared for the climax of the poem, the final lines in which the rejoicing, which the poet asks his people to indulge in at the impending dismemberment of their country is expressed as a grotesque version, or a travesty, of mystical fervour and spiritual ecstasy during a dervish ceremony:

> If it be said to you, 'Your country, folk, will be divided.'
> Then offer your thanksgivings and gratitude, and dance and sing.

As for his social themes, Rusafi, like Zahawi, sometimes chose to embody them in narrative form, as in his well-known poems 'The Orphan's Mother' (p. 39), 'The Suckling Widow' (p. 206), 'The Divorced Woman' (p. 54), and 'The Orphan on the Feast Day' (p. 58). In most of his poetry there is a melancholy tone, which sometimes deepens into real grief and at other times changes into anger and frustration. But it must be admitted that often in these narrative poems as, for instance, in 'The Orphan's Mother', there is an excess of emotionalism, and their sentimentality is reminiscent of the sentimentality of the tearful tales of the ornate Egyptian prose writer al-Manfaluti, which they resemble greatly. Like another Egyptian author, Hafiz Ibrahim, Rusafi was interested in describing natural disasters. In fact, his editor devoted a separate section in his Collected Works to the poems he wrote on fires. Poverty and destitution, especially those suffered by widows with children, are among his favourite topics, but he did not omit to deal with other social evils of contemporary Iraq and the Arab world, like their backwardness, ignorance and superstitions. Like Zahawi he dealt with the question of women's rights, preaching the emancipation of women, their education and their casting-off the veil. In poem after poem he lamented the passing of Arab glory, particularly the intellectual aspects of Arab civilization, as in his poem on Nizamiyya School (p. 380). Like other neoclassicists Rusafi wrote much poetry of social occasion, which his editor collected in a separate section of his *Diwan*. Poems composed to celebrate the setting-up of a school or the establishment of an Arab textile plant or a newspaper were in fact very largely versified journalism.

There is much description of natural beauty in Rusafi's *Diwan*, particularly the beauty of Lebanese landscapes of which he was fond. Like Shauqi's, this description is generally neoclassical in tone: nature is viewed by both poets in a civilized context in which, for instance, flowers in the meadows are likened to jewels and pearls worn by beautiful women (p. 239). An excellent example of Rusafi's general attitude to nature can be found in his charming poem 'The Nightingale and the Rose' (p. 245) which is written in an unusual stanzaic form based on the traditional *muwashshah*. Its theme is the love between the Nightingale and the Rose: nature is here completely humanized and set within the context of the old Persian tradition of mystical poetry, the tradition of Hafiz of Shiraz, but largely divested of mystical implications. Yet the attitude to nature revealed in this neat drama, with its conventional role assigned to each character, an attitude akin to that of the authors of Persian miniatures, gives way at least on one occasion to an almost romantic stance. In the poem 'Sunset' (pp. 198–200), written as early as 1894,[92] the sensibility expressed is close to that of the pre-Romantic author of *An Elegy in a Country Churchyard*. The sight of the setting sun, the herd wending its way back from the pasture, the fields near Baghdad, the smoke rising to the sky in the far horizon and the sound of the waterwheel – all fill the poet's heart with melancholy and romantic gloom. It is worth noting, however, that the poem ends with the comforting appearance of the stars in the night sky and the reassuring thought that nature, 'this book of the universe', contains the detailed signs of God's handiwork for those who care to read it. It is indeed because Rusafi was capable, although rarely, of such sentiments, quite alien to the neoclassical idiom, that he had come face to face with the frontiers of speech and of the limitations of language. In a poem entitled 'A Poet's Thought' he states that there are ideas and sensations too subtle for language:

> There is that in the soul which no words can reveal
> Which is beyond the reach of both verse and prose (p. 182).

Like Zahawi, Rusafi simplified the language of Iraqi poetry, especially in his political and social poems. A satire like his recently recovered 'The Folly of the Times'[93] is written in a most direct language, utterly free from all archaisms and conventions. One scholar claims that he was the first Iraqi poet to dispense with the conventional amatory prelude, at least in his political poems, and that he was followed in this by Zahawi.[94] This is perhaps inaccurate, since Rusafi does sometimes weep over ruined encampments even in a context of social criticism (for instance, on p. 534). His elegies tend to be conventional in approach, theme and imagery. There are still many verbal echoes in his poetry from the work not only of Abbasids like Mutanabbi and Ma'arri – both of whom provided subjects for whole poems, in one of which Ma'arri is described 'not as Arab poet, but the poet of all mankind' (p. 270) – but also from pre-Islamic poets like Ṭarfa and Samau'al. It is interesting to find, for instance, in a poem on Baghdad Prison, pre-Islamic idiom and phrases wedged into what is on the whole a thoroughly modern use of language in which is rendered a vivid, graphic description of dirt and squalor (pp. 42, 394).[95] However, Rusafi evinces a remarkable ability to evolve imagery of powerful impact, especially in his radical poems. In this as well as in his outspoken and rebellious feelings against feudalism and the authoritarianism of hereditary power and in his praise of socialism (p. 408) he points forward to the poetry of al-Jawahiri.

Jawahiri

The development of political poetry of a very high quality in Iraq (which may very well have its roots in a fairly continuous tradition of political verse[96]) must have contributed in no small measure to the appearance in that country of Muhammad Mahdī al-Jawāhirī (1900–), who is the angriest and most committed of all neoclassical Arabic poets. But, more significantly, in many ways Jawahiri represents a continuation and a further development of Rusafi. Rusafi was aware of the affinity between himself and Jawahiri, and in a poem addressed to him he acknowledged him as his successor.[97] In his turn Jawahiri, who has written more than one poem on Rusafi, says in his long poem composed on the occasion of the sixth anniversary of Rusafi's death: 'Alike we are and your fate is close to mine.'[98]

Jawahiri was born in Nejev to a family of some distinction, particularly in the field of religion and traditional learning. He was sent to a traditional school of Shi'i denomination and at home he received a solid grounding in the Arabic language, philology, rhetoric and traditional Islamic sciences. The great advantages of the poet's early background have been stressed by his biographer who has tried to show how much the young Jawahiri had been helped by the unbroken poetic tradition of Nejev and its lively atmosphere at the time.[99] Jawahiri developed a passion for poetry early in life which, we are told, seems to have adversely affected the progress of his general academic studies. His first job was in the field of education. He worked as a school teacher in Baghdad in 1924, a post from which he was dismissed as a result of his publication of a poem which the authorities found offensive. He was subsequently reinstated, but in 1927 he resigned his post and was employed in the royal court where he remained for three years, after which he resigned. (Strangely enough, despite his criticism of conditions in Iraq under the monarchy Jawahiri managed to maintain good relations with the royal family.) He then held several positions in the Ministry of Education, but on account of opposition to government policy expressed in his outspoken poems, his career there was punctuated with orders for his dismissal – later reversed by his reinstatement – until he finally resigned in 1936. He then took up journalism, a career in which he showed remarkable courage. He edited no fewer than twelve newspapers, most of which for political reasons were short-lived. In 1937 he was jailed for publishing a critical article. As a result of continued harrassment by the police, Jawahiri left for Syria where he lived in self-inflicted exile from 1956 to 1958. Jawahiri, who had never tired of attacking the policy of Nūrī al-Sa'īd, naturally welcomed the Iraqi revolution and the end of monarchy in 1958. The last of his newspapers, however, the leftist *Al-Ra'y al-'Ām* (Public Opinion), was noted for its bitter opposition to Kasim's authoritarian rule and was forced to close down, upon which Jawahiri left Iraq. In 1961 he went to Prague, and returned only in 1968 at the invitation of the Minister of the Interior and was offered an adequate monthly pension.

Jawahiri has published a great deal.[100] His first volume of verse, which contains mainly 'imitations' of renowned poets, past and present, appeared in Baghdad as early as 1922. The second was published in 1928 and included some poems from the earlier volume, but as the poet points out in the preface it contains mainly nationalist and descriptive verse. The third collection, *Diwan al-Jawahiri*, which appeared in Nejev in 1935, is marked by the dominance of poems of social and political protest in which the poet's revolutionary stance is pronounced. The next edition of *Diwan* was published in three volumes (1949, 1950 and 1953), with a most interesting preface to the first volume, together with the following dedication:

> To those who have deliberately chosen the path of freedom, light and liberation, and who have been steadfast in their choice, eagerly enduring all the suffering and deprivation which it entails. To the victims of injustice, malice and vengeance. To those who could have been otherwise had they so wished.

Another edition of *Diwan* of which only the first volume was published appeared in Damascus in 1957. In 1959 a volume of poems written to celebrate the achievement of the Iraqi revolution in its first year appeared in Nejev. A further edition of *Diwan*, described as the fifth edition, came out in Baghdad in two volumes (1960, 1961), but the third volume never saw the light of day as the poet soon emigrated to Prague. A collection entitled *Exile Post* was published in Prague in 1965. The *Diwan* was published again in Sidon (1967) and Beirut (1968–70), but none of the different editions of the *Diwan* are identical in their content or in the order in which the poems are arranged, which is a cause of much confusion. In 1969 *Return Post* was published, to be followed in 1970 by a long poem inspired by the restoration of peace with the Kurds. Finally, the volume entitled *To Sleeplessness* came out in Baghdad in 1971, comprising mainly the poet's reflections on the theme of exile.

In many respects Jawahiri's early exposure to the classical Arabic literary tradition had had a lasting effect upon his poetry, even in his latest work. Jawahiri has never been able to resist the temptation of using archaic diction. Critics have often complained of the difficult language of his poetry, which arises mainly from his tendency to use far-fetched vocabulary, a feature which is no doubt due to his early traditional philological training.[101] In his view the only training that an Arab author can profitably receive is the traditional training in the Arabic classics, for 'there can never be a poet or an author of genius who does not stand on the foundation of his own language'.[102] Clearly Jawahiri is thinking here of his own 'foundation'. He was widely read in the Arabic poetic tradition, and he knew most of al-Buhturi's poetry by heart. He had great admiration for poets like Mutanabbi and for Ma'arri, on whom he wrote a poem. His traditionalism shows itself in the high esteem he had for neoclassicists such as the Egyptians Shauqi and Hafiz, and the Syrian Badawī al-Jabal Sulaimān Aḥmād; he regarded Shauqi as the supreme modern poet.[103] In the preface to his first volume of verse, which consists largely of imitations (*mu'āraḍāt*) of poets ancient and modern like Ibn al-Khaṭīb and Shauqi, he states that his deliberate aim was to imitate his examples, both in their intention and in their techniques and method.[104] The influence of Shauqi and Rusafi on Jawahiri's later poetry is unmistakable, the former, to mention but one example, in the poem celebrating the opening of a school in 1947, and the latter in the well-known political satire *Ṭarṭarā* (1946), which is clearly indebted to Rusafi's 'Freedom Under Imperialist Policy'.[105]

Despite a somewhat romantic view of poetry expressed in an untypical poem, 'The Poet', written when he was twenty-one (III,205ff.), in which the poet is viewed as someone whose eye sees the hidden mystery of things, Jawahiri's poetry is generally neoclassical in form and spirit. The monorhyme and monometre are hardly ever abandoned, and although in his more recent poetry, such as his latest volume, *To Sleeplessness* (1971), he displays a greater freedom in the use of rhyme, the traditional metres remain intact. Apart from his strongly neoclassical language, the great care he takes over polishing his style[106] and his tendency to use archaic diction, Jawahiri's poetry is often loud in tone and displays many features of the oratorical style, particularly his fondness for repeating key words or phrases in order to produce an almost incantatory effect. This last feature can be seen in his famous poems such as 'Lullaby for the Hungry', 'My Brother Ja'far' and 'Descend, Darkness'.[107] He sometimes repeats the opening line of a poem at the conclusion, thereby giving it a circular shape, as in 'Lullaby for the Hungry' and 'Descend, Darkness', a device which is particularly effective in oratory.

Jawahiri treats the usual themes of the neoclassicists, such as panegyric, elegy and description. He even eulogized King Faisal I, Faisal II and Prince 'Abdul Ilāh.[108] He attempted to write erotic poetry and to describe nights of revelry, dancing and drinking, and indulgence in sensual pleasures.[109] However, such attempts are usually solemn and heavy: they generally lack the charm and obvious *joie de vivre* which one finds in Rusafi's poetry, although his warmly sensuous poem on Aphrodite is an exception.[110] Likewise, his nature poetry seems artificial, conventional and devoid of any fresh vision, as is obvious in 'After the Rain' (I,158). On the whole Jawahiri's range is much more limited than Rusafi's. His real achievement lies in fact in his political poetry, where there is no doubt that he is without peer among the neoclassicists.

Like other neoclassicists Jawahiri resorts to the use of narrative in his political verse, as in his poems 'The Mob' (III,109), professedly inspired by Emile Zola, and 'A Refugee Woman on the Feast Day' (III,183). The latter is a moving account of the plight of a young refugee woman whose father was killed by Israeli soldiers, and who was driven to sell her body in order to provide for her little brother. Such instances of the use of narrative, however, are rather rare in Jawahiri's work. He prefers to make his political comments directly, and often with an overwhelming effect upon his readers, despite the inordinate length of many of his poems. Time and again we are told of the truly galvanizing effect his poems had on the Iraqi public on certain occasions. He mercilessly lashed out at every form of social and political injustice in Iraq (and in the rest of the Arab world). He attacked British and French imperialism, in Egypt, Algeria or Iraq: in 'Precious Blood, or Say to the Youth of Egypt' (I,109) or 'Algeria' (I,115). In 'Port Said' (I,125) he lamented the Anglo-French-Israeli aggression on Egypt in 1956. As early as 1931 we find him in 'Blood speaks after Ten...' (I,223) boldly denouncing social inequality and calling upon the masses to rise and rebel against the feudalistic forces of oppression in society, and take up arms in a bloody struggle. In a poem with the explicit title 'Feudalism' (*Iqṭā'*), published in 1939, he describes various aspects of the appalling gap separating the rich from the poor and warns the former against the wrath and impending revolution of the deprived masses.[111] What is falsely described to the hapless people as Fate or God's will, he points out in another poem (III,113), is only 'a government decree'. In 1960 he addresses the working classes in 'The Workers' Day' (I,183), glorifying their struggle. Nepotism, corruption, false values and lack of self-respect all come in turn under his heavy fire. In 'The Diggers' (I,161) he ferociously attacks those who, motivated by excessive hero-worship, attempt to falsify history by digging up social or political figures from the past and bestowing upon them a greatness which they did not deserve. The Arabs in general and the Iraqis in particular, he says, must first face the grim reality of their present situation before they can begin to reform:

> Nations strive hard while we idly play . . .
> And live like water moss by the bank,
> Parasites on life, now floating, now sinking (I,203).

Jawahiri is the political poet *par excellence*. What is unique about his mature political poetry is that while the form is obviously classical and the diction is at times archaic, the degree and kind of political consciousness and the fervour of the revolutionary impulse are thoroughly modern. That is why he is fully accepted by the neoclassicists as one of them while even extreme modernists claim him as their mentor. His poetry is highly charged with emotion, and the explosive nature of his violent and often original imagery has an almost physical impact on the reader, with the result that the poet's anger at social injustice, political corruption and the degradation of man becomes infectious and reaches a degree of intensity that is at times truly terrifying. Listen to him giving vent to his grief and anger in his powerfully moving elegy on his brother, who was brutally killed during a demonstration held in Baghdad to protest against the Portsmouth Treaty in 1947 ('My Brother Ja'far' (I,139)):

> It is not fancy what I say, my brother,
> For he who has to take revenge is always awake; he never dreams.
> But inspired by my patient endurance
> For sometimes inspiration can reveal what is hidden in the future
> I see the heavens without stars, but lit up with red blood
> And a rope, rising like a ladder, on which to climb up from the earth;
> Whoever reaches out to cut it has his hand chopped off
> By a figure rising from the huge corpses around, where glory is even more huge.
> And I see a hand stretching beyond the veil, writing on the horizon
> A generation gone and a generation come
> [And] before them [rose] an enkindled flame.

or listen to the opening lines of his well-known poem 'Descend, Darkness', which by its repetition and diction has an effect analogous to that of magical imprecation or curses (I,149):

> Descend, darkness and fog, and clouds without rain,
> Burning smoke of conscience and torture, descend,
> Woe and destruction, descend upon these who defend their own destruction.
> Punishment and retaliation upon the builders of their own tombs

Descend, croaking [of crows], and let your echoes be greeted by the
hooting of owls. Ruin, descend.
Descend upon those sluggards of whose laziness even flies complain.
From too much cringing of their necks they cannot tell the colour of the
sky
Their heads trampled underfoot as often as dust.
Descend upon those hungry goats that are still taken to be milked
Upon those misshapen creatures to whose life even dogs would not stoop.

3

The pre-romantics

Mutran

The revolt against the limitations imposed by the neoclassical conventions goes back as far as the turn of the century, if not earlier still. The germs of it could certainly be seen in the work of Faransīs Marrāsh and Rizq Allah Ḥassūn, minor poets who in what was then known as Syria, attempted to revolutionize themes, diction and imagery in modern Arabic poetry.[1] But for our present purpose it is convenient to start with a major figure like Mutran who both in theory and in much of his practice showed his dissatisfaction with classical conventions. In previous attempts to describe the development of modern Arabic poetry I have called Mutran a pre-romantic poet.[2] The term is perhaps a little misleading, since it may suggest that the only or chief value of Mutran's poetry lies in its foreshadowing of something to come, something much more important and valuable. I should like at the outset to dispel any such suggestion. That Mutran is less important than any of the poets who precede or succeed him in this survey is completely untrue; that he is, on the contrary, one of the most gifted modern Arabic poets is beyond any doubt. The late distinguished author and critic Taha Husain once described him as 'the leader of modern Arabic poetry and the teacher of all contemporary poets without exception'.[3] The term 'pre-romantic' is chosen here not to convey any value judgment, but to describe, for lack of a more convenient term, a number of qualities in Mutran's poetry, which will be dealt with later.

Khalīl Muṭrān (1872–1949) was a versatile genius who distinguished himself in a number of fields: in journalism, in finance and commerce, in agricultural economy, no less than in poetry. He was born in Baalbek and after receiving his elementary education in a primary school in Zaḥla he was sent to the Catholic seminary in Beirut where he learnt French and obtained a solid grounding in Arabic language and literature, under the distinguished sons of Nasif al-Yaziji, Khalīl and Ibrahīm. Like other young intellectuals of his time Mutran took an active interest in politics. Inspired by the principles of 1789, he used to gather with his friends, we are told, in order to sing the *Marseillaise*, and to attack the tyranny and oppression of the policy of the Ottoman Caliph, with the result that Abdul Hamid's spies are reported to have made an unsuccessful attempt on his life. Consequently and in order to avoid the Sultan's wrath, Mutran's family prevailed upon him to leave for Paris in 1890. In Paris he developed his interest in French literature, but he also associated with the Young Turk group, which was founded to oppose Abdul Hamid, and once more, fearing the Sultan's men, he was forced to leave his home. At first he thought of emigrating to Latin America where some of his relations had settled, and actually began to learn Spanish for that purpose, but eventually he left for Alexandria in 1892, and from that date until his death in 1949 he lived in Egypt. There he began his career as a journalist in the well-known paper *al-Ahram*, then in 1900 he started himself a fortnightly cultural review under the name *al-Majalla al-Misriyya*, which continued to appear for three years. In 1902 he set up a daily, *al-Jawā'ib al-Miṣriyya*, in which was published much poetry including his own, but the newspaper had financial difficulties and lasted only five years, and Mutran turned subsequently to commerce and speculation, making a considerable fortune for himself. However, in 1912 as a result of an unfortunate deal he lost all his possessions, which almost drove him to despair. Luckily he was soon appointed secretary to the Khedivial Agricultural Society, where he earned much respect and admiration because of his efficiency, both as an agriculturalist and as an economist. He was even entrusted with the task of planning the initial programme for the Misr Bank. For many years Mutran was Director of the National Theatre Company, a post in which he discharged his duties with great industry and enthusiasm, and which enabled him to render a great service to the cause of the Egyptian theatre.[4] As a poet he was honoured in Egypt, in 1913 and in 1947, when at impressive festivals held specially for the occasion he received the tribute of leaders of thought in the Arab world. He is usually referred to as *Shā'ir al-quṭrain*, the poet of two countries, meaning Egypt and Lebanon.

Mutran's literary output, although some of it remains unpublished,[5] was both large and varied. His collected poems, known as *Diwan al-Khalil*, run into four large volumes, the first volume of which appeared in its first edition in 1908. He wrote extensively on history, translated several works from the French in moral philosophy, economics, and natural and agricultural history, was the joint author of a book on the social and economic conditions of the Egyptian peasant (1936), and compiled the elegies written on Barudi (1905).

Not the least important of his literary activities were his translations of some of Shakespeare's plays: *The Merchant of Venice, Othello, Macbeth* and *Hamlet.* He also translated Corneille's *Le Cid*. Among his unpublished works are his translations of Corneille, Victor Hugo and Paul Bourget. This is, of course, not to count his journalistic work, which could fill several volumes.

As early as 1900 Mutran wrote in his periodical *al-Majalla al-Misriyya*:

> It is by no means imperative that our mode of composing poetry should remain the same as that of earlier generations of Arabs. The times in which those Arabs lived are different from ours, their manners, their character, their needs and their sciences are not the same as ours. Our poetry therefore should represent our own modes of thinking and feeling and not theirs, even though it may be cast in their moulds and may follow their language.[6]

In the preface to the first volume of his *Collected Works* (1908), the wording of which remained substantially the same in the second edition which came out forty years later (1948–9), Mutran was more explicit:

> The author of this verse is not a slave to it, he is not driven by the necessities of metre or rhyme to say anything other than what he has intended to say. In it the right sense is conveyed in correct and eloquent language. The author does not aim at the beauty of the individual line irrespective of whether or not it disowns its neighbour and quarrels with its fellows... rather he is concerned with the beauty of the line both in itself and in its context, together with the whole structure of a poem, the arrangement of its lines, the harmony and concord of its ideas, beside the uncommonness of the imagination, the strangeness of the subject, and yet the conformity of all that to truth and its revelation of free, unshackled sensibility, minuteness and accuracy of description.

Here Mutran, who is a highly conscious artist, introduces a number of new concepts into Arabic poetry, which were destined to become almost unquestioned assumptions in the work of the next generation of poets – a thing which makes Mutran in many ways, and more than any other poet, Shauqi not excluded, the true father of the new or modernist school of Arabic poetry. Perhaps the most important of these concepts is that of the unity of the poem. Hitherto, probably partly because of the need to observe one rhyme throughout the work, the Arabic poem had in many cases tended to be ultimately a collection of lines, in which no particular order dominates, apart, of course, from the merely external order of convention: for instance, the convention of beginning an ode or a panegyric with weeping over the ruins, or description of wine or enumerating the beauties of the beloved. Brilliant as the individual lines sometimes were, they were often very loosely connected, and sometimes there was no connection at all: the poet simply digressed or moved abruptly from one theme or part of his poem to another. Even more significantly, those Arab critics who consciously evolved theories of literature were not concerned with this question of structural unity of the whole poem. At best, all they were concerned with was the unity of the paragraph. This is true even of the great medieval critic ‘Abdul Qāhir al-Jurjānī.[7] Among the neoclassical poets we have been considering there was not one who was fully aware of the need to impose a structural unity upon individual works – although of course sometimes by a kind of artistic instinct they managed to attain unity in their poems. Even Zahawi, in some ways the most articulate of them on the nature of poetry, did not consider the question of the structural unity of the poem to be of any importance. On the contrary, he believed that digressing and moving from one theme to another in the same work was more consonant with the nature of consciousness.[8] And when he came to collect what he regarded as the best of his own poetry in the volume called *The Essence*, he cut out large portions of his poems without apparently feeling any significant loss.

Mutran, on the other hand, systematically and deliberately sought to achieve unity of structure. His poems, including his narrative poems, seem to have a clear pattern, a beginning, a middle and an end – a fact noted by the Egyptian critic Muḥammad Mandūr when he came to discuss Mutran's earliest narrative poem with which the first volume of his *Collected Works* opens.[9] We shall see later on how the alleged absence of this type of unity from most of Shauqi's poems became a major target for the severely adverse criticism written by the younger generation of poets like al-‘Aqqad.

The second important concept developed by Mutran is the primacy of meaning[10], expressed in the poet's description of himself as not being ‘a slave to his verse or to the necessities of rhyme or metre'. While not neglecting the language of his poetry, or even the traditional metres and rhymes, Mutran is never guilty of mere verbiage, or pursuing high-sounding words or figures of speech for their own sake. The significant development in this was of the poet rising at long last above the rhetorical temptations which are almost inherent in the very nature of most traditional Arabic poetry since the later Abbasid period, and to which the neo-classicists certainly succumbed. Of course, many of Mutran's poems, especially most of the contents of the three later volumes, deal with such social occasions as greetings to friends or congratulations on weddings, etc. But although at some point we shall have to face squarely the question why Mutran does not seem to have developed much beyond the first volume, it is important to emphasize at this stage that these poems do not really represent the poet in any meaningful sense. They are not even *jeux d'esprit*, but are more of the nature of social obligations which he had to carry out, and are therefore not to be given too much importance in an impartial appraisal of the poet's achievement. He himself clearly distinguished between them (together with similar political and social poems such as his multiple eulogies and elegies) and his more serious productions.[11] In the latter the tone of the poetry is very much more subdued and less declamatory or harsh than that of the poetry of either Shauqi or Hafiz. We shall see later on how the followers of Mutran went a step further in their belief in the primacy of meaning: they sought an even greater freedom and independence in their desire for self-expression. Inspired by their master, who claimed (in the same preface) that he had written his poetry in order to relieve his soul in solitude, they gave an even freer expression to their personal emotions.

Thirdly, Mutran regards the 'uncommonness of the imagination and the strangeness of the subject' as essential qualities, which he tried to realize in his poetry. These qualities, which constitute very significant departures in the history of Arabic poetry, are very far from the tendency to keep the conventional themes, the conventional poetic diction and therefore the conventional poetic vision of the neoclassicists. We are now very close to the originality and creative imagination which were the watchwords of the European Romantics. Although there are no proofs of a direct or even an indirect debt to Wordsworth or Coleridge, there is definitely an interesting parallelism between Mutran's insistence on uncommonness of imagination, or strangeness of subject, together with essential truthfulness, minuteness and accuracy of description, and the avowed intentions of the authors of the *Lyrical Ballads*. To those who criticized his poetry by calling it 'modern' Mutran replied in the preface, somewhat defiantly: 'Yes, indeed it is modern and it is proud of being modern. It has the same advantage over past poetry as that which modern times have over our past ages'. And he adds, 'I claim without fear that this new style of poetry – and by that I do not simply mean my own weak compositions – is the poetry of the future, because it is the poetry of life, truth and imagination all at once'. In this no doubt Mutran's confident prophecy came true. Abu Shadi pointed out how easy it was for most of Mutran's disciples to forget the big role he had played.[12]

Writing of the contents of his first solume of verse Mutran says in his preface:

> Most of the poetry here is nothing but tears which I have shed, sighs I have uttered and fragments of my life which I have squandered away, but by turning them into verse it seemed to me as if I had been able to recapture them.

Mutran was therefore the first to be aware of the subjective nature of much of his poetry in that volume. In a famous statement which is often quoted, he once said that two main factors had shaped his personality: extreme sensitivity and a great predilection for self-examination.[13] Mutran's extreme sensitivity is directly revealed in a number of poems of a highly subjective nature, in which he gives utterance to a deep and almost overwhelming emotion. In 'The Lion in Tears' (II,17),[14] which registers the poet's despair at the sudden discovery of the loss of his fortune, the emotion rises almost to the pitch of hysteria, although it is fair to point out that this melodramatic title was not the poet's own choice, but that of his friends, his own original title being the less high-falutin 'A Moment of Despair'. One of the best known of these poems is 'Evening', written in 1902 (I,144). In this poem, composed in the traditional metre of al-Kāmil and observing the traditional single rhyme throughout, Mutran expresses his dejection as a result of falling a prey to sickness and unhappy love; the sensibility shown in this poem is something new in Arabic poetry. It is not that in 'Evening' we meet for the first time the lonely figure of the poet in the presence of nature. Such a situation does occur in classical Arabic poetry: the best and most memorable example is the pre-Islamic al-Shanfarā. But both the poet and the nature against which he is placed have now at Mutran's hands been almost fundamentally changed. The poet here is primarily a thinking and feeling being, his self-communion and introspection make him an almost different species from al-Shanfara, whose limited self-awareness, or to be more precise, whose simple and primitive consciousness puts him almost on the same level as the animal inhabitants of the desert. Shanfara's experience belongs to the world of what Schiller would call 'naive' poetry, in his well-known distinction between naive and sentimental poetry. Mutran's, on the other hand, despite the emotion it expresses, or, perhaps, because of the quality of its emotion, is a product of a civilized and highly sophisticated type of sensibility. Basically it is a romantic sensibility, which creates a deep and intangible spiritual bond between external nature and the mind of man. This is what distinguishes it from the neo-classical attitude to nature which we have found in Shauqi and which gives us what is mainly an external observation, with the poet standing outside the object of his observations and recording what he sees. With Mutran the emotional life of the poet colours the external objects of nature, thus bestowing a life, which is ultimately human life, upon them. Here again Mutran had a great influence upon many of the younger generation of poets who further developed this romantic attitude to nature. The rock on which the lonely figure of the poet is settled is:

> Assailed by waves like the waves of my affliction which wear it out as
> my disease wracks my frame
> While the sea is heaving with grief like my heart at the hour of dusk.
> Gloom spreads over the world, as if it had risen from my heart to my
> eyes . . .

The poem concludes with an identification between the poet and the natural scene, in which the setting sun and the sky seem to him to join in the lament over his misfortune as his thoughts turn to the woman he loves.

Nature, however, is not always a mere echo of the poet's feeling in the manner of pathetic fallacy, as we find in 'Evening' or in 'The Rose and the Lily' (I,134). It is often viewed as a source of solace for the suffering poet. For instance, in 'Death of a Dear Couple' (I,66) he addresses the meadows, saying:

> Bring peace to my heart
> Be my refuge from constant sorrow . . .
> Here is my solitude to which I flee
> From a painful world where injustice is rampant.

This escapist attitude is even more striking in 'Solitude in the Desert' (II,19), where the poet openly turns his back on civilization and seeks refuge in the desert away from the vices of the city and the world of men. Mutran's passionate interest in the details of landscape, seascape and skyscape is apparent throughout his poetry. One poem in particular, 'Sunset in the Egyptian Countryside' (II,11) deals mainly with the fantastic shapes formed in the sky by clouds, the rays of the setting sun and the oncoming darkness of the night. Here we notice nature gradually assuming a mysterious character in the poet's mind and reality in the process of being transfigured. At times the physical world of the senses is seen by the poet as a door leading to another purer or greater world of the spirit. In 'The Illusion of Light' (I,165), Mutran describes a girl dressed in a white frock seen from a distance on the bank of the Nile in the moonlight, observing how the rays of the moon suddenly turn the girl into a pure spirit of transparent light, robbing her of the solid and opaque clay of her body. In another, 'Microcosm and Macrocosm: a Cup of Coffee' (I,155), we get something closer to Blake's vision which sees a world in a grain of sand and Eternity in an hour. The air bubbles floating on the surface of the cup are seen by the poet as miniature suns, stars and planets, all uniting and merging into one another. This, he says to his beloved, is the fate of the universe and the fate of all lovers. But the link between death and fulfilment of desire is an essential condition in man just as it is for the whole of the universe. The movement from the cup of coffee to the cosmos and then back to the poet and his mistress is subtly conveyed. Here the relation between man and nature acquires a philosophic significance and the whole universe is felt to be bound together in a harmonious order by means of love, much in the manner of Shelley's vision. The idea is stated even more explicitly by Mutran in his poem 'Exculpation' (I,53):

Invisible atoms coming together
Revealing themselves in visible forms
Seeds are hugged by the earth
Which renders them as gardens in bloom.
And yonder stars, are they not pearls
Floating on teeming seas?
Scattered, yet strung together in orderly constellations
Love binding them to one another
And each is perpetually seeking its like?

The intensity of Mutran's feeling for nature is intimately bound up with the depth of his love-passion. Mutran had an unhappy and unfulfilled love affair early in his life, for the woman he loved died tragically young.[15] The experience had a profound and lasting effect upon him, and, as a result he remained unmarried until his death at the age of seventy-seven. In a series of love poems under the general heading 'A Tale of Two Lovers' (1897–1903) he recorded the genesis and dramatic developments of this love, tracing its course starting from their chance meeting in a park where she was stung by a bee, to the happy times they enjoyed together, her departure as a result of malicious interference by others, to the news of her illness which led to her death and his reaction to her death. Referring to her under different names as Salma, Hind, Maria and Laila, Mutran gives expression to the many facets of his highly idealized and spiritualized love. In one poem (I,191) he claims that it is love that makes man 'real' and that without love man remains like a shadow flitting across the surface of life, with no more substance than that possessed by 'an image on a mirror'. In another (I,194) he assures his beloved that when he can no longer see her with his eyes he can still see her with his heart. In a third (I,201) he wishes he had the spontaneity and freedom of the art of a bird, so that he could borrow the bird's wings in order to fly from the troubled world of man to the carefree horizons and to drink of their liquid light. The death of his beloved inspired much moving poetry. In one poem, for instance, he says (I,216):

What use is the cup that remains
Now that the wine has gone?
Passion, the youth of the soul, has fled,
Hope has died; there is no joy
In either sleep or wakefulness.

In another (I,218) he writes about the sad memories evoked in his mind by the discovery among his clothes of her worn-out handkerchief with her embroidered initials long after her death.

Mutran's first volume of verse is full of such deeply subjective love poetry of varying degrees of emotional intensity.[16] It is therefore strange to find Mandūr and his disciple Dusūqī asserting that Mutran seldom expressed his personal emotion;[17] Mandur even attributes that partly to the poet's rigid Roman Catholic upbringing, partly to what Mutran himself described as his great propensity for self-examination which may have made it difficult for him to let himself be carried away by his emotions. However, in Mutran's poetry love is always idealized and free from any sensual or sexual overtones. In 'My Moon and That in the Sky' (I,23) the conventional comparison between the beloved and the full moon is set against a natural background drawn with such sensitivity that the poet's passion becomes ennobled and almost spiritualized. In 'The Star and I: a mutual complaint' (I,29) Mutran imagines the star to be lovesick like him and suffering from disappointed passion for an unattainable object. Here the poet's beloved is likened to a creature of light. In 'The Two Pigeons' (I,73) we find a deeply felt description of the lament of a pigeon over its departed mate which inspires the poet to lament his own solitude and to appeal to his beloved not to continue to desert him: although the situation is highly traditional, the intensity of the feeling makes the experience unmistakably genuine. Moreover Mutran's detailed account of the sufferings of the bird reveals the extension of the poet's sympathy so as to include other living creatures, which we find in many poems like, for instance, 'The Sparrow' (I,101) or 'From a Stranger to a Strange Bird' (II,21) – a feature one associates with Romantic poetry. Significantly enough the poet tells us that he composed the last-mentioned poem near the statue of Jean-Jacques Rousseau in Geneva. In fact, if we examine it we find that it embodies many of the main themes of Romanticism: complete self-absorption, nostalgia, the spiritual appeal of nature, idealized unattainable love, together with the poet's power of sympathy evinced in the detailed and loving description of the song bird. In the beginning its song soothes the poet's heart, but as it goes on it gradually arouses his grief over the loss of his beloved, whose grave he calls upon the bird to visit in order to convey the poet's feeling of longing and his yearning to be united with the spirit of his beloved. Mutran continued to write poems on the anniversary of the death of his beloved, poems which, while revealing the poet's singular faithfulness to her memory, express a quiet sort of grief, somewhat etherealized by being set against idealized natural background. Typical examples are 'A Rose that Died' (II,10) and 'The Story of a Rose' (II,288).

Mutran's excessive idealization of woman at times makes one suspect that he was probably more interested in an abstract ideal than in the warm and concrete reality of women. The suspicion is confirmed by a poem like 'A Virgin Bathing in the Sky' (I,292) (written in 1907), the theme of which is the planet Venus, pictured here as an idealized woman. But the picture, as in all of Mutran's poetry about women, is strongly marked by the absence of sensuality or even sensuousness. Here the poet declares his love for Venus and not for any mortal woman. The contrast he draws between the two is very much in favour of the goddess who is characterized by beauty, perfection, freedom from sin and from the wiles of real women who are described as the cause of so much human misery. Another poem, 'Venus' (I,124), written as early as 1901, depicts worshippers in the Temple of Venus led by an inspired poet who, in response to the worshippers' longing to see the goddess of love, predicts truly that by a miracle Venus will appear as a woman of perfect beauty to those who spend two months in prayer and fasting. Here the Greek myth is vivified and the planet is personified much in the manner one associates with, not just European Renaissance poetry, but specifically Romantic writings: the poet is now the prophet or priest of the religion of beauty. In another poem, 'The Two Roses' (I,35), even God is viewed as the supreme poet and maker, and the world is regarded as a collection of captivating poems. A related image of the poet emerges from Mutran's poem 'Eloquence' (I,55) where the poet is revealed to us as a magician and poetry is conceived as magic which transports the hearer to a higher and nobler order of reality. The figure of the poet with his lyre, gazing into the invisible world and telling stories of love, the poet, that is, as the lover, magician and storyteller all in one, draws upon elements from the classical Arabic and Greek traditions, in which we can detect echoes from Qais, the mad one, and Orpheus. The poet's search for an ideal Beauty which does not exist on earth, is unequivocally expressed in the poem 'In the Wood' which Mutran himself describes as 'an imaginative picture of a poet roaming about in a mountainous wood looking for a non-existent flower' (I,302). The poet is here obviously looking for Perfect Beauty which does not exist in the outside world, but the only approximation to which is in the poet's own mind or poetic imagination, for in the end the lover offers his mistress a poem instead of the ideal flower he could not find. On the fecundity of the creative imagination, which is yet another Romantic theme, Mutran writes elsewhere (II,288):

> The soul, like Nature, is an ever-creating mother
> Bringing to a new form all created things.
> It fashions whatever inspiration offers her
> And through memory recaptures figures
> Whose absence causes us grief.

Mutran did not always express his experience directly, but he quite often resorted to the narrative poem, and he even experimented with the dramatic monologue. He wrote many narratives dealing with the theme of love such as 'A Cup of Coffee' (I,148), 'A Martyr of Chivalry and a Martyr of Love' (I,82), 'Devotion' (I,105) and 'Two Children' (II,61). Some of these have been aptly described as ballad-like on account of their short metre, stanzaic form or rhyming couplets together with the nature of their subject matter.[18] Without a single exception they are all about disappointment or lack of fulfilment in love. The impediment may be caused by a natural disaster like death (as in 'A Martyr of Chivalry' and 'Devotion') or by an unsympathetic parent or society at large (as in 'A Cup of Coffee' and 'Two Children'). 'A Martyr of Chivalry' is the story of an engaged young couple, who on their wedding night are united by death: the hero risks his life in an attempt to rid the community of a vicious wolf while the heroine prefers death to life without her beloved. In 'Devotion' a young wife dies of consumption only a year after her marriage, to be followed soon by her devoted husband who dies of a heart attack – a story which closely parallels that of the poet's cousins and which inspired his moving poem 'Death of a Dear Couple' (I,66). Mutran was fascinated throughout his life by the theme of men and women dying young either by drowning or by sudden natural death, or by committing suicide, generally because of overwhelming misery brought about by unrequited passion.[19] In 'Two Children' a young man has to part from the woman he loves to make his fortune abroad so that he may become worthy of her hand, but in his absence her parents force her to marry a rich man she does not love. She pines away and dies, the young man comes back to learn of her death, visits her grave, laments his fate and the cruel world of men and decides to die beside his beloved. In 'A Cup of Coffee', one of the best of Mutran's narratives partly because of the poet's admirable power of creating the appropriate atmosphere for the events he narrates, both the princess and the young officer she loves are killed because of the tyranny of her father, the king: she dies of fright while he is ordered to drink a poisoned cup of coffee. In his use of narrative form in such poems Mutran was something of a pioneer in modern Arabic poetry.

Mutran's interest in narrative poetry goes back to his youth. In fact, the earliest poem he cared to preserve to include in his first collection of poems and which he composed in 1888 (at the age of fifteen), is cast in the form of narrative. It is the poem called '1806–1870' in which he treats as his subject the wars between the French and the Prussians. This, of course, indicates that already in his youth the poet had become influenced by French culture. For although there are a great many descriptions of fighting and wars in traditional Arabic poetry, there is nothing quite like this, in many ways, impressive early work –

although we have to be on our guard against the possibility of reading too much in it, since we are told by the poet that he later on modified it a little. What is new in this narrative poem, apart from its striking structural unity, its logical and emotional progression, already referred to, and its dramatic and epic quality despite its shortness, is its aesthetic disinterestedness or its impersonality. This last quality is one of Mutran's contributions, for the narrative element in traditional Arabic poetry, in which poets described fighting episodes and heroic deeds was in fact only a part of the traditional lyrical form. It remained subjective or related to the poet's self, since the poet's design behind the narrative was either to illustrate his own achievements or the achievements of his tribe or of his patron. This remained the case even in relatively recent descriptions of war as attempted by Barudi and Shauqi: the aim of the former being on the whole *fakhr* (self-praise) and the latter being the eulogy of the Ottoman Caliph. This was also the aim of Mutran himself in certain panegyrical contexts, as in his encomium on Abbas II where he describes the conquest of Sudan (I,44). But in his poem '1806–1870' as well as in many others such as 'Napoleon I and a Dying Soldier' (I,41), Mutran's narrative, on the other hand, is sought for its own sake, as a form of expressing a vision of human life, or to use the Aristotelian phrase, of imitating character in action – although his best known narrative and dramatic poems, whether their subjects are derived from historical events or from incidents in contemporary life, often contain an indirect political or moral commentary. 'The Maid from Montenegro' (I,179), for instance, narrates the story of a fair Arab girl who, disguised as a man, fought heroically against the tyrant Turkish rulers until she fell a prisoner to them and only escaped death when she revealed her identity. 'The Boer Child' (I,162), which describes the feelings of a Boer child whose father had to go to the war, expresses the poet's condemnation of the war. In 'The Great Wall of China' (I,60) Mutran indirectly laments the submissiveness of the Arab people, and in 'The Athenian Elder' (I,64) their lack of resolution, their weakness of character and their ignoble acceptance of occupation by foreigners. 'The Murder of Buzurjumuhr' (1901), the minister of Chosroes, offers an indirect eloquent comment on and a criticism of tyranny and an oblique passionate plea for freedom. A similar attack on tyranny occurs in 'Nero'. In all these poems, we discern a movement away from direct political statement of the type familiar in neoclassical poetry and towards oblique commentary.

The longest of these poems is 'Nero' (1924), which the poet himself described as 'the most daring attempt by an Oriental [i.e. Arab] poet' (III,48). He claimed it was the longest poem in Arabic dealing with a single theme and observing one rhyme throughout, consisting as it does of 327 lines. The experimental nature of the poem is stressed by Mutran who in the prose introduction wrote:

> To this day there have not been any long poems dealing with one subject in Arabic and that is because the need to observe the monorhyme has been, and still is, an obstacle standing in the way of such attempts. I have therefore wished, by making one final definitive endeavour, to ascertain the extent of the ability of a poet to compose a long poem on a single theme observing a single rhyme throughout. By reaching the furthermost limit in my experiment I hoped to show to my Arabic-speaking brethren the need to follow different methods in order to keep pace with western nations in the progress which they have achieved in poetry and eloquence.

Clearly this somewhat negative aim of the venture has not been realized, for it did not discourage Zahawi from attempting an even longer narrative in monorhyme and monometre in his 'Revolt in Hell' (1929), which, as we have seen, comprises more than 400 lines. Bearing in mind Mutran's noble aim, 'Nero' may be regarded as a *tour de force*, although the exigencies of monorhyme drove the poet to use, as he apologetically admits, archaic and difficult vocabulary. However, powerful as it is as an expression of Mutran's commitment to the ideals of freedom and democracy, it does not rank as one of his finest achievements. For a poem dealing with so many dramatic events it is surprisingly free from any dramatic tension. There is no serious attempt in it at characterization or portrayal of conflict or interaction of characters, but it contains some vivid description, particularly where it deals with burning Rome. It is of course an indirect political comment, although there is a direct enough moral, which we are given at the beginning and more especially in the end where we are told that tyranny is made possible only by the submissiveness of the people, that tyrants in fact are created by their own subjects. This is a view which Mutran advocates in his poetry with such persistence and steadfastness that one critic regarded him as the poet of freedom *par excellence*, and another wrote a book on him entitled *Khalil Mutran, the Poet of Freedom.*[20] Even in his famous poem on 'The Pyramids' he could not refrain from attacking the tyranny and despotism of the Pharaohs. It is this dedication to the ideal of freedom that prompted his angry and courageous comment when in 1909 Sir Eldon Gorst decided to curb the freedom of the Egyptian press (II,9):

> Disperse her best men by land and sea
> Slaughter her free men one by one
> The good shall remain good till the end of time
> And so shall the evil remain

Smash all the pens, would that prevent
Hands from engraving the stone?
Cut off the hands, would that restrain
Eyes from looking in anger?
Put out the eyes, would that prevail
Against the fiery breath?
Stop then the breath, for that would be
The utmost you could do to us
We would then be saved from you
And for that we would offer you our thanks!

One of the most interesting of the long narrative poems which contains a large dramatic element is 'The Martyred Foetus' (I,223) which was written in 1903 and comprises 115 stanzas with the rhyme schema *aaaaa/bbbba/cccca*, etc. In it Mutran portrays the thoughts and feelings of a poor young unmarried prospective mother about to abort herself. She chooses to put an end to the life of her baby in order to save it from the shame and misery which would otherwise fill its life. A simple, innocent but attractive girl, she had come to the city in search of employment to support her aged but unprincipled parents, but at the tavern where she was driven by them to work and where her character slowly deteriorated, she met a man with whom she eventually fell in love. He turned out to be a villain who deserted her and ran away with her earnings after he had ravished her and she had become pregnant. The dramatic monologue with which the poem ends, and which describes convincingly the sufferings of the girl, is no less moving than, for instance, Wordsworth's 'The Affliction of Margaret'. Needless to say, for this dramatic type of verse there is really no precedent in Arabic poetry.

Among Mutran's contributions we ought perhaps to include some of his prothalamia and epithalamia which possess much elegance and charm. For instance, in 'A Gift of Flowers' (I,275) the poet sings an encomium on flowers, and in a manner somewhat reminiscent of a masque, the flowers, led by their queen the Rose, prepare to arrange themselves in the form of a wreath to be presented to the bride who is spoken of as one of their kind. This is poetry written with great sensitivity and is characterized by its considerable power of fantasy and charm.

It may seem strange, after this account of Mutran's poetry, that I have not followed some Arab critics in calling him a 'romantic' poet.[21] After all, Mutran wrote poems on Alfred de Musset (I,166) and Victor Hugo (IV,362), emphasizing the hypersensitivity and the capacity for love and suffering in the former and in the latter the rebellious impulse which drove him to make a radical break with the neoclassical shackles. There are even some signs that he saw something of himself in both poets. It is not that Mutran affirms his kinship with the neoclassicists by regarding himself primarily as a moral teacher when he writes in the preface to his first volume:

> The greatest recompense that I could hope for is that in the following moral tales, unusual anecdotes, parables and imaginary representations . . . the reader will share my feelings while perusing my book, thereby approving of virtue and grieving over vice and will benefit from my counsel and derive a cure for his wounds from mine.

Poets like Wordsworth and Coleridge could boast of even stronger moral intentions. I have chosen to call him pre-romantic for a significant reason, however. Although in his sensibility, in his themes and in some of his ideas he does betray an unmasked romanticism, there is much in his use of the Arabic language which, despite its originality, points backward rather than forward. The influence on him of his early teacher and friend, the great Arabic scholar Ibrahim al-Yaziji, on whose death he wrote two eloquent poems, remained strong all through his life. Mutran's childhood reading in the work of classical Arabic poets such as Abu Tammam and Buhturi left an indelible mark on his style and language which, with few exceptions, tended to be somewhat archaic, or at least not fully modern. In his style the rational, conscious element is perhaps a little too dominant: he is constantly polishing his language,[22] constantly vigilant and self-critical, with the result that one feels that there is not enough spontaneity in his poetry to make him a thorough-going romantic. With the almost obsessive desire to observe the outward form of the language goes a fairly rigid adherence to the metres and rhymes of traditional Arabic verse, although we have to admit that he shows considerable freedom in handling the stanzaic form based upon *al-muwashshah* (I,33;35), and in one poem he uses two different metres to indicate different speakers (I,61). We even find him making an attempt at writing *vers libre* in 1907, in an elegy on Ibrahim al-Yaziji which is quite impressive with its powerful rhythm, striking imagery and biblical tone (I,294). However, there is generally some tension between the old form and the new content in his poetry and it is this tension which leads me to call him a pre-romantic, in spite of the possible misunderstanding to which the term may give rise.

Besides, there is much in Mutran's poetry that is in no way different from the conventional output of the neoclassicists. There are many panegyrics of one kind or another, there are scores of conventional elegies written on friends and public figures, innumerable poems of direct commentary on social and political occasions. In fact Mutran's innovation does not appreciably go beyond what he has achieved in the first volume of 1908. If anything, in the second volume we notice already a gradual increase in the number of poems on social and political subjects and a lessening in the poet's imaginative inventiveness. Indeed one still finds in this volume poems of considerable appeal such as the nostalgic 'Do You Remember' (II,135), the theme of which is childhood memories and in which the poet 'tries to salvage fragments of his life that float on the surface of time', or the remarkable poem 'Christmas' (II,246) which he wrote when he was forty-five years old. On Christmas Eve the poet, alone in his room, recalls how as a child he used to look forward to finding a present by his bedside when he woke up. Now he is a middle-aged man and expects nothing. He cannot go to sleep, thinks at first of drinking himself asleep, but decides not to do so on moral grounds, retires to bed and is rewarded for his virtue by falling asleep immediately. He dreams of large beautiful gardens and at dawn when he wakes up he is surprised to find a plant in a pot on his bedside table, a present his mother has surreptitiously placed for him during his sleep. The subject is an ordinary one, namely the loneliness of a middle-aged man with nothing to look forward to in life. Yet the poem is remarkable for its immediacy, its dramatic quality, created partly through the use of untypical simple language and a conversational rhythm. The poet's meditations, the movements of his thoughts on a variety of topics, his momentary self-indulgence to be followed by his apologizing or chiding himself, are all subtly conveyed, and the description of his sparsely furnished room with its crooked bedstead, its so-called wardrobe which cannot be locked, its piles of books, is admirably vivid. But it is perhaps significant that the impressive poems in this volume are poems of nostalgia and reminiscence, of looking back to the past. On the other hand, the gradual drying-up of inspiration or the creative impulse can be detected not only in the preponderance of direct political and social verse, but also in the quality of the few descriptive and nature poems. For instance, a poem like 'Sunset in Cairo' (II,186) obviously lacks the fire and feeling for nature which is so unmistakable in Mutran's earlier work. 'In the Shadow of the Statue of Ramses' (II,175) is straightforward and didactic, compared with the earlier poem 'Baalbek Castle' (I,97), in which the remains, far from being treated in an objective, descriptive, moralistic or didactic manner, are related to the poet's personal experience by being made part of his childhood memories. The third volume of the *Diwan* has few or no poems in which Mutran breaks new ground (with the possible exception of 'Nero'), but it is taken up with conventional elegies and panegyrics, poems written on social occasions to express gratitude to various bodies for receptions held in the poet's honour in different places in Syria and Lebanon, congratulations to friends on joyful occasions, celebrations of anniversaries and of establishing new buildings, and so on. In the fourth and last volume, which is no less bulky than the other three, there are hardly more than half a dozen short poems which embody what can be described as a fresh vision (pp. 56, 243, 337, 342, 351, 362). Narrative verse seems to have disappeared, except for two not very distinguished attempts (pp. 83, 106). There is a brief momentary resurgence of the poetic impulse (p. 56), but it is now virtually dead. The best poem in it is significantly enough one in which the poet, as it were, bids farewell to the Muse (p. 337).

What happened to prevent Mutran from developing his new style any further? Some have explained this sad phenomenon by saying that it was a result of the opposition with which his new style of writing was received. This explanation is to some extent supported by a statement made by Mutran himself in an article published in November 1933 in the periodical *al-Hilal*:

> The circumstances of my early background forced me to avoid shocking people by expressing all that came to my mind, particularly to avoid shocking them by the form in which I would have preferred to express myself had I been completely free. I therefore followed the ancient forms as far as it was possible for me to do so.[23]

Mutran's reversion to more conventional poetry has been ascribed not only to lack of sympathy in the reading public who preferred more traditional forms, but also to his poor health and to the need to make a living which allowed him little time or energy for more demanding 'creative' writing.[24] A more likely explanation is that Mutran's inspiration simply dried up in his forties. That he continued to write verse regardless is, as he himself put it in his 'Farewell to the Muse', to be ascribed to his almost puritanical fear of being idle (IV,338).

The Diwan Group

The tension between the old form and the new content in the poetry of Mutran can also be seen in the works of Mutran's younger contemporaries al-Mazini, Shukrī and al-'Aqqad, who, in spite of the important role they played in the development of Arabic poetry, were less gifted poets than Mutran.

Ibrāhīm Abdul Qādir al-Māzinī (1890–1949) was born in a middle-class Egyptian family, his father being a lawyer. He received his education first in the secular schools, and then at the Teachers' Training College, from which he graduated in 1909. He started his career as a teacher of translation in a secondary school in Cairo, then as a teacher of English. He later gave up teaching to become a freelance journalist, devoting his energies to politics and literature. Mazini distinguished himself as a poet, critic, essayist, novelist and translator. He began his literary career as a poet, and he published two volumes of verse, the first in 1913 and the second in 1917. Early in his career he met ʻAqqad and Shukri, and the three of them formed a distinct group of *avant-garde* writers, calling themselves *madrasat al-tajdīd* (the School of Innovation) and attacking traditional literary values. Although Mazini later quarrelled with Shukri, his friendship with ʻAqqad remained unimpaired until his death. ʻAqqad wrote the preface to his first volume of verse, and they collaborated in publishing two volumes of literary criticism, called *al-Dīwān* in 1921. Prior to that Mazini had expressed his views on poetry in two long essays: *Poetry, its Ends and Means* (1915) and *Hafiz's Poetry* (1915). Later Mazini turned away from the writing of poetry, and concentrated on prose: he was to become one of the most important prose writers in modern Arabic literature.

ʻAbdul Raḥmān Shukrī (1886–1958) was also a graduate of the Teachers' Training College of Cairo. His father was an army officer who took part in the ʻUrabi revolution and was jailed for some time; he was a close friend of the orator of the Revolution, ʻAbdullah Nadīm. When the son had finished his primary and secondary school education he entered the Law School, but was soon sent down because of his political activities on behalf of the Nationalist Party. At the Teachers' Training College, which he joined later, he developed a great interest not only in Arabic but also in English literature, and while still a student he contributed to the modernist paper of the time, *al-Jarīda*, which was edited by Lutfi al-Sayyid, who encouraged promising young authors like Muḥammad Ḥusain Haikal and Taha Husain. After he had published his first volume of verse, *The Light of Dawn*, in 1909, he was sent on an educational mission to England, where he acquired a deeper knowledge of English literature at Sheffield University College. On his return in 1912 he was appointed teacher in a secondary school in Alexandria, and, unlike Mazini, he remained in the field of education until his retirement in 1944. His second volume of verse was published in 1912, also with an introduction by ʻAqqad. The rest of the volumes followed in rapid succession and by 1919 the seventh and last volume of his collected poems or *Diwan* called *Azhār al-Kharīf* (Autumn Flowers),[25] had appeared. Like Mazini, Shukri wrote most of his poetry early in his career, for from that date until his death in 1958, he published poems in literary periodicals, but never a whole volume of verse. Besides his poetry he produced a number of prose works, the most interesting of which is a short book of remarkable frankness, called *The Book of Confessions* (1916), a book full of profound self-analysis and acute observations on art and man, life and death, and graphically expressing the malaise of the Egyptian intellectual at the beginning of the century. Shukri, however, did not acknowledge his authorship of *The Book of Confessions* but he attributed it to an imaginary friend, M. N. It is clear, however, that the author of the confessions is none other than Shukri himself. Mazini saw the point at once, and he later made use of it in the severe attack he launched on him when he tried to prove Shukri's madness. After this attack, but not entirely because of it, Shukri gradually withdrew within himself, cutting himself off from the literary society of his time. His pessimism had the better of him, and he was driven to near silence: he spent the last years of his life in morbid seclusion – a paralyzed man whose spirit was almost completely broken. The poems published in various journals after 1919 were collected and published by his editor as the eighth volume in his *Collected Poems* (*Diwan*) in 1960.

Unlike Mazini and Shukri, 'Abbās Maḥmūd al-'Aqqād (1889–1964) was largely self-taught. At the age of fourteen when he was halfway through his secondary school he left his native town Aswan for Cairo, seeking employment. Having spent some time in a junior post in the civil service, he decided to take up journalism. He also did some school teaching, which gave him the opportunity of meeting his future friend Māzini. After the First World War, both he and Mazini gave up school teaching to devote their time to journalism. He wrote many political articles for the Wafdist *al-Balāgh* and later wrote much of his literary criticism for its weekly literary supplement. He collected this and published it later in the form of collections of essays, for instance. *Reviews in Literature and Art*, *Readings in Books and Life*, and *Chapters*. During the despotic rule of Ṣidqī (1930–4), 'Aqqad wrote a passionate plea for democratic freedom, *Autocratic Rule in the Twentieth Century*. He was tried for his attack on King Fuad and sentenced to nine months' imprisonment, and in *The World of Prisons and Chains* he left us an account of his imprisonment. 'Aqqad led a full, active life, and his works, which run into more than ninety volumes, deal with practically every topic under the sun. Besides writing on politics and society, literature and philosophy, both in East and West, he wrote a novel, *Sara*, in powerful and sinewy prose, and a number of biographies, for instance on Muhammad, Abu Bakr, 'Umar and 'Ali. Unlike Mazini and Shukri, 'Aqqad continued to write and publish volumes of verse. The first volume appeared in 1916 and by 1928 he had published four volumes, which he had gathered together under the name *Diwan al-'Aqqad*. In 1933 appeared his volume of poems about the curlew and *On Attaining the Age of Forty*, and in 1937 his volume on themes and subjects from everyday life called *The Wayfarer*. Three more volumes were still to appear: *Evening Storm*, signifying old age, *After the Storm*, and a *Sequel to After the Storm* which was his last volume.[26]

Writing of this group of poets, one of them, 'Aqqad, says the following in his well-known book *Egyptian Poets and their Environment in the Last Generation.* The passage is important and is quoted at length.

> The generation which appeared after Shauqi were not in the least influenced by him, either in their language, or in the spirit of their poetry . . . They read directly the *Diwans* of the ancients, studied them and admired in their style whatever they found agreeable . . . Were it not for the similarity of their general attitude, these modern poets would have differed widely the one from the other as a result of the stylistic differences between their favourite poets, who were as distinct one from another as Mutanabbi was from Ma'arri, Ibn al-Rūmi, al-Sharīf al-Raḍiyy, Ibn Ḥamdīs or Ibn Zaidun. As it was, they only differed in their opinions on detail and in the manner of expressing them, but they were all agreed on the conception of poetry and the criteria of criticism . . .
>
> As regards the spirit of their poetry, the younger generation . . . were widely read in English literature. In this respect they differed much from the writers who appeared towards the end of the past century, and whose reading in western literature was confined to certain limited aspects of French writing. Yet, despite their extensive reading in English literature, they were by no means unaware of the works of the German, the Italian, the Russian, the Spanish and the ancient Greek and Latin poets and prose writers. In their reading in English literature they seem to have benefited more from literary criticism than from poetry or other forms of literature. I do not think it would be wrong to say that to the whole school Hazlitt was the guide in the field of criticism, it was he who led them to a true understanding of the meaning of poetry and other arts, to the various kinds of writing and the aims of each kind, and to the proper use of quotation and comparison . . . In their admiration for Hazlitt then, the Egyptian authors were not slavish imitators; what enabled them to retain their independent judgment when approaching western literature was the fact that they had previously (and even concurrently) been reading their own literature; they therefore did not enter the world of western literature blindly or without discrimination.
>
> The truth is that the Egyptian school did not imitate English literature, but it benefited from it and was guided by it. Further, it formed its own opinion of each English author in accordance with its own independent judgment, and did not mechanically adopt the estimate arrived at by the author's countrymen.[27]

Then follows a list of the authors cited as a source of inspiration to Egyptian writers, which includes the names of Wordsworth, Shelley, Byron, Carlyle, Browning, Tennyson and Hardy, and the Americans Emerson, Longfellow, Poe and Whitman.

Of course, this partisan account of the whole movement given by 'Aqqad, who is one of its staunch protagonists, is in many respects highly exaggerated. In the first place, as the eminent Egyptian literary critic Muhammad Mandur pointed out,[28] the classical Arabic poets members of the group read were obviously confined to those of the Abbasid period, to whose works they often referred in their writings. Secondly, their knowledge of western literature, ancient and modern, was not so great and intimate as is suggested here, and it was derived through the English language. Thirdly, although the poet boasts of their wide reading in English literature, when it comes to their actual poetic output we find that the main influence comes from Palgrave's *The Golden Treasury*. Fourthly, there is a cunning and deliberate omission of the significance of the role of Shauqi's great contemporary, Khalil Mutran, whose importance in the development of modern Arabic poetry 'Aqqad grossly underrates in other places. Yet, despite its exaggeration, 'Aqqad's account does reveal one or two significant points about his group: their extreme reaction against Shauqi, and their direct indebtedness to western literature and particularly English literature. The two points, in fact, are not completely unrelated. 'Aqqad's group rejected Shauqi, because they came to know specimens of English poetry which seem to involve totally different principles. Their whole position is crystallized in their attitude to the question of the unity of a poem – the very same question which, as we have seen, had occupied Mutran's mind.

'Aqqad's detailed treatment of the matter is to be found in the collection of critical essays which he wrote in conjunction with Mazini under the name *al-Dīwān* and which the authors had hoped to produce in ten volumes. In actual fact only two volumes appeared, in 1921,[29] and the main aim of the authors in these two volumes was strongly similar to that of Dr Leavis in *Scrutiny*, of debunking and attacking current orthodox values or the literary Establishment. While Mazini concentrated his attack upon the popular prose writer of the period, al-Manfaluti, the author of the sentimental and ornate reflections-cum-short stories, Shauqi was the main butt of 'Aqqad's virulent onslaught. 'Aqqad bases his spirited attack on a number of points, the most important of which being the absence of unity in Shauqi's poems. He selects as his example the Elegy on Mustafa Kamil; after a complete reshuffling in a thoroughly amusing fashion, of the individual lines of which the poem consists, in order to show that nothing is lost by a change of the order of its composition. 'Aqqad concludes that the poem is nothing but 'a heap of sand lacking in spirit, and in progression and devoid of a unifying feeling',[30] while a good poem in his opinion 'ought to be one complete work of art, in which one impulse or a number of homogeneous impulses are given a unified form . . . in such a way that if the order is changed or the proportions varied, the unity of design is impaired and the whole work suffers'. The same need for organic unity in the Arabic poem is insisted upon by Shukri, who, in the relatively long introduction to volume v of his *Collected Works*, enunciates a number of principles, including the principle that 'the value of a line (*bait*) consists in the relation between its sense and the subject of the whole poem, since the line is only a component part' and the principle that 'a poem ought to be regarded as a complete whole, not as a collection of autonomous lines'.[31] This is not the place to discuss the value of *al-Diwan* in the history of modern Arabic literary criticism, although it may be mentioned, in passing, that in spite of its obvious extremism and partisanship, it does contain some of the best practical criticism produced in Arabic in the first half of the century. What needs to be pointed out, however, is the fact that 'Aqqad succeeded to a large extent in preparing the reading public, especially the younger generation, for the acceptance of a new type of poetry, different from the neoclassical. According to 'Aqqad, there was so much demand for the first volume that it had to be reprinted only a few months later. Although neoclassicism proved to be hard to kill, and many poets like 'Ali al-Jarim and Muḥammad 'Abdul Muṭṭalib continued to write poetry in the manner of Shauqi, it can be safely said that, with the possible exception of Jawahiri and Badawi al-Jabal, from the time of *al-Diwan* on no truly major Arabic poet sought to write in the traditional neoclassical style, And it is no wonder that a radical revolutionary like the Lebanese Mikha'īl Nu'aima hailed the appearance of the *Diwan* with such rapturous enthusiasm in his own equally, if not more iconoclastic volume *al-Ghirbāl* (The Sieve) which was published in 1923.

Apart from their belief in the organic unity of the poem, these three poets, Mazini, Shukri and 'Aqqad, had much in common, although by the time the *Diwan* was published they had ceased to form a group. All three poets had a serious and lofty conception of poetry and literature in general. According to them, poetry, far from being merely a matter of verbal tricks, is, or should be, the product of a deep emotional experience, and ought to express a valuable attitude to existence or a philosophy of life. Poets, therefore, should not prostitute their talents and waste their time writing imitative panegyrics to rulers or verses on trivial social occasions. The main faults of Shauqi in 'Aqqad's view are (apart from the absence of unity in a poem) absurdity, imitativeness and preoccupation with accident rather than substance.[32] Poetry, says Shukri in the introduction to his fifth volume of verse (1916), is essential to life, and 'a true poet regards writing poetry as the greatest thing he can do in his life, and believes that poetry is his *raison d'être*, that far from being something complementary to his life poetry is in fact its essence' (p. 360). As 'Aqqad and Mazini expressed it in the *Diwan*, the aim of the modern Egyptian author is to write literature which is *insānī miṣri 'arabī*, that is, universal, Egyptian and Arabic at one and the same time.[33]

Perhaps next to their insistence on the need to create an organic unity in a poem comes the importance these three poets attached to the part played by emotion in poetry. The poetry they advocated is primarily of a subjective or personal nature. Although this does not constitute a completely new departure in Arabic poetry, in this respect the influence of English literature upon them is quite clear. As it has already been pointed out, the English poetry they were most familiar with, and which they found most appealing, was the poetry contained in Palgrave's *The Golden Treasury*, which is on the whole biassed in favour of emotional, subjective or lyrical verse. Likewise, the English literary critics they read and used as their guides (Hazlitt in the case of 'Aqqad and Coleridge in the case of Shukri, who even adopted his distinction between 'imagination' and 'fancy'),[34] were Romantic critics who seemed to set a high value on the role of emotion in poetry. 'What distinguishes a poet from the rest of men is the strength, depth and wide range of his feelings and his ability to penetrate into the reality of things,' says 'Aqqad,[35] thus combining in one sentence both the emotive and the transcendental theories of poetry. True poetry should never remain on the level of the senses, but, he tells us, should go beyong the senses to the feelings and the emotions: the only justification for a simile, therefore, is not mere apparent external likeness, but the feeling and the emotion it conveys. In the same way Shukri maintains that a true poet does not seek a simile for its own sake, and in the second edition of his first volume of verse he uses as his epigraph the following line:

> O bird of paradise, poetry is but emotion (p. 266).

The subject of his preface to the third volume (1915) is the importance of emotion in poetry:

> A great poet is not content with conveying knowledge or understanding to people, but he tries to transport them into a state of ecstasy against their will, mixing his emotions and feelings with theirs. The poetry of emotion has a particular ring and tone which you cannot find in any other type of poetry. One day people will wake up to the realization that it *alone* is poetry. (p. 209).

Mazini defines poetry as an art 'of which the end is emotion, the means imagination or a stream of related ideas directed by emotion'.[36]

The best works produced by this group of poets were, therefore, of a dominantly subjective nature, expressing the poet's own response to others or to nature or to his metaphysical condition: poems of introspection, confessional poems or poems which record a mood, usually one of sorrow and despondency.

The insistence of these poets on the need to write Egyptian literature is in fact related to their belief in subjective poetry; poetry, that is, which is the product of the poet's direct experience, and not the result of cold and mechanical imitation. As Mazini constantly maintained, sincerity is of prime importance in literature. This comes out clearly also in 'Aqqad's attempt, which is not always successful, to write about ordinary scenes from everyday life in Egypt, no less than in his well-known remarks in the preface to his volume of poems on the curlew, which are obviously inspired by the various English Romantic poems written on, or addressed to, a number of birds in *The Golden Treasury*. 'Aqqad attacks the previous Egyptian poets who address the nightingale in their works, even though, he claims, the bird is little heard in Egypt, and neglect the curlew utterly, because of their preference for lifeless literary conventions to warm and concrete real experience.

One final feature of the works of these poets is their common attitude to the Arabic language. They avoided mere verbiage and the desire to impress their readers by the wide extent of their vocabulary, which drove most of the neoclassicists to the use of archaic and far-fetched words, and which made it necessary for them or their editors to provide with their poems glossaries explaining the meaning of difficult words. 'Aqqad, Mazini and Shukri went a long way towards simplifying the language of poetry. Yet on the whole, their diction and rhythms and the spirit of their language bore some resemblence to that of the Abbasid poets, and they did not avoid the use of archaic vocabulary altogether. Unlike the *Mahjar* poets (the Arab poets who emigrated to America) they were meticulous about their Arabic, proud of the poetic achievements of the Arabs. This is clear not only from the style of their poetry, but also from the Introduction which 'Aqqad wrote to Nu'aima's *Ghirbāl*, in which he takes care to point out the difference of his own views from those of Nu'aima on the question of the language of poetry:

> The crux of the difference is that the author deems it superfluous to be concerned with diction or language, and thinks that an author or a poet is free to make language mistakes as long as his intention is clear and his language meaningful, and believes that the law of evolution necessitates that authors should be allowed to form new derivations and coin words. These views, which may be regarded as tenable by some worthy colleagues, are in my opinion in need of modification and correction.

'Aqqad then adds the Longinian remark: 'I believe that an author may be excused a fault, only when the fault is better, more beautiful and significant, than the correct version.'[37]

In their almost obsessive care for the spirit of the Arabic language, as it is revealed in the heritage of the past, together with their generally conservative attitude towards versification, these poets, unlike the romantics, especially those of *al-Mahjar*, occupy a position similar to that of Mutran between the neoclassicists and the romantics. It is true that the language of their poetry is no longer the language of pure statement, but it has not attained the full power of suggestion that the language of the romantics was later to develop.

Shukri

Of the three poets, Shukrī, much of whose poetry reminds one of Edward Young's *Night Thoughts*, is certainly the greatest: in spite of their many interesting poems the genius of Mazini and 'Aqqad reveals itself more clearly in the sphere of prose. Shukri is perhaps one of the most fascinating and complex personalities in the history of modern Arabic poetry. The clue to his personality probably lies in his hypersensitivity, a quality which 'Aqqad justly noted in his obituary of the poet.[38] This is the impression one amply receives from his clearly autobiographical book *The Book of Confessions* (1916).[39] It is because of Shukri's hypersensitivity, which borders on the abnormal and pathological, that Mazini accused him of madness in the unkind attack he launched on him in the critical work *al-Diwan*, which was provoked by Shukri's strictures on his many obvious borrowings (or plagiarisms) from western writings. In an interesting attempt to universalize his problem, Shukri claims in the introduction to the *Confessions* that the author of the book is typical of Egyptian youth at that juncture in the history of Egypt, in alternating between excessive hope and utter despair (as a result of the state of Egyptian society which inspired both extremes) and being exceedingly suspicious (and this is the product of ages of despotic rule), weak of resolve, given to day-dreaming and to entertaining wild hopes and ambitions which they can never realize because of their inactivity. They are capable only of spasmodic acts of courage and are generally timid. They are excitable but without profundity, vain and exceedingly sensitive, impatient and fond of complaining. Despite their vanity they are confused, perplexed and full of doubts, not certain which of their outworn beliefs and traditions are harmful superstition and which of their newly acquired modern ideas and attitudes are true and useful, with the result that they are harmed both by the old and the new. In his further description of the author he says that despite the sardonic expression on his face he was a very kind and compassionate man. He was in turn proud and humble, but generally melancholic because he was misunderstood and mistrusted by his society whom he in his turn misunderstood and mistrusted.

This sketch of the author and his cultural background shows that Shukri had a good deal of honesty and insight into his own character. There is no doubt that Shukri's malaise was in part a reflection of the malaise of contemporary Egypt, caught as it was in the clash between traditional Islamic and western values in a period of cultural transition. But equally Shukri's own psychological make-up contributed to it. The book fills in various details which either provide or explain themes treated in his poetry. He begins with the assumption that happiness and great sensitivity are mutually exclusive, that a man of feeling is inevitably a man of suffering (*C.* p. 13), that the taste of the masses in poetry and the fine arts is corrupt and that the conventional poetry of eulogy, elegy, satire and description of daily political and social occurrences, in short the poetry of the Establishment at the time, is poetry of the 'false heart' and that the true poet 'describes the passion of the soul' (*C.* pp. 19–20), that the soul is full of contradictions (*C.* p. 74) and is 'a temple inhabited by God who illuminates it with His light, but is also Satan's cave lit up by his fire,' (*C.* p. 85). On the different stages of the development of the poet's mind we read the following:

> In my childhood, I was very superstitious, seeking the company of old women to hear stories about the supernatural to the extent that their stories filled every corner of my mind which became a huge world teeming with magic and demons ... Later I went through a phase of religiosity during which I became immersed in books of devotion which described the characteristics of wickedness as well as God's horrible punishment. The full horrors of this unbearable punishment are so vividly depicted in these books that whenever I dreamed about them I used to wake up with a start ...
>
> I subsequently turned to reading books of poetry and literature, so I became aware of the beauty of the world and my terrors which had been inspired by religion grew less. I then passed through the stage of doubt and quest ... I denied the existence of God with the same fanaticism as that with which others asserted their faith in Him. Yet my denial alarmed me without satisfying my mind, for it never explained to me what I am, why I exist, and whither I shall be going ... I used to roam the streets of the city at night (for night seemed to accord with my feelings of despair and sorrow) looking at the stars, asking them about life and death, God and man, this world and the next. But the stars merely looked back at me as if in pity and in sadness ... and life then felt heavier than a nightmare or a horrifying dream ...
>
> Eventually I regained my faith, having learnt that the universe has a huge spirit with its own life and personality and that this spirit inspires its will to the various individual spirits and that the Fates are its subalterns. Yet despite my strong rejection of popular beliefs I experience moments in which I can accept anything, even magic and what violates or suspends the operation of the laws of nature ... (*C.* pp. 21–5).

The above quotations underline the fact that the change in the conventional idiom of Arabic poetry is, like all genuine changes in artistic expression, not simply a matter that affects the external and artificial features of style. It presupposes a change in the whole of the poet's *Weltanschauung*, his general attitude to life, man and God. What we find in these quotations is the psychological dislocation and the spiritual turmoil and confusion which attend the change from the relatively comfortable and comforting world of neoclassicism with its traditional values, in which a certain measure of agreement obtained on the major issues of life. In *Confessions* Shukri records the impact of such a change on a man of sensibility. Shukri's hypersensitivity, coupled with his vivid imagination and a tendency towards self-dramatization remain salient features of his poetry. On the subject of imagination we find this interesting comment in *Confessions*, revealing a significantly ambivalent attitude, the relevance of which we shall see later on:

> Imagination is both the paradise and the hell of our dreams. Do we not spend our life alike in our dreams and our daydreams, alternating between roses and thorns, between angels and demons? At times I feel as if I had been transported to a world other than this world, where the air is perfumed and water fragrant and people are perfect in beauty and virtue . . . I see in my reveries visions so beautiful that I cannot adequately describe them. But at other times I see black dreams of despair and sorrow, then I fear all the disasters of life which can be pictured by the imagination in its countless different forms. I anticipate them and feel their painful impact . . . The pain which I endure is the result of the folly of fear engendered by imagination. (*C.* pp. 68–70).

Already in volume I of his *Diwan*, which appeared in 1909, when the poet was only twenty-three years of age, and before his departure for England, we notice sometimes in embryo many of the main themes which were to characterize Shukri's subsequent poetry. It is true that we find a number of poems dealing with topics of public interest. He wrote elegies on the nationalist leaders Mustafa Kamil, Qasim Amin and Muhammad ʻAbduh (*Diwan*, pp. 47, 53, 54, 58). He made an appeal for fund-raising in order to help establish a secular Egyptian university, a plea for national unity and for the sinking of differences between Copts and Muslims in the national interest, for the unity of political factions in an attempt to restore past glory, an exhortation to the people of Egypt to shake off their stagnation and humiliation and to learn to be steadfast and resolute (pp. 39,40,48,69,71). Likewise he poses as a stern moralist. The very first poem in the collection 'Chosroes and the Captured Woman' opens with an address to young women, asking them to heed the story he is about to tell, showing how a young beautiful woman can protect her honour and overcome the importunities and threats of even a tyrant. He calls his story 'a tale with a moral'. The next narrative poem, entitled 'The Lover of Money' and given the subtitle 'How women are deceived', tells the story of a man who has been professing his love for a wealthy woman he is courting, but who ruthlessly spurns her once he learns of the loss of her fortune (pp. 19, 22). He warns against the danger of despair and preaches the need for resolution (*ḥazm*), a recurrent word in his poetry which is imbued with a spirit of stoicism (p. 40). Yet in the entire volume there are no more than the handful of poems listed above on public themes, and of a poem like 'The Lover of Money' more than one-third is taken up by a long detailed description of the background of nature against which the story takes place. Nature and the poet's subjective emotions, his thoughts and his attitudes provide the main themes of the vast majority of the poems.

In 'A Stranger's Nostalgia at Sunset' the sight of sunset arouses feelings of sorrow and nostalgia both in the stranger and in the poet. Nature acts as a catalyst for the poet's identification with the stranger, thereby emphasizing his feeling of alienation from his society. This is how Shukri describes the poet or creative writer:

> At home and amidst his own people he lives like a sad stranger . . .
> Nought in his heart but love, sorrow and anger against these
> untrusted times (p. 25).

Shukri can be more cheerful, as in his description of the sea or his hymn to the sun at sunrise (pp. 27, 33), but the mood is generally a sombre one; even when nature has a liberating effect upon the poet as in 'The Meadow at Night'. In 'The Garden' we are told that 'unlike man's joy the joy of the birds is unmixed with sorrow' (72,37). In 'Complaint against the Times', one of many plaintive poems, the poet is in a state of near despair in which he is 'spurned by God's mercy while being so young' (p. 40), for such is the lot of poets, as he says in 'The Poet and His Beloved': God has ordained that 'sweet hope flees from a poet's thoughts just as a healthy man flees from a leper' (p. 49). The theme of the lover as a worshipper of beauty already appears here in 'The Worship of Beauty' (p. 63). There is a large number of short poems in this volume, expressing meditations and aphorisms mainly about love and the sufferings of the lover mostly couched in conventional idiom, and the volume ends with a long poem in what he describes as *shi'r mursal* (blank or rhymeless verse), entitled 'Words of Passion', and containing his observations on various causes of the poet's sufferings and his reflections and aspirations towards a higher and happier state of affairs in the world, in a rather prosaic language which is not characterized by its verbal felicity (p. 85).

Shukri's second volume, which appeared in 1913, after his return from his studies in England, and prefaced with an enthusiastic introduction by ʿAqqaḍ, contains much of his mature work and is more typical of his productions until 1919, the date of the appearance of the last volume he published in his own lifetime. Contrary to prevalent opinion, in his mature work Shukri never loses interest in public or social issues altogether. He urges his people to accept change and progress and not to stagnate (p. 107), pointing out to them that it is only false religion that preaches resignation while true religion means heroic struggle and endurance (p. 109). He preaches the value of work and the danger of despair in his didactic poem 'Life and Work' (p. 113), drawing a painful contrast between dynamic Europe and his own stagnant society (p. 305) and stresses mankind's need for visionaries and dreamers to achieve great things (p. 298). He writes on the suffering of an orphan child (p. 111), the fear of death and the unknown expressed in a sick child's conversation with his mother (p. 122), pleads for educating criminals in prison instead of sentencing them to death, and for showing mercy to those who commit crimes driven by poverty and need (p. 134). He attacks the veiling of women (p. 152) and the attitude which regards them as mere chattels and as their husbands' private property (p. 141). He describes his country's ancient monuments like the Sphinx and the Great Pyramid, although here he is simply moralizing on man and time and the transitoriness of human life and achievements (pp. 440, 444). 'The Voice of Warning' is a passionately committed poem in which, in ruthlessly frank terms, he laments the weakness of the Egyptian character and tries to rouse his fellow countrymen to improve their lot through scientific, technological and economic enterprise (p. 277). An equally angry criticism of his backward nation for their neglect of science and knowledge, the only means to glory, appears in 'Science and Dignity' (p. 415). 'The Awaited Hero' is a Messianic poem which is an invocation to the long-awaited hero, the saviour of his nation, to come and revive the spirits of his people who will then shed their lethargy and identify themselves with him, and be infected by his determination and resolve (p. 387). In the last published volume of his poems we still find a moving poem like 'The Youthful Hag' in which the poet, ever-loyal to his country and hopeful of her resurrection, persists in his attempts to rouse her from her deep slumber despite the unpopularity that this will bring him. 'I have not been negligent in my preaching, but have been let down by deaf ears' (p. 557).

Shukri never manages to drop the stance of a moralist. In 'Black Flowers' he attacks the pleasures of life which ultimately bring pain, regret and sorrow in their wake (p. 227). In the epigraph to volume IV he points out that the function of poetry is to ennoble and raise the soul above all that is base

(p. 284). Furthermore in the poetry written after 1919 Shukri became excessively moralistic, and often his poems were no more than a string of moral observations and meditations, and his satires grew more savage and direct, as in 'Dead People' (p. 643) published in 1938, although as late as 1935 he was capable of writing such a remarkably lyrical and evocative poem as 'A Lovely Night' (p. 612). No doubt his attitude as a moral teacher was later enforced by his career as schoolmaster and educationist.

But from the second to the seventh volumes of his *Diwan* there is undeniably a growing concentration on the poet's inner world, his subjective and spiritual experiences. His complaints against his times increasingly sounded less like those of a social reformer and more like those of an 'outsider', who is at odds with a society that was incapable of either understanding him or appreciating his efforts. In 'The Poet and the Ruined Times' (p. 157) lack of appreciation and the difficulties put in the poet's path end by destroying his hopes and render his heart 'like a ruined mansion'. The same feeling is expressed in countless poems such as 'A Poet's Complaint', 'A Poet's Prophecy', 'Agitation of the Soul', 'Fear and Terror', 'Poetry and Nature' and 'A Poet Dying' (where the chief source of the young poet's sorrow is his failure to attain fame before death) (pp. 164, 167, 169, 221, 226 and 235). Shukri's agonizing awareness that he was living in a period of great cultural upheaval, where the clash between traditional and modern values had a devastating effect upon society and especially the sensitive individual (particularly fully expressed in the *Confessions*), often made him, like Hamlet, feel that 'the time's out of joint', and touched the metaphysical roots of his existence.

Shukri's early feeling of alienation, which as we have seen, is discernible in 'A Stranger's Nostalgia at Sunset', was enforced by his experience in Sheffield where he spent three years. His poems 'A Poet in a Strange Land' and 'Nostalgia of a Stranger' show that he felt very much like an exile there, cut off from his home, friends and familiar surroundings, missing the sunshine and clear sky in a gloomy city where 'Above us the sky is in mourning like the vault of a tomb' (pp. 154, 155). In 'The Humiliation of Old Age' the poet's feeling of being a stranger among his kith and kin drives him to desire death before he becomes a despised old man (p. 418).

The main themes of Shukri's poetry are philosophical and moral meditations, interesting or unusual states of mind, beauty in general and nature in particular, love, death, and the creative imagination. He wrote about man's belief in the golden age (p. 574); in 'Man and Time' (p. 136) he wonders if man's desire for a better world is the result of his soul remembering a less imperfect pre-natal existence; in 'Mixed Needs' (p. 139) the body is described as 'the gateway to the soul' while 'The Eternal Seeker' (p. 292) represents allegorically the value of the eternal quest for truth. 'The Voice of God' is a religious and mystical comment:

> Listen, in listening the soul communes, for God's eloquent voice is so near.
> Each of us is a Moses. In the eyes of the Lord all pure souls are great.
>
> (p. 349)

In the introduction to Volume VII Shukri denies the charge of lack of religious faith levelled at him, claiming that 'Doubt or questioning does not betray insufficient faith, on the contrary, it is the highest degree of faith', and that belief in God and in good is 'a basic need necessitated by the enormity of evil and misery' in this world (p. 505). This enormity prompted a compassionate angel, in the poem entitled 'The Rebellious Angel' (p. 537), to rebel against God and decide to turn his back on his blissful life in heaven and seek the earth in order to alleviate human suffering and combat evil. On earth he met with the same fate as Christ, but because he had rebelled his soul was condemned to an eternally restless existence, neither in heaven nor in hell. According to the poet, God's wisdom, which the angel had failed to understand, lies in making evil an occasion for good to reveal itself.

But it cannot be said that Shukri is as sensitive to the good as he is to the evil in man and in human society. 'The Mirror of Conscience' shows his unusually keen awareness of evil in the world of man (p. 235). Poems like 'The Nature of Man' (p. 228) and 'The Friendship between the Dead and the Living' (p. 232) show the extent of his misanthropic feeling: in the latter he says that we forget the enmity of those who die and passionately lament their death, thinking that they are loyal to us, but if they were to return to the world of the living they would prove to be faithless in their affections. Another poem is entitled 'The Mirage of Friendship' (p. 250). This sentiment is expressed in countless other poems. In 'The Futility of Life' (p. 251) he writes, 'If man were to know the full extent of his misery in life he would not have wished to be born'. In 'Boredom with Life' boredom sets in as a result of the poet being suddenly assailed by the disease of doubt when he was in the midst of his enjoyment of a comfortable and easy life (p. 161). Shukri composed poems on the duality of passion, love/hate relationships, repentance and crime which reveal his fascination with unusual states of mind (pp. 146, 282). Despite the low opinion of human nature which he held Shukri was not a cynic: on the contrary his poetry is imbued with a strong feeling of pity, as is clear in, for instance, his poem 'The Murderer' (p. 383), a dramatic monologue in which the poet evinces a deep-rooted sense of sin, together with great compassion for human suffering, in some ways reminiscent of Shakespeare's portrayal of Macbeth, by which it may very well have been inspired.

Among Shukri's other themes nature occupies a large space. In 'The Magic of Spring' he claims that 'To be fully human man must love the beauty of nature, otherwise he is no better than a stone' (p. 217). 'The worship of beauty', he once wrote in an essay in 1916, 'frees man from the bondage of prejudice, obtuseness and narrow-mindedness, and bestows upon his soul a light which illuminates for him the secrets of life and opens the gates of his heart to every aspect of the beauty of nature.'[40] And as late as 1936 he wrote a poem entitled 'Truth and Beauty' (p. 623) in which the poet's sense of human misery makes him turn away from beauty to truth, but he soon realizes that beauty is designed to be a consolation enabling man to withstand sorrow and that it is the ideal which inspires man to improve his lot, and gives him hope, fortitude and love. 'The Voice of Night' opens with the words

> 'You have filled the world with your deep breathing
> Which all who have a wakeful heart could hear'. (p. 118)

The term 'wakeful heart' is significant and it recurs again in his verse ('a happy wakeful heart', p. 121). In 'A Description of the Sea' the poet is struck by the teeming sea and by its changing moods which make him feel it has a life of its own (p. 118). 'Narcissus', which is about both the mythological figure and the flower at one and the same time, reveals the poet's romantic ability to respond to nature and yet to transcend it (p. 342). A number of poems on birds, like 'Elegy on a Sparrow' in which there is a genuine feeling of bereavement at the death of a sparrow, and 'The Caged Songbird', show Shukri's powers of empathy, of feeling for non-human forms of life (pp. 162, 301). His poem 'To the Wind' (p. 401) is Shelleyan in its dynamic Dionysian quality and in the author's desire to identify himself with the wind. As in nature Shukri, like Wordsworth and other Romantics, found in childhood a source of joy which has a healing power for the soul: 'The Child' treats the innocent and divine joy of childhood while in 'Children's Laughter' he writes: 'The laughter of children, like the words of the Lord, wipes off sin and guilt.' (pp. 571; 114).

But it is love and beauty that provide the themes of the vast majority of Shukri's poems. To explain the preponderance of love poetry in his work he wrote in the introduction to volume IV of his *Diwan* (p. 290):

> By love poetry I do not mean the poetry of lust or sexual passion, but that of spiritual love which rises above all descriptions of the body except those which reveal the working of the soul. Love is the passion most intimately related to the soul, from it derive many passions or emotions such as hope, despair, envy, regret, bravery, cowardice, love of glory, munificence or

> meanness. Because of this love has a great place in poetry ... it is not a condition that love poetry should involve loving any one individual alone, although this may be the cause most likely to produce it. The love poetry I have in mind is caused by the passion which enables man to feel keenly Beauty in all its manifestations alike in a beautiful face, or a body, a flower or a river, in the beauty of lightning in the clouds, the beauty of night and stars, morning and its breeze, or the beauty of the soul or character, an attribute or an event, or the beauty of the images created by the human mind. The love of one human being for another is only one aspect of this extensive passion which embraces all visible beauty in life. This poetic passion bestows its light upon everything, even upon those loathsome dark aspects of life, giving them an artistic beauty ... Like the painter the love poet draws upon the images of beauty in his mind... Who knows, perhaps Qais ibn al-Mulawwaḥ was singing not about the [real] Laila al-ʿĀmiriyya, but about the one who inhabited the inner world of his soul.

As is to be expected Shukri's love poetry is marked by its excessive idealization of the beloved. In 'Smiles' (p. 148) we read that her smile brightens up his soul and nearly unveils the unknown secrets of the invisible world, enables him to hear myriad songs in his soul, and her glance breathes life in him as the sun causes the hidden seeds to germinate. The terms in which she is described suggest that she is more than a mere human being. In 'To the Beloved' (p. 177) the lover's attitude is one of utter humility. He addresses her in 'I Have No Other Concern But You' (p. 240), saying:

> My soul is a sapling which you have planted,

and

> My soul is the lowly earth beneath your heights
> You are the target of all creatures, no one lives but you
> So have mercy upon me, my beloved.

Clearly the object of love is almost divine here, and just as in 'The Sought Beauty' (p. 321) where he says:

> I saw in a dream your face which I adore
> Crowned with the stars of night

or in 'Love and Eternity' (p. 269), the poet's love is love of Beauty and not of an individual human being. But although he claims, 'I am not one who loves fair maidens, nor do my eyes shed tears when they desert me' ('Love and Affection', p. 271), there are moments when the passion seems to be for a human being. For instance, in the deeply moving 'A Lover Turns Away His Glance' (p. 172), the poet is agonizingly aware that the object of his desire is, for some mysterious reason which he dares not disclose, unattainable and that he therefore ought not to indulge in daydreams about him or her. Could it be that the poet was suffering from a homosexual passion? This is not at all a fantastic theory, although Shukri's general tendency to use the traditional Arabic masculine pronoun in his love poetry cannot help us to decide either way. However, we do know that Shukri never married, and what is more interesting, there is a morbid fascination with death and the gruesome aspects of physical decay and dissolution in practically all his love poems, especially where beautiful women are mentioned.

In the powerful poem 'Beauty and Death' (p. 115) the poet, troubled and unable to sleep, sees in the dark of night a vision of his recently dead beloved, but as he embraces her she once more dies in his arms, her beauty vanishes and her flesh disintegrates, leaving behind a skeleton smelling strongly of decay. The image of the poet kissing a dead corpse occurs again in his poetry ('Memories', p. 162). In 'Women in Life and in Death' (p. 132) he sees the ugly and the dead behind the beautiful and living, expressing a somewhat diseased sensibility:

> They rose, swaying in their clothes in the dark nights,
> After they had become food for worms . . .
> They came in the dark, and struck the eyes of beholders with disease,
> Echoing the shrieks of owls till the air grew sick,
> Wearing their shrouds for modesty, lest their ugliness be seen.
> Alike in death and in life they hide defects that make their modesty a mockery.

This hysterical, melodramatic and rather nightmarish vision brings out the strong connection in the poet's mind between beauty and decay and his ambivalent attitude towards women. In his prose work *Kitāb al-Thamarāt* (Book of Fruit), a book of meditations sometimes couched in poetic prose, on man, nature, society and art, some of which are close to the themes of his poetry, Shukri defines love as 'an animal whose upper half is a beautiful woman and whose lower part is a serpent'.[41]

Nearly every poem on love and beauty ends with thoughts on death. Examples are so many that they can be chosen at random. One poem is given the title 'Love and Death' (p. 211); others, like 'Beauty, the Mirror of Nature' (p. 216), 'Love's Paradise and Hell' (p. 218) and 'The End of Love' (p. 223) and 'After Beauty' (p. 268), all – and particularly the last two – show the poet unflinchingly facing the most unpleasant aspects of physical decay. 'Would we were' (p. 257) begins with:

> Would I were a breeze and you a bloom
> We would then love one another for ever
> We would neither quarrel nor part.
> Would I were a meadow and you the rain,

> Would I were the water and you the wine,
> We would then contain one another,
> With neither jealousy nor deceit

and it ends with:

> Would I were a dead man and you were my tomb
> There would then be neither longing nor despair
> Neither prohibition nor reprimand.

Just as there is death-imagery in his love poems, death conversely is often seen as a woman, sometimes with sexual overtones felt in his courtship of death. In 'Death' (p. 542) he prays to death to deliver him from a life which is a painful riddle and invokes death by the most appealing epithets and descriptions, calling it a mother that for long has been deaf to her son's entreaties and whose breasts he wishes to suck. He loves death as a man loves the face of his beloved and yearns to quench his passion by kissing its lips. And of course it is fairly often that the poet invokes death. In 'The Misery of Life' (p. 405), as the title suggests, the poet is writing about his sufferings. Though living amidst his people he feels as if he had come to them from another planet, new and strange. Tired of his life he calls upon death to relieve him, although death here is viewed in romantic pleasurable terms. 'Moonlight on the Tombs' (p. 145) depicts the moon as weary and wan, inspiring similar sensations in the beholder, and likens it to a fair maiden worn out by disease and lying on her death-bed. In 'The Voice of the Dead' (p. 151) the poet stands amidst the tombs and hears the voices of the dead sounding now like the rustling of wind in leaves, or the bubbling of water, now like the beating of drums, the wailing of bereaved women, the howling of desert wolves or the roaring of the enraged sea. 'Between Life and Death' (p. 213) gives us the lonely figure of the poet standing by the raging sea in the middle of a thunderstorm on a dark night, a perfect 'sublime' setting for the poet whose thoughts turn to the subject of death and suicide: he admits to love of death being 'an overwhelming secret disease' and addresses the sea saying:

> O save me from an unjust and wicked world,
> My misery is teeming like your waves.

In 'Buried Alive' (p. 215) he explains that the secret of his unhappiness is a great sorrow deeply seated in his heart; he feels that the wide world is too confined for him and that he is buried alive. It is as if in his sleep his relations, mistaking him for dead, buried him in a deep grave and piled earth and stone on top of him, and the poet woke up not knowing whether he was awake or had just had a nightmare. Finally, his well-known 'Dream of Resurrection' (p. 241) is a macabre poem giving the gruesome details of physical dissolution and betraying his low opinion of men, for it shows the persistence of human greed and strife when the bodies, risen from their graves, quarrel over the missing limbs and parts on the Day of Resurrection.

In 'Ideas Beyond the Reach of Words' (p. 21), as the title suggests, Shukri deals with the mysterious aspects of the psyche which cannot be logically discussed or formulated in words:

> Part of the soul they are and how can the soul be seen by the physical eye?
> You know them only when your wakeful heart is fortunate enough to feel them.
> They are often attained by the one who keeps silent, for silence yields much eloquence and is full of peace
> The soul speaks only to those who listen in humility.

These unknown and 'virgin' regions of the soul had a deep fascination for Shukri, as they did for his Romantic successors. He even wrote a poem entitled 'To the Unknown' (*ila'l majhūl*, a word which became very potent in romantic vocabulary) (p. 396), which shows this fascination (the patently didactic and moralistic prose introduction to the poem in which he links this passion to the healthy and useful scientific curiosity was added more than twenty years later). In 'The Marriage of Souls' (p. 392) the soul of each individual is felt to be an island, a *terra incognita*, a painful mystery and a riddle yearning for communion with its like through love, without which it becomes an arid desert without water or vegetation. In 'In Paradise', a poem seen by one scholar to be intimately related to D. G. Rossetti's *The Blessed Damozel* on the one hand and to the Moslem tradition of the Heavenly Bride, houri, on the other, the poet cannot be happy if he is divorced from his soulmate.[42] Hence the poet's constant quest for the ideal object of his desire. 'The Poet and the Image of Perfection' (p. 130) depicts a poet who in the pursuit of the ideal (which is ultimately Perfect Beauty – the creation of his imagination) is lured to his destruction (p. 130). Abdul-Hai thinks this poem is inspired by *Alastor*:

> As in the case of Shelley, the theme of Shukri's poem is self-alienation and the pursuit of a perfect image of the self which, in spite of its evasive nature, is the only means of attaining self-authenticity. It is not so much a pursuit of Ideal Beauty as an attempt of the mind to counter self-alienation by an image which the mind itself has evolved.[43]

This may be so, but arguably the poem is also a variation on the theme of *La Belle Dame Sans Merci*. Imagination is regarded as a tool of insight into a higher order of reality – a reality, however, which may render those who have glimpsed it incapable of coping with this mundane world. The poem clearly shows Shukri's ambivalent attitude to imagination which we have already encountered in his book of *Confessions*: he is both fascinated and frightened by it: 'lost is the man whose fancy is his guide'; it was left for a later, younger generation of more thorough-going romantics to accept imagination without any reserve. In 'The Mouthpiece of the Invisible' (p. 128) true imagination is said to be the mouthpiece of the invisible; and because the poet feels and suffers he sees what others cannot see and communes with the Divine. Likewise, 'Death and Imagination' (p. 153) shows the value of the imagination in conferring beauty on life, making both life and death easier to bear:

> There is in poetry many a pleasurable dream
> Which enables us to endure life or death.

The poet's vision can be a source of bliss: 'The Angels' Visit' (p. 480), for example, describes the poet, uncertain whether he was awake or asleep, receiving a host of angels who cure him of his despair, purify his soul and give him a moment of eternity. But visions can also be a source of terror. For instance in 'A Step away from the World of the Senses' (p. 419) the poet while awake dreams that he has departed from the world of the senses, but the fearful vision he sees which indicates to him the full extent of the dominion of death, drives him to seek frantically to return to the real world and after several unsuccessful attempts he manages to do so. He wishes he would never again in his life have a similar experience and advises others never to stray from the concrete and secure world of the senses. Moreover, in 'The Shadow of Madness' (p. 402) the poet feels the constant presence of the image of the beloved to be painfully oppressive, like an obsession or a disease and wishes in vain he could break free from his enthralment.

There are perhaps too many poems about the theme of idealized love in Shukri's work, and their cumulative effect tends to be rather monotonous, especially as the tone is generally solemn and unrelieved by any humour. Furthermore, they are mostly in the first person: there is not enough variety in them which could have been achieved if the poet had made a greater use of the narrative and dramatic poems. Not that Shukri's poetry is entirely lacking in formal variety. He uses the narrative and the dramatic monologue deriving his material from well known pre-Islamic Arabic stories and legends, or from more modern sources (pp. 142, 156, 180, 201, 205). He experiments in the use of the multiple rhyme, the alternate rhyme or rhyming couplet. He even attempts to write blank (rhymeless) verse on a number of occasions (pp. 200, 201, 203, 205), though the result cannot be described as successful, and in one case he finds himself slipping into monorhyme in eleven consecutive lines (p. 91). The poem which adheres to the monorhyme and monometre remains Shukri's norm.

Stylistically, too, despite the profound influence of English Romantic poetry on him, Shukri's style remains in many respects traditional: the vocabulary is still quite difficult, requiring a glossary, and the verse does not flow smoothly enough for the particular themes it tries to express. As has already been mentioned Shukri addresses the beloved in the traditional masculine form, and occasionally uses conventional love and desert imagery. He has an unmistakable tendency to express himself in generalizations, sentiments and moral precepts in the manner of traditional gnomic verse. Once or twice when as a young man he talked about his great ambition he struck the note of traditional boastfulness (*fakhr*) (pp. 46, 55). He sometimes complains of his times in the manner of Mutanabbi, and even in a poem expressing *ennui*, a specifically modern disease, we hear verbal echoes from Mutanabbi's verse (p. 161). It is true that Shukri can attain a high degree of lyricism, as in his most accomplished poem 'The Bird of Paradise' (p. 266), but this does not happen frequently enough. On the contrary, he can easily descend to the level of what is largely poetry of mere statement, even in a poem about a Romantic theme, as 'The Ideal' (p. 460), which is an unabashed defence of the infinite inner world of dreams and the imagination against the drab and limited external reality.

Mazini

The subjective element in Māzinī's poetry is paramount: in the whole body of his collected poems there are no more than four poems dealing with themes of public interest.[44] His poems have an atmosphere of romantic sadness; in them the poet complains, in the manner of Shelley, of the world, of life and of time. They are after all mostly poems of adolescence.

Mazini wrote about 'The Faded Rose', 'Dead Flowers'. 'The Dying Poet', 'Life is but a Dream'. In the second volume of his *Diwan* (1917) a whole section, including no less than twenty-eight poems, is devoted to the subject 'Reflections on Solitude'. Typical of Mazini's work is the long poem in the first volume (1913), *Munājāt al-Hājir* (To a Mistress who has Deserted Him), which, we learn from 'Aqqad, was partly inspired by the Abbasid poet Ibn al-Rumi.[45] In this poem, which contains more than 200 lines and a single rhyme throughout, the poet deals with a number of his favourite themes, ranging from unrequited love, the worship of beauty and the devotion to poetry, the lover seeking comfort in nature, especially its wilder aspects, his loneliness and despair and his welcoming of death.

Mazini translated or adapted a number of English poems (by Shakespeare, Milton, Waller, Burns, Shelley, Hood, Morris, Edward Fitzgerald and James Russell Lowell). His borrowings or plagiarisms from western writers have become notorious ever since Shukri pointed out some of them in the introduction to volume v of his *Collected Works.*[46] Mazini's interest in the wilder aspects of nature, which 'Aqqad praises in the introduction to the first volume of his *Diwan,*[47] betrays at least in part the influence of eighteenth-century English ideas on the Sublime. This influence, which he shares with 'Aqqad, was at times reinforced by that of the traditional pre-Islamic convention of writing about *aṭlāl,* (ruins). This is clearly seen in a poem like 'The Deserted House' which is among the poems singled out for praise by 'Aqqad (p. 29). In 'Agitation of the Soul' (p. 42) the poet likens his heart to 'a ruined cave on the summit of a high cliff, a playground for the winds' and himself to 'a rock in the midst of the sea of events against which beat the surging waves'. The experience with its horrifying components is melodramatic and hysterical, and the voice is loud and shrieking. Mazini seems to pile up violent, grotesque, dark and terrifying images in an attempt to evoke a 'sublime' atmosphere. In 'The State of the Agitation of the Soul in its Repose' (p. 76) the poet encounters a mad lover on a dark winter night while the winds are howling by a raging sea, and the lover intends to bury himself alive in the tomb of his beloved. We read that 'the winds were, as it were, lamenting the departure of stars which had been destroyed by the dark, and the sea responded by the roar of its surging waves'; that 'the demons of the dark were chanting through the winds' and that the mad lover had a tearful eye, an aching heart and a fearful lustre in his eyes which shone on that night, while his lips were trembling as he told his woeful tale. In 'Reverie' (p. 93) the poet writes: 'I heard a clamour in the dark, as if wolves were being tortured at night', the scaring noise robbing people of their reason, echoing throughout the waste land making the poet feel as if he was surrounded by corpses of dead men. In 'The Sea and the Dark' (p. 132) the poet complains, 'Darkness before me, darkness behind and darkness in my heart. Where then can I flee?'

No doubt the poet's feelings of despondency and despair which are expressed in many poems besides, such as 'Meditations in the Dark' (p. 167) and 'Desolation of Life' (p. 194) in terms which are patently melodramatic, are partly a consciously adopted posture, in which suffering is cultivated for its own sake, and which is the result of the poet's excessively solemn self-image – all the more surprising in a man who eventually proved to be one of the greatest humorists and masters of the ironic style in modern Arabic prose. The concept of the poet as primarily a man of sensibility who wrote about his suffering is uppermost in Mazini's mind, perhaps even more so than in those of the rest of the Diwan group. It was their awareness of their own suffering as poets that bound the three poets together, as is clearly seen in the poem addressed by Mazini to Shukri entitled 'The Vanity and Futility of Life' (p. 175). Mazini held that 'the more sensitive men are, the greater is their suffering' (p. 44). And because they suffer, Mazini says in 'The Poet's Consolation' (p. 169), poets can bring comfort to the lonely and the suffering. It is clearly part of the romantic image of the poet as a man whose exquisite sensibility distinguishes him from (and probably sets him on a higher level than) the rest of the community (p. 115). In 'The Worshipped Shepherd' (p. 121), a poem indebted to James Russell Lowell, we find the image of the singer who charms his hearers, men and beasts alike, and who is endowed with supernatural qualities and is therefore little understood by the rest of mankind to whom he is a superior being. The poet both as sufferer and as visionary is clearly seen in 'The Poet' (p. 178). Another component of the romantic image of the poet is that of the superiority of imagination: in 'Creature of Fancy' (p. 162) the beauty created by the imagination is regarded as more perfect than any real human being. Even the dangerous impact of the vision of beauty on a mere mortal is shown in 'The Bewitched Mariner' (p. 206) where the poet sees himself as an enraptured sailor lured to his destruction by a beautiful mermaid. The belief in the happiness and innocence of a prelapsarian state of childhood is expressed in the poem entitled 'Childhood' (p. 195) in which the suffering poet looks back nostalgically upon his childhood, the happiest period of his life.

All these elements of romanticism in Mazini's attitude towards man and society, poetry and the imagination generally remain somehow ill-digested and not sufficiently fused together and reduced to deeply satisfying artistic form. Yet despite their melodramatic quality they are the expression of a genuine state of mind and feeling: we must not forget that in his Introduction to Mazini's first volume of verse 'Aqqad praises the poet primarily for his sincerity (p. 24). Even making allowance for the propaganda-like aims of 'Aqqad and his intention to pave the way for the appreciation of his own similar brand of poetry, it would be foolish to dismiss his judgment altogether or, as is often done, to accept Mazini's later judgment on his own poetry in which he denied that he was a poet. Both Mazini and 'Aqqad believed in the romantic relativist notion that art expresses or should express the spirit of the age (p. 17ff). They were both deeply and painfully aware of living in a period of transition during which traditional cultural values were being seriously eroded without any other firm values being put in their place. As in the case of Shukri, the poet's suffering, doubts and anxieties were in many ways the reflection of the times which 'were characterized by anxiety and hesitation between a worn-out past and an uncertain future' and in which 'there was a wide gap between things as they were and things as they believed they ought to be'. 'Aqqad even draws a comparison between his age and that immediately preceding the French Revolution, with its clashing and new and unorthodox ideas and values in ethics, politics, religion and society. Mazini's poetry was, then, an expression of the malaise of the Egyptian intellectual, at a time of insecurely hovering between Arab and western values. In that sense it is an authentic record, despite the poet's heavy and at times unacknowledged indebtedness to Abbasid poets on the one hand and to English poets on the other, and despite his wavering between the European Romantic themes and the Abbasid idiom, and his not very successful experimentation in form; in the use of rhyming couplets, his experimental rhyme and even his use of blank verse in his translation of lines from Milton's *Paradise Lost* (pp. 89, 126). Furthermore, in the few poems in which the poet retains his irony and sense of balance he achieved very interesting results. For instance, in his 'Elegy on Himself' (p. 201) the poet's feeling of self-pity is effectively counterbalanced by his lack of illusions about himself and others (almost in the manner of the address of the author of *Les Fleurs du Mal* to the reader) or about the value of his own achievement. Similarly, in a humorous poem in the third volume of his *Diwan*, published posthumously in 1961, entitled 'Look at my Face' (p. 280), he makes fun of himself and of his physical appearance – a theme common in his prose writings. It is in this volume that we find one or two of Mazini's best poems in which the tone of the poetry is less strident and the effect is much more moving. For instance, 'Where's your Mummy? – a Dialogue with my son Muhammad' (p. 248):

> I did not speak to him, but the look in my eye said
> 'Where is your mummy? Where's your mummy?'
> While he was prattling away, as was his wont
> Every day since she has gone.
> He turned to me trying to smooth the furrows in my forehead,
> But how could that be done, I thought? How indeed?
> When his hand had passed over my face I said
> Do you know of aught, aught that might help?
> Help to do what, he asked. What do you mean, Dad?
> 'Nothing' I replied and I kissed him instead.

This is poetry pitched at a much lower key than is usual with Mazini, moving and adequately expressive of the grief and the sense of loss of the bereaved widower. A much more impressive poem is 'The Conflict' (pp. 262ff.) – a work hitherto totally ignored by critics. It is a long philosophic poem of over 300 lines written significantly enough in monometre and monorhyme.

Despite some obscurities this little-known poem is perhaps Mazini's most mature work. Considering its length, its vocabulary is largely straightforward, apart from words used mainly for the exigencies of the monorhyme. The theme of the poem is a problem, akin to that which faced the aged Yeats: an old man troubled with his lust and his fascination with the world of the senses, his love of beauty and beautiful young women. Should the poet not find solace and satisfaction in wisdom and the 'monuments of unageing intellect', as befits an old man, or should he give in to the urge of his instinct and the call of the world of the senses? The poem, as the title suggests, is a debate in which the balance between the two attitudes represented by the Poet and his Soul is nicely maintained, although the Poet ends with the refusal to create idols of the sages of the past to worship them, and instead calls upon his Soul to 'worship the Truth, not those lips that murmured for a while, then grew tired and soon shut up' (p. 277).

'Aqqad

Like Mazini, but not quite to the same extent, 'Aqqād wrote mainly about himself, his emotions and attitudes. He did occasionally turn to public themes: he wrote on national leaders such as Muhammad Farid and Sa'd Zaghlul, on disasters like the death of a large party of Egyptian students in a railway accident in Italy, and important events like the abdication of Emperor William II. Volume IV of his *Diwan* (1928) which has a larger number of poems on public themes, opens with a poem welcoming the return of Zaghlul from exile in 1923, followed by a long work of 187 lines in monorhyme and comprising fourteen sections, which is an elegy on Zaghlul, revealing the extent of hero worship which he, in common with many of his generation, felt for the national leader. Like Shauqi he wrote political and moral exhortations to the Egyptian people in which he could be just as direct and his language just as much a language of statement.[48] In 'Glory and Poverty' (p. 53) he laments the wide gap between the rich and the poor. 'Aqqad wrote descriptive poems on the remains of ancient Egyptian civilization such as Anas al-Wujūd and the Statue of Ramses II, which are not very different from similar exercises in purely external description by neoclassicists (pp. 28, 195), although his poem on Karnak (p. 270) is closer to Mutran's 'Baalbek' in that it ends with a subjective meditation. In 'Cinematograph' (p. 62) we find the naive approach to modern inventions, revealing the poet's childish wonder at such miracles of science or technology which we associate with the work of some neoclassicists. 'Aqqad can also be a stern moralist, as in his 'The Lesson of Beauty' (p. 36) or 'Pharoah's Column' (p. 37), where he draws an obvious contrast between man's ephemeral and fragile existence and the durability of stone. His neoclassical roots can be seen not only in his attempt to imitate the work of the medieval mystic Ibn al-Farid in 'Divine Wine' (p. 77) – a lifeless exercise lacking the spontaneity and fervour of the original – or in his deriving inspiration from the poets, Ibn al-Rumi and Mutanabbi (pp. 41, 313), but also in his use of traditional imagery or vocabulary in a poem addressed to 'The Goddess of Love, Venus'[49] (p. 75), which is a perfect illustration of the uneasy alliance between the two elements in 'Aqqad's literary formation.

The influence of English poetry on 'Aqqad is revealed not only in his verse translations from English poetry, which include free renderings of texts from Shakespeare's *Venus and Adonis, Romeo and Juliet* and *Othello* (pp. 38, 67), and poems by Burns and Cowper (pp. 110, 114). There is a deeper influence which pervades much of his work. It is to be found even in a poem which the poet claims to have been inspired by the great classical Arabic poet Ibn al-Rumi. 'First Love' is a long poem of over 160 lines which contains many lines expressing 'Aqqad's attitude to man, nature and society. The poem opens with a description of spring and the beauty of nature, then it tells of the poet's love for all living things, which leads to an account of his passion for his beloved, and of the pleasures of love which he enjoyed until slanderers put an end to his happiness. In times of sorrow the poet says he turns to poetry for refuge: then follows a description of poetry in which he claims that the source of poetry is 'the breath of Divinity'. Among men a great poet is like a god, for poetry is creative. In fact poetry is life, since feeling and emotion mean life while reason or intellect equals death. The poet's thoughts turn again to society, the cause of his unhappiness in love, and here his sense of superiority to others and of his being a stranger amongst his own people, of his uprootedness, is most striking. Despite the traditional love situation with the stock character of the slanderer it is obvious that the poem is heavily influenced by English Romanticism, from the love of nature and all living things (Blake and Coleridge) to the conception of poetry as divine breath (Shelley) and as life itself (Hazlitt) and of the poet as a god (Carlyle, Emerson).[50] In his prose introduction to the second volume of his *Diwan* (1917) 'Aqqad rebuffs Peacock's attack on poetry on the grounds that it belongs to the infancy of mankind and that it is therefore not fit for an age of science, endorsing Victor Hugo's arguments in defence of poetry and claiming that poetry will come to an end only when life itself ceases. Poetry, he says, will disappear only with the disappearance of its springs which are the beauties and terrors of nature and the emotions and aspirations of the soul (pp. 136–7).

In a poem entitled 'The Blind Poet' (p. 33), 'Aqqad writes that a blind poet is doubly unfortunate since beauty is the main concern of a poet and it is therefore wasted if he cannot see it. Much of 'Aqqad's poetry is taken up with his meditations on objects of nature, from birds to flowers, especially the rose. He wrote for example on 'Autumn' (p. 27), 'Sunset on the Coast of the Mediterranean' (p. 31), 'The Full Moon in the Desert' (p. 73), 'Nature and Life' (p. 74), 'On the Seashore' (p. 77), 'The Melancholy Spring' (p. 78), 'Roses' (p. 94), and 'Carnations' (p. 95). Among his best nature poems are those describing winter scenes, for instance, 'Winter at Aswan' (p. 72) which he concludes with the thought that 'he sees little who only sees what is visible to the eye', and more particularly 'The Approach of Winter' (p. 108), where the poet's sensitivity to the bleakness of the winter scene is eloquently expressed. 'Aqqad's power of empathy is revealed in a number of poems about birds, like 'An Aged Eagle' (p. 33) and 'The Sparrow's Life' (p. 99), in which the poet envies the freedom and apparent joyfulness of the sparrow, but also laments the hazards of its little life in terms which evince a real feeling for the sparrow. But more often 'Aqqad's egoistic feeling drives him to see himself reflected in aspects of nature. In 'The Curlew' (p. 57) he finds in the lovely song of the curlew in the dark night an analogy to the cry of the man of genius unheeded by his ignorant society, a voice lost in the wilderness. 'Aqqad's sense of his own importance as a poet in a society unable to appreciate him or do him justice is a recurrent theme of his poetry and is in fact a further stage towards the feeling of the poet as a prophet not honoured by his own people which we shall encounter later in the work of the romantics proper. 'The Poets' Lot' (p. 85) portrays poets as madmen and dreamers lost in the world of fancy and inhabiting the clouds. Having given up worldly pursuits for the sake of their dreams they live in penury, weaving of their sufferings their sad poems. Lovers of beauty, to whom the hidden secrets of the universe are revealed, they are not appreciated or rewarded by society. In 'The Youth of Egypt' (p. 156) he complains that his contemporaries have been spoilt by life in cities. He feels that although physically they are close to him they are in fact as distant from him 'as a sheep is from a lion'. That is why the poet turns to nature. The sea in 'Life and the Sea' (p. 223) is where the poet cleanses his soul from all the stains and hypocrisies of civilized life. The same sentiment is expressed in 'On the Sea Shore' (p. 224) which begins with the words: 'On the shore of the sea is a retreat for us from the world of sin and the mansion of ruin.' The poet's salvation sometimes takes the form of an intimation of the existence of another world, a divine world of the spirit. For example, this happens in the poem 'On the Nile' (p. 226) which describes a moonlit night on the Nile.

As in Mazini, the dark night and the raging sea seem to be fit background for the poet's suffering and his song, as we find in 'Night and the Sea' (p. 36).

The theme of suffering is dominant in 'Aqqad's verse. In one poem he writes (p. 184)

> How I strive to sing the gay song of life . . .
> But soon I discover that what I have taken to be singing
> Is in truth no more than a sigh of pain.

In 'Outpourings' (p. 198) we get perhaps the clearest statement of the poet's grief: 'My verse is my tears! 'Aqqad's despair is shown in 'Al Ma'arri and His Son' (p. 188), a dialogue which he imagines to take place between Ma'arri and his unborn child whom Ma'arri chose never to beget, about the value of life, and which he concludes with the thought that on balance it is better not to be born. This romantic languor and despair, partly a pose, partly an expression of the dominant malaise of the time, gradually gives place in 'Aqqad's poetry, as he grows older, to a strong element of intellectuality, unfortunately very much to its detriment. The result is that sometimes the reader has to labour for the meaning of a line which is not commensurate with the effort involved. What is also absurd is that the author himself, anxious that the reader does not miss the point, supplies a prose explanation at times, as in 'Life and the Universe' (p. 169) which consists of philosophic meditations on the place accorded by God to man in the universe, or 'The Dead World' (p. 171), a poem dealing with a theme similar to that of Coleridge's *Dejection Ode*, namely how the poet's unhappiness robs his vision of the world of sources of joy, since 'we receive but what we give'. This is prefaced by a prose introduction on idealistic, subjective and solipsistic positions in philosophy. In his volume *The Wayfarer* 'Aqqad tries to show that the distinction between poetical and unpoetical subjects is a false one and that all subjects, however insignificant and ordinary, are capable of poetic treatment. He therefore sets out to compose poems of unequal merit on everyday-life sights and sounds like the ironer, or hawkers' cries in the street. That many of these poems, like much of 'Aqqad's later output, have no great poetic value has never been shown more clearly than by the distinguished Lebanese critic Marun 'Abbud in his spirited and somewhat vehement attack on 'Aqqad.[51]

Among 'Aqqad's most interesting poems are those dealing with 'demons'. In 'The Demons' Contest' (pp. 54ff.), which is written in a stanzaic form based upon a skilful use of the *muwashshah*, Satan, the chief devil, holds a contest among the devils in an attempt to prove which of them is worthy of controlling the Kingdom of Hell. The contest in which Pride, Envy, Despair, Regret, Lust, Sloth and Dissemblance participate is easily won by Dissemblance. Here the vices are personified in a manner reminiscent of the treatment of the Deadly Sins in the western poetic tradition. A much better-known poem is 'A Devil's Biography' (pp. 241ff.), which is also written in an interesting and more satisfactory form, the quatrain, which contributes towards the rapid movement of the story. It is a long narrative poem of over a hundred quatrains and it tells the story of a demon who grew bored with his job of tempting human beings to their perdition, since he saw that they were all alike, more to be pitied than to be envied, and that in his view there was no difference between the so-called good and bad. He repents, and God accepts his repentence and settles him in heaven in the company of angels, but he soon resents having to sing the praises of the Lord and he aspires to be as exalted as God himself. He rebels, and God immediately turns him into a stone statue. But even in his final state he still exercises an evil influence, for as a statue of perfect beauty he has the power to bewitch the beholder. The poem is interesting on account of the view of mankind it reveals and which, according to the poet, is coloured by the despair engendered in him by the shocking events of the First World War. Although the devil, clearly a mouthpiece of the author, says that all mankind is to be pitied, it is not because he believes that men are innocent: on the contrary when he was on earth the worst trick the devil could devise to play on mankind was to invent the word 'right' (*ḥaqq* which means both Truth and Right) in the name of which all human action was justified. The poet makes a repeated profession of faith and belief in God, yet it is not without significance that the charm and lure of the statue, which is seen by him simply as a work of art, is related to the wiles of the devil. Although one should not drive the point too far, it seems that 'Aqqad's view of art and the creative imagination is somewhat similar to Shukri's, which, as we have seen, involves some degree of moral danger. That 'Aqqad was drawn to the supernatural in this manner seems to be, at least in part, the result of his reading in English literature; we know that he was familiar with Milton's *Paradise Lost* and with the writings of Joseph Addison whose papers in *The Spectator* on the Pleasures of the Imagination reveal the common eighteenth-century view of the imagination which limited its creativity largely to the invention of supernatural characters.[52]

'Aqqad also wrote some memorable poems on children, and as Mandur has said, some of his most successful poems deal with childhood themes. For instance, 'A Little Girl's Jealousy' (p. 53) possesses considerable charm, while 'Elegy on a Little Girl' (p. 56) is a moving elegy strongly reminiscent of Wordsworth's *Lucy* poems. A large proportion of 'Aqqad's work, however, is love poetry. This varies considerably in quality. Although he is capable of writing a good poem on the happy experience of fulfilled love, such as 'Tell Me' (p. 314), it is on the whole the poems dealing with his doubts and disappointments in love which stand out, poems such as 'Suspicious Love' and

'The Fallen Idol' (p. 326) or 'War or Peace' (p. 335). In his best poems he is generally realistic in his approach: far from being an idealized object the beloved is in fact as much a dissembler as she is intelligent and beautiful. The lover is wracked by doubts (the type which he described at length in his novel *Sara*) and when she proves to be untrue he endures much suffering in an attempt to forget her. The following is an example of the quiet and realistic tone of this type of poetry: 'Forgetting', the mood of which is reminiscent of some of Hardy's poems (pp. 332–3):

> Time has cast us adrift on its sea, we are lost in its wastes, like two beings who have never met.
> No longer are you the dearest one to me, nor am I your sole comfort in this world; no longer are we prepared to die for one another...
> Strange is our past and strange too our present. Is it like this that the landmarks of our lives go, leaving no trace behind?
> These lips, is there in their smiles any mark of her kisses which happened not so long ago?
> These eyes, where are the traces in their looks of her merciful touch or the bliss of her breath? Nothing, not a word or a sign has remained.
> Only a memory that haunts life, sick, orphaned and fraught with shame, then it will pass as if it had never been.

This is just as disturbing as the equally muted poetry of Hardy (for whom incidentally 'Aqqad had great admiration).[54]

The romantics

'Aqqad and Mazini proved much more successful than their greater contemporary Mutran in altering the current literary taste. They did not, however, accomplish this change by their own poetry so much as by their criticism. Both 'Aqqad and Mazini were powerful polemic writers, brilliant essayists who wrote much in the leading newspapers of the day, and were avidly read especially by the younger generation. Having to a large extent succeeded in dethroning Shauqi and Hafiz, or at least in dislodging them from the seats of eminence, they made it possible for the public to be at least prepared to listen to different voices, if not actually to welcome these voices. What they were doing in Egypt was being done effectively in the Lebanon and in America by even more radical innovators, extremists like Amin al-Rihani, Jibrān Khalīl Jibrān and Mikha'il Nu'aima, whose writings were by no means confined to these regions, but found their way to Egypt almost immediately.

But the new poetic voices in Egypt were a development not so much of the poetry of 'Aqqad or Mazini or even of Shukri, as of the great Syro-Egyptian poet Mutran. Dr Aḥmad Zakī Abū Shādī began as a disciple of Mutran, who was a friend of his father's, and he acknowledged his debt to his master on many occasions. At the conclusion of the second edition of his volume of verse, *The Dewdrops of Dawn* (1910), Abu Shadi wrote an essay entitled 'Mutran's influence on my verse', and Mutran, in turn, wrote an introduction to Abu Shadi's volume *Spring Phantoms* (1933). Similarly in the case of Dr Ibrāhīm Nājī, who was much more of a thoroughgoing romantic, Mutran exercised a profound formative influence early in the poet's life. Naji was an ardent admirer of Mutran, whose acquaintance he sought and developed early in his career. Thanks largely to the efforts of these two remarkable physicians and of the young men who gathered around them, principally in the Apollo Society of which Abu Shadi was virtually the founder and Naji the vice-president, the spirit of romanticism which had already begun to make itself felt in the *Mahjar* poetry, swiftly spread and dominated much of the poetry written in the 1930s and the 1940s in most Arabic-speaking countries.

Abu Shadi and the Apollo Group

Abū Shādī was born in Cairo in 1892. His father was an eminent lawyer and orator and his mother had a gift for memorizing and composing verses. He was educated in the modern (secular) primary and secondary schools, and at the early age of sixteen, while he was still at school, he published a volume of verse and prose, *On Literature and Society,* under an amusingly old-fashioned rhyming title (1908),[1] which he followed with two other volumes in the next two years. In these early literary efforts, the influence of Mutran's poetry and of his reading in English literature is clear. Partly to recover from the shock of an unsuccessful love affair he left for England in 1912 where he studied medicine. The ten years he spent in England were full of hectic activity, in which he revealed an unusually wide range of interests. He distinguished himself in his medical studies. He set up a society for bee-keeping which had its own periodical *Bee World.* He studied English literature in some detail, especially the works of the Romantics, as is clearly shown in his two collections of articles, *Echoes of Life* (covering the years 1910–25) and *The Field of Literature* (1926–8). He admitted his great debt to Wordsworth, Shelley, Keats and Heine.[2] His mastery of the English language reveals itself in the number of quite competent poems he composed in it. In the meantime, he retained his deep interest in Arabic literature, writing poems and articles which he continued to contribute to Egyptian papers and reviews while he was away. In 1922 he returned with his English wife to Egypt, and almost immediately he resumed his literary and social activities. He founded several scientific and agricultural societies, editing their various periodicals. In the meantime Abu Shadi never ceased to write Arabic poetry. In 1932 he formed the epoch-making Apollo Society with its well-known review which, for lack of financial support and because of powerful political opposition, he was obliged to close down in its third year with the publication of the twenty-fifth issue in December 1934. He later edited two other literary reviews which did not meet with such success as *Apollo*: *al-Imam* (the Leader) and *al-Huda* (Guide). In 1942 he occupied the chair of Bacteriology in the University of Alexandria, but in 1946 after the shock of his wife's death, and feeling bitter disappointment because instead of receiving the recognition he deserved he felt he was being deliberately and actively obstructed for political and other reasons, he emigrated to the United States, where again he resumed his literary activities, contributing to the Arabic literary periodical published in America and forming the Minerva Society on analogy with his old Apollo.

Abu Shadi was a prolific poet, his volumes of verse following one another in rapid succession. His first serious volume of verse, with the typically romantic title *The Dewdrops of Dawn*, was published when he was only eighteen. In 1924 a volume of predominantly love poems appeared under the title *Zainab*, the name of the woman who in his youth aroused in him a desperate passion which seemed to haunt him most of his life, to the extent that one scholar could only ascribe it to a masochistic disposition.[3] In 1925 he published three volumes, *Groans and Echoes*, *Poems of Passion*, and *Poems about Egypt*, the last of which expresses his political and nationalist aspirations. The year 1926 witnessed the appearance of *The Land of the Pharoahs*, which deals with the remains of the glory that was Egypt, as well as a large volume entitled *The Weeping Twilight*. Then followed his *The Year's Inspiration*, in which he announced his intention to publish one volume of verse a year. In 1931 came out *Light and Shade*. In 1933 two further volumes came out: *The Torch* and *Spring Phantoms*; in 1934 *The Fountain*, in 1935 *On the Torrent*. After a pause *The Shepherd's Return* appeared in 1942. After his immigration he published *From the Heavens*[4] in New York in 1949. By 1955, the year of his death, he had already prepared four volumes for the press, which, in probability have not yet been published, although some of their contents are included in M. A. Khafāja's book on the poet. This list may give an idea of the amazing output of this highly productive man, to say nothing of his translations from English poetry, including his translation of *The Tempest*, from Umar al-Khayyam or Hafiz of Shiraz, or of his literary and critical studies, of which three volumes appeared posthumously: *Islamic Studies*, *Literary Studies*, and *Contemporary Arab Poets*, or of his countless scientific publications or of his excursions into painting which resulted in an exhibition of his paintings held in New York shortly before his death.

A curious feature of Abu Shadi's work is the very large number of critical prefaces, studies and epilogues which most of his volumes of verse contain, particularly *The Weeping Twilight* (1926) – a thing which made it swell into 1336 pages. These were written either by the poet himself or by his friends, sympathizers and disciples, who on the whole tended to treat the poetry rather favourably. Abu Shadi apologetically attributes this unusual phenomenon to the novelty of his poetry and to the need to offer some guidance to his readers hitherto accustomed only or mainly to the very different prevalent traditional verse, and he says he looks forward to the day when they would no longer need such aids. However, Abu Shadi's real motive seems to be, as the poet and scholar Kamal Nash'at suggests, his thwarted ambition and desire to obtain some recognition, since for a long time his poetry was either attacked or merely passed over in silence by influential critics such as Taha Husain.[5] One reason why he was not sufficiently appreciated was almost certainly his unwillingness to join political parties at a time when party politics penetrated the whole fabric of the literary and cultural world – with damaging results which he himself lamented.[6] The literary establishment, the guardians of traditional poetic values (including even a poet like Shauqi for whom Abu Shadi had expressed admiration on many occasions) seemed to be alarmed by the new values which Abu Shadi and his followers represented. He was therefore attacked, sometimes mercilessly, and often made fun of and represented as the physician who dabbled in poetry. Satires on him were published. Those who attacked him were not confined to the champions of neoclassicism: 'Aqqad and his followers joined the rank of Abu Shadi's detractors and denigrators because Abu Shadi dared to publish some critical remarks in an otherwise sympathetic review of a volume of verse by 'Aqqad in *Apollo*. A cursory look at the contents of the issues of *Apollo* will give the reader some idea of the extent and strength of opposition with which the poetry of Abu Shadi and his disciples met, for the periodical is full of replies to such adverse criticism. This hostile reception of Abu Shadi's work no doubt deepened his sense of grievance and isolation in his own country. Yet despite his feelings of sorrow and frustration he never ceased to struggle or to serve the cause of modern Arabic poetry. He made enormous financial sacrifices: he bore the entire cost of printing and publishing not only the periodical, but also many volumes of verse written by the younger generation of poets which he printed in a printing press he had bought with his own money for this purpose, although he was not a very wealthy man. His yearning for communication is felt in the Introduction to his volume *The Torch*, in which he claimed that his motive in publishing it was neither profit nor fame, but simply the pleasure of spiritual communion with his readers. As his disappointment increased with the passage of time he found himself printing no more than fifty copies of the volume *The Shepherd's Return* (1942) which he distributed mainly among his friends and public libraries.[7] Four years later his sense of frustration and bitter disillusionment, enhanced by what he felt to be persecution and intrigue by reactionary forces in his country on the one hand and his grief over the death of his wife on the other, drove him to choose exile in America.

It would not be surprising to find that a poet who could write so much or with such ease was liable to be uneven, and this indeed was the case with Abu Shadi. Although his poetry generally impresses us with its spontaneity, it suffers from the same defect as much Victorian poetry, of sheer bulk or verbosity. Sometimes Abu Shadi is not inspired but gives the impression of writing mechanically, of being too prosaic and diffuse. In this respect he differs considerably from his master Mutran who constantly polished the language of his poems. On the other hand, with Abu Shadi and with Naji and the rest of the poets who have been here called romantic, the diction of the poetry attained a remarkable degree of simplicity, which in moments of true poetic inspiration becomes deeply moving in a haunting manner, suggestive of unknown modes of being, a thing new in Arabic poetry.

Abu Shadi continued to experiment both in form and in content until his death. His poems are cast in a variety of forms, ranging from the traditional 'ode' or fragment which observes a single rhyme throughout, to the stanzaic form, and even to rhymeless verse, the Arabic equivalent of blank verse.[8] Under the influence of Mutran, Abu Shadi wrote a number of narrative poems dealing with historical subjects. In 1924 he produced his *The Navarino Disaster* which describes the defeat suffered at the hands of a combined Anglo-French-Russian fleet (1827) by the Egyptian navy in its attempt to defend the Ottoman Empire. In 1925 he wrote *The Pride of Rosetta*, which treats the Egyptians' noble defence of Rosetta against the British attack. Of lesser interest were his long narrative poems inspired by contemporary or social subjects, such as *'Abduh Bey* and *Maha* (1926). Abu Shadi also experimented in the field of dramatic poetry. He tried to introduce into Arabic poetry a new form, half-way between drama and opera. Influenced probably by Wagner, and believing that in the German and to some extent the French opera the literary quality of the text or the libretto is just as important as the music, he set out to write a number of Arabic operas which he hoped would be set to music some day. For his dramatic subjects Abu Shadi went to recent history as well as ancient history and folk tales, and sometimes he invented his own plot or story. For instance, *Iḥsān* (1928) is a tragedy of personal relationships set against the background of the Abyssinian war in 1876, while *Ardashīr and Ḥayāt al-Nufūs* (1928) is derived from the *Arabian Nights. Zenobia Queen of Palmyra* is, as the title indicates, based on ancient history and legend, and *The Gods* (1927)[9] is an allegorical work, in which the poet-philosopher is engaged in a dialogue with the deities of love and beauty and of lust and physical strength, and in part seems to be inspired by the work of Keats.

Interesting as his narrative and dramatic verse is, it is not really as successful as the more personal type of poetry which covers a wide range of subjects. The dominant themes of his abundant lyrical verse are love, nature, mythology (both Greek and ancient Egyptian) and artefact (paintings that inspired the poet), and politics.

In his lyrical verse Abu Shadi was a precocious poet. As early as 1910 when the second volume of his first book appeared his poetry and his views on poetry were already defined with an extraordinary degree of sharpness. As he grew older his experiences became deeper and more varied, but he never changed the direction taken so early in his life. Before he was twenty years old he had been sufficiently exposed to the direct influence of English literature to be familiar with a fairly recent work like A. C. Bradley's lecture 'Poetry for Poetry's Sake' and he felt the need to summarize it for the benefit of other young Arab poets. 'It was that', he wrote, 'together with the teachings of Mutran, which opened my eyes to the living world of English poetry.[10] The mainstay of poetry, he wrote in the same volume, is 'sincerity, faithful adherence to nature, not affectation and modish imitation and departure from nature'. Attacking the false poetry of eulogy, he said, 'We now look down upon the notion of earning our living as poets by means of artificial eulogies addressed to monarchs, rulers and wealthy men.' Abu Shadi was capable then of writing a poem like 'In the Stillness of the Dark' which opens with these lines:

> In the stillness of the dark, in the desolate night,
> When mind and feelings are fraught with awe,
> I stand all alone, a poet in self-communion,
> Thirsty for the Truth, wondering about the world
> While the world takes no heed of me,
> And all around me rushes swiftly past.

Such obvious romantic slant is equally to be seen in another poem, 'The Melody of the Orange Tree', which is similarly written not in the dominant monorhyme *qasida* form, but in rhyming couplets. The new romantic sentiment and attitudes are expressed not only in the poet's feeling that he had 'mingled with the tree and become part of its captivating scent', or in his complete absorption into nature, but also in his language which tended to be ethereal and to rely less upon statement and more upon suggestion: the poet calls the tree 'a friend singing of dreams about an enchanted world', he uses synaesthesia as in the title of the poem or in saying that he hears 'melodies emanating from the perfume of the orange tree'. He ends by describing himself as a 'worshipper of light whose song is glistening winged perfume'.[11]

In the same year (1910) his gift for writing lyrical impassioned love poetry is amply shown in his volume: *The Dewdrops of Dawn*. For instance in 'Inspired by Rain' he says:

> Raindrops are falling upon the blooms,
> Flowers pass them round and all are drunk.
> But I am all alone, looking in vain
> For my beloved to cool the ardour of my passion

and in 'Devotions'[12] – a poem in which Mandur[13] finds the incontrovertible evidence that Abu Shadi was a born poet – we find him uttering this moving and simple cry:

> What is the matter with my eyes that whenever I see you they weep?
> Is it with joy they weep or for fear that my dream be shattered?
> My hope neither fades away nor does it grow bright
> And like a man lost and weary I rush to seek refuge with illusions.

Yet Abu Shadi's poetry published after his return from England has on several counts disappointed many critics: the simple and lyrical early poetry has given place to what was felt to be stilted, forced and unmusical verse.[14] It is true, of course, that Abu Shadi deliberately avoided the facile and superficial type of verse which relied largely on music and that he wrote far too easily and far too much. Kamal Nash'at enumerated the weaknesses of Abu Shadi's style (in the poems written during the long period stretching from his return from England in 1922 to his immigration in 1946) as improvisation, lack of concentration and polish, forced rhymes, obscurity, the frequent absence of connections between his poetic statements and a tendency to think in English rather than in Arabic which had a corrupting influence on his Arabic style. Despite these numerous defects, Nash'at goes on, 'Abu Shadi has poems of a high order, free from faults and characterized by deep passion and purity of style'. These, however, are 'scattered like small oases in a vast desert' and 'most of this beautiful poetry is to be found in the work of his mature late middle age and was written in his new environment of freedom, the product of acute suffering and overwhelming nostalgia for his homeland'.[15] Yet nowhere does Nash'at show in any detail where the greatness of these late poems lies. In fact, despite the large volume of what has been written on it, Abu Shadi's work still awaits an impartial critical investigation. All too often he is either too lightly or categorically dismissed as not sufficiently poetical, or he is given fulsome and bardolatrous praise in terms that are far too general and uncritical.[16] The only possible exception is Nash'at's study in which a serious attempt is made (in chapter v) to analyse the 'new aspects in Abu Shadi's early poetry'.

Abu Shadi explained his conception of poetry in many articles and prefaces to his own and other poets' volumes of verse, but it is perhaps in his poem 'The New' (in his collection *The Weeping Twilight* 1926)[17] that we find a compact poetic statement of his interests and attitudes to the tradition. Abu Shadi describes himself as a songbird whose song pleases the ear but also moves the hearers' feelings, a revolutionary who loathes all chains because of his keen sense of freedom. He does not compose verse for the sake of glory or to display his skill, but because of his passion for poetry, the poetic ideal being the object of his dreams and all that he regards as worthwhile is devoted to it. Poetry conveys wisdom of a kind that brings comfort and bliss in its wake, not the wisdom of philosophers like Avicenna. In his wisdom he does not try to emulate the sad thoughts of Ma'arri, or the ideas of Bashshar, the wise saws of Mutanabbi, the playful bucolic verse of Abu Nuwas or the pleasurable songs of Shauqi. He scrutinizes the universe, soars to its heights and plumbs its depths, roams all over life in search of inspiration, communing with nature which reveals her secrets to him, and he in turn hands them over to the reader, but in a form in which they are made richer and more beautiful by his verse: he sings and describes them without exaggeration either in colour or in tone or sound, but every idea is given its own dignity and worth. He is the worshipper of beauty in nature to which he prays in the manner of a mystic, and the custodian of his people's glorious past which he celebrates in immortal song in an honest and courageous attempt to bring them to create a present worthy to be compared with their past. Such, he says, is the picture of the poetry he conceives, a poetry that does not care for ornament or over-elaborate phrase, that does not concern itself with eulogy, congratulations, all manner of folly, drunkenness and immorality, cheating the people or rejoicing in high-sounding titles, but a poetry that strives to breathe a new life into the people, inspiring in them the pursuit of glory and the ideal. Here we find an account, albeit idealized, of Abu Shadi's aims and themes and an implied criticism of the contemporary poetic scene which was still dominated by neoclassical poets who strove to emulate the poet or poets who rejoiced in hollow and meaningless titles. Although the poet is a worshipper of beauty he is no mere anaemic aesthete or idle dreamer but a serious moralist who is pledged to serve the wider interests of his fellow men and his country.

Abu Shadi had remarkable powers of description, especially in his nature poetry. He was one of the most important nature poets in modern Arabic: the landscape and scenes he described are varied, ranging from Egypt to England and America, and we have seen how early in his career he wrote poetry on the local orange trees. He described local Egyptian birds like crows, the hoopoe, flowers like violets, fields and canals, the Nile and the desert. In 'Evening in the Desert' he describes the desert at night and people huddled round the fire in the cold desert night. In 'The Stars' he described stars as:

> looking like holes behind which the Invisible lurks in its clouds.

'A Country Worshipper' gives a good description of a countryman performing his evening prayers in a field against the background of chirrupping birds and bubbling brook at the hour of sunset, which provokes the thought that beauty is the best means by which to reach God. 'Sunrise in Tranquillity' is a lyrical account of the way in which the whole world, 'nations' of birds, flowers, brooks, grains of sand and pebbles have all joined, each in its own language of adoration, in a fervent hymn to sunrise. 'A Cat and its Looking Glass' describes in vivid details a white cat drinking from a pond in the green park.[18] A better-known poem, 'The Autumn Leaves',[19] describes leaves as

> Pale like death with a blood-like streak of red,
> As if slain by the ruthless orders of autumn.

In his poem 'On the Melancholy Road',[2] composed when the poet was passing through the old village of Matariyya, Abu Shadi says that the world of men with its evil and corruption is not for him since 'his being is wrought of the songs of light', his 'dreams are made of the stars', and 'his cup is filled with their radiance'. In the sanctuary of nature the artist's senses are sharpened, he is enabled to hear clearly what would otherwise remain unheard or confused. To Abu Shadi nature was, as in the case of Wordsworth before him, a constant source of spiritual joy, for there is a relationship of harmony between it and the mind of man. He also seems to have been influenced by Mutran in his belief that the whole universe is bound together by the principle of love. But, unlike Mutran the Catholic, Abu Shadi developed a rather humanistic philosophy which resulted in his tacit belief in the perfectibility of man.

One particular aspect of nature that Abu Shadi never tired of describing was the sea in its various shapes and moods. As is to be expected he does not give us an external description, but he enters into a spiritual relationship with it. Often he does not impose his own mood upon the sea, reducing it to a mere echo of his own feelings, but approaches it passively in a reverential and receptive mood and lets it induce in his soul its healing power of joy. At one point (in 'From the Heavens') he addresses the sea as 'Our father . . . to whom I now return with a yearning thirst for his inspiration'. In 'The Waves'[21] he compares the waves to a feast in which light is intoxicated.

Light is, in fact (like 'thirst', 'exile' and 'fire') one of the dominant and recurrent images in his verse. Mutran realized this early in the poet's career with the result that he called him 'the Poet of Light'.[22] In 'The Beginning and the End'.[23] he says that he worships light and adores its inspiration, for it is the finest expression of the Creator, and adds:

From light we began, to light we return,
The world is made with minute waves of light.

This last statement turns Abu Shadi almost into a pantheist. There are indeed many instances in his verse which seem to indicate that at least Abu Shadi the poet held a pantheistic view of the universe. Kamal Nash'at collected some of these instances which pointed to the poet's belief that all parts of the universe are related to one another by means of love and that the entire universe is a manifestation of God. He concluded that Abu Shadi's pantheism explains his deep love of nature and his adoration of woman. The latter is particularly fitted to be a symbol of divinity, for besides being an expression of the spirit of God as much as any other element in the universe, she is the source of man's life, affection and love and is therefore the most sublime symbol of God.

This attitude to woman Abu Shadi seems to have arrived at very early in his career (even before his apparent pantheistic position was fully developed): in 1910 he wrote: 'woman deserves not only to be respected but also to be worshipped body and soul.'[24] It was confirmed later in his life: in the poem 'The Disguised God' from the collection *Spring Phantoms* (1933) he writes that divinity has assumed the form of a beautiful woman so that 'in worshipping her we only worship the God of life in his visible sign'.

Yet unlike Shukri, Abu Shadi does not turn woman into a purely spiritual entity: her body no less than her soul is an object of his almost mystical adoration. In his view the female is the finest expression of beauty in nature. He was always fascinated by the female nude (usually against a background of the sea) and he wrote many poems inspired by paintings of nude women, a rather daring theme for the generally conservative Muslim society that Egypt was at the time, and it was no doubt just as much a source of some of the hostile criticism that his poetry met with as his liberal use of Greek mythology.[25] In 'My Paradise', a poem of a strikingly lyrical quality, he says that the meadow, birds on trees, the babbling brook, the roaring sea and its cleansed pearls, the honey of bees, the refreshing rain after drought, the spring sun, the whole world with its people and their achievements – all these things put together are worth no more than 'an atom of the unique beauty of his beloved'.[26] In another equally lyrical poem, 'Wanton Beauty',[27] which is perhaps one of the finest poems in modern Arabic, and deserves to be much better known, the physical and spiritual sides of love are completely fused together. 'Souls, like bodies', he says, 'are subject to hunger and thirst.'

In kissing her I kissed my dreams and phantoms of spring;
When I embraced her I held in my arms the most precious
  light granted by a gentle god.
My soul was not satisfied, my heart did not cease to beat fast,
Greed upon greed, world without satiety or end,
Till when her garment fell off (who knows? perhaps by design)
Love rushed to Beauty, enfolding and protecting its dominion.
What lights, what hues are these bestowed by the Bounteous Lord!
Is it in this image that a painter draws bliss from the heavens of art? . . .
She smiled and sighed, a combination of light and fire.
In turn she yielded and resisted until in the end she acquiesced.
So I knelt down before her, greeting from a distance my own
  enchanting Aphrodite,
My poet's eye brimful with every passion I felt.
I gazed and gazed at her form, so lovely and bashful,
And suddenly the true meaning of life was revealed to me
(For life does not show its secret in all living things alike).
I drew closer and knelt, taking my cue from her languid eyes.
I found them filled with the vagrant dreams of love;
I peered and peered into them, stealing their secrets,
And a tremor went through my body as though it had collected
  their honey.
We were two souls created inseparable, like light and heat,
Mingling in love, and both were satisfied.
At their embrace immortality was gained,
And when they parted their lives were no longer part of life . . .
Like a mystic in the zeal of his devotions I exhausted her,
The union of our bodies was like communion with God.

The sanctity of physical union could not be more forcefully or unambiguously expressed. Yet at the conclusion of the poem night falls and the poet is uncertain whether what he is describing is a real experience or simply a vision created by the poetic imagination, and the borderline between reality and unreality vanishes. This is a love poem of remarkable subtlety which ends with a metaphysical statement. Another striking poem is 'Nefertiti and the Sculptor',[28] in which we come across the intimate connection in Abu Shadi's mind between art, beauty and love; it is by means of love that the artist perceives and recreates beauty, of which the supreme example is woman. Hence the idealization of woman who becomes an object of love and adoration for the artist. This theme Abu Shadi returns to later in 'Pygmalion' (1942), although by now there is less of the celebration of the pleasure of the flesh.[29] The beauty created by the poet out of his imagination has become a distinctly spiritual kind of beauty and the poet now makes a complete identification between himself and a prophet.

This preoccupation with beauty may lead some to think that Abu Shadi was a poet exclusively concerned with nature and art to the complete disregard of all the pressing problems of social and political reality around him. Nothing could be further from the truth, and it is important to emphasize this aspect of Abu Shadi's work, because it has not yet received due recognition. Abu Shadi's interest in social and political problems of his country was of long standing: in a poem entitled 'Art for Art's Sake', claimed to be written in 1912,[30] Abu Shadi writes:

> Should I get drunk on songs, love and fair women while tears are flowing and my country goes hungry?

He is always lamenting the degeneration of the Arabs, the passing of their glory and the present tyranny under which they are forced to live.[31] Although he is prone to idealize village life in contrast to the evils of a big city as, for instance, in 'The Jewel of the Countryside'[32] which depicts the dangers city life holds for a naive village girl, on the whole he cannot be accused of romanticizing the *fellah* in the manner Taufiq al-Hakim did in his well-known novel *Resurrection.* On the contrary he wrote about social and economic problems, and advocated the creation of co-operative societies.[33] His poem 'At the Religious Court'[34] is a graphic description which would do credit to the most committed social realist. He depicts the law court as a market place where people's conscience and dignity are bought and sold, where women appear as humiliated victims, lawyers' agents awesome figures and the whole place resounds with shouting and screaming and the utterance of false oaths. It swarms with miserable-looking and deprived children, their faces covered in flies and the bread they eat laid over with a thick layer of dirt. Mothers sit suckling their babies with breasts wrinkled and thin from hunger and suffering. The court of law is called the house of women's lamentations: women go there hoping for a redress to their just grievances and for a meagre sustenance to be granted them but they only receive scoldings and false accusations: 'They look like shrouded ghosts but to their shrouds the whole world is blind.' In his most mature volume, *From the Heavens* Abu Shadi's awareness of the social and political problems of his country grew much keener, and it gradually became so overwhelming that he was finally driven to self-imposed exile. The poem that gives its title to the volume,[35] written in 1942, affirms once and for all Abu Shadi's commitment to the 'Earth' and to its cares and problems. 'The

Kingdom of Art', he says in another poem,[36] is here on earth, 'our mother earth has created it, art flies in the sky only with regretful wings.' In 'A Tear and a Smile', a verse-letter to Mutran in which he tries to explain the reasons for his silence, he writes:

> It is not the roaring of guns around me at night, nor the approaching screeching of bombs . . .
> Which ties the tongue of a friend that is affectionate and true.
> It is the sorrow my heart feels for my kinsmen, for my heedless people,
> Who are still bewitched by idle play, even if it led to their cowardly perdition.'[37]

In 1943, despite his 'official' eulogy of King Farouk on the occasion of the conferring of an honorary degree upon him by the University of Alexandria,[38] Abu Shadi addresses to him in 'The Vagrant Dead', a powerful and frank poem in which he attacks feudalism and urges the king to redistribute land among the landless peasants who are homeless and vagrant, wearing humiliation and indignity for their shrouds, all dead, their tombs being the opulent estates of the few wealthy landlords. In the poetry he wrote in America he was naturally freer and even more outspoken: he satirized Farouk in 'White Kāfūr' (an allusion to Mutanabbi's satire on Kafur, the negro slave who ruled Egypt).[39] He celebrated his dethronment and welcomed the declaration of the Republic.[40] He also wrote about the plight of Arab refugees and the atrocities committed by Zionists.[41] Until the end of his life Abu Shadi never ceased to express his love and concern for Egypt about which he wrote many moving and nostalgic poems to be found in the second volume of Khafaja's book on the poet. He addresses Egypt as:

> Home of my youth, the dearest dream of my young days,
> You are still my dream and my sweet comfort.[42]

Despite his idealized view of America as the land of freedom, where he felt he could without restraints attack tyranny and injustice in Egypt, he continued to write poetry such as this:[43]

> Do not chide my soul for its excess of love.
> The tears which you wish to deny me are but some of her tears,
> Events have cast me away from her land,
> Yet I continue to live in her heart.
> Around me visions spring, full of her breath . . .
> Moved by my memories, I choke with grief . . .

In the minds of most people Abu Shadi's name will be associated chiefly with the Apollo Society, an indication of the great contribution he made, by means other than verse composition, towards the cause of modern Arabic poetry. In September 1932, thanks to his initiative and effort, the Apollo Society was formed with its threefold aim: to promote the cause of Arabic poetry in general, to help poets morally, socially and materially, and to support new, serious movements in poetry. The catholicity of the taste of Abu Shadi, the driving force behind the group, is revealed in the fact that membership of the Society was by no means confined to one school or to one generation or even to one country. The first to be elected president of the Society was none other than Ahmad Shauqi, and when Shauqi died in 1932 he was succeeded by Khalil Mutran. Abu Shadi, acting as secretary to the Society, was the editor of its organ, the *Apollo* magazine, the first periodical in Arabic devoted exclusively to the publication of poetry and poetry criticism. The choice of the name was itself significant of the width of the editor's outlook, although it was severely criticized by ʻAqqad. The same catholicity of taste is revealed in the poetry published in the periodical, which embraced such different types of poets as the neoclassicists Shauqi, Aḥmad Muḥarram, Muṣṭafā Ṣādiq al-Rāfiʻī, the pre-romantics Mutran and ʻAqqad, and the romantics Naji, Ḥasan Kāmil al-Ṣairafī, ʻAli Maḥmūd Ṭahā and Maḥmūd Ḥasan Ismāʻīl. *Apollo* also published works by the Lebanese Abū Shabaka, the Tunisian al-Shābbī, the Iraqis Rusafi, Jawahiri and Muṣṭafā Jawād, the Sudanese Muḥammad Aḥmad al-Maḥjūb, and the *Mahjari* (American) Iliyā Abū Māḍī, Shafīq al-Maʻlūf and Shukrallah al-Jurr.

Yet despite this catholicity of outlook it must be admitted that one school seemed to be dominant in the movement and that was the romantics. The magazine, which continued to appear monthly till December 1934, published in translation a good deal of western poetry and criticism, both of which happened to be of a dominantly Romantic character. For instance, the translations from English poetry were confined to works by Shakespeare, Thomas Gray, Scott, Wordsworth, Shelley, Hardy and D. H. Lawrence, and of these Wordsworth and Shelley had the lion's share. Moreover, the magazine became the rallying ground for a number of enthusiastic young poets, most of whom were of a romantic turn of mind. Furthermore, the political situation itself seemed to be favourable to the spread of romanticism. The early 1930s witnessed the government of Sidqī Pasha, which effectively made hollow parliamentary democracy and limited the freedom of expression, with the result that young intellectuals were driven to escape from social and political reality into a solipsistic inner world of private sorrows and vague longings, and into excessive preoccupation with depopulated nature. The extent of the contemporary malaise and day-dreaming can be inferred from the titles of some of the volumes of verse published by the young romantic poets, who either flourished or were brought up during that period. Here are some revealing ones: *The Lost Mariner* by 'Ali Mahmud Taha, *Behind the Clouds* by Ibrahim Naji, *Lost Melodies* by Hassan Kamil al-Sairafi, *Burnt Up Breaths* by Maḥmūd Abu'l Wafā, *The Dreaming Boat* by Mukhtār al-Wakīl, *The Dreaming Palm-Trees* by 'Abdul 'Azīz 'Atīq or *The Unknown Shore* by Sayyid Quṭb.[44]

One of the most interesting and gifted of these poets was Muḥammad 'Abd al-Mu'ṭī al-Hamsharī, who died tragically young (1908–38) and never collected his poems in any one volume. But together with some very fine lyrics, such as 'To Charming Jītā',[45] he published in the first volume of *Apollo* a long narrative poem written in 1929 and consisting of more than 300 multi-rhyme lines (divided into units of four rhyming lines each) entitled 'The Shore of A'rāf',[46] A'rāf being a Koranic word denoting a place between heaven and hell, but used by the poet to signify a place dividing life from death. Hamshari, who was passionately interested in English Romantic poetry and the Bible, imagines himself taking a trip after his death accompanied by the Muse in the 'magic boat of memories' to the shore of A'raf. The imaginary shore is where all life and sound come to an end, all spirits cease their wandering and come to rest, and where the landscape is bleak with nothing to see but snow-covered rocks. The poet sees the ships of death sailing silently towards the shore as processions of life heading for the tomb of nights at the end of the sea of time. The poem ends with a description of the poet in the valley of death with his lute broken and mute, forced by death to eternal silence – which is in many ways an eloquent comment on the sorrows of this generation of sensitive and frustrated romantics yearning for death as an escape from a painfully oppressive reality. Significantly enough it is the sight of the Nile in Cairo which, as he says in the introduction he wrote to the poem in *Apollo*, evoked in the poet's mind the image of the land of death.

The Egyptian romantic poets associated with the *Apollo* magazine are so many that it is clearly impossible to deal with them all in a book of this size. Lack of space therefore compels us to discuss in some detail only two: Naji and Taha, who, different as they are, may together with Abu Shadi be regarded as representative of certain facets of romantic poetry in Egypt.

Naji

Ibrāhīm Nājī (1893–1953) was born in Cairo in a well-educated family: his father was well read in Arabic and was familiar with English literature which he used to discuss with his son. After finishing his education at the modern schools Naji entered the School of Medicine from which he graduated in 1923. He worked as medical officer in various ministries, and he continued to practice medicine until his death. At an early age he developed a passionate interest in literature which he managed to sustain all through his life. He admired greatly the poems of Muṭrān, some of which he seemed to have learnt by heart. His knowledge of English and French enabled him to read much of western literature and western thought, especially in the field of psychology. His reading in western literature was selective but deep, and the authors whom he found most congenial to his temperament were the romantics. According to the poet Ṣaliḥ Jaudat, he, together with Taha, Hamshari and Jaudat himself, used to meet as young men in the Delta town of Manṣūra (where they all lived at some point) to discuss the poetry of Wordsworth, Shelley and Keats, as well as their own creative efforts.[47] Naji translated Shelley, Lamartine, de Musset and Baudelaire. He admired especially Baudelaire and D. H. Lawrence: on the former he published posthumously a long detailed study accompanied by a translation of many poems from *Les Fleurs du Mal.* His literary activities included essays on general topics, such as *The Message of Life,* and *How to Understand People* (a popularization of modern psychology), and literary criticism for instance, the book which he wrote jointly with Isma'il Adham on Taufiq al-Hakim, *Taufiq al-Hakim, The Restless Artist.*

Naji's poems are collected in three volumes: the first came out in 1934 under the title *Behind the Clouds,* the second, *The Nights of Cairo,* was published in 1951, and the third, *The Wounded Bird,*[48] was published posthumously in 1957. (A complete edition of his poetry was published in 1961 under the auspices of the Egyptian Ministry of Culture, but unfortunately by a strange error it includes more than a dozen poems by the younger poet Kamal Nash'at.[49]) Of the Egyptian romantic poets Naji is perhaps the most subjective. Practically the entire content of his three volumes of verse concerns the poet's most intensely personal experiences. There is remarkably little interest in wider issues, social or political in his work: to be exact there are four political poems, and one poem on a public theme, 'The Burnt Wings', which laments the death of Egyptian pilots in an air-crash.[50] In these public poems Naji's poetic style seems to be inappropriate: it is not declamatory enough for such public occasions. He also wrote seven elegies, six of which were on poets, four on Shauqi,[51] and eight poems close to panegyrics or social compliments addressed to people in high office.[52] The rest of Naji's poetry is about the poet himself, his feelings and attitudes, and nearly all of it turns round the subject of love. As epigraph to his second volume of verse he uses these words which can be regarded as his poetic creed: 'I regard poetry as the window out of which I look at life and eternity . . . it is the air I breathe, the balsam in which I have sought to cure the wounds of my soul when physicians were rare to find.'

Naji's extreme form of subjectivity is expressed in his view of literature in general and poetry in particular in an essay from his collection *The Message of Life*. Nature, he says, is a collection of dry data which need to be translated, interpreted and clothed by man's imagination. It is the poet who 'endows the mountain, the sky and the desert with movement and vitality and clothes them with his imagination, bestowing upon them his emotions . . . If nature was beautiful in itself we would need to do no more than reproduce it photographically.'[53] Unlike Abu Shadi, Naji finds that nature can afford only a temporary consolation. This attitude is best revealed in his poem 'Thoughts at Sunset' (p. 41), where clearly the healing power of nature is limited, for the poet's suffering is specifically human and arises from the nature of the human condition, the consciousness of his mortality: it is the Pascalian 'thinking reed' syndrome. Because of the poet's sense that nature is neutral his feeling of isolation and of being an exile in the universe is very much sharpened. In one poem he writes that 'the raging sea listens to no one, heeds no complaint', and in another he wishes his heart were like 'this earth, unaware if the houses on it are deserted or occupied; indifferent to what goes on, be it birth or death' (pp. 127, 228). This theme of exile is one of the leitmotives in Naji's poetry. For instance, in 'The Wounded Bird' he describes himself as a man who has lived his allotted time 'perplexed and tortured', 'a traveller without kinsmen', a stranger or an outsider journeying away', and typically as 'a weary man alone in a storm' (p. 66). His poem 'The Outsider' is, as the title suggests, about the exile theme (p. 153) and in 'After Parting' he writes about himself (p. 197) 'Dragging my solitude behind me in every crowd'.

The only experience that stops (temporarily) the poet's feeling of exile or, at least comforts him, is love. That is why love occupies such an important place in Naji's poetry. As is shown in 'The Wine of Contentment' and 'From N to A' (p. 149), love provides a cure, however momentary, for the poet's vague metaphysical sorrows (p. 89). In 'The Wounded Bird' the beloved is a haven for the poet to whom she has given life and a feeling of security. According to Naji those who have not loved 'have lived all their lives in vain' (p. 46), for love is the only meaningful experience in a man's life. It raises the poet to a higher and nobler existence, which he describes in 'A Journey' (p. 175) as 'a radiant summit of innocence and light', another garden of Eden. His beloved provides comfort and cure for the deep wound in the poet's soul, and the bond of love is the only bond the rebellious spirit of the poet willingly accepts since in the name of justice and humanity he has rejected all social ties and laws which seem to him to be inspired solely by greed and hatred, and to be the products of the base elements in man, of his 'clay and despicable mire'. 'Friday' describes the poet's feeling of loss and restlessness in the absence of love (albeit in a minor key), while 'The Burning Flute' shows the poet as a solitary figure in the dark, 'singing of his hopeless passion' (pp. 196, 348).

Naji is undoubtedly one of the most attractive love poets in modern Arabic: in his poems he covers the whole range of the emotion of love, from the most passionate adoration of the beloved, in which both the physical and the spiritual meet in a manner similar to the John Donne of *The Ecstasie*, to pure romantic idealization, in which the woman who is the object of love is placed beyond the reach of ordinary mortals, from joyful fulfilment to utter despair. The sheer delight in love can be felt in poems such as 'A New Joy' (p. 125) or 'The Farewell' (p. 181), where he writes:

Has love ever seen people in such ecstasy as ours?
How we created mansions of fancy around us,
Walked together the moonlit road
With joy scampering in front of us
And when we looked covetously at the stars
They came down to us and became our own
Like children we laughed together
And raced till we outran our own shadows.

In 'The Dream of Love' his happiness is such that he says

I cry for fear lest our love be a dream. (p. 264)

One day of happiness with his beloved 'brought together all the scattered joys in the world and gave them to him'; it was not a mere day like any other; it was a whole life-time and even more.

On the other hand many poems lament the dying of love or the unhappy state of the lover, including 'The Lyre of Pain' (p. 44), 'The Cairo Nights' (pp. 139ff.) and 'The Mirage Poems' (pp. 55ff.). The last of these poems, which is divided into three sections or poems ('At Sea', 'In the Desert' and 'In Prison'), records the shattering effect of unhappy love: his beloved has now become an unattainable object like a star in the night sky for which he still yearns. Life to him now seems like a desert with its deceitful mirage, and in it human beings are lost and thirsty. In the first section of the poem the three themes are introduced: life as desert, life as sea, and life as prison. They are then picked up later and developed in the three component poems almost as in an orchestral piece of music. The three themes continue to intermingle in the structure and imagery of the whole poem in an emotional and alogical manner. 'The wide sea, the lonely sky and the silent infinity' all weigh down upon the poet's heart and he now feels the expanse of the open space to be no more than a prison. The poet complains: 'In my soul night set in long before it was night time' and 'Inside me a wintry sky, with dark clouds but without rain, sterile they are in the regions of my soul'. His sense of exile returns, and once more he feels he is a stranger in his community and even in life. His rebellion goes beyond society and acquires a metaphysical dimension, becoming a rebellion against the human condition itself. The third of these poems opens with the poet addressing himself:

> O prisoner of life, how can you escape? Night and day have bolted their gates.

Even if the gates of the prison were opened and the prisoner was allowed to roam freely anywhere on earth, the poet asks where he could go, since 'his steps were heavy with despair' and he is in fact imprisoned within his soul, his chains coming from within himself: 'In vain do I try to flee from myself'. Naji's rebellion, however, never extends to a revolt against God or to a denial of His existence. In 'Clouds', when the poet rails against his fate in a moment of despair brought about by his unhappy love, and feels as if the skies had fallen and the fabric of the universe was falling apart, he hastens to ask God's forgiveness for harbouring such a feeling (p. 151). In another poem, 'A Tempest', he asserts the need to feel the existence of God in such moments of despair (p. 184).

It has been suggested that the preponderance of love poetry in Naji's work and his attitude to women were caused by the poet's experience of bitter disappointment in love very early in his life.[54] But this surely can only be a partial explanation. What is interesting (and new) is not the fact that he wrote so much about love or that he often placed himself in the situation of an unhappy deserted lover. As is well known, the volume of love poetry is very large in the Arabic poetic tradition in which the plaintive lover is a stock character. What is new to the tradition is the particular kind of sensibility expressed in Naji's love poetry, a sensibility which we have encountered in the equally large proportion of love poetry in the work of Shukri. In the writings of both poets, as indeed in those of many other romantics, love is usually the context in which so many of the poet's attitudes are revealed, such as his sense of exile, of isolation, his fear of death, his bewilderment in the face of so many pressing questions about man's place in the universe and his destiny. Like Shukri, Naji often idealizes his beloved: in 'A Sick Man's Farewell' (p. 115) he calls her 'idol of my eye' or says to her 'You are the one who has given life to a dying man', although we may point out, the situation here is a concrete one and the beloved is fully human. Unlike Shukri, Naji never loses his grasp on female reality. In the poem 'Woman' (p. 171) he wonders if woman is a mere creature or a goddess and treats her as a source of inspiration for artists. But in the process he emphasizes her 'physical' charm and never turns her into a mere spirit, as we find in Shukri. The warm and concrete aspect of love is abundantly clear in, for instance, the short poem 'Handshaking', as it is in many others:

> It was as if our souls embraced as we shook hands
> And love, an electric charge, went through both our frames
> Enkindling our eyes and inflaming our blood (p. 311).

Nevertheless Naji often employed religious language in his love poems. For instance, in 'Doubt' (p. 222) he used the words 'monotheist' and 'polytheism', while in 'Darkness' (p. 69) he said he read 'verses' from the 'book of the wonderful beauty of his mistress'. He almost developed a religion of beauty. Like Keats, whom he greatly admired (as is clear from the Introduction he wrote to Abu Shadi's volume *Spring Phantoms*), he often describes beauty in divine and ritualistic terms. The house of the beloved is the sacred mosque or *Ka'ba*, beauty is a holy shrine, the journey he undertakes to see his beloved is a pilgrimage.[55] This is not the same as the conventional imagery of Persian poetry or indeed of the poetry of medieval courtly love in Europe, where the human and divine meet and each is conceived in terms of the other. In most of Naji's poetry the warmth of feeling and the occasional use of realistic detail make the whole thing heavily weighted in favour of the human. At times it is simply that the glowing passion which the poet feels towards his beloved reaches almost the degree of worship: with Naji love, warm concrete human love, seems to be the only meaningful experience in life. But of course there are times when the figure of the beloved is fused in the poet's imagination with that of the Muse, the celestial Bride and the Ideal in a manner reminiscent of Shukri's verse. It is she who confers reality upon the poet's life. In his 'Quatrains' he writes that the world is a strange illusion when his days are empty of love:

> You have taken me on your wings past the wall of mist
> And my heart and the whole space become full of light
> Then brought me back to the earth of illusions
> And the night was dark like the raven's wings.
>
> You have shown me the secrets of the invisible world,
> Revealed to me what no eye can see.

It is clearly through love that the secrets of life and the universe are revealed to the lover/poet (pp. 226, 229). In 'Love's Prayer' (p. 263) the emphasis on the visionary power induced by love is clear: 'it has purified me, and enabled me to see, has torn away the closed curtains'. The call of love is divine, raising the poet to a more elevated level of existence where 'my heart was not of this earth nor was my body of clay'. Because woman has such spiritual power over the poet his disillusionment becomes almost unbearable when he realizes that she cannot live up to his ideal standards. This feeling of shock and horror is expressed in many poems, particularly in his long poem 'Ruins' (pp. 342ff.) which records the story of the downfall of his love from the spiritual pedestal where he had placed her.

Apart from religion there are a number of dominant images in Naji's poetry, the most recurrent of which are perhaps the desert, the mirage, the desert caravan, the road and the journey.[56] He wrote poems entitled 'The Travellers' Return', 'A Journey', 'Mirage in the Desert', 'Deceitful Mirage', and 'The Little Desert Caravan'. The word *sarāb* (mirage) is a potent word in his poetic diction: it has a peculiar fascination for him, perhaps equalled only by the word *layālī* (nights) from which hardly a poem is free: he gives his poem the titles of 'The Nights' (p. 289), 'Sleepless Nights' (p. 294) or 'A Night' (p. 301), and, as has already been mentioned, the second of his volumes of verse bears the title *The Nights of Cairo*. Apart from the musical quality of the Arabic word in its plural form, there is the undeniable influence of de Musset's work, *Les Nuits* and the significance of the appeal of night to the Romantic mind in general and the Arab romantics in particular, a point ably discussed by M. Abdul-Hai.[57] There is also the star and/or moon image, for the setting of many of Naji's love poems is starlit or moonlit night and often the beloved is likened to a star.[58] Finally there is the bird image, especially a wounded bird: the poet likens himself to a bird that loves the open sky and high altitudes being shot and wounded or being shut up in a cage.[59] He gave one of his poems the title 'The Wounded Bird'. Wounds proliferate in his poetry, though these and other disease images or terms such as sickness, pallor, pain have been attributed by one scholar to the poet's medical profession.[60]

Most of these images meet in his justly celebrated poem 'The Return' where we find the religious imagery, the desert, the journey, the nights and the wounded bird. In it Naji skilfully uses the old outworn classical convention, that of weeping over the desolate encampment of the beloved, but in a manner, typical of the great artist he is, in which at his touch the dead convention springs to life again. It acquires immediate relevance and becomes an adequate medium for the expression of a thoroughly modern sensibility. This is done in a subtle fashion. In the first place, although the poet returns to the place once inhabited by his beloved, it is not the ruins of a deserted encampment in the desert. It is clearly a house in a city, with a hall or a drawing room, a staircase and a door (in fact we do know that it is a house situated in one of the main streets of Cairo).[61] But the delineation is left deliberately vague and no further details are given; we are only told enough to make us see that the poet is writing about a real personal experience and not merely engaged in a literary exercise in poetic imitation. Yet the total situation of the poet, mournfully returning to the vacant site which had once been occupied by his beloved, together with the use of the term *ṭalal* (ruin), ensures that in the mind of his reader an emotional charge is released, the feelings aroused by the long-established tradition of *nasib* brought into play. Secondly, the whole scene is internalized, for when we reach the last quatrain of the poem where the poet describes himself as 'a wanderer, eternally exiled in the world of my grief' we realize that the ruins he talks about may not be an external reality so much as a vision in the poet's mind. This possibility makes the poem undeniably an expression of a modern sensibility. Thirdly, the poet's manner of evolving imagery is somewhat alien to the older tradition. For instance, that night should crouch like a camel is a traditional enough image, but it is not traditional to make the shades of night flit in the hall. Moreover, for the poet to feel the breath of Weariness/Despair filling the air or to see with his own eyes Decay weaving cobwebs with its hands, or to hear the footsteps of Time and the sound of Loneliness climbing the stairs, argues an unusual and a daring power of personification, too individualistic for the main body of the Arabic tradition. (Naji's fondness for personification, his ability to objectify states of feeling and personify abstractions is revealed most strikingly in a well-known poem called 'Longing' (p. 322) where the feeling which gives the poem its title is turned into a person to plague the poet by his constant company and by feeding on his blood and youth.) This is to say nothing of the freer form of the poem, written not in the *qasida* form but in quatrains, the quiet meditative tone of writing, and the remarkably lyrical and tender quality of style and the utter simplicity of language.

It is in fact these last two qualities, lyricism and simplicity, that largely account for Naji's enormous appeal and distinguish his poetry from that of, for instance, Shukri. The evocative power of his simple language is most striking. In *The Message of Life*[62] Naji defines poetry as the best words in the best order (thus unconsciously echoing Coleridge), and then proceeds to say that the poet uses the 'souls of words', that is he uses words with all their powers of suggestion, in all their subtler shades of meaning, thereby creating what is called internal music. The distinction he draws between what he calls 'direct or straightforward words' and 'the soul of a word' is at bottom a distinction between the poetry of statement and the poetry of suggestion, and it is beyond any doubt that he prefers the latter. To help create this 'internal music' it was necessary to abandon the traditional declamatory style, and for this purpose Naji resorted to the use of short metres, of multirhyme and of quatrains. Even when he employed the traditional monorhyme and monometre form he tended to write short pieces, probably in an attempt to avoid padding and such devices that might make it declamatory. On the whole Naji was successful in his freer handling of the formal features of Arabic verse. Despite the exceedingly limited range of his poetry, unlike Shukri, Naji managed to avoid creating the effect of monotony, and that is probably partly because he succeeded in describing different and wider aspects of love, the joys as well as sufferings of lovers, their desperate longing and their anxious waiting, partly because he has a remarkable sense of humour and considerable charm – amply illustrated in such poems as 'The Night Shirt' (p. 76), 'A Hair' (p. 112), 'At a Lentil's Party' (p. 206), and even in his rather malicious satire on an unpleasant blind man married to a beautiful woman (p. 189). He was capable of writing frivolous verse and even an 'Elegy on a Puppy' (p. 312) which, however, is not entirely devoid of pathos. But, clearly, what he called his poet's heart, which enabled him to see the suffering behind the gay appearance of the dancing girl in 'A Dancing Girl's Heart' (p. 267), did not utterly crush his sense of humour – a valuable asset in a romantic poet who is often a rather solemn creature whose vision tends to be one-eyed.

Taha

Unlike Naji, whose poetry impresses us primarily by its intensity of emotion, Taha is chiefly a cunning artist, who, like Shauqi, is gifted with a highly developed sense of music. And indeed a comparative study of these two poets on their use of verse music would be exceedingly useful in shedding light on the interesting stylistic differences between neoclassical and romantic poetry. Such a study would reveal how more akin is Shauqi's verse to rhetorical declamation. The music of Taha's verse, on the other hand, is pitched at a lower key, and produces its effect on the level of suggestion, through a carefully chosen diction.[63] For romantic poetry soon developed its own poetic diction, no less than the neoclassical – although, of course, very different from it.

'Alī Maḥmūd Ṭāhā (1902–49)[64] was born in the town of Mansura in Lower Egypt, where he received his early education in modern schools. He did not receive a university education, but after finishing his primary school he entered the intermediate School of Technology and qualified as an architect in 1924. As we have already seen in Mansura he became friends with Hamshari, Jaudat and Naji, all of whom were to become distinguished poets. They all later moved to Cairo, where Taha held a number of posts in the Ministry of Commerce and in the House of Parliament. He published some of his work in the *Apollo* magazine whose editor gave him much encouragement. Shortly before the Second World War, in 1938, he was drawn to

Europe, especially to the landscape of Italy, Switzerland and Austria, about which he wrote some descriptive and nostalgic poems. Although he was widely read neither in classical Arabic nor in western literature, he knew English well and some French: in fact, he translated Lamartine and Verlaine, John Masefield, and Shelley. In Mansura he benefitted from his association with Naji and other young poets who read and discussed the English Romantics. He also derived some of his knowledge of the western Romantics, or at least he received their influence, indirectly, through his contact with the Apollo group, and his readings of *Mahjar* poetry. His volume of essays, *Vagrant Spirits*, contains brief accounts of his travels in Europe and essays on English and French writers such as Shelley and H. G. Wells, de Musset, de Vigny, Verlaine, Rimbaud and Baudelaire (although in his writings on French poetry he seems to have relied mainly on English sources).[65] He was particularly drawn to Verlaine and Baudelaire: he regarded the former as a victim of wine and the latter as a victim of women while considering himself to be a victim of both wine and women, thereby flattering himself with the thought that in his person both Verlaine and Baudelaire met!

Taha's poetic output consists of seven volumes: *The Lost Mariner* (1934), *The Nights of the Lost Mariner* (1940), *Spirits and Shades* (1942), *Song of the Four Winds* (1943), *Flowers and Wine* (1943), *The Return of Longing* (1945), and lastly *East and West* (1947).[66] The dedication of the early volumes is significant: the first is dedicated 'to those enamoured of longing for the unknown, those lost on the sea of life, those who haunt the deserted shore'. These words, in fact, set the keynote to the whole of his work. The poems are variations on these themes of mysterious longings for strange and undefined objects, the strong appeal of the unknown, the vague metaphysical doubt as to the end of existence, the feeling of loss of direction. The picture conjured up by the title, of a mariner lost on a sea, is a pregnant comment upon the whole of his poetry. The student familiar with western Romantic poetry may be tempted to find little that is particularly striking about these themes or images, but it must be admitted that in Arabic literature, by Taha's time they had not yet become the commonplaces they now are. In fact it was Taha himself, who by his exceedingly skilful handling of them in a highly musical verse, encouraged a whole generation of younger men among his admirers to imitate him, thereby rendering such themes and images the mere stock-in-trade of facile romantic poetry. It was Taha's followers, therefore, who were largely responsible for their demotion.

Two of the poems in Taha's first collection are called respectively 'The Lost Mariner' and 'The Deserted Shore'. The volume ends with a verse translation of Lamartine's *Le Lac* which probably inspired the title of Taha's poem as well as that of his collection, since one of the dominant images in Lamartine's poem is that of man journeying on the ocean of time with no harbour in sight, and being carried for ever into eternal night. In 'The Deserted Shore' the poet appears as a wandering wretch weeping by a lonely shore.[67] Except for a handful of poems, mainly elegies on poets and statesmen, the poems in *The Lost Mariner* are all intensely subjective. The themes that attracted Taha are mainly poetry and the poet, human suffering, love and nature. Of these the most important is the first on which the others are often directly or indirectly brought to bear. The two longest poems in the collection are 'A Poet's Birth' and 'God and the Poet'. The former, with which the volume opens and which was first published in the *Apollo* magazine, shows us the remarkable change that had occurred in the meantime in the conception of the poet, or in the Arab poet's self-image. This is how Taha describes the birth of a poet (p. 11).

> He descended on earth like a ray of celestial light,
> Bearing the wand of a magician and the heart of a prophet.
> A spark of the iridescent spirit has dwelt in the folds of a human frame,
> Inspiring his heart and tongue with every elevated thought from the
> world of wisdom and light.

The romanticizing is now complete, and instead of being a skilful craftsman, as he was generally thought of in classical Arabic poetry and criticism, the poet is now regarded as a winged and ethereal being, a thing of the spirit, a magician, a 'mighty philosopher', a 'seer' and a prophet all in one. The conception of the poet as a creature of light, hinted at by Abu Shadi, has by now become an assumption fully accepted and explicitly stated. In his description of his poet's birth Taha uses the language in which only the birth of the Prophet has hitherto been traditonally celebrated in Muslim religious or mystic verse. Interestingly enough, the conclusion of this poem has unmistakable echoes from de Musset's *Nuit de Mai*. But clearly in the manner in which he has expressed his conception of the poet as a prophet and a visionary, Taha has drawn as much on sources from western Romantic poetry as on the traditional idiom of Sufi writing.[68]

In 'The Poet's Room' (p. 38) we see the lonely figure of the suffering poet sitting up until the small hours of the morning in his silent room, unable to sleep from excess of care in an unjust world which is not a fit place for an innocent, sensitive and gifted spirit. Likewise, 'The Fugitive' (p. 191) presents the poet as a symbol of freedom of thought and of the spirit and an apostle of the Truth who is misunderstood and unappreciated by his society. Yet, despite his view of himself as a nobler, more spiritual being, the poet's feeling of pity for his people is boundless. In 'God and the Poet' (pp. 87–115) he poses as the mouthpiece of suffering mankind, regarding it as his duty to communicate to God humanity's complaint. He begins by expressing doubts regarding His justice since man has been created by Him imperfect, with the eternal struggle raging inside him between his soul and his body and made to inhabit an imperfect world whose nature, despite her enthralling beauty, is red in tooth and claw (p. 103). Pain is unavoidable and men fall helpless victims to natural disasters such as the earthquake, the dire effects of which the poet describes (pp. 108–9). But the poet ends with the affirmation of the positive value of pain as a necessary means of cleansing and softening the heart, and of the pressing need for all mankind to join in a moving and humble prayer to the Lord. Throughout the poem the poet's function as the intermediary between God and suffering man is emphasized. This view Taha seems to have held all his life, although it must be admitted that in his later work his affirmation of it sounds somewhat mechanical and lacking deep conviction. In the long poem 'Spirits and Shades' (p. 434) Hermes describes the poet as 'The Child of Heaven', suffering acutely from the conflict between his body and his soul because of his keen awareness of the beauties of the spiritual world; he is 'an angel who resents being ruled by his humanity' (p. 440), he is a visionary because he derives his gift from God.

Just as the birth of a poet is celebrated by the entire universe, so is his death mourned by the whole of creation. In 'A poet's Grave' (p. 158), an elegy on the Syro-American Fauzī al-Maʿlūf, inspired by a reading of his long poem 'On the Carpet of the Wind', Taha describes the poet's tomb in idyllic terms which suggest an extraordinary degree of sympathy between nature and the poet: leafy branches lean over it and wild flowers form a border round it, a palm tree keeps it company, its leaves rustling in the breeze and making melancholy sounds, the turtle dove sings a sad song faithful to his memory, the gentle dawn bestows its loving light upon it and at night the stars sadly search in vain for their missing brother who chose the earth for his abode. Nature is a dominant subject in the whole of the collection: there is hardly a poem which is entirely devoid of some nature description, while there are many devoted to it, such as 'On the White Rock' (p. 72), 'The Rock at the Meeting Place' (p. 115), 'The Pole' (p. 126), 'The Lover of Flowers' (p. 155), 'To the Sea' (p. 185), and 'In the Village' (p. 203). These descriptions are rendered in a language of great lyricism and simplicity: for instance, in the 'Lover of Flowers' he says:

> Would that I had wings like butterflies
> I would then fondly float in the air
> Flapping my wings eastwards towards the light

Intoxicated with its radiance . . .

Until night spread over me its shade
Then I would lie awake amidst roses
Inhaling their breath as their hearts throbbed
In tenderness and love for the spring. (p. 155).

Love is a theme often linked with nature in Taha's first volume, the natural scenery which forms the background of his love poems generally ennobling and idealizing the poet's passion, which in turn bestows upon various aspects of nature the ability to share the poet's emotions of love. An excellent example of this dual process is furnished in his 'A Pastoral Song' (p. 52), where water 'caresses' the shadows of trees, clouds 'flirt', with the moonlight, the ring dove 'moans with love', the breeze 'kisses' every passing sail, yet the poet is eternally faithful to his unattainable mistress. This melancholic idealized love which we have encountered often in the work of romantics is the dominant variety of love in Taha's first volume. Despite its trials and sufferings it is welcomed by the poet: in 'The Return of the Runaway' (p. 41) he prefers bondage in love to freedom without it. As in 'A Singing Girl's Boudoir' (p. 45), where he declines an invitation to a night of sensuality, it is the spiritual aspect of the sentiment that the poet wishes to assert, although in the highly sensuous and sensual quality of the description of the woman and her boudoir we may detect a tendency in Taha's poetry which will be further developed in his later productions.

In Taha's second volume, *The Nights of the Lost Mariner* (1940), a significant change takes place. It is true that in it we still find a poem such as 'The Statue' (p. 313), which is a dramatically moving and somewhat allegorical work, representing the loss of hope at the approach of old age. This poem however, is not typical of the general mood of the second volume, any more than a poem like 'She' (p. 266) in which the poet expresses regret at having defiled his spirit by indulging in carnal pleasures. *The Nights of the Lost Mariner* celebrates the pleasures of the flesh in a manner that is perhaps new in modern Arabic poetry. It represents the poet's liberation from the narrow teachings of a puritan society, mainly as a result of his exposure during his travels to Europe in which he found not only a different kind of landscape of breathtaking beauty, consisting of lakes and mountains hitherto unfamiliar to him, but also a way of life that is colourful and gay. With the opening poem in the volume 'Song of the Gondola' (p. 225) a musical poem written in an accomplished stanzaic form, a new note is struck: a romantically idealized picture of the West as the embodiment of glamour, pleasure-seeking and fun-loving begins to enter modern Arabic poetry. The poem describes in graphic and lyrical terms a gondola trip during a Venetian carnival. Taha's lust for life and his hedonism are expressed for the first time in an uninhibited manner, totally free from a sense of guilt.

In the second poem in the volume, 'The Enamoured Moon' the sensuous nature of Taha's poetry is again emphasized and the language acquires a transparency and a soft silken quality admirably in keeping with the theme. Needless to say, this degree of transparency can rarely be found outside modern romantic poetry. The poem is addressed 'to her who lies in her bed asleep, wearing a thin garment and with the bedroom window open on a moonlit summer night' (p. 231):

> When the languid moonlight visits your chamber window
> Coming to you shimmering like a dream or a radiant thought,
> While you are lying on your chaste bed like a lily asleep,
> Then pull together your uncovered body and protect your beauty.
>
> For I am jealous of that enchanter whose light seems to have melodies:
>
> Whenever black-eyed maidens hear him sing their hearts beat faster with longing.
> A rogue, whose caress is soft and who chases every beauty,
> He is bold, and at the call of desire ever ready to storm castles.

The poem goes on in this vein, with the moonlight not simply personified but the natural phenomenon raised by the poet's imagination to the order of mythology. Yet despite the ethereal, dream-like quality of the vision, despite the air of mystery evoked by the description of the moonlight, this is a very sensuous poem indeed, and points forward to Taha's more earthly and sensual work, especially of later years. The next poem is 'Khayyam's Wine Cup' (p. 236) which is preceded by this significant comment:

> Al-Khayyam was one of those poets who tried to probe the secrets of the universe and glimpse the unknown..., but were denied their object because of the limitations of the human condition. Consequently they were plunged into grief and sorrow, which drove them to seek comfort and consolation from their powerlessness and despair in the pleasures of wine and women.

This seems to shed more light on Taha than Khayyam for he is clearly thinking of himself as one of these poets. It is this feeling of kinship with the Persian poet that drove him to imitate him in 'Khayyam's Wine Cup', where he says of him:

> Monstrous and unnatural,' they said [about you], 'A reckless lewdness that is never sober!'
> Little did they know what depths of sorrow rage in your heart. (p. 246)

Taha's hedonism is amply illustrated in the rest of the collection, for instance in 'A Night's Dream' where he addresses his mistress:

> Do not deny me. Only nights of love and song matter in the world
> (p. 259)

and in 'To a Dancing Girl' (p. 261). But perhaps the most succint statement of his attitude is to be found in 'The New Thais', where he says,

> Lord, I have worshipped Thee in the lips of a woman,
> a liberal hand and a radiant face.
> Were it possible I would make the beads of my rosary
> nipples of women's breasts.
> A most sacred rosary that would be. (p. 324)

There is general agreement that it is *The Nights of the Lost Mariner* which brought to Taha great popularity throughout the Arab world, a popularity which was not due exclusively to the fact that 'Song of the Gondola' had been set to music by 'Abdul Wahhāb. In her study of Taha's poetry (a study which is full of perceptive remarks, although at times vitiated by the author's moral and poetic prejudices) the distinguished Iraqi poet and critic Nāzik al-Malā'ika points out how in the Arab world many favourable reviews of the collection quoted lines not only from 'Song of the Gondola' but also from 'The Rhine Wine', 'Como Lake' and 'The New Thais' – what she describes as the 'western' poems in which Taha advocated *joie de vivre* and the need to shake off conventional ties in order to join western civilization – as well as 'The Enamoured Moon' because of its sensuousness. She also explains quite rightly how the combination of Taha's music and his sensual tendency influenced many young poets writing in Arabic during the 1940s.[69] In her attempt to explain Taha's great popularity she says that he appealed on many levels and to a wide variety of tastes: alike to traditionalists and modernists, to the average reader and to the intellectual elite, to those who believed in commitment and to the champions of art for art's sake, for he combined traditional prosodic forms with modern content, music of verse and depth of ideas.[70] This is of course true, but it is also true, as the other poet and critic Salma Jayyusi points out in her excellent unpublished study of modern Arabic poetry, that Taha's poetry provided one of the greatest outlets for the emotionally and sexually suppressed youth of the Middle East. Another reason which Mrs Jayyusi rightly suggests is of some cultural significance:

> A new Romantic element is introduced in *Layāli*. For [just as] the East with its exotic charms and supposedly mysterious ways was an element of attraction to western Romantics, the West [too] with its seemingly liberal

> enjoyment of life, the freedom it allowed to the individual and its own exotic charms constituted a great appeal to the Arab youth of the forties. This was depicted at its best in *Layāli* ... In this volume, moreover, Taha is fully accepted by his European associates, without any barrier. Europe is immediately transformed from the land of the snobbish imperialist to a land of peace and beauty where wine, women and song reign supreme. This is very significant in a society that had, up till that date, regarded the West as the stern-faced representative of usurpation and superiority.[71]

It is interesting to see how many of the women the poet writes about are European and how often his mistresses are described as fair and as having golden hair. As an expression of his romantic attitude to the West Taha sets many of his poems in Venice, Capri, Cannes, Como or Lugano, makes allusions to Greek mythology and writes about the wine of the Rhine, the effect of the music of Wagner and the waltzes of Johann Strauss. It is remarkable that the vogue of writing hedonistic poems with a European setting and describing affairs of varying degrees of innocence with fair women which was started by Taha affected even an established 'neoclassical' poet like Jawahiri whose poem 'Shahrazad' (1948) shows unmistakable signs of Taha's influence.[72]

There is no doubt that from his second volume of verse to the last Taha's main attitude continued to be more or less consistently hedonistic, despite al-Mala'ika's prudish denial in such statements as 'I believe that sensuality and the search for pleasure are accidents in 'Ali Mahmud Taha's life, because his nature is basically spiritual' and 'The most sensual of his poems are hardly completely devoid of a spiritual or intellectual background'.[73] His volume *Flowers and Wine* contains poems entitled 'The Poet's Tavern', 'A Kiss'. 'The Poet's Wine', and 'Dancing Girl in a Tavern'. In the volume *Return of Longing* he writes in 'Question and Answer'.

> My life is a story which began with a wine cup
> And a fair woman. For both I made my song. (p. 567).

His sensuous imagination is apparent in poems such as 'The Island of Lovers' (p. 573) and in 'Lovers' Dreams' (p. 579). In 'The Slaughtered Love' (p. 650) the poet seeks his consolation in the bosom of prostitutes. In his final volume *East and West* we find together with a poem like 'Philosophy and Imagination', describing a brief passionate affair in which the poet claims that through the pleasures of the flesh a great beauty is revealed to the soul (p. 699), many poems of strikingly sensual quality which express an unashamedly hedonistic view of life, such as 'The Andalusian Girl' (p. 731) and 'The Woman Cyclist' (p. 739).

Taha is chiefly a lyric poet, although two of his seven volumes represent interesting excursions into fields other than that of lyrical verse. *Spirits and Shades* is a long dramatic poem of about 400 lines, a dialogue between various characters, a hotch-potch, in fact, of many figures from Greek mythology and the Bible. The theme of the poem is the conflict between body and soul, represented in man's relation to woman, and the style used is highly evocative, relying heavily upon sheer profusion of imagery. Similarly, *Song of the Four Winds* is a dramatic experiment, based upon a fragment of an ancient Egyptian song in which a sailor makes an unsuccessful attempt to capture four maidens, representing the four winds, by luring them to his ship. Around this Taha weaves a dramatized story, pointing out the unhappy end met by a dissolute and lecherous Phoenician pirate given to the pursuit of illicit earthly pleasures. With the exception of a number of poems in the last volume *East and West*, which deal with political and nationalist themes, the whole output of Taha concerns the poet's personal experiences. These he managed to express in a highly musical verse in which he evolved a very skilful strophic form based on *muwashshah*, and made a successful use of the quatrain, especially to convey philosophical meditations in poems of unusual length.[74] His achievement encouraged a whole generation of younger men among his admirers throughout the Arab world to imitate him, often in a facile and derivative manner. This is true of his hedonistic themes and images no less than of the other aspects of his own brand of romanticism which combines a fondness for sensous pleasures and a tendency to suffer from vague metaphysical doubts. Without Taha neither the Syrian Nizār Qabbānī, nor the early Iraqi Sayyāb would have been possible.

Abu Shabaka

Taha's hedonism is not so loud or so theatrical as that which we sometimes find in the work of the Lebanese Abu Shabaka who, in spite of the feverish tone of his writings, seems to have developed his obsession with sensual pleasures, at least for a while, into a conscious pose. Taha's pursuit of sensual pleasures, particularly in his later work, is marked by a conspicuous absence of a real sense of guilt: his is a simple, almost pagan attitude, and if there is a feeling of grief in the poems he wrote later in his life such as 'The Return of Longing' (p. 572), that was not because he lamented his misspent youth, but because he was no longer capable of indulging in the pleasures he had enjoyed so much in his younger days. Different indeed was the Christian Abu Shabaka, who whilst celebrating the pleasures of the flesh, was aware of the expense of spirit which these pleasures entail, much in the manner of Baudelaire who seems to have exercised a profound influence upon him.

Ilyās Abū Shabaka (1903–47) was born in America while his parents were on a visit there, but was brought up in Lebanon, and educated in Aintura

School where he says he was taught French properly.[75] He left school in 1922 before he had finished his education, according to some as a result of a quarrel he had with one of the teachers. But he continued his studies on his own: he was widely read in French literature and developed an early passion for Alfred de Musset. After a brief spell as a school teacher he took up journalism: he wrote articles in various papers and periodicals such as the Lebanese *al-Maʻriḍ*, *al-Jumhūr*, and *al-Makshūf* and the Egyptian *al-Muqtataf*, thereby eking out a very meagre living.

Besides poetry and a number of unsuccessful short stories, marked by their overtly moral and religious character, Abu Shabaka wrote some literary criticism, including an interesting but rather amateurish booklet on the intellectual relations between the Arabs and Europe, in which he acknowledges the great debt modern Arabic literature owed to French literature,[76] as well as long essays on French and English writers such as Lamartine, Baudelaire and Oscar Wilde. He contributed shorter articles to periodicals such as *al-Maʻrid* and *al-Barq* on western authors like Dante, Petrarch, George Sand, Victor Hugo, Saint Beuve, de Musset, de Vigny, Paul Valéry, Goethe, Byron, Shelley, Tennyson and Browning. He undertook a large amount of translation from the French, mainly of novels and plays and some poetry: for instance four plays by Molière, *L'Avare*, *Le Malade imaginaire*, *Le Bourgeois gentilhomme* and *Le Médecin malgré lui*, a work by Voltaire, *Micromégas*, two works by Bernardin de St Pierre, *Paul et Virginie* and *La Chaumière indienne*, and Alphonse Karr's *Madeleine ou Sous les Tilleuls*. Among his numerous other translations were Lamartine's *Jocelyn* and *La Chute d'un ange*.

Abu Shabaka, however, is best known for his poetry. Apart from his early collections of juvenilia, *The Lyre* (1926) and *The Silent Invalid* (1928), he produced five volumes of verse: *The Serpents of Paradise* (1938), *Melodies* (1941), *The Call of the Heart* (1944), *To Eternity* (1944) and *Ghalwā'* (1945)—which is an anagram on Olga, the name of the woman with whom he had fallen in love early in his life and who later became his wife after an engagement which lasted ten years on account of the poet's poverty. Parts of this last volume had already been published in the volume entitled *Melodies*. One other volume, *From the Gods Above*,[77] posthumously published in 1959, largely contains elegies on Arab poets such as Shauqi, Hafiz, Jibran, Fauzi al-Maʻluf, and Ilyās Fayyāḍ. These reflect the current romantic conception of the poet which we have already encountered in the work of other poets.

Abu Shabaka's first volume, *The Lyre*, was published when he was barely twenty-three years old, and it therefore not surprisingly shows the marks of the formative influence on the poet's style and attitudes. There are some verbal echoes from classical Arabic poets such as al-Maʻarri and Abu Nuwas; and in his predilection for simple diction, muted music, short metres and multiple rhymes the influence of his readings in *Mahjar* poetry is unmistakable. His passion for French poetry is revealed in, among other things, his verse translation of poems by Lamartine and de Musset. But despite the obvious signs of immaturity and even of occasionally shaky grammar, the volume, as some critics realized, bears the marks of true poetic talent.[78] The book is dedicated to the memory of the poet's father whose murder had a devastating effect upon the ten-year-old boy, and seemed to colour his general attitudes for most of his life. It is full of poems expressive of deep sorrow and a loss of direction, despair and a desire for death.[79] Some of them, such as 'Song of Sunset', clearly betray the influence of *Mahjar* poetry.[80]

The same romantic pessimism and desire for death found in *The Lyre* is expressed indirectly in the next published work, *The Silent Invalid*, a long narrative poem woven round the true story of a young Lebanese who falls in love with an Egyptian girl but contracts tuberculosis and soon dies in Zaḥla, to the anguish of his heart-broken sweetheart. As it has been put, 'The young man who prepares to die in silence is none other than the poet of *The Lyre* himself.'[81] This poem does not seem to represent any significant advance on the earlier work and is not entirely free from sentimentality. But with *Ghalwa'* which was written between 1926 and 1932, although not published till 1945, Abu Shabaka really breaks new ground.

Ghalwa' is a narrative poem in the best romantic tradition, clearly a development of Mutran but much more subjective, complex and subtle than anything written by the older poet. The subject is an unusual one. The poem is in four parts: the first, which begins with an idyllic description of a winter's landscape, tells the story of Shafiq returning home in an idealized Lebanese village late one wintry night to find his mother still awake because she has heard the disturbing news of the serious illness of a neighbour's daughter, Ghalwa. Later that night Shafiq has a vision of Ghalwa, first in the beauty and bloom of her youth, then as a dead corpse in all its hideous aspects, and he soon discovers that he is in love with her. The story of her illness is then related. Ghalwa, a young and innocent maiden of rare beauty, goes to Tyre to visit a relation called Warda who is a very attractive woman of enormous sexual appeal. In the middle of the night Ghalwa is woken up by moaning sounds and she discovers to her horror Warda, who occupies a bed next to hers, in the arms of a man engaged in sexual intercourse. Ghalwa runs away from the house, distraught, and makes for the rocks on the seashore, passing through a cemetery on her way. The shock makes her very ill and feverish and nearly unhinges her mind. She falls a prey to hallucinations and delusions, and when she wakes up she is convinced it was she and not Warda, who has committed the sin of fornication. The first part of the poem ends with a 'vision' in which Shafiq, anxious and troubled, by a mysterious kind of affinity, goes through the same painful experience of guilt as Ghalwa. The second part describes the tortures of conscience and ends with Ghalwa's contrite prayers in the Church and Shafiq's profession of love to her; while in the third part, entitled 'Revelation', the poet recounts how his heart has been purified by suffering and he dreams of visions of beatitude in which he sees hosts of angels and chaste beautiful maidens and hears divine music. In the fourth part, Ghalwa's slow recovery from her illness takes place when she feels she has been forgiven. The lovers are united, but it is a sad, chaste reunion ennobled by suffering and in the end Ghalwa is told by Shafiq what in effect is the obvious moral of the poem:

> Pain is the ladder to Heaven
> Those who have suffered inherit the Garden of Eden.[82]

Yet the poem is more than a statement of this romantic commonplace and is an extraordinary achievement. For one thing this thought is not expressed in general abstract terms, but is rendered obliquely in some very powerful poetry which relies occasionally on vivid imagery, as, for instance, in these lines:

> The heart is the source of all true feeling
> The heart is the site of inspiration.
> Unless you suffer, and dip your pen
> Into the very depths of your sorrow
> Your rhymes will remain mere glittering ornaments,
> Dry bones in a marble tomb.[83]

Or,

> Old women with their arms shaking
> Like bent candlesticks
> In which the candles had dried up.

Furthermore the poet has a remarkable power of creating atmosphere as in the scene in the church where Shafiq finds Ghalwa at prayer.[84] But above all the value and originality of this poem lie in its being a product of a state of consciousness bordering on dreaming – hence its haunting quality and its enormous power of evocation and suggestion, the dominance of dreams and visions in it, its rich complex texture which, as in the case of dreams, allows a multiplicity of symbolical interpretation. Because it is the creation of the twilight of consciousness the poem does not seem to have suffered much from the fact that the poet was apparently forced to destroy a large section of it (because he was afraid lest people should read into it too much of the poet's personal life and his relation to his Olga).[85] One does not expect to find in such a poem the Aristotelian formal virtue of a cool and highly conscious work, nor is one seriously disturbed by the many digressions which would otherwise mar or impede the flow of a more controlled and less subjective narrative, whether these digressions consist of an idealized description of the happy life of a simple peasant, or of the ancient Phoenician glory to which the remains in Tyre testify, or of the poet's self-preoccupations, his memories or thoughts about his enemies. Yet despite some obscurities, on the whole, *Ghalwa* is a well-organized poem. There is ample evidence that the poet chose his words with the utmost care: we read in his diary that sometimes he wrote no more than ten lines of the poem in a whole day.[86] For instance, the difference between the imagery he uses in his description of Ghalwa and Warda is striking: the former's beauty is likened to the loveliest aspects of nature, but these seem to be very carefully selected – they are of a pure, chaste, cold and elevated character such as flowers, breeze, clear sky, mountain grass and snow; while Warda's physical attractiveness is described in terms of lust, fire, blood, earthquake, snake's fang, disease, scorpion and hell. The name Warda means Rose and the epithet she is given '*al-ḥabība*' means loved or desired. At a deeper level of response the two women are in fact two different facets of the same person, and the poet's psychological insight shows itself most convincingly in making Ghalwa suffer from the obsession that it was she who has committed the sin. Warda is no more than the primitive lustful woman lurking underneath the chaste and innocent Ghalwa: she is her relation and symbolically the poet makes her inhabit the ruins of the ancient world in Tyre. It is Ghalwa who seeks Warda and not the other way round, hence her feelings of guilt which the sensitive reader does not dismiss as altogether groundless: unconsciously she is in fact punishing herself for her sexual impulses and fantasies, otherwise the full extent of her horror at the discovery of Warda engaged in the sex act would be found to be somewhat exaggerated if not incomprehensible. Likewise Shafiq (whose name means sympathetic) evinces considerable complexity in his relationship with Ghalwa: he discovers he is in love with her only after her illness, that is after she has, in one sense, lost her innocence. In a vision he seems to divine the nature of her suffering and he goes through the same experience of remorse and expiation, even though he knows that she has not in fact committed any sin. It is as if the poet would like woman to be experienced while at the same time retaining her innocence.

This ambivalent and self-contradictory attitude to woman as the diabolical beauty, the fatal woman, Dolores our Lady of Sensual Pain, is of course typical of Romantic sensibility.[87] Abu Shabaka's creation is a symbolic transference of his fiancée Olga much in the same way as La Belle Dame in the poem *La Belle Dame sans Merci* may be regarded as a symbolic transference of Keats's betrothed, Fanny Brawne. As a further instance of the complexity of Abu Shabaka's poem it may be pointed out that Ghalwa's illness occurs in the winter while her recovery begins to take place in the month of May which the poet describes as the 'nuptial' of Nature and Ghalwa is then seen by the poet as 'Eve amidst delicious fruit' and as 'having known good and evil'.[88] The immediate implication is that she recovers when she accepts her own sexuality. The seasonal background to the events lends them a larger significance and seems to lift them to the level of myth: Ghalwa becomes the Female principle, Mother Earth which 'recovers' in Spring.

The full tragic impact of the contrast between the two sides of woman, the angelic and the diabolic, is felt in Abu Shabaka's celebrated volume *The Serpents of Paradise*. This volume, which contains thirteen poems written between 1928 and 1938, is certainly his best-known work and the one which created the image of Abu Shabaka as the Arab *poète maudit*.[89] In a short poem under the title 'Lust for Death'[90] the poet poses as a complete rebel, who has revolted against all laws, human and divine; a misanthrope and a lover of gloom, a sadist with a distinct preference for the sight of blood, and in whose life the only things that matter are drink and women. By means of the violent sensations induced by lust and wine he can obtain his escape from loathsome reality even in the certain knowledge that this escape means death. In this poem, in fact, we have many of the basic motifs of the whole volume.

In the long introduction to *The Serpents of Paradise* entitled 'Talking of Poetry', in which significantly enough the discussion is virtually confined to current French theories of poetry, Abu Shabaka attacks Paul Valéry and sides with the Abbé Bremond (on some points). The main issue involved is the role of inspiration in poetry. Valéry's well-known belittling of the importance of inspiration is rejected outright by Abu Shabaka who makes poetry exclusively a matter of inspiration, and, therefore, questions the validity of all attempts to theorize about the nature of poetry, or to find in poetry anything that approaches a system. When Valéry claims that a poet can compose poetry at will and is not utterly dependent on chance, he is, in Abu Shabaka's view, relegating the poet to the position of a craftsman, and 'nothing can be further from the truth or can involve a more scandalous degradation of the essence of poetry', than to regard it as a mere matter of craftsmanship. Abu Shabaka even denies that a true poet has the power to choose the right word since, prophet-like, he receives his poetry from above and 'poetry descends upon him fully clothed'.

Two relevant points emerge from this introduction. The first is the high value Abu Shabaka sets upon inspiration in poetry – a thoroughly romantic principle, leading to minimizing the role of conscious control. The second point, which is a concomitant of the first, is the complete reversal of the traditional Arab image of the poet. As we have seen in the case of Taha, here too the poet is no longer conceived of as a conscious craftsman: rather he is believed to be an inspired, prophet-like creature, who is in communion with a higher and mystical power.

But if the poet feels he is endowed with the power of prophecy it is only natural to expect him to feel, too, that he is meeting with the fate of most prophets, namely, that he is little understood or honoured by his own people. In his poetry Abu Shabaka assumes the attitude of an 'outsider', and laments the fact that he does not get the recognition he deserves. He turns his back on humanity, and has to maintain the position of a rebel because he feels he must be true to himself and to his own feelings: sincerity must always come first. In one poem Abu Shabaka wrote that truthful poetry is the best,[91] contrary to the old Arabic saying that the best poetry is that which feigns most. Like Shukri before him, he claims that the purest art evolves from emotion.[92] With a group of Lebanese writers known as the Group of Ten, although only four of them were active, he waged an unflagging war on the literary and even political establishment on the pages of the review *al-Ma'rid* until the review was forced to close down by the government three years later. In one article (published in 1930) we read: 'There is not one among the leading writers of the Lebanon who deserves to be called a writer, as the west understands the word.' In another article: 'Our main objective in this criticism is to liberate poetry from those heavy chains which still impede its free movement. We want poets to listen only to the voice of inspiration and to look only within the depths of their souls when they compose their poetry.'[93] In the same year Abu Shabaka wrote in *al-Ma'rid*:

> We want a new literature of our own which carries the imprint of our souls and which stands on the basis of a revolution in our thinking and in our institutions and traditions. We want a literature which departs from the rules set down by our forefathers, however violently we may be attacked.[94]

In a poem entitled 'Day of Judgment' in *Serpents of Paradise*[95] he makes Satan announce that all those who compose verse without feeling belong to him and hell shall be their lot.

In order that he may be true to his feeling a poet does not hesitate to write frankly about his personal experiences, even those which are generally regarded as taboo in his society. Abu Shabaka's anger and fulmination against his predicament of being hopelessly caught in the grip of sexual passion, powerfully expressed in several poems in *Serpents of Paradise*, we now know were inspired by an actual passionate affair which he had in 1928 with a married woman with a child, even at the time of his engagement to Olga.[96] The poem 'Red Prayer' (1929) is the first of such poems:[97] it begins with these two lines in which the poet humbly begs for God's mercy:

> Lord, I crave your mercy, for I am an infidel and a miserable sinner
> I have starved my soul and fed my mortal love

of which the first is used as a refrain. Yet the poet is unable to free himself from the yoke of his passion: he cries plaintively:

> O woe is me! In my heart there are still hopes and desires
> For an ecstasy of shame.

The poet's sense of sin acquires enormous proportions and he finds himself thinking of great sinners of the past such as Cain, Nero and Jenghiz Khan, with whom he unconsciously identifies himself, and in this part of the poem the tone becomes much louder and more melodramatic, the angry voice turns into shrieking and the style becomes rhetorical. But towards the end the poet returns to his own private predicament.

Despite its rhetoric and melodramatic quality, 'The Red Prayer' is a remarkably powerful poem and its force lies in the inner conflict it expresses, in the fact that while praying to God for forgiveness the poet is wading deeper and deeper in sin. Abu Shabaka was not unaware of the contradiction in his attitude to carnal pleasures: he even defended it on the grounds of the inherent complexity and ambivalence of human emotions.[98]

Abu Shabaka's ambivalent attitude is seen throughout the whole volume. For instance, in 'The Undefiled Shadow' (1929) he writes:

> There is still a shadow of chastity in my debauched heart
> Undefiled by women of sin.[99]

That chaste shadow, the poet says, belongs to another (clearly Olga). In the poem entitled 'The Serpent',[100] while desiring her he condemns his adulterous mistress for being unfaithful to a husband 'whose sweat is still damp', for causing 'a red stain' to appear on her 'wedding garment which was gleaming white', and he feels ashamed that he has brought her child a trifling toy to distract him, a 'price for his mortal sin'.

In 'The Altar of Lust',[101] where women are described as having the temperament of the serpent of paradise, he is pathetically torn between desire and fear of temptation at night:

> The colours and shades on your lovely pale face
> On which the flame flickers with desire
> Strike terror in my soul.

But he urges her to

> Pour out the wine and spare no heart
> The waves of youth break against your feet.

Likewise his torture is powerfully expressed in 'Red Lust',[102] to choose a final example, which begins with this apostrophe to the night:

> Put out thy light, be dark like me, O night! . .
> Lest a star should wake me to virtue . . .

Yet even in 1929, the year in which the last five poems discussed above were written, Abu Shabaka could write a poem of a much quieter tone, of great beauty and pathos and a remarkable atmosphere of mystery like 'Dialogue in the Hut', certainly one of his best works.[103]

Abu Shabaka's experience of the attraction and revulsion of sex, his merciless self-laceration and inner conflict, his sense of shame at his spiritual degradation and his view of a beautiful woman as a diabolical creature and a serpent of paradise, are not always expressed in direct confessional poems. The poet also manages to render his feelings obliquely by resorting to themes and stories from the Old Testament. These stories Abu Shabaka does not relate in the form of objective narrative poems: assuming that his readers are more or less familiar with them he gives only some of the salient events, and he plunges *in medias res*. He addresses some of the characters, thereby achieving a dramatic effect, impersonates others, and offers his own authorial comments on the action. The result is that these poems are no less subjective or expressive of the poet's attitudes and feelings than the rest of the volume. As a rule he chooses biblical themes of violent passion or those which have strong sexual implications such as 'Sodom' (1931) or 'Samson' (1933). These he treats in a fiery style, full of images of violence, and he describes sexual passion in frank terms, always showing woman as a cunning temptress and the cause of man's downfall. The fact that he resorts to the Bible for some of his poems obviously reflects the strong hold it had upon him. As it has already been indicated, Abu Shabaka was no thoroughgoing hedonist and his rebellion was not as absolute as he sometimes liked to think. For throughout he retained his belief in God whose judgment he feared, although he was powerless to rise above the weaknesses of the flesh. However, without underrating the extent or depth of his religious feeling, it would be wrong to omit to mention the importance Abu Shabaka attached to the Bible as a source of literary inspiration. Clearly he came to hold this view of the Bible as a result of his readings in French and European literature in general. In 1930 he wrote, 'For a long time the Bible has been a source of true poetry, inspiring Victor Hugo, Lamartine, Dante, Goethe and most European and world poets'.[104] In his booklet *Intellectual and Spiritual Ties between the Arabs and Europeans* (1943), he urges Arab authors to follow his example.[105] It is an undeniable fact that Abu Shabaka's 'Samson' was partly inspired by Alfred de Vigny's poem *La Colère de Samson*, in which assuming the person of Samson the poet says angrily:

> Et, plus ou moins, la femme est toujours Dalila.

However, as has been shown by a recent critic, this fact in no way diminishes the force, intensity and individuality of Abu Shabaka's poem.[106] The Arabic poem is full of animal imagery: it is teeming with birds of prey and wild beasts suffering from uncontrollable sexual drives, and the poet's anger expresses itself in a variety of images of filth and disgust: 'In beauty, Delilah, lurks a serpent whose hissing is often heard in bed', 'You are not my wife but a wild female hawk in my raging heart', 'Flatter him, for between your breasts death gapes in the soft bed'.

The impact of Abu Shabaka's personal experience upon his whole outlook on life and society was vehement indeed. This is seen in many of his poems in *The Serpents*, particularly in 'Dirt' (1934), a poem in which he piles on images of disgust of great intensity and variety to a degree almost unparalleled in modern Arabic poetry (except perhaps in the otherwise very different poetry of Jawahiri). In it he regards the world as a nightmare, 'an eternal prison', and he tries to escape from it by means of the violent sensations of lust and wine. It is a vision of hell that has affinity with Dante's *Inferno*: the poet wades in the dark mire, around him lechery is riotous, sins of all kinds are rife, humanity is viewed as a filthy quagmire and corrupt men move about and twitch like 'drunken worms', pieces of dirt scuttling about in life, singing joyfully, their songs echoing in the tombs. Men are 'mummified phantoms', the poet laments their condition in his own private hell, while they, unaware, are feasting all the time. The whole of humanity is condemned whether in love or in power or politics. Women are described in terms of base insects, and like 'Samson', 'Dirt' swarms with images of animals and insects, but here they are mainly creatures of a very low order: rats, bats, frogs, worms, locusts and cockroaches. But although the poet urges the pure maidens of love to shut the gates of paradise in his face as he is a poet who sings of hell, he says of himself:

His soul feels the paradise of life
But his eye can only see a manacing hell.

He has reached the point of *non plus ultra* in disgust, because of his soul's yearning for paradise his vision of hell is so overpowering.

It is difficult to see how the poet could go further in his rejection and condemnation of the world than he has already done in the poems we find in *The Serpents of Paradise*. The next volume he published, *Melodies* (1941), does in fact represent a great change: the turbulence and violence of passion, the incessant inner conflict, the loud screaming voice of condemnation, the hectic imagination, have all gone. The spiritual suffering of *The Serpents* has already had a cathartic effect upon the poet, and now nature seems to be slowly healing his soul. *Melodies* is composed mainly of pastoral poems in which the simple life of Lebanese shepherds and peasants is idealized and its joys and blessings celebrated in verse characterized by exceedingly simple diction and free stanzaic form with multiple rhymes, approaching in language and music the structure of folk songs. By implication the complicated and artificial life of the city with all its vices is, of course, condemned. The volume contains songs of reapers, of winter, spring, summer, songs of the village, songs of the birds (which include the blackbird, the goldfinch, the nightingale and the mountain quail), poems on the wine press, the peasant, a village wedding and a festival. Occasionally traces of the poet's purgatorial sufferings can be felt[107] but the dominant mood is one of acceptance and content, the calm of mind when all passion is spent. Such calm and peace we find in the remarkable short poem 'Night in the Mountains' when the trees, the river, the birds and even the wind are all tranquil while the poet hears the bells ringing in the valley beneath, 'melting the spirit of the Lord in the souls of the tired ones', and he finds his own soul 'bowing', his breath listening, and his love and longing rendered chaste and pure.[108]

With the next volume, *The Call of the Heart* (1944), it can be said that the poet has managed to put the experience of *Serpents* entirely behind him. The themes of these poems are no less personal or subjective than those in the earlier volume: they are almost exclusively love poems. But the attitude to woman has suffered a marked change from what we find in *Serpents*. In *Serpents* we do not really find love, but lust; woman is regarded in the traditional terms of Pauline Christianity, as basically a powerful temptation, a snare of the devil, and the poet could only see in her a means of arousing his lust and a symbol of his damnation. Now this mean view of woman disappears altogether, lust is replaced by love, a noble and ennobling passion. Woman has become nothing short of an angel of mercy: by means of love she delivers the poet from the hell he inhabited when he wrote *Serpents*. In 'This is my Wine' he contrasts his present state of bliss, joy and certainty with the doubt, sorrow and pain of the poisoned experience of *Serpents*: thanks to his beloved (probably as some scholars maintain he means the gentle Laila) who has provided the balsam for his soul, he now regards the painful experience of the past as 'Purgatory leading to his present Paradise'.[109] The fire and smoke, the blood-red and black imagery which dominated the earlier poetry has now given place to images derived from the world of vegetation. To his beloved he now writes:

When you came along my writing turned green and noble
My love sang, my rhymes became fresh and succulent
Until then my life had been dry and from my despair
A wretched shadow crept over my blood.[110]

It is now the chaste look in her eyes that holds a mysterious attraction for him and she is endowed with divine attributes. In another poem he calls her 'the Promised Land', and says[111] that at her touch 'All my sins died away.'

In 'You and I'[112] his union with his beloved is so complete and spiritualized that it is expressed in the language of pantheism, and the poem is full of echoes from the poetry of the great Sufi martyr al-Hallaj:[113]

Is this your beauty or mine?
Your love is as beautiful as mine.
And that by which I live
Is it you or me?

Because the poet has found peace and recovered his faith in love he can now much more easily bear his predicament as a poet with a message who lives in a society that cannot appreciate him. This is very clear in his poem 'The Cup'.[114]

The final volume, *To Eternity* (1944), confirms the position reached in *The Call of the Heart*: it uses as epigraph two lines from the earlier collection. Abu Shabaka's rebellion is now a thing of the past, its place securely and definitely taken by a full acceptance and recognition of the beauty and harmony of the universe. He now joyfully addresses his beloved: 'I have mingled you with my being as wine is mixed with dewdrops'. And the beloved now brings the poet nearer to God: 'In your tenderness I find my ascent to God and a ladder in your lovely voice'. The mystical dimension of love already felt in *The Call of the Heart* is further emphasized here: 'Beloved, you were already within me even before I set eyes on you'.[115] Instead of the tales about lust and sexual appetite Abu Shabaka now related to his own love the world's great stories of idealized love, both in the Arab

East and in the West: the stories of Qais and Laila, Jamil and Buthaina, ‘Urwa and ‘Afrā, as well as of Tristan and Isolde. *To Eternity* is in fact an eloquent celebration of a highly idealized love, lacking perhaps the fever or the heat of passion which characterized *Serpents*, but at the same time much freer from the theatricality of some of the poetry in the earlier volume, and there are moments in it of unparalleled serenity, beauty and lyricism. In the change that took place in his attitude to love Abu Shabaka forms an interesting contrast to ‘Ali Mahmud Taha who moved in the opposite direction, starting from a position of idealized love and ending with a hedonistic attitude in which the pleasures of sex are dominant.

Shabbi

There is nothing in the least theatrical about the poetry of the Tunisian al-Shabbi who is one of the most appealing modern Arab poets. He was one of three romantic poets who died tragically young, the other two being the Egyptian Hamshari and the Sudanese al-Tijānī Yūsuf Bashīr. But Shabbi was obviously the greatest of them all. More books have been written about him than about any other romantic Arab poet.

Abu'l Qāsim al-Shābbī (1909–34) was born in a town near Tauzer, where his father was a *qāḍī* (judge). After he had learnt the Koran he was sent to the famous school of al-Zaitūna mosque, where he was taught the traditional Islamic sciences, Arabic language and literature. He subsequently studied law in the Tunisian Law School, from which he graduated in 1930. In 1929 he first felt the symptoms of the heart disease which was to be the cause of his premature death at the age of twenty-five. His father's death in 1929, which meant that he had to assume responsibility for the family, cast a shadow over his life which was darkened by an unhappy marriage. Furthermore he seemed to have been disappointed in an early love which ended in the death of the young woman he loved.

Shabbi was familiar with the work of the chief classical Arabic poets such as the Abbasid Ma‘arri, Ibn al-Rumi and Ibn al-Farid (together with Khayyam), as well as with the writings of the moderns, both their original works and their translations. He was particularly influenced by his readings in *Mahjar* literature and in Arabic translations of western notions of literary criticism. Shabbi knew no European language, but through translations he came to know something of European thought and literature, including a certain acquaintance with Greek mythology. The astounding thing is that his poetry and his criticism reveal a much deeper influence by, and a much greater understanding of, western literature than that which we find in the works of many poets who mastered one or more European languages. But it is characteristic of genius to possess an extraordinary power of assimilation. One remembers Eliot's remark that Shakespeare managed to get more of the spirit of classical civilization from North's translation of Plutarch's *Lives* than many classical scholars did from the original texts. What al-Shabbi got from the Arabic translations of western literature was the spirit and attitudes of the Romantics. But then the Arabic translations available were themselves often confined to Romantic works. Besides, the Arab creative writers and critics whom he read at a very early age, and through whom he indirectly derived his western ideas, people like the *Mahjar* poets and chiefly Jibran Khalil Jibran,[116] or like 'Aqqad, Mazini and Abu Shadi, were themselves influenced by western Romantic authors. In this respect, as his correspondence with him shows, Shabbi also benefited from his friendship with the poet and critic Muḥammad al-Ḥilaiwī, who used to show him and discuss with him translations from de Musset and Lamartine. They also often discussed contemporary Egyptian literary periodicals and the general literary scene in Egypt to which Shabbi looked as his source of cultural sustenance.[117]

Shabbi's poems were first published in periodicals and newspapers, especially in Abu Shadi's *Apollo*, which, according to his most devoted scholar, was chiefly responsible for spreading his reputation in the Arab world.[118] However, he died while preparing his collected poems for publication, his *Diwan* which he was to call *Songs of Life*, and it was not until 1955 that it saw the light of day.[119] Besides the poems, he published a number of articles in various periodicals, and only one book of literary criticism, *The Arab Poetic Imagination*, which came out in Tunis in 1929. This critical essay, originally a public lecture which understandably shocked his predominantly conservative Tunisian audience, is in many ways an impressive performance, coming as it did from a young man of twenty, with no knowledge of a single European language. Whatever be its limitations, which arise from the headiness of youth and its proclivity for making sweeping generalizations, supported only by unconsciously highly selected evidence, two qualities it did not lack: courage and integrity. The book opens with a general discussion of imagination, then deals in separate chapters with the poetic imagination in relation to Arab mythology, Arab attitudes to nature, to women and to narrative literature, and ends with a general discussion of Arabic literature and (predictably, for the period) the Arab spirit or the Arab mind.

Like the thorough-going romantic he is, Shabbi is keenly aware of the importance of imagination, which he regards as essential to man in apprehending and interpreting reality as the air he breathes,[120] and of course he sees the relation between it and metaphorical language. Shabbi finds Arab mythology deficient in poetic imagination, compared with the Greek, Roman or Scandinavian. He reviews the treatment of nature in Arabic poetry, both pre-Islamic and Islamic, compares it with the European treatment as revealed in two examples from Goethe and (inevitably) Lamartine, and finally concludes that:

> Arab poets have not expressed such deep poetic feeling because their attitude to nature lacked reverence for its sublime life: they only looked at it as they looked at a beautifully ornamented garment or pretty embroidery.

Their response to it was no more than crude admiration (p. 67). Poetic imagination according to him is the product of deep emotion, while the Arabs, he claims, 'did not feel the current of life flowing in the heart of nature, except in a crude and superficial manner, devoid of keen sensibility or imaginative ecstasy'. Shabbi does the same thing with the Arab attitude to woman, which he finds superficial and limited to the world of the senses (p. 91). Here his condemnation is even more extreme:

> The attitude of Arabic literature to woman is base and ignoble, and sinks to the lowest depths of materialism. It only sees in woman a body to be desired and one of the basest pleasures in life to be enjoyed.
>
> As for that noble view which combines love and reverence, fondness and worship, as for that deep spiritual attitude which we find in the Aryan poets, it is totally or almost totally absent from Arabic literature (p. 72).

Shabbi goes on to point out the irrelevance of old Arabic literature:

> Arabic literature no longer suits our present spirit, temperament, inclinations or aspirations in life ... We must never look upon Arabic literature as an ideal which we have to follow or whose spirit, style and ideas we have to imitate, but we must consider it simply as one of those ancient literatures which we admire and respect and no more ... (pp. 105ff).

The reasons why Shabbi considers Arabic literature irrelevant are significant: 'Everything the Arab mind has produced in all the periods of its history', he writes, 'is monotonous and utterly lacking in poetic imagination', superficial and 'does not penetrate into the reality of things'. The two chief characteristics of the Arab spirit are oratory and materialism. Materialism stops at the level of the senses, while oratory and keen sensibility generally do not go together. The effect of these two tendencies of the Arab spirit is that 'the Arabs did not view the poet as we now do, namely as the prophet or messenger who brings life to the children of the world lost in the paths of time; they did not distinguish between him and the orator who defended his tribe and protected its honour with his tongue' (pp. 121ff.).

As is to be expected this rebelliousness against traditional values, which was also manifest in Shabbi's other writings, aroused a good deal of indignation and hostile criticism among the more conservative elements in his community. By turns Shabbi was called a rebel, a heretic, an atheist and the Voltaire of the Arabs, and in fact to this day many of the numerous writings or commentaries on al-Shabbi's life and works, not only in Tunisia, but in other Arab countries too, seem to suffer from a spirit of partisanship,[121] even though he is generally acclaimed, not the least in his own country, to be Tunisia's greatest modern poet. We shall see later how the hostility which this work aroused contributed in no small measure to the poet's sense of grievance and isolation.

It is not the intention here, of course, to discuss Shabbi's ideas or their relation to their sources, the chief of which was 'Aqqad who, as has been demonstrated, in turn derived his ideas about Aryan myth-making (once a fashionable subject) from Herbert Spencer, Ernest Renan and Tito Vignoli.[122] This remarkably inconoclastic work has been quoted, partly in order to show the full extent of the revolutionary impulse in some of the Arab romantics, partly because the words in which the author expresses his views on literature, poetry and mythology, on nature, love and women, provide an admirably faithful description of the attitude to these topics revealed in his own poetry and indeed in much of the best work of the Arab romantic poets.

Songs of Life was primarily the work of a romantic rebel. But it is very different from, for instance, *The Serpents of Paradise*. Unlike Abu Shabaka, Shabbi does not seem to strike attitudes; despite his deep passion, his voice never rises to the point of screaming: that is why his passion sounds to us all the more genuine. Because of his early training in the traditional type of *madrasa* Shabbi's command of the Arabic language is (despite some weaknesses pointed out by 'Umar Farrūkh) much greater, a thing which, together with his great gifts and acute sensitivity, enabled him to attain heights of poetic utterance not easily reached by Abu Shabaka who in *Serpents* seemed to cultivate what is perilously close to a *fin-de-siècle* type of attitude, confining his poetry to the world of sensations, of sex and drink. There are no prostitutes in the poetry of Shabbi: on the contrary, the women he addresses in his poems are all highly idealized and, as in the case of Naji, described in religious terms. While Abu Shabaka writes 'The Red Prayer', we find Shabbi composing his 'Prayer at the Altar of Love'.[123] This is a full poetic statement of al-Shabbi's reverential attitude to woman already expressed in his essay on *The Arab Poetic Imagination*. In structure it is similar to Shelley's 'Skylark', in which the poet tries to define his feelings by a series of comparisons and analogies drawn from a wide range of experience. The result is that the poem strikes us mainly by its rich profusion of imagery, for at times the images seem to be only tenuously related to the main theme. The poet's beloved is sweet like childhood, dreams, melodies, a new morning, a bright cheerful sky, moonlight, roses or a baby's smile. She is gentle and youthful, and her innocence inspires reverence even in the most obstinate and hardened heart, her gentleness would nearly cause blossoms to grow out of stone. She is both Venus and an angel from paradise, for she brings both joy and peace to a troubled world. She is the epitome of the mystery, depth and beauty of the universe, she is the spirit of spring. She is the Song of Songs, yet she is sung by the God of song (Apollo). She is a woman whose voice is as soft and lovely as the echo of a distant flute, whose figure, steps and movements are full of melody. Everything about her, such as the movement of her neck and the swaying of her breasts, observes a beautiful rhythm. Yet she is more than a woman: she is 'life in her sublime sanctity', she is 'raised above imagination, poetry and art, above mind and above all limits'. She is the poet's sacred idol, his goddess. He calls her 'daughter of light' who will deliver him from a sad and imperfect world. Surely the terms in which she is described suggest that the poet's beloved is much more than an idealized mistress, she is nothing short of his soul, the creative principle within him. His yearning for her is the romantic poet's longing to be reunited with his self, from which, as we have seen in a number of cases, he feels he has been exiled. Conversely, because he either projects himself in the outside world or assimilates the outside world to himself, when he feels united with his beloved he is, as he says in another poem, 'When I see You',

> Filled with an infinite joy as if I had been raised above all men
> Wishing to embrace the universe with my soul, and all its men and all
> its trees. (p. 125).

Already, when he was barely nineteen years old, he could write in a poem entitled 'Love' (p. 45) that love is 'a torch of enchanting light descended from heaven', 'a divine spirit' which transfigures the world, and 'a river of wine, whoever tastes it wades through hell without fear of burning' and that since it is the ultimate end of life he should not fear being enclosed in a tomb.

When, on the other hand, the poet is deprived of love, 'Chaos is come again', nothing in nature can afford him sufficient comfort. This agonizing sense of the indifference of nature to human suffering is expressed in a precocious poem written when the poet was only seventeen, under the title 'Love's Funeral' (p. 20). Such a poem, written in a language of utter simplicity and with deep pathos and overwhelming emotion is saved from sentimentality by the relative intricacy of rhyme scheme in its five-lined stanza form which shows that the poet is still in command of his experience. The same grief is expressed in other poems, for instance 'The Poet's Song' (p. 64) or 'The Voice of the Lost One' (p. 81), where he writes about his soul's exile.

In another early poem, 'The Strange Grief' (p. 22), which clearly underlines the metaphysical dimension of the poet's sorrow, he writes:

My grief is different from all others
It is strange in the world of sorrow
My grief is a thought that sings
But is unknown to the ear of Time.

Yet I have heard its sound in my heart
In the midst of my intoxicated youth
And ever since I have been sad at heart
Singing of my sorrow, like a mountain bird . .

Other people's grief is like a torch
That fades and dies in the course of time
But mine is settled in my soul
Where it will remain till eternity . . .

I am a sad stranger in the world of sorrow
No one bears a tenth of what I feel
So bitter is my grief, yet when my soul screams
My very own body can hear nothing.

In 'The Orphan's Complaint' (p. 29) nature again cannot be of any avail, so profound is the poet's sense of isolation. The poet's cry is lost in the roaring of the unheeding sea, ignored by the totally uncomprehending woods and likewise by the indifferent river. He asks Mother Nature for help but she cannot hear him. Feeling orphaned he ends by urging himself to shut up.

Because of Shabbi's keen awareness of the ultimate indifference of Nature, unlike Abu Shaḍi, he does not find joy in her, but rather a confirmation of his own feelings of sorrow. Projecting his own suffering on Nature he believes that there is a bond between her and man, since both are subject to the tyranny of cruel times and are therefore united by common suffering (see for instance his poem on 'The Faded Lily' and 'The Remains of Autumn', pp. 31, 62). Indeed Shabbi's attitude to nature remained unchanged all his life. In moments of acute spiritual (and later physical) suffering his thoughts about death (and perhaps his premonition of his impending death) could not allow him to see nature as a healer or as a source of joy. In 'Song of Sorrows' (p. 47) he writes:

Whoever has heard the voice of death and the echo of tombs
Is not lured by the songs of birds
Amidst the enchanting spring flowers
Or the smiles of life revealing the glory of the Lord.

To the rebellious poem 'To God' – in which he claims that he has not found in this world the compassionate God who is alleged to create his creatures in joy, comfort them and show them Divine Mercy, finding in their lives His sublime spirit and signs of His perfect art – Shabbi writes a short prose introduction in which he explains how he has occasionally experienced emotional crises during which all certainties are destroyed by sorrow and despair, and his faith is shaken to the roots. In such moments, man feels as if the relation of kinship which binds him to the rest of the creation had been severed, and he becomes a stranger in a world that feels strange in his soul and then life feels as if it were a tedious but frightening kind of absurdity that deserves neither preservation nor sympathy (p. 98). This is clearly an existentialist experience of *angoisse*, in which a person feels he is beyond the reach of the outside world, nature and man alike. However, although nature never becomes a source of ecstasy for Shabbi, he gradually regards it as a place of escape from the world of men as the latter grows more and more oppressive. In 'To a Sparrow' (p. 55), a poem imbued with the romantic sentiments and attitudes popularized partly by *Mahjar* authors like Jibran, partly by Arabic translations of Shelley's 'To a Skylark' as well as poems inspired by it and poems on similar themes, Shabbi contrasts the world of nature and of man:

> Moved I am by the songs of birds . . .
> But there is nothing in the world of men
> That pleases my soul or satisfies my heart
> When I listen to their talk I find it trivial
> Pallid, poor and dull chatter . . .
> They grumble when I am silent, yet when I speak
> They complain of my sentiments and my thoughts.

He attacks city life because it breeds vice and evil, and he openly resorts to nature as an escape from the corrupt world of man. Typically Shabbi idealizes childhood which in a poem on the subject he calls 'life's dream' and likens to 'sweet visions in sleep', and he contrasts the innocence of sweet childhood with the disillusionment of the adult world of experience (p. 56). In 'The Woods' (p. 188) nature appears as the place where the poet finds 'the world of imagination, vision, poetry, meditations and dreams', although this is chiefly because it is far from the absurd world of men, with their sins and illusions.

However, it would be wrong to conclude from the preceding remarks that Shabbi was a purely subjective poet who was exclusively concerned with his own personal emotions. Nothing in fact can be further from the truth, although as in the case of major poets it would be difficult to disentangle what is subjective in his work from what is not, so passionate was his apprehension of reality in all its aspects – physical, social, political, psychological or metaphysical. It is true that in his conception of poetry the emotional and subjective element looms rather large: in poems like 'My Poetry', 'To Poetry', 'I Have Said to Poetry' and 'The Idea of the Artist'[124] poetry is regarded as a direct expression of emotion, providing relief for the poet and solace to man in a world full of suffering.[125] The artist is the man who develops his capacity for feeling and sympathy (the kind of sympathy that made it possible for Shabbi to write such a moving account of the experience of a bereaved mother in the poem 'A Mother's Heart', p. 129) whereas intellect leads to sterility. In Shabbi's actual practice it is clear, even from this brief account, what a large role emotions play. One scholar has counted no fewer than 1118 words signifying suffering in the collection *Songs of Life*.[126] Yet from his earliest work such as the poem 'Fair Tunisia', written in 1925 (p. 13), Shabbi has shown his commitment to Tunisia, his pledge to continue to be the voice ('the divine voice') to awaken his country, whatever be the ill-treatment or persecution he might receive at the hands of his society. In moments of impatient anger, for example in the poem 'Let Them Die' (p. 14), he says that a people that willingly and passively submits to injustice and tyranny deserves to be allowed to die and be forgotten. A similar sentiment is expressed in poems written as late as 1933 ('To the People') and 1934 ('The Dead World') (pp. 175–84). Like many aspects of the work of this poet, his attitude to the Tunisian people has provoked much controversy.[127] But there can be no doubt whatsoever regarding the degree of his involvement with the Tunisian people. In 'A View of Life' he urges his people, in almost direct neoclassical hortatory fashion, never to lose their serious outlook or give in to despair (p. 15). In a series of powerful poems, including 'The Roaring Storm' (p. 42), 'To the Tyrant' (p. 43), 'Thus Spake the Days' (p. 58), 'To the Tyrants of the World' (p. 185) and the celebrated 'The Will for Life' (p. 167), he predicts the heroic struggle of his people against foreign occupation and tyranny and the certain downfall of the latter. 'Son of my Mother' (p. 88) urges man, who was born free like the breeze or light, to sing like birds and roam freely in nature, but is content to live in humiliation and passive obedience to those who chain him, to liberate himself and move 'to the light, sweet light which is the shadow of the Lord'. One can go on citing examples. It is sufficient to remember the basic humanity of a man so sensitive to the suffering of the world; he could write in a poem entitled 'Glory':

> It is not glory to get the earth drunk with blood
> And ride a high steed to the war
> But to stem the tide of sorrow with all your might
> From a stricken world (p. 52)

Like Abu Shabaka, Shabbi viewed himself as a prophet in his society, who, alas, meets with the same fate as most prophets. This is revealed in much of his poetry, especially in an interesting poem entitled 'The Unknown Prophet' written in 1930 (p. 102), which invites comparison with Abu Shabaka's very similar work 'The Cup', both clearly showing the profound influence of Jibran.[128] Shabbi writes:

> In the morning of life I perfumed my cups, filled them with the wine of my soul
> I offered them to you, my people, but you spilled my wine and trampled on my cup
> I grieved, but I suppressed my pain and restrained my feelings.
> Then I arranged the blossoms of my heart into a garland
> Which I offered you, my people, but you tore my roses and trampled them under foot.
> Then you gave me a garment of sorrow to wear and crowned my head with mountain thorns. . .

So the Christ-like poet/prophet, having been scorned and humiliated by his fellow men, who accuse him of madness and of being in communion with evil spirits and who expel him from their temple on the grounds of his being a wicked infidel and an evil spirit himself, goes to the woods in order 'to lead a life of poetry and sanctity', hoping to forget his people and to find happiness, sympathy and understanding in nature. Here Shabbi paints an idyllic picture of the poet spending his days in the woods, away from the wicked world of men, a Pan-like figure, his hair streaming in the wind, piping away his songs, accompanied by joyful birds. Yet Shabbi realizes too well that this can only be a dream, as is clearly shown in his poems 'A Poet's Dreams' (p. 114) and the even more painful 'The Limitations of Dreams' (p. 115). We must not, however, underrate the extent of his real sufferings as a result of his not being understood by his community.[129] A poem like 'The Lost Longings' (p. 112), with lines like

> O heart of life, how I feel a stranger in this world, suffering from my exile
> Among people who do not understand the songs of my heart or the meaning of my sorrow
> In a world bound in heavy chains, lost in the darkness of doubt and misfortune.

is almost a paraphrase of an entry in his diary dated 7/1/1930:

> Now I feel I am a stranger among my own countrymen. I wonder if the day will ever come when my dreams will be embraced by the hearts of the people and my songs will be chanted by the awakened spirits of the youth

> and the longings and aspirations of my heart will be appreciated by thoughtful minds even in the distant future. As for now I have lost all hope. I am a strange bird living among people who do not understand a single word of the beautiful language of my soul.[130]

This sense of being an exile was, as J. Berque once rightly observed, typical of many Arab intellectuals at the time and no doubt had its cultural significance in a changing society.[131] It also must have contributed greatly to Shabbi's 'metaphysical' sense of exile in the world.

The poetry of the last two or three years of Shabbi's life is among the most interesting and moving in modern Arabic literature. Understandably, with the approach of death and the deterioration of his health, it shows the poet's preoccupation with the subject of death, but the early romantic welcoming of death which we find in a poem like 'To Death', which depicts death as a 'beautiful spirit hovering above the clouds' and a place where 'naked heavenly brides appear swaying and singing lovely melodies' (p. 76), gives place to a much more convincing, passionate and urgent concern. The poem 'In the Shadow of the Valley of Death' (1932) ends with these lines:

> Life's blossoms fall in silence
> Sadly, boringly at my feet;
> The charm of life has dried up
> So come along my heart, let us now try death. (p. 143)

Here is another poem typical of his last period, 'A Storm in the Dark' (1933), quoted in full:

> If I had time in the clutch of my hand
> I would scatter the days to the wind like grains of sand
> And I would say to the wind, 'Wind, take them away,
> And disperse them among distant hills,
> Nay, in the mountain passes of death, in a world
> Where no light dances, nor shade.'
>
> If I had this world in the clutch of my hand
> I would hurl it into the fire, the fire of Hell,
> For what is this world? What are these men?
> This sky and those stars?
> Fire is a more fitting place
> For sorrows' slaves, this stage of death and this nest of cares.
>
> I say to the past that is gone
> Folded away in death and the eternal night
> I say to men's present that still is
> And to the future that is not yet born:
> 'Absurd is this world of yours
> And lost in a darkness without end.' (p. 181)

Life now appears as 'A Strange Play', the work of 'a master of irony' (p. 164).[132]

However, Shabbi's mood in these years alternates between despair and a sense of the futility of existence on the one hand, and on the other, a passionate love for life as we find in 'Confession' (1934). We even find a heroic defiance of death, typical of the man, who, because he was acutely aware of suffering both within himself and outside, rebelled against everything that tended to restrict the freedom of the human spirit, whether intellectual and social, like reactionary conservative modes of living and thinking, or political, like tyranny or colonialism, even to the extent of denying at one point the existence of a merciful God. Shabbi, the author of the somewhat Nietzschean poem 'The Will of Life' (p. 167), made famous all over the Arab world by being sung by a celebrated Egyptian singer, advocated a basically heroic attitude to life which, while not ignoring the element of suffering, preaches the value of the struggle for its own sake, life being a value in itself: this is best expressed in his 'Hymn of the Mighty or Thus Sang Prometheus' (1933), in which, assuming the persona of Prometheus, the poet declares triumphantly (p. 179):

I shall live despite sickness and foes
Like the eagle on the highest summit,
Looking at the bright sun, mocking
The clouds, the rain and the storms.
I shall not look down at the gloomy shadow,
I shall not peer into the bottom of the dark pit.
I shall roam in the world of feeling,
Dreaming and singing, for such is the poet's bliss.
Listening to life's music and inspiration
Melting the world's soul in my creation,
Harking to the divine voice which breathes life
Into the dead echoes in my heart.

And I shall say to Fate which for ever fights
Against my hopes with every blow,
The bright flame in my blood shall not be quenched
By sorrow's waves or tempests of misfortune,
Buffet my heart as hard as you can
It shall remain steadfast as a solid rock.

Of course, Shabbi finally welcomed death as the only means to end his suffering. But what is interesting is that his address to death is by no means an expression of total defeat: it is not simply that the poet's view of death is no longer fraught with elements of romantic glamour, which make dying a 'rich' experience, to use Keats's epithet in the *Ode to a Nightingale* — elements which exist in Shabbi's earlier poetry. Paradoxically enough, and as is abundantly clear from a study of his imagery, Shabbi now regards death as a means of attaining a fuller and more significant life. This we find in, for instance, his poem 'The New Morrow' (1933), which is certainly one of the most haunting poems in modern Arabic (p. 159). Here, partly by means of dominant light imagery which, like Wordsworth, he tends to use in order to express moments of ecstasy or spiritual revelation, Shabbi manages to convey a profound experience of mystical dimensions, which makes the final image, in the poem, of the poet unfurling the sails of his lonely boat on a strange and vast sea, welcoming the hazards of the unknown, a perfect and moving symbol of frail but heroic man, viewed almost *sub specie aeternitatis*.

Tijani

Even more striking in his fondness for light imagery is the Sudanese poet al-Tijani – which is not surprising since much of his poetry deals with his mystical experience.[133] He even chose for his collection of poems (published posthumously in 1942) the significant title *Ishrāqa*, meaning 'illumination'. Al-Tijani, whose poetry will be treated very briefly in the survey, has often been compared with Shabbi: neither of them knew any European language, both were brought up in conservative traditional families but grew up to become rebels, both died tragically young.[134] Al-Tijānī Yūsuf Bashīr (1910–37) was born in Omdurman in a family which had a long history of promoting the teaching of Islam and of establishing Koranic schools. The boy received his elementary education in such a school run locally by an uncle, then he went to the Religious Institute where he distinguished himself; but as a result of an argument with his fellow students over the respective merits of the poetry of Shauqi and Hafiz, we are told, he was misreported to the authorities, falsely accused of religious heresy and dismissed from the Institute.[135] He had a passionate desire to complete his education in Egypt, but his authoritarian father wanted him to stay in Sudan and foiled a desperate attempt made by his son to flee. For a while he worked as payment collector for a firm, then as a journalist contributing literary articles, first to the cultural review *al-Fajr*, then to *Omdurman*, but in 1936 he displayed the first symptoms of consumption which proved to be the cause of his death in the following year.

Like Shabbi, Tijani looked towards Cairo as his intellectual inspiration, reading avidly its publications, both books and periodicals, and following with great interest all its literary news and controversies. In his articles in *al-Fajr* he refers to the work of 'Aqqad as well as younger romantic poets such as Naji and 'Ali Mahmud Taha. Like Shabbi, too, he read *Mahjar* literature, especially the work of Jibran. The influence of western Romantic poetry upon him was therefore equally indirect, but no less profound. Tijani was also fond of reading classical Arabic literature, particularly the works of Sufi writers like al-Ghazālī.[136]

In the opening poem of his Collected Works Tijani describes his poetry as flowing from 'the world of beauty and love, the heart, its passions and its longings'. The majority of his collection is of a subjective character, with very few poems dealing with public matters, and also a number of elegies. It is not that the poet lacked an awareness of the social or political problems of his century, as is clear from poems such as 'The World of the Poor' in which he showed his sensitivity and compassion for the poor, or 'Rebellion' which attacked the economic exploitation of the Sudanese by foreign businessmen such as the Greeks and Armenians.[137] But on the whole in his poetry Tijani dealt with what he clearly regarded as more suitable subjects: his feelings about God, nature, love and poetry. He was aware that the poetry he wrote, so different from the traditional neoclassical imitations dominant in the Sudan in his time, was 'the poetry of life and noble feelings' and the fact that it was lost on his people who were not only incapable of understanding it, but who attacked him for his obscurity and even heresy, naturally caused him much suffering, as we can see in his poem 'The Lost Literature' (p. 59). Nevertheless, considering that he actually suffered expulsion from school, Tijani's reaction was not as violent as that of Shabbi, and was even free from bitterness. This may be due to his mystical outlook which generally results in an attitude of ultimate acceptance of the world. It is also noteworthy that Tijani was singularly free from self-pity, despite his fatal illness. Only in one poem do we find him complaining of the disease and giving an account of his physical suffering, and this in a poem addressed to his friend and fellow poet Maḥmūd Anīs, which has the tone and character of a private letter (pp. 110–11).

It is not that Tijani's acceptance was a facile attitude, mechanically or thoughtlessly maintained all the time. On the contrary, there are a number of poems which record states of doubt, some of which must have been the source of the false accusation of religious heresy or lack of faith hurled at him by his enemies. But the doubt is only momentary and is followed by certainty and firm belief in a benign providence which is the source of all beauty. This is true of poems such as 'Yesterday I Bade Farewell to my Faith', 'My Doubt Gives me Pain' and 'Uncertainty'. His poem on God, which adopts as epigraph one of the most famous verses of the Koran for its use of the image of light, is resplendent with light imagery, and expresses the poet's faith in God's power and beauty and His omnipresence. Tijani's mystical position was in fact very close to pantheism. His poem 'The Philosopher's Heart' ends with this thought:

Here in my heart is the Truth, here is a spark from Heaven,
Here in my heart is God. (p. 19)

which is strongly reminiscent of utterances by al-Hallaj. In 'The Passion of a Mystic' he writes:

How vast in the soul true Being extends,
How closely to the soul pure silence is linked.
Inside all that is in the universe the Lord moves.
This minute ant is an echo of Him
He lives in its belly and in His soil it lives
And when it gives up its soul God is there ready
To catch it in His hands.
It does not die, for in it God lives if only you could see Him. (p. 91)

This Blake-like awareness of the sanctity of life also enabled Tijani to write poems about nature and simple aspects of everyday village life, in which there is a feeling of innocence and a freshness of vision and of a blessed universe somewhat reminiscent of Blake's *Songs of Innocence*. Such is his poem 'Tūtī in the Morning', Tuti being a little island opposite Khartoum, a charming description of the island coming back to life at daybreak. The poet lovingly records many details such as processions of pikefish going solemnly round it, birds waking from their sleep, fluttering in their nests, each nest turning into a monastery where morning hymns are sung, an ox bellowing, a sheep bleating, or an ass braying, 'bright drops of dew hanging like little lanterns from branches', beasts roaming about and fields looking fertile and green, water-wheels beginning to moan and girls fetching water in their jars, flocks of geese with dark wings and boats sailing up and down the river.

The same spirit is shown in his poems on childhood, a period during which Tijani, like many mystical poets before him, felt man was closer to God. Here is a poem inspired by his recollections of his days in the Koran school, not entirely free from gentle irony:

He sprang from his sleep; rubbing his eyes, he turned his face away from the morning
Grumbling and cursing heaven and earth, and all their inhabitants, alike people and ghosts
Joyless and powerless, irked by the loathsome thought of going,
Urged on by morning shadows as they spread in the open spaces of the village and the valleys,
Fearful memories wandering in his imagination and once more was aroused in him the familiar desire to play the truant.
But reluctantly he plodded on, dragging his feet and weeping in his sad heart,
His garment reeking with the smell of his inkpot, a powerful scent in which his head was drenched. (p. 57)

Tijani never takes for granted the physical beauty of the world, he never ceases to be surprised that so much beauty has been created for the enjoyment of man; it is an attitude one finds in mystics whose sense of beauty is unusually acute, such as G. M. Hopkins. 'Dawn in the Desert', virtually a hymn to 'sacred light', ends with these lines:

> O the wonder of this glorious beauty in its different forms, both violent
> and calm,
> Weaving of this dawn a sublime garment of love for a poet sublime,
> Who from the profound depths of his being praises the Lord, from his
> soul cries, shouting like a boy:
> 'Lord, is it possible that all that beauty, splendour and magic are for
> the sake of this one mortal?' (p. 85)

Tijani's mysticism is therefore the mysticism of a poet: his awareness of beauty leads him to God, just as his profound and intense experience of God sharpens in him his sense of beauty. This two-way movement is expressed in his poem 'Hope' (p. 42), where the poet asks beauty to 'bestow the spirit and mystery of the Lord upon the world', to 'unlock his soul and uncover its hidden dawn', and at the same time he relates an experience on a glorious night when surrounded by beauty he found himself walking to the place where the veil was lifted from the world, and where he says 'he burned his soul in the perfumed censer of the Lord'. Although the meeting of the aesthetic and religious or mystical is obvious in much of Tijani's poetry, it is especially so in a poem of remarkable complexity entitled *Fi'l Mauhā* (pp. 83–4), which must be translated as 'At the Site of Inspiration and Revelation' (the Arabic root *wḥy* can mean both terms, and is used here in such a way that poetic inspiration becomes equated with divine revelation or *tanzīl*, a word used in the poem). The poet, described as the 'prophet of feelings', is urged to go to the site of revelation; the right atmosphere is set for the creative moment: nature at night, bathed in moonlight, completely still and silent, exuding rich perfumes. The senses are aglow and the poet is in a state of complete receptivity. In the moment of poetic creation the world is transfigured and indeed miracles occur, for, as the poet says, solid stone ceases to be solid; things go beyond the limits assigned to them by the natural order of things:

> God will open to your awakened feelings a sublime world of splendid
> images,
> Release for you the springs of the unknown, reveal before your eyes a
> world of treasures
> To choose, describe and paint the revealed visions, to forge and make
> a new world.

Clearly here the poetic and mystical experiences became one and the same thing.

Abu Risha

There are no such mystical moments in the work of the Syrian poet 'Umar Abū Rīsha (1910 –).[138] Abu Risha was born near Aleppo in a well-to-do literary family and received his early education in Syria, but he pursued his later studies in the American University of Beirut, and subsequently in England where he studied industrial chemistry in Manchester. He did not complete his studies in England but returned to Aleppo in 1932, and from that time onwards he concentrated on poetry and politics. For some time he occupied the post of librarian of Aleppo Public Library, and later held a number of diplomatic posts ranging from Syrian cultural attaché in the Arab League in Cairo to Syrian and United Arab Republic ambassador in Brazil, India and Austria. Abu Risha has published four volumes of verse:[139] *Poems* (1936), *By 'Umar Abu-Risha* (1947), *Selections* (1959) and finally *Collected Works*, vol. I (1971). He has also written several verse dramas: *Dhi Qār, The Poet's Trial, al-Ḥusain ibn'Ali* and *Semiramis*.[140]

In an interview Abu Risha is reported to have said that in the beginning of his poetic career he loved the great classical poets of the Abbasid era: al-Buhturi and Abu Tammam, and their followers among the modern neo-classicists such as Shauqi, but he gradually grew tired of them and began to look for the more individualistic voices in the tradition. In England he fell in love with Shakespeare (whose *Venus and Adonis* he regards as the greatest poem ever written on the subject of love), Shelley, Keats, Baudelaire, Poe, Morris, Hood, Milton, Tennyson, Browning, Thomas Gray and Oscar Wilde. He admitted he was not fond of Hugo and Lamartine, but that his favourite poets were Poe and Baudelaire.[141] To these two strands of his literary formation we should add the influence of the *Mahjar* poetry, which was strengthened by an early disappointment in love on account of the death of his beloved at the age of seventeen, whom he commemmorated in an elegy 'The End of Love' (1932). However, it is interesting that Abu Risha has declared that he was not fond of poets such as Lamartine, for his poetry suffers less from the tearful sentimentality of the French Romantics than many of his contemporary Arab poets. Early in his career he developed in his poems a robustness and a virility of tone, a joyful, fun-loving and pleasure-seeking outlook, and a hedonistic and a masterful attitude to beautiful women, which in some ways reminded his readers of his namesake the celebrated Early Islamic love poet 'Umar ibn Abī Rabī'a.[142] His verse play *The Poets' Trial*, in which the best-known modern poets from Iraq, Syria, Lebanon and Egypt, both neoclassicists and romantics, are tried by Apollo and Minerva and other Greek deities, is a satirical attack on the neoclassical style and a plea for romanticism. In it Abu Shadi is made to recite lines written by Abu Risha on the *Mahjar* free-verse writer Amin al-Rihani which reveal Abu Risha's conception of the poet as a winged creature of light, an inspired being to whom are revealed the secrets of the universe, a child of nature to whom she discloses all her beauties and attractions.[143] This is the romantic conception of the poet which we have already encountered in the work of other romantics.

Abu Risha's poetry shows clearly the blend of Arab and western culture which he received. During his residence in England he was able to acquire first-hand knowledge of western thought and literature. The influence on him of the second generation of the English Romantics (Keats, Shelley and Byron) is pervasive, particularly that of Keats whose *Ode on a Grecian Urn* left its mark on at least two poems 'A Woman and a Statue' and 'Kagyurpa'. Baudelaire's ambivalent attitude to woman is reflected in some form or another in many of Abu Risha's poems.[144] Like Shabbi, he displays an admirable command of the Arabic language, and more than in the case of any other romantic poet so far discussed, his language attains a degree of crispness, hardness and precision which is almost classical. Although he is well versed in the Arabic poetic tradition of which he is extremely proud, it is obviously the 'romantic' streaks in this tradition which appeal to him most: the pessimism of al-Ma'arri, his rebellion against the human condition, or the morbid sensibility of Dīk al-Jinn of Hims, who is said to have killed the woman he loved in a fit of jealousy (as a result of his realization of his impotence) and to have made his drinking cup out of the ashes of her burnt body. This story of Dik al-Jinn provided the theme of one of Abu Risha's poems, 'Dik al-Jinn's Drinking Cup',[145] which he has included in every subsequent volume of verse that he has published.

Al-Ma'arri provides the epigraph as well as the conclusion to the first work in Abu Risha's first volume of verse, a short verse drama entitled 'Flood'. Al-Ma'arri's line signifies that the world is in need of a flood to cleanse it and wash away its sins. The scene is a tavern where we meet the landlord, a waiter, a crowd of drunken men, and a young debauched man who spurns his wife and turns to a prostitute. A poor man comes in begging, but he is promptly turned away, then a couple of merchants enter quarrelling. A mad priest comes in and begins to preach to all the sinners and warns against God's wrath and His impending punishment by means of a Flood. At this moment a storm breaks out accompanied by thunder and torrential rain. When the scared waiter reports a flood they all believe it is the flood prophesied by the priest. This produces a dramatic change in them, for they all repent. But as soon as the storm passes they mock the priest and everybody returns to his sinful way of life. This disillusioned and cynical view of mankind is shown in another short verse drama in the same volume, called 'Torture', in which a painter surprises his wife, the model of his pictures, with his best friend and as a result of his torture and her feelings of guilt she is driven to commit suicide by throwing herself out of the window. Infidelity and treachery are further aspects of a sinful world.[146]

There is relatively little experimentation in stanzaic form in Abu Risha's poetry, and in this respect he tends to be more conservative than many of the romantic poets. However, his vehement passion, his fiery imagination, his profusion of vivid and at times violent imagery (which has particularly struck his critics)[147] and the peculiar quality of his sensibility make his poetry belong undoubtedly to the romantic school. Abu Risha wrote not only dramatic but also narrative verse such as 'Muḥammad' and 'Khālid'. But he is primarily a lyric and subjective poet. Even in his nationalistic and political verse the subjective element is very strongly pronounced. In his poetry one meets with many of the themes of the romantics: descriptions of the spiritual effect of nature, especially the beauty of the Syrian and Lebanese landscape; descriptions of storms, of bare autumn landscape ('The Starved Meadow'[148]), meditations among the ruins of ancient civilization; human suffering such as that of an innocent child deprived of love and affection ('The Orphan'[149]), the alienation of creative genius driven to cruel and premature death by lack of recognition and the insensitivity of society, which drive the artist to drown his sorrows in drink ('Death of an Artist'[150]). In 'Light', Abu Risha laments the disappearance of mystery from the world as a result of the spread of light. The same idea occurs in 'The Poet of Nature' where beauty is felt to lose its mystery in broad daylight. Likewise, in 'Morphine' the poet asks his woman companion to leave him 'before dawn can dissipate the remaining mystery of the dark', which implies that the poet prefers not to know the truth.[151]

Woman and politics are the main subjects of Abu Risha's poetry. As has been suggested, his attitude to woman is ambivalent: it is one of physical attraction and moral revulsion, of approval and condemnation. In 'Tranquillity' the poet describes a raging snow storm outside his room at night after his passion has been spent, the naked and seductive mistress unable to arouse in him any more sexual feelings. Despite his indulgence, or perhaps because of it, he is a profoundly melancholic man, woman being the source of both his joy and his sorrow. In 'A Woman' he urges his mistress to forget their passionate past, try to rise above the desires of the flesh, 'to set free their souls to reach what lies beyond the world of illusion, to meet like two angels whose longing for one another does not go beyond the meeting of their lips'.[152] In 'Ennui', a poem with a Baudelairean title about man's eternal restlessness, the poet illustrates his theme by resorting to the two contrasting aspects of woman (common in much romantic poetry), woman the enticer, the temptress, the object of physical passion, and woman the angel, the heavenly bride – although it must be admitted that the conflict between the two does not possess the same degree of intensity or even reality as in that between the soul and the body which we have seen in the case of Abu Shabaka.[153] At times he attacks woman mercilessly, as in 'Storm' in which the disturbed and unhappy poet condemns a prostitute at the very moment he is asking her to make love, or in the much later work 'Delilah', the title of which is sufficiently indicative of the poet's feelings. Likewise in 'The Wretched Woman' a prostitute avenges herself on her clients by passing on to them venereal diseases.[154] But Abu Risha is also capable of writing poems of great tenderness about women. For instance, 'Lamp and Bed', which appears in a later volume in a revised form under the title of 'Deprivation', describes how the force of the poet's love for his mistress who has deserted him makes him imagine her lying on his bed as he enters his room, so vividly that it is only by touching the bed that he realizes she is not there. In 'An Attempt' the desolate poet in his lonely room resorts to drinking in the hope of forgetting all around him and inducing an image of his mistress who has deserted him.[155] But perhaps the most moving of his love poems is 'The Ghost of the Past',[156] which shows the poet's inability to forget an unfortunate old love, as the ghost of his past love haunts him in the midst of his enjoyment of a subsequent affair. The woman is described in vivid and attractive detail as she lies asleep on the couch in the poet's bedroom at night while he, unable to sleep, finishes his glass of wine in the stillness of the room disturbed only by 'the breath of darkness'. Fearful silence flows in the room and with it flow his thoughts. He watches her as she sleeps, light casting a faint shadow on her cheek, her tired arm resting on her forehead, displacing a lock of her black hair. His eye slides down her neck, resting on the cleavage of her breasts, partially uncovered. Gradually his certainty that his old love has been overcome and forgotten is undermined, as the sad ghost of the past appears as if to chide or to mock him. The poet cannot tell. The scene is set by means of a skilful choice of details and a number of vivid images and the strikingly sensuous description of which Abu Risha is a master (as is clear in poems as diverse as 'Ennui' and 'Joan of Arc'), all of which render the experience sufficiently concrete and individualized, for the peculiar emotional blend of nostalgia and hopeless despair aroused by the highly evocative language to become totally free from the taint of sentimentality.

There are, however, two basic themes which crop up continually in Abu Risha's poetry: time and change, and art and life. Beauty withering away, youth passing, and power and glory giving way to weak and decrepit old age: these are ideas which appear frequently with a cumulative haunting effect in his work. At times, as in his poem 'Persistence', they reduce the poet to melancholy and quiet grief, but at other times they drive him to violent rage against what seems to be the natural order of things, as we can clearly see in his remarkable poem 'An Eagle'.[157] For the poet is essentially a very proud man, who finds the loss of youth, power and dignity deeply humiliating. (In fact critics have likened him to Mutanabbi, with whom he clearly identifies himself, as is seen in his poem on the great classical poet.) The underlying theme of the poem on Dik al-Jinn's wine cup, already alluded to, is the poet's inability to accept old age and impotence, which drives him to murder his mistress. In 'Stagnation'[158] he expresses his love for energy, movement and life, stating his theme in terms teeming with sexual implications: the poem ends with

> Life is but storms, and those that rage
> In my blood and bones are the ones I love most.

Related to this theme of time and change is the poet's preoccupation with the world of art, since art represents man's heroic attempt to overcome the ravages of time. Like Abu Shadi before him, Abu Risha wrote much about artefacts, although in his case it is sculpture and architecture rather than painting which provide subjects for his poems. But unlike Abu Shadi, he often wrote about these subjects in strongly passionate terms. Yet, paradoxically enough, in the Keatsian contrast he draws between the transitory and ever-changing nature of life and the permanence of art he seems to favour the latter. In his well-known poem 'A Woman and a Statue'[159] he wishes his beautiful woman could have turned into a statue so that her beauty might have frozen and withstood the onslaught of time and the damaging effect of old age. But it must be emphasized that there is nothing cold about his description of the world of art; in fact his response to the statue of Venus in this poem is so passionate and his description of it is so warm and throbbing with life that it is somehow difficult to believe that the poet is thinking only of a statue. One suspects that what the poet desires is not so much the permanence of art as the permanence of life. Like other romantics, he wants to eat his cake and have it.

Women and love are by no means the sole subjects of Abu Risha's poetry, although it is remarkable that in his first published volume there are no more than four poems on nationalist themes, the rest concerning the poet's subjective experiences. But the development of his poetry shows a rapidly growing interest in politics and Arab nationalism, which must be related to some extent to the political development in the area before and after the Second World War, culminating in the creation of Israel at the expense of Arab Palestine. Abu Risha's interest in Arab nationalism, however, goes back to the early years of his career as a poet. The verse play *Dhi Qar*, which he wrote when he was barely twenty years old, deals with the wars between Arabs and Persians.[160] His early poetry shows the poet's propensity for heroic themes, as in, for instance, 'Joan of Arc'. 'Martyr' is an elegy on an Arab youth martyred for the cause of Arab nationalism, and 'Glimpse' reveals the poet's anger at the eclipse of Arab glory and the decadence of present-day Arabs.[161] In the succeeding volumes, however, Abu Risha's political themes become much more pronounced. 'Muhammad', which is designed to be a prologue to his epic on the Prophet sketching out the birth. rise and struggle of Muhammad, ends with the hope that the glory of the Arabs may be revived:

> Life may bloom again after it has faded
> And time may go our own way.

In the other narrative poem on early Islamic history, 'Khālid' which deals with the career of the great Muslim general, Abu Risha writes bitterly:

> My people woke up in might and glory
> But their evening is submerged in shame,
> Their tattered throne made of invader's spears,
> Their banners of shrouds.[162]

He celebrated the French evacuation of Syria and wrote many poems inspired by the Palestine tragedy, including one, 'Talk in a Trench', describing the heroic death of a soldier who dies in the battle. In 'After the Disaster' he draws an angry contrast between the noble behaviour of the Abbasid Caliph, al-Mu'tasin, in sacking Amorium in response to the cry of help uttered by an Arab woman (celebrated in Abu Tammam's famous poem) and the shameful and treacherous actions of some modern Arab leaders in the first Arab-Israeli war:

> How can the wolf be blamed for his aggression
> When the shepherd proved to be the sheep's foe?[163]

In the course of time in response to Arab military defeat, Abu Risha's attitude became one of sorely wounded pride, utter despair and merciless self-condemnation, as we see in a poem entitled 'Those' written in 1970:

> You ask what is it that keeps alive those wretches,
> Weary as they are, their road deserted and their target is nought.
> Before the coffin of their pride they stand, speechless and distraught.

Suffering their wounds patiently, their heads bowed down in shame,
Time has made them forget life's laughter and tears,
Has ridiculed their world, leaving them no hope . . .
Please do not ask me, lady. Can't you see that I am myself one of them?[164]

Because of his essentially passionate apprehension of reality Abu Risha manages, at his best, to write political and nationalist poems of a high degree of complexity, in which many disparate experiences are unified and fused together in the heat of his passion. For instance, in his poem 'The New Year' (1959)[165] the poet draws an ironic contrast between the messages of a Happy New Year on the cards displayed in his room and his mood of depression on New Year's Eve, when he finds himself at midnight sitting alone in his room, drowning his sorrows in drink, and looking back in grief and bitterness on the past ten years of his life. But the poem is not only about the destructive effect of time on the poet's personal life: it is not simply a poem of individual or private sorrow. The tragedy of his country and of the whole Arab world is present, forming an integral part of the poet's mood. So while it remains an intensely personal experience, the poem is also a national or political utterance.

An even clearer instance of this complexity can be seen in his poem on the 'Eagle'. Here the poem ostensibly describes in vivid and moving terms the last moments in the life of an aged eagle, an image which for a long time had been haunting the poet's imagination, judging by its occurrence in at least three of his earlier poems, but which is given its most satisfactory expression in this poem.[166] Hungry and weak, the eagle is too powerless to fly to the summits as was its wont, but enraged at being pushed about by inferior birds that dwell in the lowlands it summons just enough strength and courage to make one final leap to the top of the mountain, thus putting an honourable and dignified end to its life. But in the final line of the poem, the poet makes an identification between himself and the bird, thereby making the poem appear to be as much about the poet himself as about the bird. And on closer reading one discovers that the poem has a further dimension: it is also about the poet's own country, whose symbol is the eagle. Thus the three levels on which the poem operates are tightly and organically interrelated; there is nothing forced or contrived here. We have at one and the same time a poem about nature, a poem about the poet's personal experience and a political poem. Needless to say this mode of political expression is beyond the reach of neoclassical poetry.

5

The emigrant poets

The *Mahjar* poets, i.e. the Arab poets who emigrated to America, form such a distinct school of writing that they deserve separate treatment. Moreover, they exercised a profound influence upon their contemporaries in the Arab lands, an influence which can be clearly seen not only in the works of minor poets. Both historically and culturally the *Mahjar* poets are an extension of Lebanese and Syrian poetry. Although they fell under the influence of western Romantic poetry, directly or otherwise (and some of them did that even before they emigrated to America), their early social, economic, political and cultural background in their homeland helped, to some extent, to shape their later output – although it is difficult to go as far as some recent scholars who tend to attribute the romanticism of these poets almost exclusively to their native background.[1]

Like the distinguished authors who emigrated to Egypt, where they settled and took an active part in its intellectual and literary life, the Lebanese and Syrian poets who turned to North and South America left their homeland mainly for political or economic reasons or for both. The autocratic rule of Sultan Abdul Hamid made life generally difficult for these educated and freedom-loving Arabs who had enjoyed a modern education in European and Russian establishments. At the same time because of the increasing role of Europeans in the commercial life of the Lebanon after the 1860s there were fewer possibilities for the Lebanese at home than abroad and especially in the virgin lands of the New World.[2] The movement of immigration into America began in the last decade of the nineteenth century and gathered momentum in the course of time, so that we find no less than 9210 people emigrating to North America alone in the year 1913.[3]

One or two general introductory remarks about these emigrants, most of whom were enterprising individualists, are in order. In the first place they were Christians and the educated amongst them were brought up in missionary schools, and were imbued with modernist and anti-traditional ideas. In America they found greater freedom for literary experimentation: there they did not meet with the moderating influence of traditional Arab culture to which their compatriots were subjected in Egypt. In America they, or rather their intellectual leaders, fell under the influence of the latter-day romanticism and transcendentalism of American literature which characterize the work of Emerson and Thoreau, Longfellow and Whitman. Secondly, unlike those who settled in Egypt, the immigrants to North and South America suffered from a feeling of exile, of lack of belonging. Living in countries where the language of their literary efforts and of their tradition was not spoken, they felt that their very cultural existence was at stake. Hence their association into societies, their setting-up of literary reviews to guard jealously their cultural interest and to provide them with an organ to express their views. Hence, too, their striking feeling of homesickness, no doubt intensified by their awareness of being outsiders. This feeling is common to all the emigrant poets without exception, and often underlies their yearning to return to nature and to simple rural life. And related to that feeling is an idealization of their homeland, and an opposition between the spirituality of the East and the materialism of the West, an idea repeated *ad nauseam* in the work of all these poets. Some of the romantic features which we find in the work of these poets, like the sense of isolation and the heightened feeling of individualism, are therefore not entirely consciously developed intellectual or psychological attitudes, nor are they merely the result of imitating certain postures in western Romantic poetry. They are, in fact, based upon the real facts of their concrete situation in an alien community or culture. In the United States, Jibran, their intellectual leader, in the words of one scholar 'neither participated in the real life of the people nor acquired an imaginative sympathy with their outlook, but became a rootless outsider'.[4]

The need for local Arabic papers and reviews to give them the chance to publish their work and consolidate their position was felt very early by the immigrants. Arabic journalism in America started as far back as the last decade of the nineteenth century, with the appearance of *Kaukab Amrīka* in 1892. This was soon followed by *al-Huda* in 1898, and in 1899 by *Mir'āt al-Gharb* in which Jibran and Abu Māḍī, among others, published their work. In 1913 the poet Nasīb 'Arīḍa together with Naẓmī Nasīm set up *al-Funūn* review which played a significant role in the *Mahjar* movement, and when *al-Funun* ceased publication part of its function was taken over by *al-Sā'iḥ* (founded in New York in 1912 by 'Abdul Maṣīḥ Ḥaddād). Other reviews followed, one of the most interesting of which is *al-Samīr* founded by Iliya Abu Madi in 1929. Similarly Arabic journalism flourished in Latin America, with, for instance, the illustrated literary review *al-Andalus al-Jadīda* in Rio de Janeiro edited by Shukrallah al-Jurr, and *al-Sharq* founded in San Paolo.[5]

Although in the Arab world the *Mahjar* poets are sometimes referred to as one school of writing, there is, however, a noticeable difference between the poets of the North and those of the South. On the whole the ones who settled in Latin America are less extremist, and certainly less unanimous in their reaction against traditional Arab culture; both in their theory and in their practice, they show more concern for the preservation of traditional cultural values: For instance, while a poet like Fauzi al-Ma'luf advocated a rejection of what he regarded as the outmoded Arabic poetic tradition, we find another like Ilyās Farḥāt confirming his relationship to it. The difference can be seen even in the names they chose for their literary societies. In Brazil, for instance, they called themselves *al-'Usba al-Andalusiyya* (the Andalusian League), a name clearly harking back to the Arab past and designed to establish a link with tradition, while in North America the colourless name *al-Rābiṭa al-Qalamiyya* (the Pen Association) was used. One reason for this is, of course, the dominant influence of the revolutionary Jibran upon the North American immigrants.

In the United States

It is not my intention to assess here the whole literary achievement of Jibrān Khalīl Jibrān (1883–1931), but merely to discuss very briefly the significance of his contribution as a poet. Jibran is one of the distinguished products of the Ḥikma school in Beirut. In 1895 he left for America via Egypt and France. After spending three years in Boston, he returned to Beirut at the age of fifteen to study Arabic and French. In 1903 he returned to Boston where he remained for five years, after which he spent three years in Paris, studying painting. In Paris he is claimed to have known the sculptor Rodin, and was introduced to the work of William Blake, whose poetry and painting, together with the work of Nietzsche, were destined to have a profound effect upon him. When he had finished his art training Jibran returned to America where he lived (in New York) till his death in 1931. In America he was the most influential figure among the immigrant literary community. His rebellion against outworn social customs and religious tyranny, no less than his total rejection of outmoded literary modes and values, made him an inspiration for the younger generation of writers. He was the driving force behind the formation in 1920 of *al-Rabita al-Qalamiyya*, who elected him President. The association included the distinguished poets Nasib 'Arida, Mikha'il Nu'aima and Rashīd Ayyūb.

The aim of the association was clear: it was to unite their efforts to infuse a new life in modern Arabic literature by turning away from the traditional excessive preoccupation with mere verbal skill, and by seeking to write a literature that suited the requirements of modern times, a literature distinguished primarily by keen sensibility and subtle thought. 'True poetry', Jibran writes, in terms which border on the sentimental, 'is the incarnation of a divine spirit born of a smile that revives the heart or a sigh that brings tears to the eyes', and 'the poet is an angel sent down by the gods to teach men divine things'.[6] Most of the products of the members of the association appeared in the periodical *al-Sa'ih*, which rendered a great service to the cause of *Mahjar* poetry after the disappearance of Nasib 'Arida's review *al-Funun*. Not long after the establishment of the association Nu'aima published his well-known book of criticism *al-Ghirbāl* ('The Sieve'), which appeared in 1923, with an introduction by the Egyptian al-'Aqqad, who as we have seen was the joint author of the equally iconoclastic work of criticism *al-Diwan* (1921). Nu'aima's book is in many ways a manifesto of the *Mahjar* movement in North America. The two-fold aim of the Pen Association, namely the repudiation of traditional excessive verbiage and conventionalism, and the attempt to rise above provincialism by making literature primarily the expression of universal human thought and feeling, are given a clear and vehement expression in *The Sieve*. An interesting short chapter in the book is a piece entitled 'Let us Translate';[7] in which the author strongly advises Arab authors to concentrate upon translating the literary masterpieces of the human spirit as a necessary step in order to bring Arabic literature back into the main current of world literature. From Nu'aima's lengthy study of Jibran,[8] first published in 1934, it is clear how important and extensive Jibran's influence was on the rest of North American *Mahjar* poets. Jibran's output is enormous. Besides painting, he wrote essays, short stories, books of meditations, poems both in traditional forms and in *vers libre*, as well as much poetic prose with strongly marked biblical echoes. He wrote both in Arabic and in English: he is, in fact, one of the few Arabs who managed to produce best sellers in English. Most readers of English, especially in America, must have come across copies of his book *The Prophet*, a work of fairly popular mysticism: by 1958 it had sold a million copies.[9]

As an *Arabic* poet it must be admitted that, interesting as he is, Jibran does not occupy a very high rank, and that is partly because of his exceedingly small output, partly because of what some regard as excessive sentimentality, but chiefly in the opinion of most Arab critics because of his rather weak Arabic style. Nevertheless, because of his great influence on *Mahjar* poetry, it is necessary to pause for a while and examine his poetry. His fame as a poet rests chiefly on his long poem *The Processions,*[10] which was first published in New York in 1918. It consists of over 200 lines arranged in a rather irregular stanzaic form, the regular stanza consisting of a quatrain of one metre (*al-Basīṭ*) followed by another quatrain and a couplet of another metre (*Majzū' al-Ramal*). The first quatrains in all the stanzas have the same rhyme throughout, while the rhyme in the second quatrain as well as in the couplet varies from one stanza to another. The rhyme scheme therefore is: *aaaa bbbb cc/ aaaa dddd ee*. But the poet does not follow this scheme rigidly throughout, and the conclusion of the work is not a stanza at all, but simply three rhyming lines, although here it is clear that the author designed it to be different in order to set it off from the rest of the poem. Thematically there is such a pronounced parallelism in all the stanzas that after a while the reader cannot help feeling a certain monotony.

Although structurally the poem is interesting, in that it rejects the monorhyme *qasida* form, a feature which is to be found in the work of most of the *Mahjar* poets, it is mainly in its ideas and themes that *The Processions* occupies such a crucial position in the poetry of *Mahjar*. In it, in fact, we find most of the themes with which the *Mahjar* poets dealt, some of them more successfully than Jibran. *The Processions* is a philosophical poem treating metaphysical and moral questions, like the problem of good and evil, the relation between the soul and the body, the problem of happiness, of social and political institutions, of what man has made of man. In introducing philosophical meditations on ultimate human questions in his poetry, Jibran was doing in North America what in Egypt, at about the same time, 'Aqqad, Mazini and Shukri were insisting that a poet should do, namely think deeply and develop a philosophy of life, instead of writing a primarily social type of poetry designed to flatter a patron and please a literary coterie. This tendency, which aimed at enriching the content of the Arabic poem by metaphysical or philosophical speculation, is common to the major figures in the *Mahjar* literary world. And one manifestation of it is the great interest which they showed in those Abbasid poets who were noted for their predilection for philosophic meditations, more specifically al-Ma'arri, whose poetry was translated into English by the well-known *Mahjar* writer: Amin Rihani (1876–1940) in 1903. 'Umar al-Khayyam's poems became popular reading, and no less popular was Avicenna's *Ode on the Soul*. A very good example of this philosophizing tendency is Iliya Abu Madi's long poem

'Riddles',[11] which although by no means one of the greatest achievements of this poet, is certainly one of his most celebrated poems.

But what is the philosophy of Jibran's poem *The Processions*? In a word it is the need to return to nature, or, as he puts it, *al-ghāb* (woods). The poem is called 'the processions' because it presents in stanza after stanza mankind engaged in different types of human endeavour in the pursuit of happiness, but straying far from the right path, which, in the poet's view, is the path to nature (or the woods). It is ultimately a romantic, primitivistic philosophy, with an admixture of Blake's mystical respect for life and Nietzsche's glorification of it. The poem opens with a description of corrupt human society, in which injustice reigns and people are divided into master and slave, leader and led, and this is followed by an account of nature where all creatures are equal and the division into master and slave totally absent. The same juxtaposition between the tragic shortcomings of human society and the perfect state of nature is found in every stanza. Needless to say, nature here is not red in tooth and claw, but is highly idealized; in it there is no clash or opposition between good and evil, love and hatred, soul and body, light and dark, joy and sorrow, religion and heresy; there is not even the opposition between death and immortality. There is only life and the celebration of life in song. Here obviously one sees the quintessence of a romantic attitude to existence, the yearning for unity where all antinomies are lost, and all conflicts resolved, the rejection of the complexities of civilized life in favour of a primitive simplicity, the harking back to a pristine and prelapsarian state of innocence, to a mythical golden age, the revolt against all human institutions, motivated largely by a hypersensitivity to human suffering. No doubt, to some extent, the poet's rejection of the complications and artificialities of civilized life and his longing for the woods or nature, is a reflection of the immigrant Arab, bewildered by the mechanized life in New York, secretly yearning to be back in the much simpler life of the Lebanon, the rhythm of which was still close to nature. But only to some extent. For while not ceasing to stand for the rural life of the Lebanon as well, the woods are a much larger symbol of nature, in which a more embracing romantic attitude is crystallized, although it is fair to point out that in the surprising conclusion to the poem the author is sadly aware of the impossibility of a complete return to the woods. Jibran's poem would have been more effective had he used a less discursive and more concrete style, had he resorted to fewer bare statements and more oblique comments and more imagery. Moreover, in the discursive parts the poet's mastery of the Arabic language is not great enough to enable him to write the sort of crisp and pithy style which bare statements need in order that they may be converted into poetry. Taha Husain's judgment on the *Mahjar* school is perhaps truer of Jibran than of many others: he describes the *Mahjar* poets as 'people endowed with a fertile nature, strong talents, wide-ranging imagination, naturally qualified to be good poets, but they have not perfected the means of poetry: they are either ignorant of the language or they have ignored it and proceeded to adopt their ignorance as a method or system'.[12]

Typical of the Pen Association movement is the work of Jibran's life-long friend, Mīkhā'īl Nu'aima, undoubtedly the movement's great critic and apologist, just as Jibran was its sage and philosopher. Nu'aima had an interesting and varied education. Born in Biskinta in the Lebanon, in 1889 he received his primary education in a Russian school, then moved to the Russian Teachers' Training College in Nazareth. After completing his four-year course there he was sent to Russia in 1906 to pursue his further education at the theological seminary in Poltava. In 1911 he returned to the Lebanon, having acquired a wide knowledge of Russian literature and language: he even wrote some of his poems like 'The Frozen River' first in Russian, but in the following year (1912) he emigrated to America. He studied law in Washington and graduated in 1916. During his studies he contributed literary articles to *al-Funun* and *al-Sa'ih*. His first venture in literary criticism was a review of Jibran's book *The Broken Wings* which, in spite of its critical impartiality, expressed enough of the author's revolutionary spirit to make Jibran seek to develop his acquaintance. In 1918 he joined the American army and was sent to the French front, where he had first-hand experience of the horrors of the First World War. After the war he was awarded a government scholarship which enabled him to study French history and art and literature at the University of Rennes.

Nu'aima wrote very little poetry. His poems, most of which were composed early in his career, between 1917 and 1928, were collected and published in one volume, *Eyelid Whisperings*,[13] in 1943. His prose output, however, was large. As a prose writer he is known in the Arab world chiefly by his book of criticism, *The Sieve*, which, together with the *Diwan* by 'Aqqad and Mazini, is regarded as the most important attack on orthodoxy at the time. But Nu'aima's prose works are not confined to literary criticism; they range from drama to the novel, from essays and meditations to biography. *The Sieve* contains much violent criticism of the shortcomings of the classical Arabic poetic tradition, some of which reveals an extremist attitude. In this short account there is not the space for a discussion of the whole book; however, there is one passage which we might quote because of the light it throws on the aims and assumptions not only of Nu'aima, but also of the whole *al-Rabita* movement. It is a definition of the poet:

> Now we may ask ourselves, what is a Poet? A Poet is a prophet, a philosopher, a painter, a musician and a priest in one. He is a prophet because he can see with his spiritual eye what cannot be seen by all other mortals. A painter because he is capable of moulding what he can see and hear in beautiful forms of verbal imagery. A musician because he can hear harmony where people can find only discordant noise.... To him the whole of life is but a melody, sad and gay, which he hears according to which way he turns. That is why he gives expression to it in ringing and metrical phrases.... Metre is necessary in poetry, rhyme is not, especially if it is, as is the case in Arabic poetry, a single rhyme that has to be observed throughout the whole poem. There are now many poets among us who plead the cause of free verse, but whether or not we agree with Walt Whitman or his followers, we cannot but admit that the Arabic type of rhyme, which is still dominant, is nothing but an iron chain by which we tie down the minds of our poets, and its breaking is long overdue.
>
> Lastly, the poet is a priest because he has his God whom he serves, namely the God of Truth and Beauty. This God appears to him in different conditions and guises.... He sees Him alike in the faded flower and the fresh flower, in the blushing cheeks of a maiden and in the pale face of a dead man, in the blue sky and in the clouded sky, in the noise of the day and the quiet of night.[14]

In his poetry Nu'aima remained faithful to the principles of *al-Rabita*. He never wrote poems on social or political occasions. The work of his nearest to public poetry is perhaps *Akhī*, 'Friend',[15] which, in a sense, is a war poem, even a patriotic poem, inspired by the author's experience of the horror and destruction of the First World War and the humiliating and pointless involvement of the Middle East in it. But even this remarkable poem, surely one of the finest achievements of modern Arabic poetry, is far more universal in its appeal than poems on political occasions can be: it is ultimately a *cri de coeur*, rather than a political speech, a comment made by a highly sensitive individual, with a great capacity for compassion, on a situation which was humanly degrading. Unlike patriotic poems, this one is deliberately low pitched: he opens it by addressing his friend, telling him neither to exult with the western victors, nor to rejoice over the misfortune of the defeated, but to kneel in silence with a bleeding heart and weep over their dead who achieved no glory but were the hapless victims of a cause not their own. He proceeds to describe the misery and ravages of war which he finds on his return to his homeland – the hunger, the loss of shelter, the death of friends. He calls upon his comrade to follow him silently with his pick axe and shovel to dig a pit for the dead. In the last stanza he tells his friend to dig another pit to bury the living as well, for they too are really dead and their stench fills the air; asleep or awake they wear ignominy and shame. The anger which is expressed by the thought of burying the living as well, and which comes out only in the last line, in fact the very last word in the poem, is much more moving than in any full-length declamatory ode.

The absence of declamation and rhetoric, the bringing of the tone of poetry to that of half-uttered thoughts, with the resulting feeling of intimacy which this creates between the poet and his reader is a feature of much of the *Mahjar* poetry, and more specifically of Nu'aima's work. It is this feature which has led the late Egyptian critic Muhammad Mandur to describe this kind of poetry as poetry *à mi-voix* (*al-shi'r al-mahmūs*,[16] i.e. the poetry of whisper or of the quiet voice, a phrase that has gained currency in Arabic literary criticism, and which is used to distinguish it from the rhetoric and declamation of neoclassical Arabic poetry).

Nu'aima turned his back on the traditional subjects of classical poetry: there is no panegyric, no eulogy or self-praise in his poetry. Instead we find poems expressing the poet's innermost thoughts and feelings, and more specifically those related to his spiritual life. In this respect Nu'aima's verse is purely subjective. Significantly enough it was his reading of the work of the Russian Romantic poet Lermontov (who was heavily influenced by western Romanticism and especially by Byron) which aroused in him an overwhelming desire to compose poetry.[17] Yet in Nu'aima's poetry there is little turbulence or vehemence of passion, which is not the same thing as saying that it is devoid of feeling. On the contrary, there is a strange and almost other-worldly serenity in his best poems, unmatched elsewhere. Even when he writes about the conflict between good and evil (as, for instance, in his poems 'Good and Evil' or 'The Conflict',[18] which he wrote when he was involved in a passionate love affair with a married American woman)[19] the tone of the writing is muted and low: there is no feeling of conflict, but an account of conflict given by someone who has made up his mind about the universe and whose vision of life remains undisturbed. When he writes about 'Autumn Leaves' we do not find the 'wildness' of the 'West Wind'. It is not an accident that one of his best-known nature poems is about a frozen river. The vehemence and aggressiveness of the critic, the author of *The Sieve*, are totally absent from his poetry. Instead there are quiet meditations on the passing or the coming year ('From Time's Book'), the gentle nostalgia of the poet for his childhood and for his native village ('The Echo of Bells'), and a simple, but poignant devotional feeling that runs through most of his poems (as in, for instance, 'Prayers' and 'The Lost Traveller'). Indeed, like the rest of the *Mahjar* romantics, Nu'aima raises the heart above the head, imagination above reason: he is alarmed when he finds that his heart is not capable of feeling (as for instance in 'The Frozen River') and rejoices when it is awake once more ('The Heart Was Awakened'),[20] but compared with other romantics like Abu Shabaka, Shabbi or Abu Madi, Nu'aima's feelings, though deep, never reach the point of overflowing.

Part of the serenity which characterizes Nu'aima's poetry may be due to the wonderful simplicity of his language, his choice of homely, almost colloquial words which has been attributed to the possible influences of Lebanese folk-songs,[21] to his use of the rhythm of prose, to his preference for short metres and stanzaic verse, to the muted tone of his writing. But much of it is no doubt due to his calm spiritual life. His attitude to outside objects is marked by his withdrawal into an inner world of the spirit, against which things of this world are implicitly measured ('If Thorns But Knew'). Real life for him is life of the spirit: for wisdom we must not look anywhere outside ourselves ('The Road'). In his poetry there is more of divine love, coloured by Plotinus' view of emanation, than of human love, 'the fury and the mire of human veins'. Nu'aima's steadfastness of spirit, his unshakable religious faith are given a powerful expression in a poem with the significant title 'Certainty',[22] in which he claims that he is proof against all manner of misfortune since 'Fate is his ally and destiny his mate'. In the opening poem in the volume from which the collection derives its title, 'Close Your Eyelids and You Shall See', Nu'aima advises the reader to look inwards in times of trouble. If ever he finds the sky covered in clouds or the earth in snow, or if he discovers that he is afflicted with an incurable disease, or is fearful that death is approaching, he should close his eyelids, for then he will be able to detect stars beyond the clouds, meadows beneath the snow, disease itself will turn into cure and death becomes life. In this poem one scholar quite rightly finds the keynote to the whole of Nu'aima's poetry, for

> holding to the vision within him, Nu'aima feels he has arrived at the secret of life . . . . Everything in the world of appearance begins to fall into place . . . . In 'The Autumn Leaves' the poet tells the falling leaves . . . to go gently and lovingly down, without remorse or bitterness.[23]

There is nothing of this spiritual certainty or consistent philosophical outlook in the poetry of Iliyā Abū Māḍī, perhaps the greatest poet of the Pen Association. Unlike Nu'aima, Abu Madi (1889–1957) did not have the advantage of a regular or systematic education. Born in the Lebanon about 1889, Abu Madi moved to Egypt in 1900, later working as a tobacconist in Alexandria until 1911, the year of the publication of his first volume of verse. He then emigrated to the United States, engaged in business for some time, but later devoted himself to poetry and journalism. In 1916 he joined the literary circle which was later to form the Pen Association in New York, although he was not himself one of its founding members. His second volume of verse appeared in New York in 1919 under the title *Diwan Iliya Abu Madi*, with a preface by Jibran. In 1925 he published his third volume, called *The Brooks*, which contains most of his best poems, and the preface to which was written by Nu'aima. In 1929 he set up a fortnightly literary review in New York, *al-Samir*, which soon became one of the most successful of such periodicals in America.[24] He was able to turn it into a daily in 1936 and continued to edit it until his death in 1957. Abu Madi published his last volume of verse, *The Thickets*, in 1940, although a subsequent volume was posthumously published under the title *Gold and Dust*.[25]

Although largely a self-taught man, Abu-Madi, unlike many of the members of the Pen Association, had a strong grounding in the Arabic language and literary tradition. This, in part, is due to his having spent his formative years in Egypt, where the forces of conservatism at the time, much stronger than in the Lebanon, curbed the extremism of authors and made for a generally more moderate attitude. As it has recently been put by a distinguished Lebanese critic, it was the Egyptian intellectual climate that was 'chiefly responsible for Abu Madi's general attitudes, his moral and intellectual tendencies'.[26] The result is that even in his later productions we find him, not infrequently, using the more traditional single-rhyme *qasida* form. Moreover, he managed to retain his own independent personality when he came into contact with the Pen Association group; unlike others he was not completely dominated by the powerful figure of Jibran, nor did he share his extremist views. This, of course, does not mean that he was not deeply influenced by them. In Abu Madi's early writings the traditional element is, as is to be expected, strongly pronounced. Poems of a public nature, comments on political or contemporary events tend to recur, and although they never quite disappear from his work it is the subjective kind of poetry that dominates his later writings. The early declamation is replaced by a much quieter tone and a meditative, almost philosophical attitude. Besides, the optimistic note which marks his early work (as, for instance, in his poem 'Life's Philosophy')[27] gradually grows less audible, giving place at times to doubt and uncertainty, and even despair, as we find in the well-known poems 'The Phoenix' which is clearly a symbol of human happiness, and 'Riddles',[28] both of which come from his volume *The Brooks*. But here, too, we notice that the poet's optimism does not desert him altogether, for in the later volume *The Thickets* we find a poem brimful of hope, like 'Smile',[29] where the poet is capable of enjoying fully the pleasures afforded by life.

In fact, Abu Madi's poetry is essentially poetry of moods. In it we cannot discern a clear and unbroken progression, or a development in a straight line, in the poet's attitude to life. Instead, what strikes us is his eternal restlessness. There is indeed a clearly marked development in his style, for Abu Madi's individual voice begins to make itself heard unmistakably in his volume *The Brooks*, where he announces his new conception of poetry. Addressing the reader, he says: 'You are not of my party if you regard poetry to be nothing more than words and metre. Our paths will never cross and there is nothing more between us'.[30] But once Abu Madi has attained mastery of his medium he does not adopt a consistent attitude to reality. For instance, at one point he regards the heart as the only reliable guide, at another he clearly admits its insufficiency. In one poem he runs away from the city and civilized life to seek his refuge and solace in nature.[31] In another (as in his poem 'In the Wilderness') he falls a prey to boredom and then nature is no longer capable of healing the poet's soul: its silence then is mere emptiness. But that is not because the poet prefers the noise and bustle of the city, but because the poet's feeling of *ennui* is so deeply rooted in his soul that he carries it with him wherever he goes: in such rare moments as this he cannot find his escape in nature, and even nature appears to him as hopelessly inadequate.

Abu Madi, then, is a romantic poet throughout. The titles of his volumes indicate the extent of his interest in nature. To him nature is often a source of moral teaching in a Wordsworthian fashion. He laments the encroachment of the city upon the country as for instance in his poem 'The Lost Wood', where he expresses his grief on finding that the natural scene which used to give him so much joy has disappeared and been replaced by a town and human habitation. Of course, his view of nature is highly idealized, and is synonymous with 'beauty', the positive value for which alone the poet is exhorted to live (in a poem called 'Live for Beauty'). As in most *Mahjar* poetry the poet's yearning for nature is a reflection of his homesickness, a nostalgia for the Lebanon which in Abu Madi's poetry reaches its highest degree of idealization, as, for instance, in his poem 'The Poet in Heaven'. Among his favourite themes is the celebration of human love against the background of harmonious nature, as in 'Come' which is strongly reminiscent of Shelley's short poem *Love's Philosophy* (a poem that proved to be popular with Arab romantics), or the ennobling influence of human love and its greater efficacy than institutionalized religion and fear of hell as a means of knowing God ('The Night of Longings'). Abu Madi's poetry is also riddled with 'obstinate questionings' of the human condition: he writes about meaningless and unnecessary suffering ('The Dumb Tear'), the vanity of worldly glory ('Clay'), metaphysical doubts ('Riddles'), man's eternal restlessness ('In the Wilderness'). Although not a mystic, Abu Madi has expressed his vague mystical longing for the ideal in a memorable poem called 'The Hospitable Fire'.[32]

In his introduction to the second volume of Abu Madi's *Diwan* Jibran comments on the poet's great power of the imagination. It is this imaginative power which makes Abu Madi the great poet he is, enabling him to express his attitudes, feelings and ideas in terms of images and concrete situations. When it deserts him, as it seems to do in his well-known poem 'Riddles', the result is often merely abstract thoughts, bare statements, cold and mechanical. But in his best poems Abu Madi's imaginative power is striking indeed, and this may account for his skilful use of the narrative and dramatic elements in his poetry. It may explain why his meditations on the mystery of life and death arise naturally from a concrete situation vividly and poignantly portrayed, as, for example, in his poem 'Evening',[33] where the sight of a girl resting her cheek on her hand and looking sad at 'the dying of the light' and the approach of night inspires the poet to write a poem about the human predicament, as moving if not as concise as Hopkins's poem *Spring and Fall*. The poem ends with this exhortation:

> Dead is the light of day, the morning's child; ask not how it has died.
> Thinking about life only increases its sorrows,
> So leave aside your dejection and grief,
> Regain your girlish merriment.
> In the morning your face was like the morning, radiant with joy:
> Cheerful and bright;
> Let it be also so at night.

Unlike Abu Madi, Nasīb 'Arīḍa (1887–1946) shows very little optimism in his poetry. He was born in Hims in 1887, received his primary education in a Russian school and then he moved to the Russian Teachers' Training College, where he met Nu'aima and Abdul Masih Haddad who was also to be a member of the *al-Rabita* in New York. In 1905 he emigrated to the United States and settled in New York where he had difficulty in earning his living by means of commerce. In 1912 he set up the Atlantic Press and in the following year he cooperated with Nazmi Nasim in founding the literary review *al-Funun*. With the disappearance of the review in 1918 he was compelled to give up journalism, but after an unsuccessful venture in business he returned to live by his pen. He lived in great financial straits, fell ill in 1942, after which date he ceased to write poetry, and died in 1946. His poems were collected and published in 1946 in one volume called *Troubled Spirits*,[34] though apparently some of his work remains unpublished.[35]

The title of his *Diwan* is in fact indicative of the nature of its contents. 'Arida's poetry is an expression of the quintessence of romantic sorrow: to him more than to any other *Mahjar* poet Shelley's words are applicable: 'Our sweetest songs are those that tell of saddest thought'. His poems deal with the dark side of life, with loss and uncertainty, with the cruelty of fate, with poverty and misery, parting and pain, loneliness and all kinds of human suffering. The loss of his young brother after the war, on whom he wrote a moving elegy,[36] had a profound and lasting effect upon the poet's whole attitude to life. Besides, his constant failure in business did not help to change his outlook. In his poem 'The Poet' which he addressed to Jibran (in 1914)[37] the stress in his conception of the poet (and of Jibran's role) is not so much on his love of beauty or the sympathy or affinity between nature and the poet as the poet's sensitivity to human suffering and his rebellion against social injustice, hypocrisy and corruption. This is how the poem starts:

> He walks without seeing what lies before him,
> His spirit dwells in the sky above the clouds,
> His ear listening to a secret whispering
> Which is the cause of this smile on his lips.
> As he walks the meadow lovingly reveals to him
> Its roses and its lavender,
> The nightingale perched high on the tree
> Calls out to him to listen to its song.
> Shades beckon to him offering him shelter
> Where silence has pitched its tents.
> But on he goes, unconcerned,
> Saying, 'This is no place for me.'
> His destination is wherever Truth
> Is found weeping, tied, gagged and silenced,
> There he goes to set her free. . .
> Or hastens to wherever misery lurks
> And despair spreads out its gloom
> There no nightingale sings, no shade is found,
> No joy, no comfort, no safety.

The theme that sorrow should have a claim on the poet's attention prior to beauty recurs in 'Arida's work.[38]

'Arida was troubled and nauseated by having to live in a society where money seems to be the only dominant value. His poetry is full of condemnation of the materialism of American society, and all his life he dreamt of returning to his native town in the Lebanon, Hims, which he called the City of Black Stone (*Umm al-Ḥijār al-Sūd*). One of his most successful poems, in which he expresses his condemnation of New York life and his nostalgia for the Lebanon is 'A Fruit Basket' (1920).[39] The poet, unable to sleep at night, goes for a walk in the streets of New York where the crowds, the bright lights, the bustle and indifference of people rushing in pursuit of their pleasures and sophisticated entertainment all make him feel very much of an outsider and intensify his loneliness. His eye falls on a basket full of grapes, figs and pomegranates displayed in a grocer's shop, and the sight of these 'oriental' fruits sends him dreaming of a past of pristine beauty and simplicity in the part of the world of his own origin. By an unconscious association of figs, grapes and pomegranates with the *Song of Solomon*,[40] it seemed to him that he could hear the Song of Songs and see King Solomon, on his knees humbly confessing his love to the poor lowly Shulamite shepherdess, the object of his passion, singing her praises, likening her cheeks to pomegranates and her breasts to clusters of grapes. Homesick, and longing to be with the people he loves in the Lebanon, where fruit is plentiful, the poet awakes from his reverie to find himself standing before the basket of fruit in the shop.

It is clear that here, as elsewhere,[41] the poet obtains his release from the painful present by means of imagination. But in 'Arida's poetry the world of imagination has its own validity. Far from being simply a means of escape from harsh reality it is in fact essentially a superior and richer world. In 'The Nu'āma Wind' (one of the few poems in his collection which express an experience of joy – an exuberant celebration of the coming of spring), for instance, he writes, 'Life is richer and dreams are more splendid and delightful for him who lives by imagination'. At one point he seems to go as far as saying that the only real world is that of the imagination, while the world of external reality, 'what the eye can see', is a mere illusion, 'a mirage in a desert'.[42]

In a poem entitled 'What the Poet says'[43] 'Arida says:

> Let my heart dwell with those who lament
> The conditions of men in the funeral of life.

These very sombre words faithfully reflect the poet's preoccupations. Here are the titles of some of his poems: 'Drink Alone', 'Sleep and Death', 'Leave Me Alone', 'The Stricken Mother', 'I have Reached Rock Bottom', 'The Path of Confusion', 'Do Not Cry, My Soul', 'The End', 'O Stranger'.[44] Some of his recurrent images are the road, the caravan, the mirage, sunset, darkness and tombs. The significance of these images is self-evident: hope is nothing but a mirage and the end is dusty death. His poetry is dominated by a feeling of loneliness and isolation, of lack of communication and understanding, of every man being an island. One of the poems he translated from the Russian, *Silentium* by Tyutchev (who was heavily influenced by German metaphysical Romanticism), deals with the futility of attempts at communication, the feeling of the poet as a romantic outsider; another is a strange lullaby about the connection between sleep and death by the pessimist Sologub.[45] The poet's pathetic feeling of isolation and helplessness is given expression in several poems, especially a poem bearing the significant title: 'I Have Reached Rock Bottom'.[46] It is a cry of despair coming from the depths of his heart, moving in its utter simplicity and direct, unadorned language. This poem displays one of the features of 'Arida's poetry, his fondness for desert imagery, which, however, is not merely an unconscious attempt on the poet's part to relate himself to the classical Arabic poetic tradition, but is often symbolic of the poet's utter sterility and despair.

Despite the highly subjective nature of this poem, the suffering described by the poet is not a private sorrow, for the poet attempts to universalize his experience, by regarding himself as Everyman, and what he offers here is a lament on the human tragedy. This becomes quite clear when we relate this poem to another entitled 'Come Closer to Me' in which the poet uses the same image of the lonely traveller in the desert to describe not only himself but his interlocutor as well. In 'What Are We?'[47] we have the poet's full comment on mankind's disappointed hopes, its eternal restlessness and boredom, its unquenchable thirst, its conflict between body and soul and its longing for death.

Like the rest of the *Mahjar* poets 'Arida deals with metaphysical issues, such as the relation between soul and body, as in his rightly celebrated poem 'To My Soul'. He also finds comfort in the return to nature, although in his case the comfort is very short-lived. But nostalgia and homesickness are not absent from his poetry: his attachment to his homeland is very deep. In fact, one of his most impressive and technically accomplished poems is 'The End',[48] a short poem which he wrote on the misfortunes of his homeland after the war. It is reminiscent of Nu'aima's poem on the same subject, 'Friend', but more violent and without Nu'aima's great compassion. The poet begins with the idea with which Nu'aima's ends: namely that death is the only cure for a people that is too weak to struggle but quietly suffers all manner of humiliation. It opens with a series of imperatives conveying the urgency and vehemence of the poet's feelings, proceeds to argue that such a people, utterly lacking in dignity and sense of shame, deserves to be buried unmourned, and ends with upbraiding the emigrant Lebanese for failing to give it a helping hand, content as they were with making money and boasting of their virtues in the safety of their exile. The poet's rage and vehemence of feeling nearly caused him to break the form of the metre (*al-Kāmil*) into its constituent parts (i.e. *taf'īlāt*) and make the foot and not the combination of feet or the line the basic unit of the poem, a fact which has led some people to assume with some exaggeration that he anticipated the much later metrical developments in Arabic poetry which we begin to see after the Second World War.

Perhaps the most striking example of Jibran's influence on *Mahjar* poetry can be seen in the work of Rashīd Ayyūb (1872–1941). Ayyub is not of the same calibre as Abu Madi, 'Arida or Nu'aima. He wrote some interesting poems of great spontaneity and unquestioned sincerity, such as 'Spring', in which the return of spring does not bring joy to the poet, but only arouses his memories of the spring of his childhood in his native village in the Lebanon, or his portrait of the poet, obviously a self-portrait, under the title 'He Is Gone and We Knew Him Not', a poem moving in spite of, or rather because of, the vague feelings it evokes.[49] But even these poems are thin in their intellectual content, compared with the best work of the other poets. Yet a word about Rashid Ayyub seems necessary in order to illustrate the extent of Jibran's influence on *Mahjar* poetry. Rashid Ayyub was born in the Lebanon in the same village as Nu'aima. In 1889 he left for Paris where he spent nearly three years, after which he returned to his native country, only to leave again for Manchester. From Manchester he emigrated to the United States, where his life was never free from financial worries. He joined the New York circle of expatriates and with them founded *al-Rabita*. He published three volumes of verse, all in New York: *al-Ayyūbiyyāt* in 1916; *Songs of the Dervish* in 1928 and finally *Such is Life*[50] in 1940. He died in the United States in 1941.

The largest part of Rashid Ayyub's first volume was written before he fell under the influence of Jibran. The difference between it and the other two volumes is so great that Nu'aima says in the introduction to Ayyub's work: 'it is as if it had been written by another man'.[51] In *al-Ayyubiyyat* the reader finds many of the features of neoclassicism, such as the use of long and stately metres, of resounding words, stock imagery and hyperbole, of traditional genres like panegyric, elegies and descriptions, the imitation of classical models.[52] His descriptive poem of New York is neoclassical in tone and language. Ayyub writes about social and political occasions, like the meeting of an Arab conference in Paris, the famine in the Lebanon, and the First World War; he also writes about major events like the Titanic disaster.

Yet it would be wrong to claim that the author of *al-Ayyubiyyat* is a thorough-going neoclassicist. Already in this volume one detects signs, or the germ, of his future development. For instance, the poet uses quatrains many times; he writes verse narrative in stanzaic form, reminiscent of Mutran's narrative poems, such as 'The Old Man and the Maid', dealing with the suicide of a young woman after the death of her lover, or 'The Cottage Girl', depicting an innocent but attractive simple peasant girl, lured away from her simple lover and village folk by a rich philanderer. The poet also reveals some interest in nature, writing poems about a brook or a bird and expressing the desire to return to the idyllic life of a shepherd. Towards the end of the volume we find an attempt to versify Jibran's philosophy, and even a prose poem (clearly under the influence of Jibran) entitled 'What am I?' in which the poet is romantically conceived as a solitary and melancholy man who is at peace only in nature.[53]

When we turn to Ayyub's two later volumes, however, we find that the neoclassical elements in his early poetry, enumerated above, have completely disappeared. The declamation and rhetoric have been replaced by a much quieter tone; short metres and multiplicity of rhymes are now dominant. The poet has turned his back on social and political issues, seeking escape in nature and withdrawing himself into an inner world of 'romantic' dreams. He writes about 'Lost Hopes', 'The Meaning of Life', 'The Trembling Leaf', 'Isle of Oblivion', 'Through the Mist' and 'The Distant Light'.[54] He now appears as a dervish, a name by which he was known to his friends of *al-Rabita* circle, although his mysticism, in fact, remains more of a poetic pose than the result of profound spiritual experience. So complete was Jibran's influence upon Ayyub that the only link with the outside world that remained in his poetry was his nostalgia for his homeland, a feature which we have already encountered in the poetry of the whole movement.

In Latin America

The five authors whose work has been briefly discussed above are the chief figures of *Mahjar* poetry, though by no means the only ones, in North America, and their output can be regarded as typical of the entire movement. When we turn to the poetry of *Mahjar* in Latin America we find that it is relatively difficult to generalize, simply because the picture it presents does not have the same degree of consistency. For one thing, the revolt against neoclassicism was not so unanimous. The Latin American poets made as much effort to relate their activity to the Arabic tradition as to break new ground. Moreover, among them there was no dominant personality like Jibran to leave his imprint upon their work. Another factor which may be relevant here is the less developed cultural standard in Latin America compared with the United States, where the Arab poets could not avoid falling under the cultural influence of the West. At the same time the industrial and economic pressure of life in the United States was undoubtedly greater: in New York the immigrant Arab had more reason to feel isolated and to suffer from the effects of a materialistic society. There were, therefore, more grounds for him to adopt an attitude to life which is regarded as 'romantic'.

Compared with the United States poets, the Latin American poets were, therefore, on the whole much more moderate, and their attitude to the achievements of their Northern brethren varied considerably. Both Ilyas Farhat and Rashīd Salīm al-Khūrī (better known as al-Shā'ir al-Qarawī) vehemently attacked their extremism. The latter, in fact, regarded any deviation from the high standards of classical Arabic as a sign of lack of faith in Arabism and the Arabs. On the other hand, Fauzi al-Ma'luf stressed the need for modernity, the need for emancipation from the shackles of the outmoded traditions of the desert Arabs. Ni'ma Qāzān opposed Jibran to the ancient Arab grammarians, regarding him as an example to follow, but the extremism of Qazan is obviously the exception in Latin America (Brazil) and the date of his long poem *Mu'allaqat al-Arz* ('The Cedar Ode'), 1938, shows how much later Jibran's influence began to spread there.

Yet it cannot be said that the work of the chief Latin American poets was merely a continuation of neoclassicism. In spite of individual differences, their work as a whole contains some of the general features of *Mahjar* poetry. In what follows the work of three fairly representative figures will be briefly discussed: Ilyas Farhat, Rashid Salim al-Khuri and Fauzi al-Ma'luf.

Ilyās Farhāt was born in the Lebanon in 1893, in the town Kafr Shima, which produced other distinguished writers such as al-Yaziji and Shummayyil. His parents were poor and he was, therefore, obliged to earn his living while still a child, having had only an elementary education. In 1910 he emigrated to Brazil to join his brothers and improve his fortune. At first he had great difficulties and worked as a travelling salesman in haberdashery. In 1919 he helped edit a review called *al-Jadīd*, on which he continued to work until it ceased publication in 1928. He published his first volume of verse, his *Quatrains*, in 1925, his *Diwan* in 1932, and *The Shepherd's Dreams* in 1953. In 1954 an edition of his complete works appeared in San Paolo.[55]

Farhat is a powerful poet who shares with the pre-romantics their concern for the polish and correctness of their language. The occasional stylistic weaknesses to which most Arab critics objected rather too strongly in *al-Rabita* poetry are completely absent from his work. In fact, his style is at times reminiscent of that of Mutran. Much of his output is cast in the single-rhyme *qasida* form, and he has no particular preference for short metres or stanzaic form. He has written poems on political, social or religious occasions. For instance, 'To God's Prophet' was occasioned by the birthday of the Prophet, while a poem like 'To the Refugees' is obviously a political poem. His poetry is not totally free from traditional features, such as his occasional typical classical Arabic imagery. For instance in an interesting poem called 'A Life Fraught with Difficulties'[56] he gives a vivid account of the difficulties he encountered in order to earn his living, his arduous journeys in the wilds with a horsecart laden with the goods he tried to sell, the deserted hovels he had to sleep in on the way, the dirty water which he had to share with the horses, the dreaded highwaymen he had to arm himself against. But he concludes his poem by writing about himself in the manner of a classical poet writing a *fakhr*, and praises his pride in turning his back upon easy living, as if he were a latter-day al-Shanfara; the poem is strewn with the type of moral precepts and wise saws characteristic in a classical poem, with the result that some Arab critics likened him to al-Mutanabbi.[57]

However, couched in rather traditional verbal forms one often finds in Farhat's poetry certain romantic themes and attitudes which one associates with *Mahjar* poetry, like, for instance, the poet's feeling of isolation, his attack on the materialism of the age in which he lives, in poems such as 'To The Evening Star' or 'The Golden Calf', his nostalgia and homesickness for the Lebanon and his interest in nature. In his autobiographical poem 'Springs of Poetry' the poet replies to those who wonder how he could write poetry if he had not received much schooling, by saying that from childhood he has been looking into the book of nature, birds, trees, the breeze and the running brooks, the stars, and so forth from which he learned his lessons. In 'To The Evening Star' he tries to escape from the materialism of contemporary society to the world of nature. But in his poems about nature, homesickness and nostalgia, Farhat's emotional attitude is much simpler than that of *al-Rabita* poets. In his work one finds a straightforward feeling of homesickness. For example in 'To the Feast' the poet is unhappy at not hearing from his mother at Christmas. In his nostalgia there is no admixture of philosophy or mysticism, as for instance, in his poems 'Homeland' and 'Image of the Homeland'.[58] The Lebanon remains a geographical location; it does not become a symbol or a state of consciousness: it never becomes the embodiment of a consistent attitude to life based upon the desire to return to nature. His volume *The Shepherd's Dreams*, most of which was written between 1933 and 1934, contains strange pastoral poetry in which the poet, posing as a shepherd, has a series of dreams. In these dreams man invariably appears as an evil creature who occupies a place lower than that of animals, and the book ends on a somewhat uncharacteristic note of disillusionment and pessimism.[59]

Farhat's sensibility is, on the whole, remarkably unsophisticated. He is chiefly a love poet, gifted with a sensuous imagination. His most celebrated poem, 'The Lock of Hair', is a love poem, which, though good of its own kind, has a rather narrow range of feeling. But it has the narrative element which is often found in the poetry of *al-Rabita*, an element which one encounters in some of his best poems like 'The Nun' which reveals the poet's rich and sensuous imagination: a beautiful woman who becomes a nun after having been deserted by her lover notices, while picking flowers for the altar, a solitary flower on the convent wall. When she undresses before sleep at night, the memory of the flower arouses doubts in her breast as regards the point of shutting herself up and condemning her beauty to this solitary existence. But perhaps Farhat's powerful imagination and his general poetic gifts are best illustrated in his love poem 'The Eternal Ecstasy',[60] a poem which is woven around an almost metaphysical 'conceit', the idea that the love between the poet and his beloved has existed from the beginning of time and has endured in spite of the multiplicity of forms of life in which both their souls have appeared, and that compared with their love states and kingdoms are short-lived. The idea is obviously far-fetched, but as often in 'metaphysical' poetry it is felt and sustained throughout the whole of the poem, and conveyed through a series of rich images.

Like Farhat, Rashīd Salīm Khūrī opposed the extremism of *al-Rabita*. His belief in the Arab heritage and Arab nationalism is such that it earned him a decoration from President Nasser of Egypt. He was born in the Lebanon in 1887 and, having received his early education in his village school, moved to an American school in Sidon and then to the American University in Beirut. On his graduation he worked as schoolteacher for some time, but his father's death in 1910 left him with so many debts that he was forced to emigrate to Brazil in 1913, in the hope that he would make enough money to pay them off. But, like Farhat, he had to struggle hard as a wandering salesman to keep himself alive. However, he was able to play an active role in the Arabic literary life of Brazil, and at one point he became president of *al-ʿUsba al-Andalusiyya* (Andalusian League). Khuri inherited his love of poetry from his father, and this may explain his traditionalism and passionate concern for the future of classical Arabic. He regards any deviation from the established canons of correctness as a danger to Arab nationalism, the extent of his commitment to which the reader may get some idea from the preface to his volume *Tempests.*[61] It is not surprising that a man so deeply involved in political issues should write many poems on political and social matters – this feature alone, to say nothing of the language of his poetry, should be enough to distinguish it from the poetry of *al-Rabita*. It is this, too, which accounts for the large bulk of his verse, most of which is written on public or social themes. Like Farhat he wrote even on the occasion of the birthday of the Prophet and similar Moslem religious occasions.[62] His collected works, which were published in Brazil in 1952, run into nearly a thousand pages. His first two volumes appeared as early as 1922.[63]

Yet Khuri wrote about his feelings of homesickness, and much of his poetry is really nature poetry. In a poem entitled 'Rebirth'[64] he points out the need for man to be born again, to recapture the child's freshness of vision and joy in nature, and condemns the lack of interest in nature which a business life, centred on money-making, breeds. The idea is almost Wordsworthian: 'getting and spending we lay waste our powers'. But despite the fact that Khuri's poetry is remarkably rich in natural descriptions, nature is never endowed with a spiritual or mystical quality such as we find in the poetry of *al-Rabita*. Even in a poem like 'The Fallen Tree,' a dramatic monologue in which trees complain of selfish man who ruthlessly cuts them down and denudes forests for his own material purposes,[65] nature remains for Khuri something of a decoration. There is no real emotional involvement with it; on the contrary, the poet seems to stand outside it, looking at times enviously at it. In a poem called 'Men and Cows' he solemnly compares cows and human beings, to the disadvantage of the latter. But although lacking in spiritual quality, Khuri is capable of great charm and simplicity. He has written a few excellent love lyrics, such as 'The Great Lure', a charming and graceful poem in which the poet shows how love makes him forget everything: prayer, business, beauty of landscape, and even his poetry. Another example of his love lyrics is 'Embracing the Universe', in which he expresses his feeling that by embracing his beloved he is embracing the essence of the beauty of the universe. His simplicity is indeed most striking in a poem dealing with the birth of Christ, called 'The Mother's Bosom', which has the haunting beauty of folk poetry, strongly reminiscent of a ballad or a carol.[66]

Unlike Khuri and Farhat, Fauzī al-Ma'lūf (1899–1930) represents the progressive and revolutionary element in Latin American Arabic poetry. He belonged to one of those distinguished Lebanese literary families, like the Yazijis or the Bustanis. Born in the Lebanon he was educated first in an Arabic and then in a French school. In 1921 he emigrated to Brazil (San Paolo) where he became a prosperous business man. He died prematurely in 1930 as a result of an operation. Ma'luf's best-known work is a long poem, 'On the Carpet of the Wind', which has been translated, either wholly or in part, into many western languages.[67] It was first published in the Egyptian periodical *al-Muqtataf* in 1929 and was later reprinted in book form in Rio de Janeiro, with an extremely precious introduction by Francisco Villa Spasa, who translated the work into Spanish.[68]

The plan of the poem is simple. The poet dreams that he is flying in a plane to the upper regions of the sky. He first meets the birds, then the stars and finally he enters the realm of the spirits. He has the chance of hearing what these beings think and say about mankind. As a human being he is met with suspicion and hostility wherever he goes, especially because of the shape and noise of the plane which is taken for a strange and weird bird. But the poet apologizes for his humanity stating that he is a poet, an ethereal creature who rises above the world of matter and flesh and yearns for the world of the spirit. The spirits, who recognize him to be nothing more than a fallen creature, turn away from him in anger and disgust, but one friendly spirit draws near him: it is the poet's own spirit, which explains to the others the spiritual nature of the poet's self. Then follows a moment of ecstatic union between the poet and his spirit, a moment when the truth of the universe is revealed to him. But the union does not last long and the poet feels himself descending back to earthly existence, his spirit having joined the other spirits. He wakes up from his dream to find himself alone holding his pen: he only has his poetry to comfort him.

Ma'luf's poem is not without an element of absurdity, for it is difficult to see the point of the poet's use of the aeroplane device. If it is all a dream anyway, and an ancient dream that has haunted the imagination of poets and others at that, why does not the poet fly on the wings of his poetic imagination, instead of using an aircraft to invade the world of the spirits, whatever that may be? However, the poet's urgency, seriousness and depth of feeling are such that one responds fully to some of his emotional utterances, disregarding the rather facile framework of the poem. The whole thing is intended to be a poetic comment on the human condition, on the tragic conflict between soul and body, an allegory to show how man's yearning for the world of the spirit can be satisfied only in very brief moments of dreaming during which the romantic poet's self-alienation ceases and he is once more united with his soul.

The romantic elements, of which this poem is full, bear a close affinity to the poetry of *al-Rabita*. In fact, both Fauzi and his brother Shafiq, the author of the long, imaginary narrative 'Fairyland', were deeply influenced by Jibran (in his long poem 'The Dreams' (1923) Shafiq quotes Jibran in an epigraph to his second dream).[69] The basic theme of Fauzi's poem, the relation between body and soul, is one of the important themes in Jibran's work, although, as we have seen, Jibran himself was able to conceive a possible reconciliation between the two. In Fauzi Ma'luf's poem the poet's age-old dream of rising to the world of the spirit is really motivated by a desire to escape from reality, a rejection of the sorrows and sufferings of this world and of what it stands for. By means of his poetry he flew high above the earth in search of the tranquillity of the spirit, 'away from the wrongs of this world'. 'Voluntarily', he writes, 'he turned away from the earth, to which he had come against his own will. To the earth he belongs, yet he is not of it, so he remains a stranger amidst his mother's children.'[70] These words, which occur in the first of the fourteen cantos of which the poem consists, provide the keynote to the whole work. From it emerges a highly romantic picture of the poet as an idealized figure, an ethereal being, above the order of ordinary mortals, suffering from a sense of isolation and from a morbid sensitivity to the pain and sorrows of the world, and yearning for death which would set his soul free from the shackles and misery of clay. In fact, Fauzi al-Ma'luf's romantic pessimism and despair were such that even the romantic poet Abu Shadi condemned his attitude on the grounds that it is too negative and extreme.[71] But on the whole the picture of the poet which is depicted in 'On the Carpet of the Wind' and which was identified with Ma'luf himself, struck a sympathetic cord in the Arabic romantic poets. The poet's early death occasioned many elegies, of which one of the most moving is 'A Poet's Grave'[72] by the Egyptian poet 'Ali Mahmud Taha, who both here and elsewhere, as we have seen, gives expression to a similarly idealized view of poetry and the poet.

'Mahjar' poetry and romantic poetry

In fact, despite the geographical distance that separates them, there is a real and close link between *Mahjar* poetry and the romantic poetry which we have seen developing in the Arab world.[73] No doubt, there were mutual influences as well as common sources. Both were deeply affected, directly or indirectly, by the European Romantics. Even those *Mahjar* poets who, like Nu'aima and 'Arida, had acquired a deep knowledge of Russian literature, found the Russian romantics most appealing, 'Arida chose to translate someone like Tyutchev who wrote romantic poems on metaphysical themes. The heyday of the romantic movement in Arabic poetry is the period between the two world wars, and that is in the *Mahjar* no less than in the Arab world. Most of the major *Mahjar* poets are now dead, or have ceased to write, or have returned to their homeland after long absences, and there are no signs that a new generation of powerful poets with clearly marked characteristics are taking their place. In the Arab world itself, however, after the Second World War, we find different trends beginning to appear in poetry, and a younger generation with their own definite views on form and content. The excessive individualism which marked life both in the Arab East and in the West is beginning to disappear in the East, giving place to different forms of social and political life. The Middle East has its own problems, social, political and cultural, distinct from those that may face those Arabs settled in America. The poets in both parts of the world are now preoccupied with different matters. At the same time immigration to the United States is no longer unrestricted, and it is difficult to see how the second generation of Arab immigrants who have been totally absorbed by American culture could continue to speak Arabic, let alone compose poetry in it.

But although it is hard to see any future for Arabic poetry in *Mahjar*, no one can deny its past achievement or the extent of its influence on the rest of Arabic poetry. We have already mentioned how deeply indebted to that poetry Shabbi was, and Shabbi was by no means the only one who fell under its spell. In fact, it can safely be said that the whole generation of romantic poets who reached their maturity in the inter-war period came directly or indirectly under their pervasive influence. By introducing a new conception of poetry, by adding a spiritual dimension to it, so to speak, by turning away from rhetoric and declamation, by concentrating on the more subjective experience of man in relation to nature and ultimate questions, by introducing biblical themes and images into their poetry, by their preference for short metres and stanzaic forms, the *Mahjar* poets, especially of the United States, exercised a liberating influence upon modern Arabic poetry. Indeed their extremist views were often rejected, the revolt of some of them against Arabic versification which resulted in the once fashionable prose poetry of Rihani and Jibran, proved to all intents and purposes to be a dead end, at least until recently; their language was sometimes severely criticized for not being sufficiently correct or even grammatical, and the tendency of many of them to turn their back on the Arab cultural past was often violently attacked. Nonetheless, it would be difficult to exaggerate the significance of the role they played in the development of modern Arabic poetry, and of the subtle influence they exercised in shaping modern Arab sensibility. Without their seminal minds the course of modern Arabic poetry would in many ways have been different.

6

The recoil from romanticism

The general background

Romanticism in modern Arabic poetry reached its momentum between the two world wars. There were obvious signs that it was on the wane immediately after the Second World War. This is not at all surprising, for the war was an important landmark in the literary no less than in the political, social and economic history of the Arab world: the traumatic changes it had brought about, both directly and indirectly, had a powerful impact on the poetry of the time. Despite its distinguished contribution romanticism had by that time developed its own conventional diction, imagery, themes, phraseology and attitudes, thus becoming increasingly irrelevant to an Arab world that was growing painfully aware of its harsh political and social realities. It was criticized on the grounds of being escapist, immature, wanting in reality, as devoid of a hard core of sense, as too vague and lacking precision, as sentimental, false, sugary, facile and verbose.[1] Whatever be the degree of justice in these accusations, in the work of the best romantic poets we have noticed an unmistakable accentuation of the subjective element in experience. In their poetry romantic sorrow, nostalgia, vague metaphysical doubts and yearnings, the sense of mystery in the universe, the idealization of women and the transfiguring effect of love, became common themes. It is true that with the exception of very few poets who like Abu Shabaka or Naji were almost exclusively preoccupied with their inner personal experience, at no point do we find in Arabic romantic poetry, whether in the Arab world itself or in America, a complete withdrawal from the events of the external world.

Yet it cannot be denied that the centre of interest in Arabic romantic poetry, just as it is in Romantic poetry in general, is the individual rather than society, and its vision of society tends to be expressed in somewhat idealized terms, in a language and diction more suited to the communication of subtle subjective and evanescent feelings and moods, and therefore relatively incapable of conveying the shock and immediacy of harsh reality.[2] The reaction against romanticism began to make itself felt in Egypt, but it was soon to spread in other Arab countries like Iraq, the Lebanon and Syria. It is noteworthy, however, that towards the end of the 1940s the distinguished Iraqi poets 'Abd al-Wahhāb al-Bayyātī (b.1926) and the late Badr Shākir al-Sayyāb (1926–1964), both of whom were Marxists (although the latter was subsequently disenchanted with the Marxist ideal) were still writing in a romantic vein, just like other Iraqi poets of their generation such as the interesting Buland al-Ḥaidarī (b.1926), while romanticism was being openly condemned in Egypt.[3] In 1945 'Abd al-Raḥmān al-Sharqāwī (b.1920), better known for his novels (of which one has been translated into English as *Egyptian Soil*), published a poem entitled 'The Riot of Spring' in the periodical *al-Risāla*, an interesting mixture of romantic and nascent 'committed' poetry.[4] In 1946 the Marxist poet Kamāl 'Abd al-Ḥalīm (b.1926) expressed his dissatisfaction with nature and the world of imagination in a poem with the significant title 'To an Errant Poet', in which he wrote:

> When you sing you turn to the stars, to the flowers and birds,
> The god of wine has blessed you, so you sing nonsense, and seek the wine jug.
> But fold your wings in the sky of fancy, that you may drop down amidst us and become one of us,
> Leave aside the beauty of imagination, enter the caves of the millions and tell our story to the world,
> Art is but a tear and a flame – fancy and wandering are no art.[5]

The idea that Arabic literature in general should reflect and help to modify social reality was not altogether new in modern Arabic thought and literary criticism. It was one of the fundamental principles advocated early in the century by the radical thinker Salāma Mūsā (1887–1958) who carried on the work of the early Lebanese secularizers such as Shiblī Shumayyil. He returned from England full of the ideas and ideals of the Fabian society, published his progressive review *al-Majalla al-Jadīda* between 1929–30 and 1934–42, and had among his disciples and followers distinguished people like Muḥammad Mufid al-Shūbāshī, Luwīs 'Awaḍ and even at one time Najīb Maḥfūẓ. Salama Musa's socialist ideas, his belief that literature should be written for the people, about the problems of the people, and in a language that the people could understand, his defence of rationality and the scientific attitude, his attack on the rhetoric and artificialities of the 'literary' style, were expressed in trenchant prose which is itself a model of directness and clarity (though perhaps a little too bare) in many articles, later to be collected in volumes bearing such indicative titles as *Literature for the People* and *Censored Articles.*[6] What *al-Majalla al-Jadida* was doing in Cairo was being done by the Leftist reviews *al-Ṭalīʻa* (1935–48) in Damascus and *al-Ṭarīq* (1941) in Beirut. Leftist and Marxist ideas were propagated in Syria by ʻUmar Fākhūrī who attacked the literature of the ivory tower and in the Lebanon the distinguished critic Ra'īf Khūrī (1912–67) strongly advocated a consistently Marxist view of literature over a number of years. In the early 1930s the time was not ripe for Musa's teachings to produce immediate and spectacular results in Egypt.

It was during the war years, in fact, that the young Egyptian and Arab intellectuals in general became increasingly interested in Marxist philosophy. As Russia was one of the allies, favourable information about Russian literature and the Soviet regime became available for the first time (though still on a very small scale) in the cultural centres of the Middle East, obviously as part of the war propaganda effort.[7] At the same time the passionate interest in Marxism which young European intellectuals showed in the 1930s, and which culminated in the experience of the Spanish Civil War, was transmitted to young Arab intellectuals almost a decade later. Among the contributions to Taha Husain's *al-Kātib al-Miṣrī* (1945–8), one of the finest cultural periodicals ever to appear in Arabic, were the influential articles by Luwis ʻAwad (b. 1915) on modern English writers (in particular his article on T. S. Eliot) in which he put forward a clearly Marxist interpretation of literature inspired by certain Marxist English literary critics. In 1947 ʻAwad published his *Plutoland and Other Poems* (later to be suppressed by the censor) with a revolutionary introduction calling for the need to write the poetry of the people and to overthrow the dominant traditional metrical forms, although the poems themselves have been aptly described by one perceptive critic as: 'caught in the paradox of popularism and elitism'.[8] In 1945 a greater and more influential critic, Muḥammad Mandūr (1907–1965), gave up his academic career in order to engage in active Leftist politics and was later (after the 1952 revolution) to become editor of the Arabic Soviet cultural periodical *al-Sharq* and one of the apologists for a mild form of socialist realism.

From 1944 onwards a stream of heavily documented novels of angry social protest began to pour out, much more detailed and infinitely more concerned with the horrors and degradation of Egyptian urban life than anything that had appeared before. Social injustice and class struggle were now added to national independence as political themes. The tendency to write in a socially realistic strain in the 1940s was by no means confined to the younger generation of novelists like ʻĀdil Kāmil and Najib Mahfuz. It can be found in the work of older authors like Yahya Haqqi and Taha Husain as well as in the work of other Arab writers such as the Iraqi novelist Dhu'l Nūn Ayyūb.[9]

A frontal attack on romantic literature generally was made in a celebrated article published in the Egyptian periodical *al-Thaqāfa* in 1951 entitled 'The Erring Literature' by Mufid al-Shubashi, who dismissed the whole of 'romantic' literature as 'adolescent'. Shubashi pointed out the serious shortcomings of the literature of the ivory tower and called for the need for socialist realism and for the writer's commitment. Just as Kamal 'Abd al-Halim had criticized the errant lost poet (*al-tā'ih*), Shubashi attacked what he called 'erring' literature (*al-ḍāll*), which for him was both the literature that sought its inspiration and ideals in the Arab past and that which derived its models from western Romantic literature. He found the latter no less harmful than the antiquated Arab models, for according to him European Romanticism appeals only to adolescents, and those Egyptian writers who fell under its spell were in fact still adolescent 'despite their grey beards'.[10] (It is worth noting perhaps that as early as 1934 Amin al-Rihani attacked the tearful sentimentality of his contemporary Arabic poets in his book *You Poets*, and the Lebanese poet Sā'id 'Aql, inspired by French Symbolist poetic theory and practice wrote poetry such as *Magdalen* (1937) in which he reacted against the emotionalism and dilution of romanticism and tried to produce works of serene beauty which, however, tended to be rather cold and lifeless.)[11]

It is in the early 1950s that the debate about commitment began. The Arab word for commitment (*iltizām*) has been an essential part of the vocabulary of any Arabic literary critic for many years. Since its introduction to the literary scene, most probably around 1950, in an obvious attempt to translate Jean-Paul Sartre's *engagement* (*Qu'est-ce que la littérature?* was published in book form in 1948 but it appeared a year earlier as articles in his review *Les Temps Modernes*), the word has grown steadily in popularity and is now repeated as a stock phase. Its meaning has become so diffuse that it sometimes means adopting a Marxist stand, or sometimes expresses an existentialist position, but at all times it denotes at least a certain measure of nationalism, Arab or otherwise. But perhaps the most common denominator in all the usages is, to put it simply and a little crudely, the need for a writer to have a message, instead of just delighting in creating a work of the imagination.

In January 1953 Suhail Idrīs produced the Beirut monthly periodical *al-Ādāb*, which, perhaps more than any other, helped to determine the course of modern Arabic literature, by publication of both creative work and of criticism and evaluation of contemporary literature. In the editorial note to the first volume the editor announced that the policy of the periodical was to publish and promote the cause of *adab multazim*: 'committed literature'. The two events which in the meantime had contributed significantly to the wide spread of this attitude of commitment were the Palestine tragedy of 1948, which exposed the basic political weaknesses and corruption of Arab regimes, and hence the total irresponsibility of authors in taking refuge in a romantic world of beauty and daydreams, and the 1952 Egyptian Revolution (itself an indirect consequence of the Palestine war) with its advocacy of the cause of the masses and the proletariat and its far-reaching repercussions throughout the Arab world.

The Sartrean implications of the manifesto-like editorial of *Adab* are fully brought out in the second issue, in an article entitled 'Committed Literature', written by Anwar al-Maʻaddāwī, of the editorial board of *Adab*. Maʻaddawi finds that Sartre is not committed enough. Whereas Sartre exempts poetry (together with music and painting) from the duty of commitment, Maʻaddawi thinks it is clearly wrong to limit it to drama and the novel, since poetry ought to aim at the same noble social ends. Fifteen years later Bayyati expresses a similar view. In 1968 he writes: 'I disagree with Sartre when he exempts the poet from commitment. In my view the poet is immersed up to his ears in the chaos and welter of this world and of the revolution of man'.[12]

Quite early in the 1950s the word 'committed' had already become a term of praise. In 1954 one contributor to *Adab* wrote that 'the idea of committed literature dominates the Arab world now'.[13] The Syrian writer Muṭāʻ Ṣafadī began to expound his own peculiar blend of 'commitment', partly existentialist, partly Arab nationalist, but in any case 'revolutionary'.[14] Bayyati tells us in his account of his intellectual development, that what appealed to him in existentialism was what he could reconcile with social realism, a combination of Gorky, Sartre and Camus.[15]

In 1954 an important, though noisy, controversy arose in Cairo newspapers about the relation of form and content in literature, which on the face of it could be taken as another version of the battle between the old and the new. What was significant, however, was that the dispute was not so much over novelty of technique or approach as over the issue of commitment. The older generation was represented by Taha Husain and ʻAqqad, while Maḥmūd Amīn al-ʻĀlim and ʻAbd al-ʻAẓīm Anīs spoke for the young. The last two published their contributions in book form in Beirut in 1955, under the title *On Egyptian Culture*, with an introduction by the Lebanese Marxist critic Ḥusain Muruwwa. The book had a seminal effect in the Arab world and in the following year Husain Muruwwa published in Cairo his own equally Marxist book of criticism, *Literary Issues*.[16] The question was in fact to be raised again in 1955 in a celebrated formal debate held in Beirut between

Taha Husain and Ra'if Khuri on the subject 'Does the writer write for the élite or for the general public?' Taha Husain's contribution to this last debate[17] ramains the most convincing and eloquent refutation of 'commitment'.

From the middle of the 1950s onwards commitment, whether moderate or extreme, seems to have been the rule rather than the exception. Exactly two years after his first article on the subject in *Adab*, Anwar al-Ma'addawi wrote in the February 1955 issue of the same periodical, 'As for committed literature I do not think there is any longer a need to define it'. In the writings of most critics a work, whether a novel, a short story, a play or a poem, had to be in one way or another committed in order to earn the stamp of approval. The critical contribution of 'Alim and Anis, itself an expression of the dominant mood of the time, exercised a profound and pervasive influence on many of the younger generation of writers, particularly in Egypt. Young poets who began writing in the romantic tradition were soon attracted to social or socialist realism. Poets with obvious Marxist leanings, like the Iraqis al-Bayyati, al-Sayyāb and Kāẓim Jawād, had a large following throughout the Arab world, particularly as their names became linked with what was then a new revolutionary verse form which afforded the poet a greater freedom of self-expression, although the new form was by no means the sole prerogative of the Marxists. Bayyati remained loyal to his early Marxist beliefs, but Sayyab later on recanted and in a confused paper on 'Commitment and Non-Commitment in Arabic Literature' which he read at a conference on Modern Arabic Literature held in Rome in 1961, he launched a venomous attack on Marxist commitment. Traces of the influence of socialist realism are visible in the work of most of the younger poets at the time, especially in Egypt: Iraqis like Buland al-Ḥaidari, the Egyptians 'Abd al-Ṣabūr, Hijāzī, Faitūrī, and the Sudanese Tāj al-Sirr Ḥasan, Jīlī 'Abd al-Raḥmān, although some of them, like 'Abd al-Sabur, became increasingly interested in mysticism later on. Even a poet such as the Syrian Nizar Qabbani, whose themes were generally confined to love and women, often treated in a somewhat romantic adolescent manner, began in 1955 to turn to writing poetry of such frank and biting social criticism as his poem 'Bread, Hashish and Moon' which created a violent reaction in Syria. A basically 'romantic' poet like the Egyptian Kamāl Nash'at also tended to use more of the familiar imagery, diction and themes of socialist realism at about the same time. Those poets who opposed Marxism were in fact not entirely free from commitment, although they were committed to other causes and ideals. Adūnīs, for instance, was at first a supporter of Syrian nationalism, Hāwī a champion of Arab nationalism, and Yūsuf al-Khāl owed some allegiance to Lebanese nationalism, just like Sa'īd 'Aql before him.

Bayyati and the committed poets

This then is the general cultural and critical background of the recoil from romanticism, against which much of Arabic poetry written after the Second World War has to be read. The poet who is generally regarded as the most committed Arab poet and as the leader of the socialist realist movement in modern Arabic poetry is the Iraqi 'Abd al-Wahhāb al-Bayyātī (b. 1926). Bayyati, a graduate of the Teachers' Training College in Baghdad, was forced on account of his Communist beliefs to wander abroad in Arab countries and in Europe, particularly in Eastern Europe and Russia where he lived and lectured for some time. Understandably, much of his poetry has been translated into Russian and Chinese. Bayyati is a prolific writer who has published several volumes of verse: *Angels and Devils* (1950), *Broken Pitchers* (1954), *Glory be to Children and the Olive Branch* (1956), *Poems in Exile* (1957), *Twenty Poems from Berlin* (1959), *Words that Never Die* (1960), *Fire and Words* (1964), *Poems* (1965), *The Book of Poverty and Revolution* (1965), *What will Come and will not Come* (1966), *Death in Life* (1968), *The Dead Dogs' Eyes* (1969) and *Inscriptions in Clay* (1970). In 1971 appeared his Collected Poems (*Diwan*), together with a prose work (first published separately in 1968) giving an account of his poetic experience and his reflections as poet, in two volumes. His latest collection of verse is entitled *Love Poems on the Seven Gates of the World* (1971).[18]

Bayyati read widely, including Mayakovsky, Nāzim Hikmet (who became a friend to whom he addressed poems), Paul Eluard, Aragon, Lorca and Neruda among others. He translated Aragon (to whom he also addressed a poem), and Lorca's death is a theme that haunts him in at least two volumes: *What will Come and will not Come* and *Death in Life*. All these poets clearly left their mark on Bayyati's style and attitudes. In the recent edition of his poems he quotes with approval Boris Pasternak's statement that 'Romanticism is only the poetic content of the *petit bourgeois*' (II,373). Yet, as has been said earlier on, Bayyati began by writing poetry in the romantic idiom. This is clearly seen in his first volume *Angels and Devils*, particularly in poems such as 'A Poet's Dream' and 'Solitude'.[19] It is in the second volume, *Broken Pitchers*, that he finds his true voice. In one of its best-known poems, 'The Village Market', Bayyati inaugurated a fashion of writing poems about the countryside in which only the poor peasant is idealized, while every grim detail of his wretched life is realistically portrayed, in great contrast to the 'romantic' image of the village made popular in works such as *Songs of the Hut* by the Egyptian Maḥmūd Ḥasan Isma'īl. Likewise, in Bayyati's work the city is a menacing place where fear is born, crimes are committed and the wretchedness of the sick and starving masses is doubled, as we find in the poem entitled 'Night, the City and Tuberculosis'. In the title poem, 'Broken Pitchers', the poet expresses his boundless hope for the emancipation of the proletariat:

God and the radiant sky! The slaves feel their chains
'To-morrow you must build your cities close to erupting Vesuvius.
You must not be satisfied with anything beneath the stars,
Let violent love and deep joy set your hearts aflame.'
Whoever sells his eagles dies of starvation.
Those who ape men stand at the new crossroads,
One-eyed and confused. (I,157–9).

Here we have images such as the 'one-eyed' and those who 'ape men', which, like dwarves, fly-swatters, spiders' webs, history's rubbish heap and the green moon, are recurrent motifs in Bayyati's poetry. The poet is not always able to maintain this strident, loud and Mayakovskyian tone of voice. At times sorrow and grief dominate, as in 'Camp No. 20', inspired by the plight of Palestinian refugees.

The optimistic note which the poet strikes at the end of the poem cannot hide the extent of his impotent fury and overwhelming sense of injury. Bayyati's next volume of verse, *Glory be to Children and the Olive Branch* (1956), opens with a series of poems entitled 'Diary of an Arab in Israel' in which the poet, committed to the Arab cause, sounds more hopeful: in 'Return', for instance, he writes:

The night is banished by the lanterns of eyes,
Your eyes, my hungry brethren, scattered beneath the stars.
And it seemed as if in a dream I had paved your road
With roses and tears,
As if Jesu had returned with you to Galilee,
Without the Cross. (I,297)

The Christ theme recurs in many poems, in which the poet thinks of the suffering, persecution and exile which he endured, in his attempt to deliver his people from tyranny and despotism and to bring about social justice, in terms of Christ's passion and crucifixion. For instance, in 'Song to my People', from the same volume, he writes: 'Here I am alone on the Cross' (I,307). And in *Poems in Exile* we find: 'I die that I may give life to others', (I,395ff.). In 'Spring and Children' he complains that 'they crucify the sun in my city's public square' (I,370). Bayyati is, in fact, one of the few Arab poets responsible for propagating the theme of Christ's passion and crucifixion and making it one of the stock images in contemporary Arabic poetry, especially that of a revolutionary political character.

Bayyati welcomed the Iraqi Revolution of 1958 in a jubilant poem of unsurpassed simplicity entitled 'July 14':

In my city the sun is shining,
Bells are ringing to honour the heroes.
Arise, my love, for we are free,

Like fire, birds and daylight.
No more walls stand between us now,
No ruthless tyrant rules over us. (I,546)

although one may mention in passing that the poet's imagination has clearly been affected by his exile which has made him resort to non-traditional Arab imagery expressing joy such as the ringing of church bells to honour heroes. Even the sun is here used with a different emotional significance from what we find in the opening of 'The Village Market' where it is accompanied by flies, lean donkeys and worn-out boots. In 1965 he wrote in a poem addressed to President Nasser, obviously inspired by his enthusiasm for Nasser's Arab socialism:

O generation of defeat, this revolution
Will wipe out your shame, dislodge the rock,
Peel off your crust, and in the barren wastes
Of your life cause a flower to bloom. (II,5)

This excessive optimism may explain why the disastrous Arab defeat of 1967 had such a shattering effect upon Bayyati, as indeed it had on most Arab writers. In 'Lament for the June Sun' (1968), (published in his collection *Dead Dogs' Eyes*), a poem which managed to reach a large English audience in a translation which appeared in the periodical *Encounter* (Oct. 1971, p. 22), he ruthlessly expressed the kind of bitter self-criticism and self-condemnation which was typical of the feverish soul-searching and breast-beating that Arab intellectuals went through soon after the Six Day War. Speaking in their name he says:

In the cafés of the East we have been ground
By the war of words,
Minced by wooden swords,
Lies and horsemen of the air.
We did not kill a camel or even a sand grouse
We did not try the game of death . . .
In the cafés of the East we swat the flies
We wear the masks of the living in history's rubbish heap,
Aping men.
We dared not ask the one-eyed charlatan, the anti-Christ,
Why did you escape?
We are the generation of free death
Recipient of alms. (II,336)

Bayyati had remained a committed Marxist giving expression to his political creed in volume after volume. In 1960 he wrote, in 'Art for Life', in a somewhat aggressive tone:

I shall trample underfoot.
The champions of 'art' and the pedants,
The beggars and the old hags of poetry,
I shall smash their poems on their heads,
For lifeblood flows in my veins.
And I shall not betray the cause of man,
No, that I shall not betray.
So to Hell, Thou Muse of lies.
Here my inspiration comes
From my great love. (I,515)

In the course of time, especially starting from *The Book of Poverty and Revolution* (1965), the tone becomes less aggressive,[20] but the political position remains consistent even when his symbolist style grows in density and his imagery becomes more surrealistic in *What will Come and will not Come* (1966), and the subsequent volumes *Death in Life* (1968) and *Inscriptions in Clay* (1970). In the later poetry the facile optimism and the strident tone often give place to a quieter and more mature voice, enriched and deepened by disillusionment and the tragic complexities of experience. For instance, in 'Nightmare of Night and Day' from *Inscriptions in Clay* we read:

What did the song say?
Birds are dying on the pavements of the night,
The long-awaited prophet
Is still asleep in his cave, and rain is falling
Upon the walls of old dilapidated houses,
Upon the roofs of the pregnant city and the notices of estate agents.
The birth and the death of the Word is written in blood
While in the street I walk holding a corpse,
Hiding my face from God and you. (II,290ff.)

However, he never loses sight of his commitment to his political ideal as witness, for example, 'Elegy on an Unborn City' from the same collection (II,299) and more particularly the majority of the poems in *Dead Dogs' Eyes* and the poem which gives the collection its title (II,330ff.). Bayyati is of course aware of the change that has taken place in his style of writing as from *What will Come and will not Come* (and which has rendered it more opaque, visionary and surrealistic) (II,400ff.). But in 1968 in his prose work entitled *My Experience of Poetry*, he hastens to defend himself, making a somewhat unconvincing attempt to dissociate himself from other stylistic experiments in contemporary Arabic poetry (II,404–5).

In vague and rather melodramatic terms Bayyati attributes the change in his style to 'suffering, silence, death' and the rise of reactionary counter-revolutionary forces which 'have swept over the world', as well as 'the death of that great revolutionary Ché Guevara whom I regarded as the symbol and the only remaining hope for the wronged and oppressed workers and intellectuals of the world' (II,406). He claims that these factors have led him to seek a mode of self-expression in which he 'tried to reconcile the mortal and the eternal, the finite and the infinite, the present and that which transcends the present'. He therefore searched for suitable artistic masks in the worlds of history, symbols and myths, through which crisis could be expressed on social as well as cosmic levels. The mask, he says, is 'the name through which the poet speaks divested, as it were, of his own subjectivity'. By deliberately creating an entity that has its own independent existence 'the poet transcends the limitations of lyricism and romanticism which have beset most Arabic poetry', In this manner ' the poem becomes a world independent of the poet, although created by him', free from the masks of 'distortion', emotionalism and 'psychological ailments with which subjective romantic poetry abounds' (II,407–8). The masks which Bayyati uses in his later poetry include a wide variety of personages, historical and fictitious, such as the classical Arab poets Tarfa, Abu Firās of Ḥamdān, Mutanabbi, Dik al-Jinn, Ma'arri, the Persian poet and mathematician Khayyam, the Sufi martyr Hallaj, Alexander the Great, Hamlet, Sindbad, Ché Guevara, Picasso, Hemingway, Nazim Hikmet, Albert Camus, and 'Ā'isha the Iraqi girl killed by despots; the symbols include the Koranic many-columned city of Iram, books such as *The Arabian Nights*, Harīrī's *Maqāmāt*, cities and rivers such as Damascus, Naisapur, Granada, Madrid, Cordova and Euphrates. Many of these had been used by him earlier, not as masks or symbols, but as allusions, for Bayyati's poetry, at least starting from the volume *Twenty Poems from Berlin*, is full of allusions, not only to people and places, myths and events, but also to particular poems. This is a feature which he clearly adopted from the poetry of T. S. Eliot. But now the problem with which he is concerned seems to be 'how to present the ideal hero of our time (and of all times) in an extreme situation', how to get under his skin and 'portray his feelings when he is passing through the most meaningful moments in his life', and 'how to express the social and cosmic crisis faced by such a personage' (II,409). In the final analysis the ideal hero, we learn, is the revolutionary who is also the poet/artist and the lover. Referring us to his poem on the suffering of Hallaj, he says, 'The death of lovers, rebels and artists is the bridge which civilization and mankind cross to reach a more perfect existence' (II,415). Bayyati seems to adopt a strangely materialist philosophical position, fraught with elements of pantheism and mysticism, for which he finds support in ancient Babylonian literature. Put simply, it is that the spirit of life is ever renewing itself and death is merely the return of the part to the whole (II,476), or, on a political level, revolution is to be kept up by a succession of revolutionaries. As philosophical speculations Bayyati's prose work *My Experience of Poetry* is in parts no less idiosyncratic than Yeats's book *The Vision*, from which, however, Yeats derived the raw material of some good poetry. But it is remarkable to see Bayyati posing as the revolutionary poet *par excellence*: the portrait he paints of himself is full of self-dramatization and totally unrelieved by humour (II,440–1).

Bayyati's most recent volume, *Love Poems on the Seven Gates of the World* (1971), includes among the personae or masks the Muslim mystic Ibn al-'Arabi and the Arab lover Waḍḍāḥ al-Yaman, as well as poems addressed to the Muslim jurist Shāfi'ī and to Ikhnatun. Now the mystical and surrealistic elements become dominant features of his style, in many places to the point of unintelligibility. A more moderate example of this style is the last poem in the collection, entitled 'The Nightmare', which in five sections asserts the poet's faith in the value of the struggle and dissent in art and in life, and the continuity of the spirit of revolution despite the fall of revolutionaries. The second section is quoted here and it may give the reader some idea of the last stage of Bayyati's development, in its least impenetrable form:

> At the gate of Hell stood Picasso, and the guitar player from Madrid
> Raised the curtain for the ravished theatre queens,
> Restored to the Clown his virginity,
> Hid weapons and seeds in the earth until another resurrection.
> He died in a café in exile, his eyes turned towards his distant land,
> Gazing through clouds of smoke and the newspaper,
> His hand tracing in the air
> A mysterious sign pointing to the weapons and seeds.
> The guitar player from Madrid dies
> In order that he may be born again,
> Under the suns of other cities and in different masks,
> And search for the kingdom of rhythm and colour,
> And for its essence which activates a poem,
> Live through the revolutions of the ages of Faith and Rebirth,
> Waiting, fighting, migrating with the seasons,
> Returning to mother earth with those wearing a crown of torturing light,
> The dissenters and the builders of creative cities
> In the bottom of the sea of rhythm and colour.[21]

Although Bayyati himself may hotly deny it, it is most likely that one of the factors that have led to his change of style is the growing influence of Adunis's poetry which, as we shall see later, reveals a mystical outlook, and which seeks to destroy all logical connections, relies heavily on surrealistic imagery and resorts to the use of masks. In this respect Adunis's influence helped to strengthen and confirm whatever effect on his poetry was exercised by Bayyati's earlier fascination with the work of Marxists like Mayakovsky, Aragon, Eluard and Neruda which, besides being Marxist, was also either futuristic or surrealistic or opaquely symbolist.

Like Bayyati, the Egyptian Ṣalāh 'Abd al-Ṣabūr (b.1931) wrote realistic poetry about the village which reveals the degree of his social commitment. In a poem which gives his first volume of verse its title, *People in my Country* (1957),[22] and which was first published in *al-Adab* in 1954, he says:

> People in my country are predatory like hawks,
> Their singing is like the winter wind blowing through the trees,
> Their laughter like the hissing of wood consuming fire.
> When they walk their feet wish to sink into the earth,
> They murder and steal, they belch when they drink,
> And yet they are human.
> When they have a handful of money they are good,
> And they believe in Fate.

The poet proceeds to give a picture of his pious old uncle sitting at the entrance of his village, whiling away the hours of dusk surrounded by men, all listening intently to him telling a tale of 'the fruit of life's experience', a painful tale that made them sob, bend down their heads and gaze into the stillness, 'into the deep waves of terror'. The narrative power of the tale set them wondering about the end of man's toil in this life and the inscrutable ways of the Lord, who sends his Messenger of Death to apprehend the soul of the rich man who had built castles and 'owned forty rooms filled with glittering gold', and despatched it, rolling down into the depths of hell. This is how the poem ends, with the poet revisiting the village, and learning that his poor uncle has died and that:

> Behind his old coffin there walked
> Those who, like him, possessed only one old linen gown.
> They mentioned neither God nor the Angel of Death, nor the mysterious
> words,
> For it was a year of hunger.
> At the mouth of the grave stood my friend Khalil,
> The grandson of uncle Mustafa,
> Lifting his muscular arm to the sky,
> And a look of scorn surged in his eyes
> For it was a year of hunger. (I,29–32)

Together with a number of verse plays 'Abd al-Sabur published several volumes of verse after *People in my Country: I Say unto You* (1961), *Dreams of the Ancient Knight* (1964) and *Meditations on a Wounded Age* (1971). His Collected Works (*Diwan*) appeared in two volumes in Beirut in 1972. Unlike Bayyati, he turned from such poetry of commitment to the humanist and socialist ideal which we find in his first volume to an increasingly personal vision which alternates between a mild form of mysticism and melancholy meditations on death, and even at times despair. A mystical trend begins to be noticeable in *I Say Unto You*, in, for instance, lines such as

> One morning I saw the truth of the world
> I heard the music of stars, of flowers and water
> I saw God in my heart. (I,177)

The poet's tendency towards introspection increases in *Dreams of the Ancient Knight*. The first poem, after a brief verse introduction in which the poet apologizes for the poor fare he is going to offer his companions, as 'this year's trees have not borne fruit', is entitled 'Song for the Winter'. It begins:

> This year's winter tells me that I shall die alone
> One such winter.
> This evening tells me that I shall die alone
> One such evening,
> That my past years have been lived in vain,
> That I inhabit the open air, with no roof over my head.
> This year's winter tells me that inside me
> My soul is shaking with cold,
> That my heart has been dead since the autumn,
> That it withered with the withering of the first leaves,
> And dropped to the ground with the first drop of rain,
> Receding deeper into the stony ground with every cold night. (I,193–4)

In the same poem he states that his sin has been his poetry, for which he has been 'crucified' (I,195). The poet's overpowering pessimism is obvious, especially in the last poem of this collection, entitled 'Memoirs of the Sufi Bishr al-Ḥāfī' (I,263ff.), where the world is felt to be infected and diseased beyond all cure and where man is a sorry sight in the eyes of the Lord. The gloom is unrelieved in the next volume, *Meditations on a Wounded Age*: here the poet suffers from a recurring nightmare in which he is shot, disembowelled and made to hang as an exhibit in a museum. He amuses himself by pretending to dismember and reshape the passers by and by evolving similarly violent ideas, as for instance in 'Conversation in a Café' (I,318ff.). What comes through the *Meditations* is a sad world in which unhappy man finds in sex a temporary escape from disillusionment and misery, as in, for example, 'Female' (I,332). In his book *My Life in Poetry* (1969) 'Abd al-Sabur puts forward a basically moral and spiritual view of poetry which he now regards as closely akin to mysticism, and he devotes much space to an attack on the conventional Marxist view, pointing out that poetry affirms values like truth, freedom and justice. This position, obviously a continuation of a development which began earlier, was no doubt accentuated by Arab military defeat in 1967, which encouraged a withdrawal from painful external reality and is not confined to poetry, but can also be noticed in other aspects of Arabic literature.[23]

Another Egyptian poet, Aḥmad ʻAbd al-Muʻṭī Ḥijāzī (b.1935), gives his first collection of poems the self-explanatory title *Heartless City* (1959), and writes movingly about the loneliness, bewilderment and anxiety, the feeling of loss and fear of anonymity experienced in the great and impersonal metropolis of Cairo by those simple souls drawn to it from the countryside.[24] In 'Good-night' he says:

> The streets of the big city are pits of fire,
> At noon they ruminate the flames they have absorbed in the morning.
> Unhappy is the man who has known only their sun,
> Their buildings and their railings, their railings and their buildings,
> Their squares, their triangles and their glass. (pp. 128ff.)

In his elegy on a village boy run over by a car in the city street Hijazi says ruefully, since nobody could identify the boy:

> Eyes met
> No one answered
> In the big city people are mere numbers:
> One boy came
> One boy died. (pp. 143ff.)

Hijazi's attitude to the city later loses something of its intensity in the two subsequent volumes: *There Remains Only Confession* (1965) and *Elegy on the Handsome Life* (1973). This is due partly to the fact that the poet was no longer the bewildered newcomer to Cairo, but had grown more accustomed to fairly complex urban living, partly to the measure of recognition he had received which made him feel less of an outsider. He was now in fact writing songs for the Arab Socialist Union in which he hoped to find the answer to problems of urban life (p. 326). Hijazi's first volume, however, is, as the author of the somewhat wordy introduction to the first edition says, 'a document that bears witness to our age and depicts our generation' (p. 95). It is interesting to see how far the reaction against romanticism has gone in the poet's generation. The first poem in that volume, 'At the Age of Sixteen', shows us the poet in effect saying that he has outgrown Naji's poetry and the values it represents, its conception of the poet as a solitary, suffering being, hopelessly in love with an ideal and full of vague longings. Such poetry soon came to be regarded as poetry of adolescence.

In his later poetry Hijazi became increasingly interested in Arab nationalism. In the preface to his poem 'Aurès', which was inspired by the Algerian revolution and attained great popularity, he wrote (1959): 'I have found in the idea of Arab nationalism an embodiment of the spirit of the people, as well as my own personal salvation from a violent intellectual crisis which nearly drove me to a psychological breakdown' (p. 390). Like other Arab poets he was drawn to Paul Eluard because of his political position: in 'Aurès' he quotes from a poem in which Eluard laments the death of a man belonging to the French Resistance who had been shot by the German Nazis (p. 409). Hijazi is a committed Arab nationalist and a Nasserite who wrote more than one poem on Nasser in which he gave expression to his feelings of hero-worship. This is particularly true of his moving elegies on Nasser in 'The Journey has Begun' and the title poem of the last volume, 'An Elegy on the Handsome Life' (pp. 484, 546). In his recent poetry Hijazi too shows the dominant influence of surrealism, in his tendency to break down logical sequence and his predilection for surprising imagery.

A similar sense of compassion for the victims of city life to that we have seen in Hijazi's early work is sometimes shown in the work of the Sudanese poet Muḥammad Miftāḥ al-Faitūrī (b. 1930), who was born and brought up in Egypt. For instance, in a well-known poem, 'Under the Rain' he writes:[25]

> O driver, have mercy on the jaded horses,
> Cease, for the iron of the saddle has cut into the horses' necks
> And made them bleed,
> Their eyes can no longer see the road.
> Thus death was chanting around the coach
> As it went down swaying under the rain in the dark.
> But the black driver with sick emaciated face
> Pulled the overcoat over his face in despair,
> Casting a faint light on the road, like the light of setting stars,
> And his crying whip sang on the horses' backs,
> So they winced and staggered and plodded on in a trance. (pp. 193–4)

Clearly in Faituri's treatment both the horses and their driver, 'with sick emaciated face', indeed the entire world which they inhabit, is in great need of mercy. This poem comes from his collection *Songs of Africa* (1955) which, as the title suggests, includes poems denouncing colonialism and the exploitation of the black by the white, written in a dense, euphonious style, rich in imagery and remarkable for its vividness and vitality, Some of these poems, such as 'Sorrows of the Black City' or 'He Died Tomorrow' (which describes the death of a black political victim), express a profound feeling of anger and bitterness:

> He died
> Not a drop of rain wept for him,
> Not a handful of faces looked sad.
> The moon never looked benignly upon his grave at night,
> Not even a lazy worm turned round
> Or a stone cracked.
> He died tomorrow,
> A soiled corpse and a forgotten shroud,
> Like a bad dream
> – And then the people awoke
> Or an unwholesome storm
> Passing over the fields of roses at the hour of dawn.
>
> He died.
> And his black burning soul was full to the brim
> Of a past overlaid with the blood of gallows,
> The screams of the rebels confined in prisons,
> The painful and cracked faces of old women
> Raising to heaven, in helpless sorrow,
> Crooked, scythe-like arms,
> And eyes in which was buried deep the shadow of the gallows.
>
> (pp. 101ff.)

Faituri pursued the theme of Black Africa in further collections entitled *A Lover from Africa* (1964) and *Remember Me, Africa* (1968). Writing about his experience as poet he once said, 'In 1948 I wrote my poem "To a White Face", which is my first poetic experiment in which my little self was fused into a larger self, namely the African' (p. 22). In 'Voice of Africa', a poem from the collection *A Lover from Africa,* he claims that the voice of Africa is the poet's own voice as well as the voice of God; in it we find a complete identification between the poet and his political cause and an intimation of the way the appeal of the cause operates on three levels: the personal, the political and the religious.

In Faituri's latest collection, *Music for an Itinerant Dervish* (1970), the poet turns to mysticism. This change he defends by saying that the mystical experience was not at all a new thing to him, but on the contrary it was 'part of his being', since he was brought up on mysticism (p. 34).

Whatever the early history of Faituri the man, there seems to be a connection between the resurgence of religious feeling and the vogue of mysticism in general and the shattering Arab defeat of 1967. After all, the title poem of this last volume was written in that year, and in 'Journal of a Pilgrim to the Sacred House of God' (1968) the poet addresses the Prophet, saying:

> To you, Sir, I convey the best greeting
> From a nation that is lost, who cannot do well,
> Driven by a civilization of darkness and destruction
> To you every year in the hope you will intercede
> For its blind sun in the crowd.
> Sir, since we filled up the sea with dykes
> And put up barriers between you and us,
> We have died and been trodden by the cattle of Jews. (p. 486)

On the whole, Faituri's Sufi and religious poetry does not sound as convincing as some of his political verse, and one may instance his comments on the Arab situation after the defeat in the long poem 'The Fall of Dabshalīm', in which the poet assumes the persona of the philosopher Bidpai from the well-known Arabic/Indian classic *Kalīla wa Dimna.*

As a measure of the spread of committed realistic writing it suffices to point out the change in the style of a poet such as the Syrian Nizār Qabbānī (b. 1923), already alluded to. Qabbani had attained enormous popularity across the whole Arab world through his love poetry, in which he expressed his amorous feelings in a sensuous and elegant vocabulary, of great simplicity and immediate appeal. His collections of poems, which are numerous, often ran into six or seven impressions.[26] From the date of publication of his earliest volume in 1944, until 1955, love and woman remained his main themes, although his attitude to woman gradually changed. In the first volume, it was one of sexual starvation (which according to the poet was typical of the whole of his generation), a mode heavily influenced by the Abu Shabaka of *The Serpents of Paradise* and by the growing gap between the poet's readings in Baudelaire, Rimbaud and Verlaine and his own experience of conservative Damascus society. With his departure for Cairo, where he worked in the diplomatic service (1945–8) and was exposed to the sophisticated social life of diplomats, he began to develop a more 'aesthetic' interest in women, his crude sensuality giving place to civilized and refined eroticism which marks some of the poems in his second and third volumes, where he describes in loving detail society women with their dress, jewels and perfume. His subsequent service in London deepened his experience and sharpened his awareness of the complexity of human relationships. A note of melancholy begins to creep into his verse, but even in his mature period love and women remained his primary concern. He would write a poem such as 'Her

Birthday' where the poet's sole problem upon receiving a card from his mistress informing him of her birthday was what present to give her. From this type of verse which, despite its elegance of phrase in the original Arabic, suffers from a limited range and a narrow sensibility that borders on the sentimental and adolescent, Qabbani suddenly moves on to a more responsible and adult poetry which reveals real concern with social and political issues, such as his outspoken criticism in his 'Bread, Hashish and Moon' (1955) of an Arab society that lives in daydreams and a world of pleasant sensations invoked by drugs:

> What does a disc of light do to my land;
> The land of the prophets and of the simple people
> Who chew tobacco and trade in narcotics?
> What does a disc of light do to us
> That we lose thus our pride and importune heaven?
> What has heaven to offer to the lazy and weak
> Who turn into dead men when the moon is born?[27]

Or his more bitter and sweeping condemnation of Arab leadership after the Six Day War, in *In the Margin of the Book of Defeat* (1967).[28]

Among the committed poets who suddenly attained great popularity after 1967 are the Palestinian poets known in Arabic as 'Poets of Resistance', *shu'arā' al-muqāwama*, and 'Poets of the Occupied Homeland'. For understandable reasons their popularity is not always related to their poetic merit: the poets themselves vary greatly in talent, but among the names that have come to the foreground are Maḥmūd Darwīsh, Samīḥ al-Qāsim, and Taufīq Zayyād, and their works, together with others by minor Palestinian poets, were published in one volume in Damascus in 1968 under the title *The Collected Poems of the Occupied Homeland*[29] with an introduction by Yūsuf al-Khaṭīb. Of course these poets have continued to publish other works since that date: in fact if there is a charge to be levelled at their writings from the purely *literary* point of view, it is that they have been overproductive, with the result that their poetry is in danger of sounding too facile and mechanical. Partly because most of these poets are Marxists their poetry, particularly their early poetry, betrays the influence of Bayyati and Sayyab. For the most part they use the new form, which consists of an irregular number of feet, and they follow the technique of their contemporaries in all its main features, including the use of Greek, ancient Egyptian, Babylonian, Arab, Islamic and Christian mythologies. For instance, in the poetry of Darwish and al-Qasim, Ulysses is the dispossessed wandering Arab, and Penelope is Palestine, Telemachus is the poet who chooses to stay with his mother and work towards the return of Ulysses.[30] For the message in their poetry is not one of despair, or defeat; on the contrary, without minimizing the difficulties they preach the need to continue the struggle. For instance, in a well-known poem 'A Lover from Palestine' (1966), which gave its title to the whole volume, Darwish movingly describes the sufferings and tribulations of the Palestinians, but far from indulging in self-pity his chief emotion is anger and the message of the poem is one of hope. In 'The Winter Moon' he has no romantic illusion:

> I shall say to the poets of our glorious nation
> 'I have killed the moon to which you have been enslaved.'[31]

In 'Roses and the Dictionary' he says:

> I must reject death
> Even though all my myths die,

and in 'Promises from the Storm'

> If I sing to joy behind frightened eyes
> It is because the storm has promised me
> Rainbows and wine.

For he says in 'My Country':

> My country is not a bundle of tales
> Not a memory or a field of moons,
> It is not a story or a song:
> This earth is the skin on my bones,
> Above its grass my heart hovers like a bee.

Similarly al-Qasim writes in *Road Songs* (1965 [?])

> Despite doubt and sorrows
> I hear, I hear the footsteps of dawn

and in the volume entitled *My Blood on my Hand* (1967):

> On the horizon there is a sail
> Defying the wind and waves, weathering out the storm:
> It is Ulysses returning from the sea of loss.[32]

Experiments in form

Besides the spread of social realism and Marxist and Arab national thought one of the factors that contributed greatly towards the downfall of the romantic ideal was the greater knowledge Arab poets acquired of western post-Romantic poetry, the French Symbolists and in particular the strangely powerful influence of T. S. Eliot. Eliot's name seems to occur for the first time in Arabic literary criticism in 1933 and 1934 in two articles published in Egyptian periodicals in which Mu'āwiya Nūr (1909–1941), a young Sudanese intellectual, launches the 'earliest attack on romantic poetry and poetic theory from a "modernist" point of view'. Influenced by T. E. Hulme and F. R. Leavis, Nur criticizes the poetry of Naji and Taha for its reliance on 'poetical' subjects such as breezes, birds, waves and desolate shores, its neglect of aspects of urban life and its lack of modernity, or lack of 'awareness of the age in which they live'.[33] But as Abdul-Hai points out, Nur's articles passed completely unnoticed because the literary scene, especially in Egypt, was dominated by the romantic poets of the *Apollo* group. It was Luwis 'Awad who really introduced Eliot to the Arabic reader in 1946 in a long article published in *al-Katīb al-Miṣrī*. As has been rightly observed:

> The tone of the article shows that it was intended not only to inform the reader about a contemporary Anglo-American poet, but mainly to 'create' the Arab reader who would appreciate a 'new poetic method', which is 'obscure', 'allusive' and 'does not conform to the familiar patterns of the traditional verse we know'.[34]

Since the publication of 'Awad's article Eliot began to assert his presence in Arab cultural life. In the 1950s much of his poetry and criticism was translated into Arabic and published in leading literary reviews such as *Ādāb* and *Shi'r* in Beirut and *Adab* and *Majalla* in Cairo. In the late 1950s and early 1960s Eliot became the subject of broadcast talks, and of many heated arguments on the literary pages of Cairo newspapers in which leading Egyptian critics took part.

The influence of Eliot is shown not only in the structure and style, the use of myth and allusion and of the interior monologue, in Iraqi, Lebanese and Egyptian poetry, but Eliot's attacks on the English Romantic poets, his reaction against what he regarded as their limitations both in style and subject matter, no doubt affected the attitude of the younger generation of Arab poets towards their own romantic poetry, making them reject the false simplicity, the sentimentality and sugary poeticality of some romantic poetry in favour of a pregnant style more capable of expressing real-life experience in all its complexity and harshness.[35] But the interest taken in Eliot, which seems to be common to all the major figures in Iraq, Lebanon, Syria and Egypt, is an expression of a much wider concern with modern western poetry in general. Scholars have shown, for instance, the impact of Lorca and Edith Sitwell on Sayyab, of Saint John Perse on Adunis, and of Yeats on M. M. Badawi.[36] Among those intimately acquainted with modern western poetry are the symbolist or surrealist poets connected with the *avant-garde* magazine *Shi'r* (1957–64; 1967–1969) – itself a powerful means of propagating modern anti-romantic attitudes. It is true that these poets generally opposed social realism and Marxism: on more than one occasion Yusuf al-Khal claimed that any form of political ideological commitment is harmful to art and distorts its nature, and those 'who call for the exploitation of literature and art in the effort of construction or reconstruction [of society] do harm to literature and art'.[37] However, they share with the Marxists their dislike for Romanticism which some of them regard as 'a disease'.[38]

The revolt of the so-called 'new' poetry was not confined to its rejection of romantic themes and style. Formally at least, it was more extreme than any other revolt modern Arabic poetry had seen so far. It has rejected most of the basic conventions of Arabic verse. Put superficially, a printed page of 'new' poetry looks different from Arabic verses written before the late 1940s: what is known in Arabic as *bait*, the line that consisted of two hemistichs of equal length or metrical value, has disappeared and has been replaced by lines of unequal length. So fashionable has this revolution in prosody proved to be that some poems which really follow the traditional metrical pattern have been arranged by their authors on the page in such a way that they are made to look metrically new (this was done even by distinguished poets like the Sudanese al-Faituri and the Palestinian poet Mahmud Darwish).[39] For a long time poets had been searching for new metrical forms which would allow a greater freedom of self-expression and would enable the poet to realize a truly organic unity in his work, would extend the scope of Arabic poetry so as to make possible the writing of verse drama that was truly dramatic and not lyrical, like Sa'īd 'Aql's plays, or rhetorical, like those by Shauqi or 'Azīz Abāẓa. Recently the story of this long quest and hectic experimentation with verse form has been thoroughly studied by at least two scholars of the period.[40] The new form that has found acceptance virtually throughout the entire Arab world is that connected with the names of the Iraqi poets Badr Shakir al-Sayyab and Nazik al-Mala'ika, and which relies upon the use of the single foot (*taf'īla*) as the basic unit, instead of a fixed number of feet or a combination of certain different feet per line. Like Bayyati, both Sayyab and Mala'ika are graduates of the Teachers' Training College in Baghdad. Which of these two poets was the first to use this new form has been the subject of keen controversy, and claims of priority have been made by each poet and for each poet by several writers.[41] The issue was complicated by the fact that both poets published the poems in which they used what they regarded as a new experimental form, in December 1947. Nazik al-Mala'ika's poem 'al-Kūlīrā' (Cholera) appeared in the Beirut magazine *al-'Urūba* (1 December 1947), while al-Sayyab included his, entitled 'Hal kāna ḥubban' (Was it Love?) in his volume of verse *Azhār Dhābila* (Withered Flowers). But it has been pointed out that the two poets did not develop this form independently, but that on the contrary they frequently met in Baghdad to discuss poetry and exchange ideas, and that far from being an entirely new departure the new form, known as *al-shi'r al-ḥurr* (literally = free verse), was a culmination of a long series of prosodic experiments started early in the century, and that in fact externally the new form had been developed before these Iraqi poets by the Egyptian Muḥammad Farīd Abū Ḥadīd and the Indonesian-born Egyptian Bākathīr, in their attempt to write (or translate) poetic drama. It is indeed futile to try to establish which modern Arabic poet was the first to use this new form, nor is there any glory attached to such precedence. For the fact is that poets of the generation born in the 1920s were searching for a new, freer form around the same time (during or shortly after the Second World War), and it is more than likely that several poets quite independently worked out the same or similar solutions simultaneously. The present author can affirm that his own experiments, which were made along similar lines at roughly the same time (and which were subsequently published in the volume *Rasā'il min London*, 1956), had been arrived at in England completely independently. Likewise, Yusuf al-Khal tells us that he pursued his own independent experiments in complete isolation when he was living in New York between 1948 and 1955.[42]

What is interesting, however, is the close link between these post-war experiments and the conscious reaction against romanticism. Writing about this new form in the periodical *Adab*, Sayyab says that it had arisen to destroy the 'vagueness or dilution of romanticism' and the 'literature of the ivory tower', no less than the stagnation of classicism, as well as the declamatory verse which the political and social poets have been in the habit of writing, and although Nazik al-Mala'ika insisted on more than one occasion that the new form is primarily a prosodic phenomenon, she claimed that one of the main factors that led to its appearance is the tendency towards realism and away from romanticism, because of the greater freedom and simpler diction afforded by the new form.[43] It was no wonder then that this new form, used with or without rhyme, was strongly opposed by the literary establishment, even ironically enough by a former rebel like 'Aqqad,[44] for apart from the general cultural considerations involved in this phenomenon which represented a direct threat to traditional values, romanticism itself had by that time lost its revolutionary zeal and become part of the literary establishment.

An even more extreme form used by some poets does without the principle of prosody altogether; it is either free verse or the prose poem (which, according to one moderate poet, might well become the form of the future).[45] The prose poem *Qaṣīdat al-nathr* which is related to, but not identical with, free verse (in Arabic *shiʿr manthūr*: prose poetry) is a form connected with the names of the Lebanese Unsī al-Ḥājj, whose writings are exclusively in this form, and of Adunis and Yusuf al-Khal who make occasional use of it. Free verse has been in existence in modern Arabic since the beginning of the century and we have seen how Mutran composed an elegy on Ibrahim al-Yaziji in this form. Born under the influence of western poetry, particularly that of Walt Whitman, it was used by Amin Rihani and more successfully by Jibran and Mayy Ziyāda (1895–1941). As the name indicates, free verse does not adhere to any of the traditional metres, nor does it follow any regular pattern whatsoever, though it may heavily rely upon euphony, rhythm, imagery and occasionally rhyme. Ever since the beginning of the century (and particularly during the 1930s when the movement of Arabic translations of European poetry gathered momentum), free verse has been a popular medium particularly with highly westernized Arab intellectuals. In Egypt Muḥammad Munīr Ramzī (1925–1945) (whose works, alas, still remain unpublished) wrote in this form poems of an unusual emotional intensity which reveal an exquisite sensibility of a profoundly romantic nature.[46] For obvious reasons (related partly to the fact that its authors claimed to be writing under the influence of the unconscious mind, partly to a revolt against the Arab heritage) free verse was also used by the writers of surrealist poetry in Egypt, such as Jūrj Ḥunain, and the Syrians Urkhān Muyassar and ʿAli al-Nāsir in their volume *Siryāl* (Aleppo, 1947). Similarly, Albert Adīb (b. 1908), the editor of the well-known Lebanese periodical *al-Adīb* (1942–), published a whole volume of free verse entitled *Liman* (For Whom) in Cairo in 1952. The most significant users of free verse in the postwar period are the Palestinian Jabrā Ibrāhīm Jabrā (b. 1926) (who has been living in Iraq since 1948 and who has exercised a seminal influence on major Iraqi poets such as Sayyab), Taufīq Ṣayigh (1924–1971) and the Syrian Muḥammad al-Māghūṭ (b. 1934). Jabra has published two volumes: *Tammūz in the City* (1959) and *The Closed Circuit* (1964), and Sayigh produced three: *Thirty Poems* (1954), *The Poem K* (1960) and *Taufiq Sayigh Ode* (1963), while al-Maghut has brought out *Grief in Moonlight* (1959), *A Room with a Million Walls* (1964) and *Joy is not My Profession* (1970). It would be pointless to try to give here in translation examples of what these poets were trying to achieve in this respect, though we may later on refer to their work in our discussion of other, non-formal aspects of modern Arabic poetry.[47]

Unlike free verse the prose poem appears on the page as prose, and is generally divided not into lines but paragraphs. Whereas free verse starts from verse, as it were, prose is the starting point of the prose poem. According to its apologists Adunis and al-Hajj (both of whom are indebted to Suzanne Bernard's book *Le Poème en Prose de Baudelaire jusqu'à nos jours* (Paris, 1959), to which they refer in their writings on the subject) the prose poem is the medium best suited to the expression of modern sensibility. In his introduction to his first collection of poems in this form, entitled *Not* (1960), Hajj describes the prose poem as 'the highest point in language to which the poet has so far aspired', pointing out that in French literature, where it 'occupies its natural place', it 'represents the strongest aspect of the poetic revolution which broke out a century ago'. He claims that the only form in which the liberated Arab poet can fully express his modern attitudes is the free form of the prose poem and that the author of the prose poem 'has great need to invent his language continuously'. Hajj's introduction brings out in the clearest but at times rather colourful terms the revolutionary thinking underlying the prose poem experiment. 'The true poet of today', he says, 'cannot possibly be a conservative', and

> Facing this attachment to the official heritage, surrounded by this conflagration of tumultuous forces of reaction prevalent in Arab countries, Arab schools and Arab authors . . . we may ask: Is it possible for any young and tender literary experiment to sustain life? My answer to this question is certainly not. There are in fact only two alternatives open for such an attempt: either suffocation or madness. Through madness the revolutionary triumphs and can make his voice heard. He must stand in the thoroughfare and at the top of his voice swear and curse, pour abuse and proclaim . . . Destruction is the first duty . . . It is vital and sacred.[48]

It is of course significant that the poet chose as a title for his collection the negative particle *Not* (in Arabic: *lan*) which denotes his general attitude of rejection and dissent.

It should be clear by now that what we have been dealing with in this chapter are not purely matters of the external form of verse, but questions intimately related to attitudes taken with varying degrees of consciousness towards traditional Arab society and culture. Leaving formal considerations aside, however, we find that the 'new' or 'modern' poets vary considerably in the degree of their revolt against convention. Some, like Nāzik al-Malā'ika (b. 1923) are basically writing in an extension of romantic sensibility; despite her use of 'new' techniques, she is a conservative at heart, as her book *Questions in Contemporary Poetry* (1962) clearly shows.

In the recent edition of her Collected Works, her two-volume[49] *Diwan* of 1970, Mala'ika published for the first time her long poem *Life's Tragedy* which runs to 1200 lines (in rhyming couplets), written between 1945 and 1946, together with two revised but incomplete versions of the poem composed in the same form of verse in 1950 and in 1965, and entitled respectively *Song for Man I* and *Song for Man II*. The poem, clearly influenced by Abu Madi's 'Riddles' and Taha's 'God and the Poet', is, as Mala'ika herself was aware in the introduction, an extremely romantic work, the title of which indicates the extent of her pessimism and her agonizing sense of life as an overwhelmingly painful riddle. The theme is the poet's quest for happiness, which is occasioned by the sufferings of the Second World War and which drives her to seek it in vain, first in the palaces of the rich, then in the monasteries of the ascetics, the dens of sinners, in the simple life of the shepherd and the peasant, among poets and lovers, until finally the poet finds her rest in the presence of God who, as in the conclusion to Taha's poem, provides the answer. There is nothing in the least unusual or surprising in the young Mala'ika writing such a poem on a theme of this type in the mid 1940s. What is obviously significant and indicative of her apparently permanent romantic cast of mind is that she should later on feel the need to go back to the poem and to revise it at two different periods of her life. As she says in the introduction, comparison between the styles of writing might give the reader an idea of her poetic development. Indeed the diction of the latest version is much less unabashedly romantic than that of the earliest one, although the earliest version would seem to be much more successful because in it the language is more in keeping with a theme that belongs to the heart of the romantic tradition in modern Arabic poetry. Furthermore, the change in the title of the poem from *Life's Tragedy* to *A Song for Man* suggests, as the poet rightly claims, that the extreme pessimism of the earlier poem may have gone. However, if we compare the passages in the earliest and latest versions which attempt to depict the poet, we find that Mala'ika's conception of the poet did not undergo any *fundamental* change from 1945 to 1965. He is still the romantic poet: a visionary, a singer of sweet songs, a lover of beauty, of man and the universe, a person of hypersensitivity, a tragic being and a rebel who endures great suffering 'in the silence of his soul' on account of his awareness of the sufferings of mankind (I,450–5). Perhaps one should not dismiss as altogether irrelevant in this context her remark, written as late as 1970, that the form of the New Verse (which relies not on the symmetrical hemistichs but on the use of an irregular number of feet) is 'unfit for long poems . . . dealing with philosophical ideas and complex and conflicting feelings' (I,18).

Although Mala'ika's first published volume, *The Lover of Night* (1946), shows the unmistakable influence of established romantic poets, in particular Taha, it does contain poems such as the one which lends the collection its title, or 'Sunset' which can be regarded as among the minor contributions of Arabic romantic poetry (I,556ff., 549ff.). Her second collection, *Splinters and Ashes* (1949), is perhaps her most revolutionary work, and at least the introduction in it reveals the poet's dissatisfaction with the limitations of the tradition, in prosody, themes and diction alike. Apart from her experimentation in form, perhaps her most interesting contribution in this volume is her attempt to describe the subtler shades of feeling and the twilight state of consciousness in poems such as 'The Train has Gone' and 'The Snake', poems which she says 'treat states of mind relating sometimes to the inner self, and at other times to the Unconscious, and these are states seldom dwelt on in Arabic poetry' (II,22). Another interesting feature of the collection is the use of allusions to Greek mythology and to a work by Longfellow, *Hiawatha*. But the states of feeling which the poet successfully depicts in her poetry often belong to a romantic experience, expressed in a romantic or post-romantic style. Among the best is 'The Bottom of the Stairs' (II,108), where she writes:

> Days have passed, whose light has been snuffed,
> When we did not meet, not even in imagination,
> While all alone I have been here feeding on the footsteps of the dark
> Outside the cruel window pane, outside the door.
> Days have passed while all alone I have been here,
> Cold days creeping, dragging along my suspecting impatience,
> And I have listened and counted the anxious minutes.
> Was it time that has passed or have we been wading through timelessness?
> Days have passed, made heavy with my longings,
> And I? I am still gazing at the stairs,
> The stairs that begin here, but I know not where they end?
> They begin here in my heart where it is all dark,
> But where is the door, the shadowy door
> At the bottom of the stairs?

In the two succeeding volumes, *The Bottom of the Wave* (1957) and *The Moon Tree* (1968), Mala'ika has not gone much further than this experience. For instance, in 'The Fugitives' the poet tries in vain to escape from herself and from her painful feeling of being an outsider in the universe (II,302), while in 'The Visitor who Has not Come' (II,329) she clearly prefers her dreams to reality. There are a handful of political poems in her work, but nature and nature descriptions dominate her poetry, especially in the last volume where we also find her romantic sense of suffering driving her to write the moving but rather masochistic 'Five Songs to Suffering' (II,458) in which she expresses her love for pain (II,460), saying:

> At dawn in our sleep we have crowned you a god
> And wiped our foreheads on your silver altar,
> Our love, our pain. (II,466)

Unlike al-Mala'ika, other poets, such as some members of the *Shi'r* group, are extreme revolutionaries who wish to cut themselves off from Arabic literary conventions and align themselves with the cause of contemporary poetry in the West. This is true, for instance, of Adunis and more particularly Unsi al-Hajj, whose rejection of Arab traditional values is, at least in theory, absolute, with the result that they came to be known as the poets of rejection or dissent (*shu'arā' al-rafḍ*). Those who fell under French Symbolist and Surrealist influence (notably Adunis) have formed a view of poetry which has metaphysical and mystical implications, a view which in the case of Adunis has been translated into practice, resulting sometimes in poems of a rare and haunting kind of beauty. Others on whom the influence of modern poetry in English, particularly that of Eliot, is apparent (like al-Khal, Khalīl Ḥāwī and al-Sayyab) have resorted to the use of aside, interior monologue and mythology, allusions to popular songs and beliefs, and occasional use of colloquialisms. But the two influences have not been kept separate in the writings of these poets, and each group has learnt something from the techniques of the other. After all, Adunis translated Eliot and Sayyab Aragon. And perhaps the most important common feature of the New Poetry is its syntax and its peculiar use of imagery. This is the feature that links it to contemporary western poetry. The modern Arabic poet, whether he is a Marxist or an existentialist, deliberately avoids the language of statement: in this he has learnt from the experience of romanticism, which relies upon the evocative power of words, but he has gone a step further in resorting to an oblique style, to imagery as a means of objectifying his emotional experience. In thinking in imagery, as it were, he sometimes transcends logic, and it is often the absence of logical relationships, and all explicit connections that makes the syntax of this poetry as difficult as in the case of the most obscure modern western poetry. Bayyati was absolutely right when he wrote in 1968: 'Innovation in poetry is not so much a rebellion against metres, prosody and rhyme, as some seemed to think, as it is a revolution in expression' (*Diwan* II,411).

Adunis and the New Poetry

The most articulate and sophisticated apologist for the New Poetry is undoubtedly Adūnīs ('Alī Aḥmad Sa'īd), who was born in a little Syrian village near Latakia in 1930, but who has enjoyed Lebanese nationality for many years. Adunis graduated in philosophy from the Syrian University in 1954, but in 1956 he left Syria where he had been engaged in hectic political activity in connection with the Syrian Nationalist Party at a time when most Syrian students belonged either to it or to the Communist Party. His revolutionary political activity at one point landed him in jail, a thing which occasioned some poetry of violent social and political protest against the authorities. He then fled to Beirut where he has been living ever since, except for one year (1960) which he spent in Paris, studying at the Sorbonne at the expense of the French government. Adunis has published several volumes of verse: *Delilah* (1950), *The Earth has Said* (1952, then 1954), *First Poems* (1957), *If I say, Syria* (1958), *Leaves in the Wind* (1958), *Songs of Mihyar the Damascene* (1961), *The Book of Metamorphosis and Migration in the Regions of Day and Night* (1965), *The Stage and the Mirrors* (1968), *A Time between Ashes and Roses* (1970) and most recently *A Tomb for New York* (1971): an edition of his *Complete Works* (from which some of the early poems have been deliberately omitted) appeared in 1971. At least in his earlier period, Adunis shows himself to be a meticulous craftsman who continually revises his poetry, generally shortening it, making it tighter, and getting rid of the more explicit statements and of many poems of political and social criticism which are of a more direct nature, especially his severe attacks on Syrian authorities for jailing him and his wholesale condemnation of Syrian and Arab society.

Adunis's pronouncements on contemporary Arabic poetry have recently been collected and published in one volume (in 1972) under the title *The Time for Poetry.*[50] They include several articles, papers read at various conferences, as well as letters sent to other Lebanese poets, and cover the period from 1959 to 1971. They show a remarkable degree of consistency, integrity and seriousness, indicating a mind of great subtlety and originality, and a prose style which is at once sensitive and clear, and a gift for making challenging and provocative statements. There is not the space here to discuss all the main ideas in that book, but some of these ideas, particularly in the first essay, are immediately relevant since they provide the best comment on the work of not only the most influential single figure in Arabic poetry today, but also of some of the *Shiʿr* poets.

The essay is given the significant title (borrowed from the French poet René Char) 'Exploring a World Constantly in Need of Exploration', but was first published in *Shiʿr* magazine in 1959 under the title 'An Attempt to Define the New Poetry'. Drawing upon such French writers as René Char, André Malraux, Rimbaud and Baudelaire to support his argument, Adunis begins his essay with these words:

> Perhaps the best way to define New Poetry is to say that it is a vision. By its nature a vision is a jump outside the present concepts. It is therefore a change in the order of things and in the way of looking at them. Thus at first glance New Poetry appears to be a rebellion against the forms and methods of old poetry, a rejection of its attitudes and styles which have outlived their usefulness (p. 9).

New Poetry expresses the eternal anxiety of man, the existential problems which the poet experiences in his civilization, in his nation and inside himself:

> It therefore issues from a metaphysical sensibility which feels things in a revelatory manner suitable to their essence and true nature for these cannot be apprehended by reason and logic but by imagination and dreams. From this point of view New Poetry is the metaphysics of human existence (p. 10).

Not even the romantics whose view of poetry was serious enough made such large claims for poetry as these. Because of its metaphysical preoccupations New Poetry dismisses what is purely accidental, and rises above realism, which in Adunis's words brings poetry closer to ordinary prose in which 'words are used in their familiar sense' and is therefore contrary to the function of true poetry which 'empties words of their old and opaque weight and charges them with a new and unaccustomed significance'. Adunis deplores the limitations of most modern Arabic poetry which attempts to do no more than express the personal feelings or psychological problems of the poet, whereas the New poet aims at expressing feelings which are at once subjective and objective, personal and universal (pp. 12–13).

Because it is 'a vision and a revelation' New. Poetry is 'obscure, hesitant and illogical. It is therefore inevitable that it rises above formal requirements because it needs greater freedom, greater mystery and prophecy' (p. 15). The music of New Poetry arises not from 'a harmony between external parts and formal patterns', as we find in traditional metres, but from 'an inner harmony'. 'The poet is not a person who has something to express but the one 'who creates his things in a new way' (p. 19). If New Poetry goes beyond phenomena and is an immediate apprehension of inner truth, words must be deflected from their ordinary sense which can only lead to a familiar common vision: in New Poetry language is 'made to say what it has not been taught to say', and in this case poetry becomes a rebellion against language. New Poetry is 'a kind of magic'. New Poetry reveals our modern life, in its absurdity and dislocation: hence the absence of logical sequence and comparisons, the occurrence of apparently pointless imagery, the merging of images and symbols into one another. 'The truth is that it is not necessary to fully understand poetry in order to enjoy it' (p. 24).

These statements amply illustrate the profound influence of modern French poetry and thinking about poetry on Adunis, but they do not bring out clearly enough the full extent of his passionate concern for the cause of contemporary Arab society and culture. The social and cultural implications of his New Poetry, and of his views on poetry – which we may remind ourselves were regarded as applicable to the whole movement of New Poetry associated with *Shi'r* magazine (p. 8) – can be seen in the text of a most interesting lecture he gave at a conference on Modern Arabic literature held in Rome in 1961, entitled 'Arabic Poetry and the Problems of Innovation' (pp. 30ff.). After a brief historical introduction in which he sketches out previous attempts at innovation in Arabic poetry, Adunis sets out the three principles on which the New movement is based, namely a radical rebellion against traditional mentality, a rejection of the old Arab conception of poetry which regards poetry as something static and as no more than emotion and craftsmanship, and a rejection of the view that ancient Arabic poetry is a model to be imitated by all subsequent poetry, or that it is an autonomous and self-sufficient world independent of all the poetic heritage in other languages. He then discusses the novelty of New Poetry on three levels: artistic form, language and civilization. On the last point he says: 'In order that the New Arab poet may liberate himself from these static values in poetry and language it is necessary for him to free himself also from these values in the whole of Arab culture.' Adunis believes that this lack of change in poetry and language is probably due to the religious nature of Arab culture, which stresses 'obedience not freedom, learning not discovery'. He laments the fact that it is still difficult for an individual to question the fundamentals of religion or to deny the existence of God in the way Nietzsche has done in the West. Yet:

> It is essential for the modern Arab poet . . . to reject the static values in his ancient poetic heritage and in his cultural heritage generally in order that he may be able to create poetry that reaches the standard of the civilizational movement in which he lives. Just as he should not see any ultimate value in his own poetic heritage, he should likewise learn to view his cultural heritage. In this way, the Arab heritage, poetry and culture alike, becomes part of human civilization. . . . Thus the contemporary Arab poet will not seek his sustenance in the sources of his Arab heritage alone, but in the totality of human civilization.

On the need for radical cultural change Adunis is emphatic: 'It is impossible for the poet to write New Poetry unless he himself has changed inwardly and has lived a new experience'. (pp. 47–51). Adunis has remained committed to the cause of reviving Arab culture, as is clearly shown in the last document published in his collection of essays, his letter to Yusuf al-Khal dated 20 December 1971: 'Arab existence and Arab destiny', he writes, 'constitute my reality, not only as a poet, but as a man . . . We have no identity outside the Arab identity' (p. 286). His feeling of responsibility towards Arab culture is enhanced by his conviction that Arab life at present has sunk to its lowest ebb since the fall of Baghdad at the hands of Hulagu.

Adunis's commitment, however, differs radically from the political commitment of, for instance, Marxist poets. In 1967 he wrote:

> The poetry that aspires to nothing more than serving the Revolution and describing its aims and achievements in an optimistic spirit, at times to the point of naiveté, is a poetry that in the end betrays the spirit and meaning of Freedom and the Revolution.

For by its nature the Revolution is constantly in need of reexamination and renewal, lest it should become frozen into institutions and achievements, and it can be renewed only by 'a creative critical force which will give it another dimension or a further impetus', by

> creativity and freedom, the spirit of questioning, inquiry and progress, by poetry which is constantly beginning afresh, constantly moving, arousing and suggesting. By definition the poet is a revolutionary . . . he can only be on the side of change (pp. 116–17).

In 1969, in an important address to the Soviet Writers' Association, he said:

> The role of the poet is to replace the language spoken by present society with a revolutionary language. For the present language, like present society, is something inherited: they both belong to a bygone age and must be superçeded (pp. 179–80).

And again in 1970 he says, 'It is impossible to create a revolutionary Arab culture except by means of a revolutionary language' (p. 199).

The progress of Adunis the poet can fairly be described as the story of his attempt to create this revolutionary language: it is a journey from the poetry of direct social and political protest to that which suggests more than it states, and sees a deeper significance in phenomena, a hidden meaning behind the form linking it to mysticism and surrealism.[51] The revolutionary stand which he adopted in the 1950s, when together with Yusuf al-Khal he edited *Shi'r* magazine (1957), he came to regard as not sufficiently revolutionary in the 1960s and he dissociated himself from the magazine. In his own *avant-garde* magazine *Mawāqif* (1969) he claims that his intention is both to complement and supersede *Shi'r* in the sense that the aim is now not simply to establish the new *poem*, but a new *writing* altogether, which is an exploration of the unknown, in which the emphasis is on total originality and creativity, and traditional distinctions between literary forms like poetry, drama and narrative disappear.[52] How far he has succeeded in this unrealistically ambitious objective of creating metapoetry and metalanguage is very doubtful. What is beyond doubt, however, is the enormous influence his 'surrealistic' style has had on younger poets throughout the Arab world, sometimes with happy results as we can see for instance in the interesting work of the Egyptian poet Muḥammad 'Afīfī Maṭar (b.1935).[53] But that the results can at times be disastrous can be readily admitted by any impartial reader of the many effusions published in his journal *Mawaqif*. As we have seen, not even a major poet like Bayyati has escaped this influence.

In Adunis's early poetry such as *The Earth Has Said* the revolutionary content is clear: the poet urges the young to rise against the established stagnant order. It is full of optimism and contains many direct statements, although the obvious interest in natural phenomena and the sensitive handling of the language, together with the occasional originality of imagery, point to the later symbolist poet of *First Poems*. It is here, in this later volume, and not in the work of Bishr Fāris (d. 1963) or even of Sa'id 'Aql, who is generally regarded as the first major symbolist poet, that we find Arabic symbolist poetry of a very high order. Consider this brief poem: 'The Frontiers of Despair':

On the frontiers of despair my house stands,
Its walls like yellow foam,
Hollow and disjoined like clouds,
My house is lattice work of dough.
My house consists of holes.

It is shaken by the wind until the wind grows tired,
And is then relieved by the gale.
My house is deserted by the sun, despite its nearness;
It is deserted even by sparrows.

My house has been turned by its convulsions
Into something invisible, transcendental,
Fixed beyond the invisible world.
In it I sleep and around me the world
Lies asleep, with voice muted and choked. (I,24)

Here the complexity of structure is such that the purely subjective elements of the experience are completely fused with the impersonal comment. It is difficult to discard the symbol altogether once we have arrived at what we regard as the meaning, for the symbol itself has become an essential part of the meaning.

The poet's passionate concern for his generation is no less obvious in the next volume *Leaves in the Wind*, for instance in the poem that bears this title and particularly in the powerful poem 'Emptiness' (I,227,241) written in Damascus in 1954 when Adunis was engaged in political action. According to the poet, it is 'Emptiness' which drew Yusuf al-Khal's attention to Adunis: in it we find a diagnosis of the ailments of modern Arab society in mercilessly frank terms, but also at the same time the hope for the revolution to be led by the poet and his generation, expressed in bold and effective language. One of the most bitter satires on modern Arab society, it is also one of Adunis's most optimistic poems: the poet is confident that Phoenix-like Arab society will renew itself.

In *Songs of Mihyār the Damascene* Adunis adopts the mask or persona of Mihyār, the medieval Arab poet, to express his feelings and attitudes to reality, political, social and psychological. But Mihyar is identified with other figures from Greek and biblical and Koranic mythology, such as Noah who survives the Flood and destruction of the world to rebuild another better one, or Shaddād ibn 'Ād who created a world of great architectural beauty and splendour, or Ulysses the eternal wanderer, the symbol of restless man in an endless quest. The poet is mystically aware of a deeper truth behind the world of appearances and the distinctions between good and evil, and he gives expression to a twilight state of consciousness where man and God are one, a pantheistic experience marked by its fluidity and dream-like quality. Despite the growing mysticism and inwardness in this volume, Adunis is tragically concerned about the future of his society and of Arab culture. He can write a poem charged with mystical feeling like 'I Said to You':

> I said to you I have listened to the seas
> Reciting their poetry to me, I have listened
> To the music that lies dormant in shells.
> I said to you I have sung
> At the devil's wedding, at the banquet of fables.
> I said to you I have seen
> In the rain of history, in the blaze of distance
> A fairy and a mansion.
> Because my sea journeys take place in my eye
> I said to you I was able to see all
> At the very first step I took. (I,388)

He can also write 'You Have No Choice' which is a metaphysical as well as a cultural comment:

> What? You will then have to destroy the face
> Of the earth and form another.
>
> What? You will then have no choice
> Other than the path of fire
> Other than the hell of denial –
>
> When the earth becomes
> A dumb guillotine or a god. (I,431)

or 'The Little Times' which similarly operates on two levels (I,481), or the even more complex 'Homeland':

To the faces that harden behind a mask of gloom
I bow, and to streets where I left behind my tears,
To a father who died, green as a cloud
With a sail on his face, I bow,
And to a child that is sold
In order to pray and be a bootblack
(In our land we all pray and are bootblacks).
To a stone I inscribed with my hunger
Saying it was lightning and rain, drops rolling under my eyelids,
And to a house whose dust I carried with me in my loss
I bow – all these are my homeland, not Damascus. (I,453)

While prose poetry is used very sparingly indeed in *Songs of Mihyar* (only in the so-called psalms introducing the sections of the collection and in the last section where it is interwoven with the new and freer form of verse), in *The Book of Metamorphosis and Migration in the Regions of Day and Night* (1965) very large sections are written in prose poetry. Here Adunis's mystical pantheistic experience grows in depth, and the fluidity of the universe, the Heraclitus-like vision, is more pronounced as the poet portrays a world in which things become their opposites. As the poet's wife, the distinguished critic Khālida Sa'īd, says in a statement quoted on the dustjacket of the first edition, 'This is the poetry of a journey in the continents of the interior where the self is in a constant mystical night journey moving to and fro between the regions of the body and those of the soul.' Yet, although Adunis even here does not lose sight of his people and their plight (see, for instance, his passionate lines on Damascus (II,52–3)), there is no doubt that he is now moving to a much more solipsistic universe and that his language is becoming increasingly obscure. Here is a short poem which may give the reader some idea of the original, 'The Tree of Fire':

A family of leaves,
Sitting beside a water spring,
Wound this earth of tears,
Reading aloud to the water from the book of fire.

My family did not wait for my coming,
They went, and now there is
Neither trace nor fire. (II,18)

Clearly, after *Songs of Mihyar*, which represents the peak of his poetic creativity, Adunis's poetry has become increasingly cerebral.

In *The Stage and the Mirrors* the form is much freer: it even contains brief dramatic scenes. Here Adunis seems to be more interested in external issues such as the relation between the poet and the powers-that-be. For instance, 'Taimur and Mihyar' deals with the problem of the poet versus authority. In the story around which the poem is built, which shows how Mihyar, after being put to death and dismembered by the orders of Taimur (Tamburlaine), returns to life in order to plague the despot, we clearly see the martyr or Chirst-like figure of Mihyar, the poet, into whose conception elements from the myth of Adonis have entered. Likewise, episodes and characters from early Islamic history are used to indicate the relation between the artist and authority: for instance, Hajjāj, the bloodthirsty Umayyad governor of Kufa, is the tyrant while the martyr al-Husain is the Christ-like poet. Some of the dramatic scenes are striking: for instance in 'A Woman's Funeral' (II,279) the ritual burning of a woman sacrifice is rendered in poetry of strange and uncanny beauty.

The Stage and the Mirrors touches again upon the poet's primary concern, for instance, in these lines from 'The Mirror of the Earth':

> That which persistently haunts my heart
> Uproots palm-trees, domes and bells,
> Strikes the face of the earth,
> That dissenting blood, that dissent
> Is but another yearning, another flame
> In the name of the rising tomorrow, in the name of the earth. (II,362)

In the final poem in the volume, in which he makes a complete identification between himself and his people, the poet poses the question:

> How do I walk towards myself, towards my people
> While there is fire in my blood and my history is a heap of ruins?

Then he says:

> Histories are mirrors
> Civilizations are mirrors
> They are all breaking . . .
> I can hear voices singing in my ashes
> I can see them walking like the children of my country. (II,575)

He wishes his song to be 'like the edge of a knife, wounding the cold city with its hoarseness and weeping' (II,555). This is not the voice of despair: even though the poet confidently prophesies the rise of 'the sun that loves to destroy and annihilate', the annihilation is not final, but it is essential for the present order to die before another is born (II,563–4).

The next volume, significantly called *Time Between Ashes and Roses* (1970), contains a poem entitled 'Prolegomenon to the History of Kings of Petty States' (1970), described as a greeting to Nasser, 'the first modern Arab leader who worked towards ending the age of Kings of Petty States and beginning the new age' (II,581). Much of the poetry is very obscure, but in a poem such as 'This is My Name' (1969) we can detect what is in effect a lament for Arab defeat:[54]

> I have said this broken jar
> Is a defeated nation . . . (II,631)

Elsewhere in the poem he says, 'We rave, I rave so that I may die well', and at one point, in anguish:

> I try to spell and draw a star,
> Fleeing from my country in my country,
> I try to spell and draw a star,
> In the wake of its defeated days.
> O ashes of the word,
> Is there a child in store for my history in your night?
> ONLY MADNESS REMAINS (II,642)

It seems that here the poet evinces a desperate and extreme reaction to the Arab tragedy. For to bring about a rebirth everything has to be changed, including the basic rules of logic and sanity. Hence the incomprehensible and illogical language of Adunis's poetry. It is a sad irony that a poet who is motivated by an overwhelming desire to change Arab reality and recreate Arab society should, by the very means he adopts towards that end, namely to recreate the Arabic language, simply end in such solipsism.

One of Adunis's most recent works to date is entitled *A Tomb for New York* (1971). In it we read:

> New York, a woman, the statue of a woman holding in one hand a rag called liberty by paper we call history and with the other hand strangling a child called the Earth (II,647).

Here in prose poetry revealing obvious biblical influences in rhythm and structure of sentence, the poet gives expression to his political preoccupations, recording, among other things his response to the horrors of New York and of American civilization, with its dehumanizing features, especially the brutalities of American foreign policy in Vietnam and the Middle East. Towards the end of the work the poet asserts his absolute freedom from all rules:

> Thus I end all rules and for each moment I make up its rule. Thus I approach, but do not go, and when I go I do not return (II,671).

It may be wondered whether this last stage of Adunis's development is not in fact a dead end, which if universally followed could spell the end of all Arabic poetry. In any case, many of his young admirers have produced modish works which are no less ephemeral than the psychedelic popcrete/concrete verse of which the present Oxford Professor of Poetry has recently complained in his Inaugural lecture, 'Alternative Poetry' (printed in *Encounter*, June 1974).

Khal and Hawi

Of the major figures connected at some time or other with *Shi'r* magazine only three will be briefly discussed here: the Lebanese Yusuf al-Khal, Khalil Hawi and the Iraqi Badr Shakir al-Sayyab, none of whom is as extreme in his approach to the language of poetry as Adunis has become, although ironically enough at the start of the *Shi'r* venture Yusuf al-Khal was considered by the most enthusiastic and sympathetic critic of New Poetry to be 'the most extremist of the innovators because he is the one whose aims were clearest'.[55]

Yūsuf al-Khāl (b.1917), a graduate of the American University of Beirut, where he studied philosophy and English, left Beirut for America in 1948 to work first in New York for UNO, then in his own export business, while at the same time editing the Arabic *Mahjari* paper *al-Hudā*, which because of Khal's Protestant religion was, according to him, opposed by the Maronites and strongly criticized by Abu Madi in *al-Samir*. After a spell in Libya on a United Nations mission Khal returned to Beirut, where he worked for a very brief period in journalism, then as a research assistant at the American University. It was then that the project of *Shi'r* was conceived. He gathered a number of young people around him and was joined by Adunis when the latter heard about the project. The magazine was set up in 1957 and continued to appear until 1964, and was resuscitated (for a relatively short time) in 1967. It was the rallying ground for most of the *avant-garde* poets in the Arab world (for instance, the first volume published Khalil Hawi's well-known poem 'River of Ashes'), and played a role in the development of Arabic poetry similar to that of Abu Shadi's *Apollo* during the 1930s, a role shared by the other great Beirut magazine, Suhail Idris's *al-Adab*. In 1961 he set up another literary magazine, *Adab*, which had to close down two years later. Concurrently with editing *Shi'r*, Khal ran a publishing firm which brought out a large number of volumes of verse by the most experimental of Arab poets and which, not surprisingly perhaps, eventually went bankrupt. He also owned a modern art gallery (Gallery One) in which for many years he and other *avant-garde* poets and writers had their lively weekly meetings. The poets included Unsi al-Hajj, Shauqī Abi-Shaqra, Fu'ād Rifqa, 'Iṣām Mahfūz and Taufiq Sayigh, men of widely varying talents, but their sessions contributed towards the lively literary atmosphere of Beirut during the 1950s and 1960s.

Khal began as a follower of Sa'id 'Aql who was known to be the leading symbolist poet in Lebanon. His first two volumes, *Liberty* (1945) and *Herodia* (a verse drama published in New York in 1954), do not show many signs of the poet Khal was to become a few years later.[56] In America Khal came to know the poetry of Pound and Eliot and younger poets of the English-speaking world. In fact later – in 1958 – he published an anthology of his translations from poets ranging from Emerson, Longfellow, Poe, Thoreau and Whitman to Emily Dickinson, Hilde Doolittle, Wallace Stevens, E. E. Cummings, William Carlos Williams, Marianne Moore, John Crow Ransom, Auden and Robert Lowell among others, as well as a translation of *The Waste Land* (done jointly with Adunis in 1958) and a selection of Robert Frost (in 1962). It was partly his readings in modern English and American poetry that turned Khal away from the rarefied atmosphere of ʻAql's cold craftsmanship. Khal published at least two volumes of verse in the new style: *The Forsaken Well* (1958) and *Poems at the Age of Forty* (1960). There is also his *Selected Poems*, selected and introduced by Adunis (1965 [?]), which contains some of the poems not included in the two earlier volumes.

In the first poem in *The Forsaken Well*, 'To Ezra Pound' (p. 9), two things at once become clear: first, Khal's poetic ideal, derived from the work of contemporary English poets, and secondly, the conception that the poet is a Christ-like figure, who not only brings life, but also has to make the ultimate sacrifice towards that end, namely crucifixion. The conception is further enforced in the second poem, entitled 'The Poet':

> Crucified, I bleed while my hands touch the heavens
> But tomorrow I rise from my grave . . . (pp. 11–13)

The Christian image is not merely a myth whose primary function is to organize Khal's poems; like Taufiq Sayigh's impressive 'free verse' Khal's poetry is in many ways religious and specifically Christian poetry: in a recent interview fully reported in *Mawaqif* (June 1971), he explicitly and proudly asserted his Christianity, and Adunis once described his poetry as 'the first Christian experience in the purely metaphysical sense in Arabic poetry'.[57] Furthermore, like other contemporary Arab poets what occupies his mind is not simply the question of breathing life into what seemed to him to be stagnant and dead poetry. Poetry is only one of many symptoms of what appears to be a dying culture, and Khal is concerned with the whole Arab culture and society. He opens a poem by asking:

> Will the morning arise or will the end of day
> Die with us? Our faces are deserts
> Trampled over by barrenness. (p. 20)

In 'The Loss' (pp. 22–4) he writes ironically about the prevalent attitude in his society of seeking refuge and comfort in the distant past instead of facing courageously and constructively the grim reality of the present. In 'The Black House' (p. 32) the only thing the poet is capable of is prayer:

> My black house is full of bones
> From which the light of day has fled.
> Who will bury them, so that one day
> They may come back to life,
> Pushing aside the rock?

The poet has no energy to bury them, and he can only pray.

Khal's best-known poem is that which gives the volume its title, 'The Forsaken Well' (pp. 36ff.). Superficially, it is the story of the poet's neighbour and old friend Ibrahim, an ordinary man in the eyes of the world which is not aware of his existence, but whose belief that his death might bring about peace and plenty, remove injustice and put an end to evil and misery on the earth, prompts him to walk straight into the enemy fire, totally deaf to the warning and the advice given to him to seek safe refuge in a nearby shelter. The verdict of the world is that he was simply mad, but the poet knows otherwise. The poem is clearly a modern variation on the theme of crucifixion, and it emphasizes the need for the deliberate act of self-sacrifice to revive society. Ibrahim is the poet and the man of vision who in the pursuit of his ideal runs counter to self-interest, with the result that he is taken by lesser mortals, men of cruder substance, to be mad. However, by making Ibrahim an ordinary man in a sense, the poet asserts his hope in the salvation of his culture: we only have to turn to the well we have forsaken, the inner spiritual depths within each of us; it is an arduous process demanding nothing less than total self-abnegation, but, nevertheless, it is possible. The same theme is treated in 'Memento Mori' where the need for self-sacrifice is further emphasized (p. 52).

The water image is not accidental in 'The Forsaken Well'; it is part of the contrast between water and desert, life and death, which is to be found in the work of Khal just as much as in that of Adunis, Hawi and Sayyab, and which plainly has an ultimately religious (and anthropological) significance.

But there is another symbol in Khal's poetry, namely the sea, which stands for the spirit of adventure, the passion for the unknown, the metaphysical quest so essential to the rebirth of the Arabs. This comes out very clearly in the poem 'The Call of the Sea' (pp. 65–78) which consists of three parts: 'The Prayer', 'The Journey' and 'The Return'. In 'The Prayer' he urges his soul 'to tear off the black veils, to look out on the new and rebel'. In 'The Journey' we read that the narrator and his companions are the adventurous few who gave up the comfort of their homes in search of heroic ideals. By the use of terms such as Halleluja and the mention of sacrifice to Astarte, Adonis, and Baal, the journey is given a religious, sacramental and spiritual significance. 'The

Return' is a song of hope in which the glorious return of the hero is anticipated and his achievements celebrated.

Khal's next volume, *Poems at the Age of Forty*, contains several poems of fulfilment rather than of yearning. The spiritual experience which is regarded as the means of salvation is to some extent lived in a poem such as the attractive 'A Poet's Wish' (p. 30), which is at one and the same time a poem about love, God and poetry: the love between man and woman, physical love, is sacramental and sanctified. Such love brings man closer to God and makes the poet's song appeal to the Heavens. The poet's wish is

> Lord, when you take me back to your bosom
> And wipe out my sin,
> Bring me back my beloved alone
> So that what I say will be a song
> Which the Heavens would be pleased to hear.

Likewise, in 'Prayer at an Altar' (p. 36) we have a love poem celebrating sexual pleasure, which is also a religious and devotional piece of writing, full of biblical overtones, a prose poem (one of many in this volume), in which he says 'My beloved is with me, My body is with me. God is with me. Get up Fate and let me take your place.' The poet's beloved is 'a god whose paradise is free from sin', and yet although he says 'On your body runs my boat, its oars are endless desire' he also writes 'My body recedes from me, it departs like a stranger, an unknown knight whom I have not seen before.'

In the introduction to his selection of Khal's poems, Adunis writes, in a relatively less opaque sentence than the rest of the introduction, that 'it is the poet's belief in an ultimate truth which makes his poetry in the end dominated by a sense of the presence of the world and satisfaction with it'. This presence, however, he adds, 'is not horizontal but vertical, it gives man a dimension not so much social as metaphysical' (p. 13). Khal's vision of the world is a hopeful Christian vision, for despite the many images of suffering in his poetry there is the promise that there is that which transcends death. The final answer, it must be emphasized, does not lead to facile optimism. On the contrary, even if it is true, as Adunis claims, that in Khal's experience time is not regarded as the enemy of life, its passage is not the less poignantly felt, a thing amply illustrated in the poem entitled '[Old] Age',[58] which ends thus:

> We wipe off the frosty wave
> And tell it the story of all the seasons of the year.
> Yet it sinks deep into our veins and is gone,
> Or we think it is gone,
> For it suddenly appears
> Here in a hair turned grey,
> Or a lip that wants food.

But Khal does not lose interest in the wider issues of Arab culture, as is clearly shown in his poem 'The Departure' or 'The Long Poem'[59] (a prose poem) in which he denounces in the manner of an Old Testament prophet contemporary society with its artificiality, lack of authenticity, its death and stagnation, mediocrity and false values, and paints a horrifying and vivid picture of it in a series of powerful images rendered in a style that is biblical in its rhythm and associations: he complains bitterly that 'mountains move every day while there is no faith in the homes, the new is a breast that is not yet round'; 'Eyes are eaten by flies in the city of the Lord', 'our women's thighs are displayed on the pavement, their breasts are sold in shops and their lips are neon signs'. It ends with the prophecy: 'The last days are at hand, their hours are counted on the fingers. Defeat is a raised banner, labour pains are burning seas. Give us a sign O Lord'. Lately, Khal bas become increasingly dissatisfied with the limitations of literary Arabic – the language of writing as opposed to the spoken language – and has been advocating the use of the language of speech for serious literary purposes such as the writing of poetry.

Equally concerned about the position of Arab culture in the context of the modern world is Khalīl Ḥāwī (b.1925) who, like Khal and Taufiq Sayigh, also uses dominantly Christian symbolism which seems to express a specifically Christian sensibility and outlook although he claims that he uses Christian symbols not for their doctrinal content, but for their universal significance as archetypal images. However, as an epigraph to his first volume of verse *The River of Ashes*, he uses these words from his poem 'The Bridge', dedicated to the rising generation:

> They will cross the bridge nimbly in the morning,
> A firm bridge wrought with my ribs,
> From the caves and the marshes of the East
> To another East that is new.

which embody the conception of the poet as the Redeemer whose sacrifice will save his people and take his society out of the stagnant marshes of the Arab East and lead them to the new East.

Hawi is a graduate in philosophy and Arabic from the American University of Beirut where he took his M.A. on a thesis in Islamic philosophy dealing with the question of reason and faith in Ghazāli and Averroes from a Kantian point of view. For his doctorate he went to Cambridge (1956) where he wrote a thesis on Jibran (published later as *Gibran Khalil Gibran, His Background, Character and Works*, Beirut 1963), and deepened his knowledge of English literature, which he acquired as a student in Beirut, reading, together with the French Romantics, Baudelaire and Saint-John Perse, Shakespeare, the English Romantics, Yeats and Eliot. Among the formative influences in his poetry are the *Mahjar* writers and Abu Shabaka. In many ways, stylistically Hawi is a modern development of Abu Shabaka: both poets are masters of rhetoric. Hawi has published three volumes of verse:[60] *The River of Ashes* (1957), *The Flute and the Wind* (1961), and *The Threshing Floor of Hunger* (1965).

It is not surprising for someone who was preoccupied with the problem of reason and faith to write a poem like 'The Mariner and the Dervish' with which *The River of Ashes* opens and which is one of the best known of Hawi's poems.[61] The poem seems to concern the question of the poet's choice between two ideals: science or reason and mysticism. The mariner who is western man (Ulysses/Faust/Huxley) or the poet who has followed in their footsteps, is disenchanted with science, rationality and the spirit of inquiry, with the humanist ideal as well as heroism, and therefore goes to the ideal of mysticism in the hope that it will provide the answer, but he finds mysticism no more satisfactory than rationality, and the poem ends with the disillusioned mariner saying that he will be saved by neither 'heroic deeds' nor 'the humility of prayer', (pp. 30–1).

Although the problem appears to be a personal one, relating to the poet's own salvation, it is significant that the conflict between science and mysticism or dynamism and stillness takes the form of a polarization of East versus West: a less crude version of the popular opposition between the spirituality of the East and the scientific materialism of the West. There is no doubt that the poet's failure to identify himself with either science or mysticism, with either the dynamic West or the stagnant East, his disillusionment and his loss of clear objectives and the blotting-out of the lighthouses on the way have more than just a personal relevance: they are a reflection of the position of the poet as a modern Arab intellectual. The rest of the poems in the first volume bear out the truth of this remark. In fact all the thirteen poems in this volume, we are told by the poet at the end, are not intended to be entirely independent poems but sections or cantos of one long poem: it is worth noting that they are all written in one metre, though in the new free form in which an irregular number of feet is used. To be properly understood, the experience of the first poem or canto must therefore be seen in relation to the rest of the volume.

In the second poem 'The Nights of Beirut', the poet (in whose eyes the light has died) is unable to face the overwhelming monster of tedium:

> In the nights of tedium and loss,
> Where the wind echoes through the labyrinthine streets,
> Who can give us the strength to bear the cross?

Who can protect us from the boredom of the desert?
Drive away that fearful monster;
When from the cave of sunset it crawls out,
Wrapping up the diseased street and the gloomy neighbourhood? (p. 32)

The poet is scared of the visions and nightmares of the night, and he has not sufficient courage to face the feeling of his insignificance during the day. His hell being in his blood, he cannot escape. He has lost his belief in a forthcoming paradise and his life cannot be given a meaning either by the pursuit of wealth or by indulgence in vice or physical pleasures. In 'The Coffin of the Drunkards' we meet the poet, together with other 'victims of accursed boredom', in a brothel: they are all drunk in a futile attempt to run away from themselves and he is railing at a prostitute who is singing of real love and chastity, in a manner reminiscent of the early Abu Shabaka, author of *The Serpents of Paradise*. Then we get a glimpse of the poet's state of mind in 'Cold Hell' when he wishes that 'this cold paralyzed being [i.e. himself] would either live or die', since black visions have turned him into an embittered, cold and hateful creature, whose 'senses have become worn out', whose nerves are now like 'cobweb threads' and whose home reeks of the smell of a tomb. In 'Without Address' there is nothing to look forward to but 'cold, hunger and madness', and all that he knows, he says in the section entitled 'Inside the Whale', is that he is 'dying, an insignificant morsel in the belly of a whale', and all that he remembers about his life in the past is that it has been a cave in which spiders crawl and bats fly. 'Laughter and Children' records how he no longer succumbs to the temptation to flee from his prison or to indulge in the idle hope of being pardoned, since in his heart time has now 'rusted'; he has become absorbed by the darkness of his prison, his eyelids eaten away by dust, this limbs have disintegrated into rotted flesh and bones scattered by rats' feet. In 'Sodom' is a clear indication that the whole of the poet's society is dead (p. 63). In the following section, entitled 'The Magi in Europe', there is a merciless satire on the poet's people, particularly in these lines so memorable in Arabic:

We are from Beirut, alas, we were born
With borrowed faces and with borrowed minds.
Our thoughts are born whores in the market places,
Then spend their lives pretending to be virgins. (p. 67)

In the tenth section, 'After the Ice', however, we detect a faint glimmer of hope which will grow brighter in the three remaining sections to the extent that the end of the poem, if it is not exactly a note of triumph, is at least a far cry from the loss and despair of 'The Mariner and the Dervish' at the beginning of the poem. The poet's recovery is helped considerably by the use of the resurrection myths of Tammuz and the Phoenix. However, before the poet reaches 'After the Ice' he has to go through 'The Ice Age' in which he fully admits that 'death has struck the veins of the earth' and *all* the veins in his people, so that their bodies are all frozen. After this realization the poet is able to offer a prayer to the god of fertility, to Baal, Tammuz and to the harvest sun to save the veins of the earth from sterility and destruction, to put some warmth into the frozen slaves in the ice desert (p. 73). If indeed nothing could revive the veins of the dead, the poet says in his prayer, except a fire that begets the Phoenix, a fire that feeds on the ashes of our death, then let us endure the hell-fire which will grant us certain rebirth (p. 77). In 'Love and Golgotha', helped by his love for his people, the young men and women and children, he 'challenges the ordeal of crucifixion and endures death in his love for life' and he regains the light of the way that he has lost. In 'Return to Sodom' he returns to his people with his all-consuming fire to destroy his people who are the children of slaves and whom the raids of the East and West have turned into 'robbers and whores, rags and the doormat of the grand hotel of the East' (p. 86). He is hopeful (in 'The Bridge') that the miracle of rebirth will take place.

In *The Flute and the Wind*, Hawi is more difficult to understand, but the poetry gains in subtlety and the subjective element in the experience becomes more pronounced. On the whole the mood is much less sombre. There are four poems in this volume: the first, 'With the Fortune-Teller', describes how, assailed by doubts about the validity of his confidence in the future and the possibility of his being deluded as regards himself and his society, the poet seeks the service of a fortune-teller, but when her prophecy does not appeal to him he has sufficient courage and self-assurance to ignore it and defy her. 'The Flute and the Wind', a poem in which symbols are used somewhat arbitrarily, shows in sinewy verse of great orginality the conflict in the poet between his family obligations, scholarship and academic ambitions on the one hand, and on the other his love of freedom which alone would make him the poet that he wants to be. But his ideal is not purely subjective, for in a subtle way his poetic creativity is intimately bound up with the creativity and rebirth of his society. In the remaining two poems, 'The Faces of Sindbad' and 'Sindbad on his Eighth Voyage', Hawi speaks through the persona of Sindbad, one of the figures from the medieval Arabic literary tradition that have become very popular in modern Arabic poetry. 'The Faces of Sindbad' is perhaps the most subjective poem in the collection: it is primarily an account of the effect of time on the poet, and describes with some irritation how the woman that he loves remains totally unchanged throughout his long absence from her when he was studying in England, and how she thinks that he has not changed 'from the youth choking with tears in the airport café', while he has had much to endure which has left its mark on his face. Besides treating the question of identity the poem contains a moving account of the emotional difficulties he faced as a young scholar in a foreign land – the loneliness, the futile attempt to escape from himself, the boredom of dry scholarship and the nightmarish temptation to commit suicide by jumping over Waterloo Bridge in London. The poem ends with a mature acceptance of the passage of time, in fact with man's eventual triumph over time. 'Sindbad on his Eighth Voyage' is an even more triumphant work: it records the poet's journey within himself, on which he throws overboard one by one his luggage which consists of old outworn preconceptions and useless inherited attitudes until he stands all alone and naked. 'When he had reached the essence of his nature he came back and brought with him a treasure unlike any other that he had found on his previous voyages' (p. 71). The outworn ideas which he discarded included preconceptions on religion and its restrictions which confine the human spirit, and excessively puritanical views of sex (represented by an amusing description of al-Ma'arri's attitude to woman as an unclean object (pp. 77–8)). The treasure he found is a vision:

> I would not have welcomed the sun,
> Had I not seen you in the morning,
> Cleansing yourselves of the stain of sin,
> In the Nile, the Jordan and the Euphrates . . .
> Gone are the crocodiles from our land,
> Stormed by our raging sea. (pp. 105–6)

It is a clear vision of Arab revival. From his eighth voyage Sindbad returned 'a poet with glad tidings' (p. 110).

Very different in mood is Hawi's third volume, *The Threshing Floor of Hunger*. The first poem in the volume, 'The Cave', depicts the poet's impatience because the prophetic vision has not yet been realized and the miracle which he had expected at the end of *The River of Ashes* is taking such a long time to happen, if it will happen at all. 'The Cave' is probably one of the most eloquent poetic statements in modern Arabic, expressing fruitless waiting that borders on despair (p. 7). In 'The Female Demon of the Shore' Hawi shows how innocence and spontaneity are misled and destroyed by sophistication and religious fanaticism. But it is in the last work in this volume, the long poem 'Lazarus 1962', that the poet's bitter disappointment in his earlier vision is expressed. Here we find some of the most disillusioned and most powerful poetry written in Arabic since the Second World War and it is in this poem that Hawi attains the height of his rhetoric, particularly in the opening of the poem entitled 'The Bottomless Pit' (pp. 41ff.). Using a modified version of the biblical story of Lazarus as a scaffolding for his poem, Hawi records his disenchantment with the dream of Arab revival, and shows how when values die in the soul of the leader of the struggle, the hero becomes a tyrant. This is a very pessimistic poem which in its unrelieved gloom can be compared only to some of Sayyab's works.

Sayyab

Badr Shākir al-Sayyāb (1926–1964), who led a life marked by failure, suffering and exile on account of his political beliefs, and of disease and slow death towards the end, is arguably one of the two or three greatest poets of his generation. A graduate of the Baghdad Teachers' Training College, he was considerably influenced by modern English poetry, particularly Eliot and Edith Sitwell, and by Lorca. He translated Aragon's *Les Yeux d'Elsa* and also published a volume containing his translation (not always accurate, and done through the medium of English) of twenty poems by poets as diverse as Pound, Eliot, Edith Sitwell, Stephen Spender, Day Lewis, De la Mare, Rilke, Lorca, Neruda, Rimbaud and Prévert, under the title *Selected Poems from Modern World Poetry*.[62]

Sayyab started as a romantic poet, an admirer of Taha and Abu Shabaka. His first volume, *Withered Flowers* (1947), which strangely enough was published when the poet was already a member of the Iraqi Communist Party, did not differ markedly from the work of any other young poet who derived his ideals from the established romantic poets. However, it included his famous poem 'Was it Love?' which shows his experimentation in form. (Later on Sayyab tried to get rid of some of the romantic dilution and vagueness by making some drastic changes in the first version of his poems.)[63] The change in Sayyab's style begins to be noticeable in the second volume, *Myths* (1950), in the introduction to which the poet draws the reader's attention to three features of the contents: the new and unfamiliar rhythm of the poems which rely on the use of an irregular number of feet, a form which he claims to have been inspired by his readings in English poetry, the relative obscurity of some poems (which, however, he hastens to point out, is not due to his being a symbolist poet – a denial which seems to be prompted by a desire not to be branded as a supporter of the doctrine of art for art's sake), and lastly the adoption of the principle of the association of ideas in the creative process as well as the mixing of the conscious and the unconscious. It is interesting that at the conclusion of his introduction Sayyab is careful to affirm the social and political function and relevance of poetry, and to assure the reader that he has already written a large number of poems on social themes. It is also significant that in a footnote to a poem[64] he refers to Eliot as a 'reactionary' English poet, although this may be due to the fact that this is how Eliot was described by Luwis 'Awad, when he introduced him to the Arabic-reading public. All the poems in this volume, except for the last two, are about love: on the whole, they are fairly stereotyped romantic poems.

Yet Sayyab seems to go beyond the general limitations of the romantic experience in at least two poems. 'In the Ancient Market Place' and 'An Ancient Song' reveal the poet's power of creating atmosphere by exploiting the poetic potentialities of realistic details, unconventional imagery and a daring use of language close to that in symbolist poetry, an incantatory use of words which relies upon repetition and strong rhythm, together with a certain complexity of structure which is an expression of a relatively complex and modern sensibility. Of the two poems, 'In the Ancient Market Place' is the less tightly organized and satisfying, but the description of the atmosphere of the old market is masterly: it is night and all noises in the old market have died down, except for the murmurs of passers-by, the footsteps of a stranger and the sad moaning of the wind. In 'An Ancient Song' we find the poet listening one evening to an old record of a love song in an outlying crowded café, while his tired eyes 'watched faces, hands, feet and flames' and 'the clock continued to strike, scornful of the noise within'. The echoes of the long song 'recede, melt away, trembling like a distant sail on the waters'. As the poet listens, his thoughts turn first to the inexplicable human tragedy reflected in unhappy love, obviously the theme of the song, wondering:

> Why should the hand of Fate
> Let fall its shadow between two hearts?

then to his own private sorrow, his unfulfilled love, how he was forced to part from his beloved and see her disappear from his vision as slowly as the tune of this song. This leads him to think of the voice of the singer, long dead, and the ancient recording. As he listens he pictures to himself the fair woman singing: whose 'image rippled in the tunes like a shadow in a river, ruffled by the breeze', and he is overwhelmed by thoughts of death and the passing of time. This brings him naturally to the last section of the poem in which he views all around him 'the faces, hands and feet' of the opening simply as 'particles of dust':

> Particles of dust
> Vibrate and dance in boredom,
> In the music-charged atmosphere.
> Particles of dust,
> The young woman, like her lovers,
> Particles of dust.[65]

After *Myths* Sayyab turned to socially and politically committed poetry by writing first long poems such as 'The Grave Digger' (1952), 'The Blind Prostitute' (1954), and 'Arms and Children' (1954),[66] all of which were to be published again in the volume entitled *Hymn to Rain* (1960) which contains some of Sayyab's best and most mature poems. The long poem is a form which had a great fascination for him, yet despite his many gifts as a poet, his extraordinary power of evolving imagery and recording vivid sensation, Sayyab was unable to write a long poem that is free from structural weaknesses. 'The Grave Digger' depicts an unpleasant type, the man who makes a living out of the death of others and to whom wars afford the most profitable times: he is therefore a symbol of all that is evil, rapacious and inhumane. Sayyab complicates the issue by making him an unlovable and sensual character who leads a debauched life, spending his earnings on prostitutes, but there is a sardonic paradox in the poet's making him recover the money he has paid a certain prostitute by being asked to dig her grave after her death. It is a gloomy poem and somewhat naive, partly inspired by the poet's experience in the sleazy quarters of Baghdad as an impecunious young man after his dismissal from his job as a school teacher on account of his membership of the Iraq Communist Party.[67] But structurally it suffers because the political and psychological interests seem to pull in two different directions. Likewise, 'The Blind Prostitute' suffers from the poet's inordinate interest in the erotic and the sensual, stimulated by the early influence of Taha and Abu Shabaka, and which became even more striking with the approach of death and his growing physical impotence during the last two years of the fatal disease that killed him so young. Salīma, the daughter of a poor farm labourer, killed by a feudal landlord as a result of alleged poaching, is raped by a soldier and is obliged to resort to prostitution for a living. She does a good trade when young, but as she grows old she loses her eyesight and in vain pathetically offers her body in order to earn enough to keep her alive. Sayyab employs the technique of flashback, the stream of consciousness in the mind of the prostitute, and he also uses many mythological allusions, both Greek and biblical, such as Cain, Gog and Magag, Oedipus, Medusa and Aphrodite, though the allusions are on the whole of a superficial nature. *Arms and Children* is based on the obvious contrast between the innocence and beauty of the world of children and the evil of warmongers who trade in arms which destroy them, a simplistic contrast between war and peace, but the description of the world of children has, as is often the case when Sayyab turns to the theme of children, a haunting beauty and pathos.

However, it is in the relatively shorter poems which he began to write around 1953, poems such as 'A Stranger on the Gulf' and 'Hymn to Rain' (and others included in the volume *Hymn to Rain*)[68] that Sayyab attained the full height of his creativity. In such poems he managed to fuse together in the heat of the imaginative act the most disparate elements of his experience, so that it is impossible to disentangle the individual predicament of the suffering poet from the commitment to a social or national ideal. In them we find an emotional complex of elements related to the man who since early childhood has been yearning for a mother's love and who has therefore been nostalgically looking back to the happy days of his early childhood in his native village with its river, its shells and its palm trees, the emotionally starved young man who seems to be constantly suffering from unrequited love, the committed Marxist dismissed from his job as a school teacher, hunted by the police in an authoritarian state and forced into exile for long periods of time in Iran and Kuwait (where he earned his keep by washing up dishes and doing domestic chores). A good example is 'Hymn to Rain'. The poem describes Sayyab's feelings as he watches rain falling on the Arabian Gulf in Kuwait where he is a political exile. The mood alternates between nostalgia for the poet's childhood and homesickness for his country, between grief over the present situation in Iraq and hope for the future. Rain is life-giving and results in flowers and crops, but in Iraq it brings only hunger for the people. However, despite the prevailing sadness of the poem it does not end on a pessimistic note.

'Hymn to Rain' opens with an address to what at first sight seems to be a woman, (which reminded Jacques Berque of the amatory prelude (*nasib*) in the traditional ode)[69]:

> Your eyes are forests of palm trees at the hour of dawn

But the exact identity of the person the poet is addressing is never explicitly disclosed and from the progress of the poem and the nature of the rich imagery used, it seems that what we have here is a composite figure: it is both the lost mother and the missing mistress, the idealized village of the poet's childhood, Iraq itself and even nature at large. Hence the apparently contradictory nature of the profuse imagery: when the eyes smile 'vines turn green and lights dance', the eyes are compared to 'moons reflected in the river': they are dark but 'in their depths stars pulsate':

> They drown in a mist of transparent sorrow
> Like the sea stroked gently by the hand of evening:
> Having both the warmth of winter and the shiver of autumn,
> Death and birth, darkness and light.
> Once more my soul overflows with the tremor of tears,
> And I am possessed with a violent turmoil embracing the sky,
> As violent as a child's fear of the moon.

By a natural process of association the poet's thoughts turn to the main subject of the poem: the rain, first to its joyful life-giving qualities, 'the chuckles of children amid vine trellises', the excitement of birds on trees as drops of rain fall, then to the negative side of rain, on the personal level: evening yawning and clouds weeping heavy tears just as he had done as a child, in his ravings before falling asleep about his recently dead mother 'lying in a grave on the hillside, eating dust and drinking rain'. The personal grief eventually turns into national:

I can almost hear the palm trees drinking rain
In Iraq, the villages groan, and exiles
With oars and sails struggling against the gusts
And thunders of the Gulf, chanting:
Rain. Rain.
Famine in Iraq.
At harvest time corn is scattered
To feed ravens and locusts
In the fields goes round
A mill, grinding grain and rock
With people around
Rain. Rain . . .
Not a year has passed without famine in Iraq
Rain. Rain.
In every drop of rain
A red or yellow flower bud
Every tear drop of the hungry and naked
Every blood drop of the enslaved
Is a smile awaiting new lips
Or a roseate nipple in the mouth of a newborn
In the youthful world of tomorrow, giver of life
Rain. Rain.
Iraq will grow green with the rainfall!

The word 'rain' (in Arabic it is the almost onomatopoeic *maṭar*) is repeated several times like a refrain at the end of each section of the poem with a hypnotic effect and creates an almost magical atmosphere in which the poet is confident that his prayer for life-giving rain (i.e. political salvation) for the whole of his country will be answered. It is interesting that the last section of the poem contains no more than these words: 'And rain pours down.' The complexity of themes, the tight organization, the swiftly moving imagery which is strictly functional and not merely decorative, the use of obliquities and symbols, to say nothing of the subtle internal music and rhythm and the incantatory effect of the language – all these features make 'Hymn to Rain' one of the most interesting poems in modern Arabic.

The same interweaving of the personal and the public and political elements is to be found in several other powerful poems. In 'The River and Death', to mention but another example, the poet's yearning for Buwaib, the river of his childhood village, particularly his longing not only to play but also to drown in it, is in part an expression of a desire to go back to the womb, a memory of the child's fascination with death and the unknown. Yet water is at the same time the element of life, hence the poet's wish to die as a political 'martyr', the yearning in his blood for a bullet 'whose sudden and awesome ice will bore the depths' of his heart and 'like hell-fire will set ablaze' his bones. But it is a death inspired by the wish to 'share the burden of mankind' and therefore by bearing the load with other men to bring back life. 'My death', he says, 'will be a victory.'[70] One may perhaps add that the intensity of Sayyab's feeling of commitment and hence his ability to combine the personal and the public did not disappear with his gradual disenchantment with the communist ideal during the 1950s.

Rain, as an archetypal image (in Arabic no less than in other literatures), is a dominant motif in Sayyab's poetry. But in this he seems to owe a direct debt to Edith Sitwell, and of course to T. S. Eliot who makes a striking use of the rain theme throughout *The Waste Land*. As has already been suggested, Eliot's use of myth has had considerable influence on Arab poets, of whom Sayyab is a conspicuous example. 'Hymn to Rain' is based on the concept of rain and fertility which underlies the Tammuz/Adonis myth, but in Sayyab's later poetry there is an increasingly overt use of this myth of death and rebirth, together with others including the Christian myth, the last of which he seems to have been led to use extensively under the influence of Edith Sitwell.[71] The myths are used in several poems of a political character, Marxist and Arab nationalist alike, such as 'Message from the Grave' (dealing with the Algerian struggle), 'The River and Death', 'Christ after Crucifixion', 'City of Sindbad' and 'City Without Rain'. It is not difficult to see the relevance of the myth of death and resurrection to Arab poets like Sayyab who are passionately concerned about the need for sacrifice to bring about a rebirth of their people. As one scholar put it: 'He resorts to the myth of Tammūz in his search for symbols to represent the victory of life over death, and finds in it all that he needs to embody his vision of a plenteous, new life for his people.'[72]

There was also the political consideration which Sayyab himself once explained in 1963:

> My first motive [in using myths and symbols] was political. When I wanted to resist the royal Saʿīdī regime with poetry I used myths to veil my intentions, for the myrmidons of Nuri al-Saʿid understood no myths. I also used them for the same purpose in the regime of Qasim. In my poem

> entitled 'Sarbarūs fi Bābil' ('Cerberus in Babel') I satirized Qasim and his regime severely and his myrmidons did not realize that. I also satirized that regime severely in my other poem 'City of Sindbad'.[73]

But the use of myth did not prevent Sayyab from writing some of the most nightmarishly horrifying comments on the bloody events in Qasim's Iraq, as we find, for instance, in 'The City of Sindbad', where we read:

> The Tartars have come, their knives dripping with blood
> Our sun is blood and our food
> Is blood served on platters.
> They have set fire to Muhammad the orphan
> And the night is alight with the blaze,
> Hot blood gushing forth from his feet,
> His hands and his eyes . . .
>
> A horseman rode in the streets,
> Murdering women
> And dyeing cradles in blood . . .
> It seems that Babel, the ancient walled city, is back again.
> With its high domes of iron, its ringing bells
> Mournful as a graveyard,
> The sky above it the courtyard of a slaughterhouse,
> Its hanging gardens planted with heads
> Cut off with sharp axes, and crows
> Pecking at their eyes.[74]

Nor was Sayyab always successful in his use of mythology: on the contrary the mythological allusion is sometimes, for his Arab reader at any rate, no more than a mere erudite reference for which the poet provides an explanation in a footnote, and at other times it is neither an organizing factor nor a device to release an emotional charge in the reader by tapping a common source of attitudes in his culture. One of the notorious examples is his long poem 'From Fūkāy's Vision', which is cluttered with forced and ill-digested allusions to literature and mythology from East and West which do not seem to serve any serious purpose or perform a valid function in the poem.[75]

With Sayyab's subsequent volumes begins a new phase in his development, in which he became gradually more introspective and subjective, and less absorbed in political or public themes. In the collection *The Sunken Temple* (1962) there is a marked interest in death, in the Persephone myth, in figures from the poet's past such as his cousin Wafīqa (who died while giving birth to a child and on whom he projected the persons of his mother and mistress): Wafiqa's gardens are identified with Persephone's in the underworld of Pluto. The volume contains a prayer to God in which the poet asks Him to put an end to his suffering. But there are still poems of public concern in the collection, such as the title poem which is a disillusioned comment on the absence of ideals from human society. In the next volume, *The House of Slave Girls* (1963), however, we find that with the exception of one poem celebrating the fall of Qasim, the entire contents of the book concern the poet's experience of disease and approaching death. He is constantly raging against the dying of the light, although at times he is pathetically trying to learn to accept death. The mood changes from self-pity, self-delusion and false hope to resignation to God's will, to homesickness for Iraq and nostalgia for the past. On the whole the style is simpler and less cluttered by mythological references. Sayyab gave this last stage of his development the name 'the Job stage',[76] for in it he adopted the persona of Job through whom he expressed his trials and sufferings and his attitude to God. In fact, one of the best two poems in *The House of Slave Girls* is the first of a series of poems entitled 'The Book of Job', which is one of the finest poems written on the theme of acceptance of suffering and shows Sayyab at his best.[77] The other is the poem that gives the collection its title, a nostalgic work about an old house in his village Jaikur, the memory of which sets his imagination on fire, and he thinks of all the diverse experiences of its generations of inhabitants, especially their sufferings, which bring him back to his own suffering and to his own condition, penniless, paralyzed and without hope, tied down to a sick bed in a London hospital in the land of snow (that was in winter 1963). Using an ancient Arabic poetic convention he calls upon rain to fall kindly and lovingly on the ruined house as well as on his own 'thirsty tomb'.

The Oriel Window of the Nobleman's Daughter (1964), which followed, contains mainly childhood reminiscences and memories of the poet's more youthful days. In 'Love Me' he recalls in powerful and sinewy verse (somewhat like the verse of the later Yeats) a procession of all the women with whom he had fallen in love. There are some very moving poems inspired by anticipation and fear of death, such as 'In the Hospital' and 'At Night' in which he is welcomed by his dead mother who invites him to share with her her grave. There is also some poetry of extreme eroticism and sensuality in the collection.[78]

Iqbāl (the volume posthumously published in 1965 and named after his wife) contains his last unpublished poems, together with some juvenilia. (More juvenilia appeared in two further posthumous collections published in Baghdad under the titles *The Wind Harp*, 1971, and *Storms*, 1972.) *Iqbal* has at least two remarkable poems. 'Ḥāmid' is about a fellow paralyzed patient who dies, and:

> When God sees him face to face,
> Crawling on his chest,

His broken crushed spirit
Shining through his supplicating eyes,
In mercy God will weep for him,
And ask him for forgiveness.

In the other poem, 'In the Forest of the Dark', the poet asks the Lord to have mercy upon him and end his life, or as he puts it, 'Your bullet of mercy, Lord'.[79]

Towards the end of his life and as the realization of the hopelessness of his health condition became apparent, Sayyab was in an almost continuous state of hectic and feverish poetic activity, so much so that poetry seemed to be the only means by which he felt he could still hold on to life, just as his excessively erotic imagery is an expression of a desperate attempt to prove to his paralyzed and impotent body that he was still alive. The abundant poetry he produced was understandably of an uneven quality, but it had the mark of authenticity and there is an almost demonic quality about it: he wrote as if he were possessed. Although it was poetry of introspection and reminiscence it did not contain any profound meditations on life and death. Yet it teems with vivid impressions and primary sensations, and at its best it is an eloquent and moving record of the terror of death, of man's helplessness when he is reduced to a physical wreck bound to a hospital bed. Alike in its moments of terror, and its moments of impotent fury, of resignation and of despair, it represents a unique voice in contemporary Arabic poetry.

General remarks on the contemporary poets

Sayyab died before the vogue for obscure and obscurant symbolist New Poetry with its predominantly surrealistic imagery swept Arabic poetry, and not only that written by the younger generation of poets – although he himself was guilty of cluttering his verse at times with a farrago of symbols and myths from East and West. In this respect he can be said to have contributed towards making modern Arabic poetry more obscure than it had been. One must also mention the influence (both direct and indirect) of French Marxist poets who also employed the Surrealist technique, particularly Aragon and Eluard. But it is the conception of poetry as a special kind of vision close to dreams and daydreams, best propagated by Adunis (and the *Shi'r* magazine generally) and made popular through his practice no less than through his theory (and later through his magazine *Mawaqif*), which had a drastic effect upon contemporary Arabic poetry from which few young poets seem to have been able to escape, and which, for the sake of the future of Arabic poetry, one can only hope will not be long lasting.

One revealing feature of the New poets is their very obsession with newness or modernity. The term has become an emotionally charged one: the cult of the 'New' has never been so widespread as it is now. 'The only thing the New poets have in common is their intention to innovate', wrote one enthusiastic critic.[80] That modernity or newness (*al-ḥadātha*) has become a value in itself, is the source of both the strength and the weakness of this poetry. On the one hand it has resulted in the most daring verbal constructions, thus enlarging the possibilities of the language, as Jaroslav Stetkevych has recently observed in *The Modern Arabic Literary Language*.[91] But this obsessive concern with newness also argues a disturbing insecurity and lack of self-confidence, for by newness the poets really understand similarity with the West. So anxious are they to become international that they stand in danger of working against the genius of the Arabic language. For instance, when in the early 1960s Maghut wrote about 'blue clouds of chestnut', 'the hissing of wild breasts', the sea 'bidding him farewell with a chesty smoker's cough', 'eagles' tears piling up like silt' and 'wild words hanging down from trees like figs', or the fingers of his dead friends and kinsmen 'embedded like thorns in the wind', or when Taufiq Sayigh described 'radiant negation growing dark', – the sensitive and enlightened reader might have regarded this as an interesting and valuable extension of the poetic image, an effective device if used in moderation.[82] But in the 1970s such language would neither surprise nor shock, but would be looked upon as the common idiom of poetry. It is as if a poem consisted of an unbroken chain of paradoxes and *non sequiturs*, so far has Arabic poetry travelled on the road of irrationality. As can be seen from the special issue of *Ādāb* devoted to Modern Arabic Poetry (March 1966), many voices from Egypt, Lebanon and Iraq have already been raised deploring this obscurity and the accompanying violence done to the Arabic language, and not all of these voices were those of Marxists – such as Ḥusain Muruwwa who understandably objected to Arabic poetry becoming dissociated from the realities of the Arab situation and identified with the inner world of dreams. But, of course, it cannot be said that the dangers inherent in obscurity have been averted, and the fear is that if this present tendency continues unchecked serious poetry will become just as irrelevant, or at least as marginal in the Arab world as to some extent it has become in the West.

What is the image of the poet that emerges from this poetry? It is that of the hero, the saviour and the redeemer. We have seen how the craftsman has given place to the spokesman of society in neoclassicism, how in pre-romanticism the spokesman has been replaced by the man of sensibility who is above society, and in romanticism he has become the seer, the prophet, but without, losing his passivity, his talent for suffering. In the last phase of the development of Arabic poetry the poet has become once again identified with his own people, but he is no longer the spokesman: he is the hero who in his personal salvation seeks the salvation of his people. Admittedly this often leads to excessive solemnity and hollow self-dramatization in contemporary Arabic poetry. But it also explains why in its best examples, the spiritual experience, which is the poem, becomes at once a political and a cultural comment. It is interesting to note how deeply, and even tragically, concerned many of these poets are about the need to revive Arab culture and society, and drag it into the context of the fast-moving civilized western world, how this theme runs through their works like a leitmotive under one guise or another. Myths of resurrection like the Phoenix, Tammuz/Adonis, are used by Adunis, Hawi, Khal, Sayyab and Jabra among others.[83] The poet thinks of himself as Noah or Christ the Redeemer, Sindbad the explorer. This is no less true of 'Abd al-Sabur, Buland Haidari and the present writer than of Adunis, Hawi and Khal. The poet is no longer the passive sufferer, but the active saviour, the one who performs a heroic act of self-sacrifice to save his people. In the context of Marxist thinking the nature of the poet's activity is clear enough, but with the *Shi'r* group the poet's action *is* his poetry, for by creating his own language, his own imagery and metaphors the poet arrives at a new apprehension of reality, thereby creating a new order and a new world.[84]

There were, of course, many angry reactions from conservative quarters against the extreme anti-traditionalism of some New Poetry. Mention has already been made of 'Aqqad who on formal grounds simply dismissed it as non-poetry. Amongst the most vociferous critics was the scholar Maḥmūd Muḥammad Shākir who expressed violent objections on religious grounds to the use of Christian symbolism and terms like sin, redemption and crucifixion in modern Arabic *Muslim* poetry. Some less tolerant minds even saw in New Poetry a threat to Arab civilization and Islam, nothing short of a 'western imperialist plot'.[85]

7 Epilogue

By contrast with earlier poetry, modern Arabic poetry is, in general, characterized by a spirit of revolt: the student of this period cannot but be struck by the variety and multiplicity of schools and styles and by the extent of restless and indeed hectic experimentation which went on and is still going on unabated. The last hundred years or so have witnessed the amazing journey which, under the cultural impact of the West, Arabic poetry has travelled from the mournful traces of encampments in the Arabian desert to the tragic Waste Land of western Europe and America, and even further still to the nightmarish and paradoxical world of the surrealists and post-surrealists and the Messianic and millenial Utopia of Marxists. *En route* it has passed through the tombs and ruins of *Night Thoughts*, known the raging seas and howling winds of the pre-Romantic Sublime, inhabited for a while the magic casements, the beautiful but forlorn fairyland, mingled with nature, landscape and seascape, meditated over *Le Lac*, held communion with the Muses and *Les Nuits*, experienced the Sorrows of Werther and the vague and almost metaphysical yearning of the Romantics in general, as well as the ritualistic, hieratic and sacred images, hints and suggestions of the Symbolists – to mention but a few of the familiar landmarks and experiences of the long, often winding and at times tortuous route.

No doubt this final stage of development is not the exclusive feature of Arabic poetry; this is also where modern Japanese poetry, to mention but one of many instances of Oriental literature, has apparently arrived.[1] Indeed there may be some useful parallels to be drawn between the experiences of both Arabic and Japanese poetry, as both were exposed to profound and pervasive western influences at roughly the same time. One could go even further and claim that there are great stylistic similarities in most of the sophisticated poetry written in the world today, irrespective of the language in which it is composed. The present vogue of poetry in translation, which is clearly noticeable in the Anglo-Saxon world at least, may indeed mean that many readers who are not acquainted with the language of the original, inevitably get only a much watered-down version of poems in other languages. But it also means that stylistic barriers between the products of different cultures are being eroded, that in fact we may be moving towards an ideal of poetry which, paradoxical as it may seem, is almost as international as science. International poetry festivals have now become a fairly common occurrence. Paris has recently witnessed the appearance of a volume of verse called *Renga*, a joint production of four poets, a Mexican, a Frenchman, an Italian and an Englishman, who during five days (in the spring of 1969) collaborated, each in his own language, in writing a single long poem (a sonnet sequence) using the collective Japanese poetic form *renga*. Of this astonishing work, which prints the original, together with a complete French translation, one enthusiastic reviewer wrote: 'It consecrates the internationalization of poetry'.[2] Rimbaud and Paul Valéry, Saint-John Perse, Louis Aragon and Paul Eluard, Rilke and Quasimodo, to choose random examples, meet not only in Stanley Burnshaw's well-known anthology of international poetry called *The Poem Itself*[3] but also on the pages of the Lebanese poetry quarterly *Shi'r* where they appear in the company of Jacques Prévert and Yves Bonnefoy, Anglo-Saxon poets like Yeats, Pound, Eliot, Wallace Stevens, Edith Sitwell and Emily Dickinson, Dylan Thomas, John Holloway and John Wain, and the academically not so respectable company of beatnik poets like Allen Ginsberg. Recently, when asked about the poets who have influenced his work, the Palestinian poet Mahmud Darwish (b. 1942) listed, among others, Eluard, Aragon, Nazim Hikmat, Lorca and Neruda.[4] This is the international cultural background of the young Arab poet of today.

It will be noticed from this survey of modern Arabic poetry, however, that in each of the stages discussed the revolt against convention was not entirely a spontaneous and indigenous movement, but was inspired by the example of western poetry, which seemed to act like a catalyst for the change or for the desire to change. Furthermore, until quite recently Arabic poetry turned to western fashions or styles after these fashions or styles seemed to have run their course in the West. Perhaps the case of romanticism is the most striking. By the end of the nineteenth century, when Arabic poetry was beginning to enter into its romantic phase, European Romanticism which had set in more than a century earlier had already given place to other movements: in France to those movements which made 'modern' poetry possible practically all over the world, in England to a Victorianism that was already showing signs of disintegration. Mutran knew of the Alexandria-born Italian futurist poet

Marinetti, but his own poetry shows only a mild form of romanticism. It is a sobering thought indeed that the Greek poet Cavafy was producing his powerful 'modern' poetry in Alexandria, to all intents and purposes unbeknown to the Arab poets who were busy writing romantic poetry at the time. Abu Shadi lived in England at a time when the most exciting experiments in modern English poetry, the experiments of Pound and Eliot, were taking place, yet his interest lay chiefly in English Romantic and Victorian poetry. Similarly, with the exception of one or two (Egyptians), Arab poets turned to the poetry of T. S. Eliot in the late 1940s and early 1950s, when it was already beginning to look old-fashioned, having in the meantime been succeeded by the work of the generations of Auden and of Philip Larkin. In fact, to the informed reader the excitement of discovery which was felt by many Arab poets and critics in the 1950s in the work of Eliot seemed somewhat naive and certainly provincial. The case of socialist realism provides another example, although the gap here is only that between the generation of the Spanish Civil War and the post-war generation.

This apparently disturbing observation gives rise to two not unrelated questions. First, What is the significance of this gap? Secondly, What is the extent of originality in modern Arabic poetry? There are many reasons, I think, why the Arabs turned to the Romantics when they first encountered western poetry. The obvious one is that at that time the popular taste in Europe was still formed on Romantic ideas and ideals, and it would be grossly unfair, if not unrealistic, to expect a complete foreigner to a culture to acquire more than the popular taste where an extremely complex cultural product like poetry is concerned. Second, Romantic poetry presents fewer difficulties than the classical which relies upon the peculiar rhetorical features of a language, particularly its formal features. (How many native English speakers can really appreciate Racine?) Because Romantic poetry is more spontaneous and emotional its appeal is proportionally more immediate. Like the Arabs, the Japanese, for instance, translated or adapted Shelley when they first met English poetry.[5] Third, while there may be 'romantic' elements in the Arab poetic heritage which would facilitate the appreciation of western Romantic poetry, the traditional Arabic conception of literature shares many of the fundamental assumptions of European classicism, with the result that, when the desire to break with their past and enter the modern world was genuinely felt, Arab poets found in European Romanticism, which was professedly anti-classical, the assumptions and ideals which seemed to them to fulfil adequately their own needs. Al-Āmidī's criticism of Abu Tammam's poetry for its unfamiliar and far-fetched metaphors[6] is strongly reminiscent of Johnson's famous criticism of the 'metaphysical' poets, where he attacks their *discordia concors*. The ideal of clarity which remained of paramount importance in the classical Arabic critical tradition[7] is the very ideal which the Cartesian spirit brought about in French and English neoclassicism. This is not to mention stylistic features in neoclassical poetry like the use of rhetoric and poetic diction in English Augustan verse, the neat balance and antithesis of the heroic couplet, with its meticulously placed caesura and its pronounced rhyme designed to emphasize the sense which is supposed to end with the end of the couplet – features to which one can find many parallels in classical Arabic poetry, if one cares to look for them.

The two hypotheses which, according to von Grunebaum, underlie medieval Arabic literature, namely the comparatively low place assigned to imagination[8] and the view of form as something external, to be 'somewhat arbitrarily joined to content',[9] are in fact true also of western neoclassical poetry. Furthermore, classicism, with its stress on polish and good form, should be seen as an expression of a fairly stable culture in which there is common agreement on fundamental issues, while romanticism is the product of a society at odds with itself and in which the individual questions the validity and relevance of traditional values. What could be more natural, then, than that the individual Arab poets should, at this juncture in their history, turn to this literature of revolt?

That the Arabs turned to western Romantic poetry first need not therefore surprise us. Apart from other considerations, they would not have been capable of taking much interest in the subsequent or *avant-garde* poetic movements, because in many ways these were further developments of the Romantic experience and they presupposed it. The Arabs had to assimilate fully the Romantic experience first, both on the psychological and on the language levels. Once they had done so subsequent movements became possible, and with each successive movement the gap became increasingly narrower, so much so that the young Arab poet of today has access to nearly as much international poetry (mainly in translation, of course), almost immediately, as his English-speaking counterpart.

Fortunately in matters of poetry the gap does not have the same significance as in matters of technology. Although romantic poetry was not the poetry of the western world in the twentieth century and poems like Mikha'il Nu'aima's 'Friend',[10] Shabbi's 'New Morrow'[11] or Iliya Abu Madi's 'Evening'[12] could not have been produced in the West at that time, the value and significance of such poems remain unimpaired. Unlike technology, poetry is not superseded – poetry, that is, which is the expression of a genuine human experience in words that exploit to the full the possibilities of a particular language. The heightened sense of individuality, the agonizing feeling of social and cultural change, the political malaise, the occasional awareness of loss of direction and of being strangers in an unfamiliar universe, were in one way or another facts of Arab existence for some time. Whatever be the foreign influences, at its best Arabic romantic poetry is, therefore, although more limited in range, no less original than the German which is heavily influenced by the English, or the French which owes much to both. When, however, the experience is lacking the result is hollow and slavishly imitative. An example of such a work is 'From Fukay's Vision',[13] in which the young Sayyab imitates the style and mannerism of Eliot of *The Waste Land*, unaware that style, especially when it is as individual as this, is not an external mould that can be borrowed, but an expression of a particular vision of life. But when Sayyab himself has something to say he does not produce such monstrosities, but works of considerable value such as 'The River and Death'[14] or 'The Book of Job'.[15] I do not think it would be exaggeration to say that at its best the New Arabic Poetry has its own original character, which distinguishes it from the rest of modern poetry. Its contribution lies in the fact that, while it expresses the anxiety and bewilderment of modern man in the face of ultimate questions, it is deeply concerned about the identity and future of Arab culture in a tragic age. It is both metaphysical and national at one and the same time.

NOTES TO THE TEXT

CHAPTER 1: INTRODUCTORY

1 A. J. Arberry, *Arabic Poetry, A Primer for Students* (1965), pp. 18–21.
2 R. A. Nicholson, *Studies in Islamic Poetry* (1921), p. 50.
3 H. A. R. Gibb & Harold Bowen, *Islamic Society and the West* (1963), vol. I, part II, p. 164.
4 See Mārūn 'Abbūd, *Ruwwād al-Nahḍa al-Ḥadītha* (Beirut, 1952), p. 39.
5 Abd al-Raḥmān al-Jabartī, *'Ajā'ib al-Āthār fi'l Tarājim wa'l Akhbār* (Cairo 1322 A. H.), vol. I, p. 83.
6 Mārūn 'Abbūd, *Ruwwād*, p. 27.
7 The story of Muḥammad Ali's innovations in Egyptian education is admirably told in J. Heyworth-Dunne's book *An Introduction to the History of Education in Modern Egypt*, (1938).
8 See J. Heyworth-Dunne, 'Printing and Translation under Muhammad Ali' *Journal of the Royal Asiatic Society* (July 1940), 325–49.
9 See Isḥāq Mūsā al-Ḥusainī, *Al-Madkhal ila'l Adab al-'Arabī al-Mu'āṣir* (Cairo, 1963), p. 27 and Jāk Tājir, *Ḥarakat al-Tarjama bi Miṣr khilāl al-Qarn al-Tāsi' 'Ashar* (Cairo, 1945), p. 113. On the impressive size of the translations undertaken in the early history of the movement see Ibrahim Abu-Lughod, *Arab Rediscovery of Europe* (Princeton, 1963), p. 41.
10 On this point see the extremely valuable chapter; 'The Violet and the Crucible: Translations and the Language of Arabic Romantic Poetry' in Muḥammad 'Abdul-Ḥai, 'Tradition and English and American Influence in Arabic Romantic Poetry', unpublished D. Phil. thesis (University of Oxford, 1973).
11 Philip P. Hitti, *History of the Arabs* (1958), p. 747.
12 See the unpublished Oxford D. Phil. thesis by the late Mrs N. Farag: 'Al-Muqtataf 1876–1900: a Study of the Influence of Victorian Thought on Modern Arabic Thought' (Oxford, 1969).
13 On the contribution of Syrian immigrants to the Egyptian cultural renaissance see Albert Hourani, *Arabic Thought in the Liberal Age 1798–1939* (1962), chaps. IV and X, and his paper 'The Syrians in Egypt in the Eighteenth and Nineteenth Centuries' contributed to *Colloque International sur l'Histoire du Caire* (Cairo, 1972), pp. 227ff.

CHAPTER 2: NEOCLASSICISM

1 See Muṣṭafā Luṭfī al-Manfalūṭī, *Mukhtārāt al-Manfalūṭī* (Cairo, 1912), p. 108.

2 See Jurjī Zaidān, *Tarājim Mashāhir al-Sharq fi'l Qarn al-Tāsi' 'Ashar*, vol. II (Cairo, 1903), p. 191.

3 *Ibid*, vol. II, p. 206.

4 These were *Nafḥat al-Raiḥān* (1864), *Fākihat al-Nudamā'* (1870) and *Thālith al-Qamarain* (1883).

5 See 'Isā Mikhā'īl Sābā, *Al-Shaikh Nāsīf al-Yāziji* (Cairo, 1965), p. 95.

6 See especially the poetry in his *'al-Ramliyya' maqāma*.

7 It is interesting to note that Bārūdī, although apparently he knew no European language (see Afaf Lutfi al-Sayyid, *Egypt and Cromer*, London, 1968, p. 9), was, like the vast majority of the eminent Egyptian poets of the modern renaissance movement, a product of the new secular education. From now on the Azhar seems to have ceased to produce great poets.

8 Bārūdī's ambition, no less than his intelligence, was commented on by English observers like Wilfred S. Blunt and Alexander M. Broadley. See Mounah A. Khouri, *Poetry and the Making of Modern Egypt* (Leiden, 1971), p. 15.

9 All the quotations from the preface, which are translated here, come from the 1915 edition of the poet's works, *Dīwān al-Bārūdī*, ed. Maḥmūd al-Imām al-Manṣuri (Cairo, n.d.), henceforth to be referred to as *Dīwān*. Likewise the references between brackets in this section are all to this edition.

10 T. S. Eliot, *Selected Essays*, (London, 1948), p. 14.

11 It is interesting in this context to note the manner in which he learned the craft of poetry, and in which he resembled the earliest Arab poets. Instead of receiving the philological training which was common at this time, and which might have warped his poetic nature and driven him to the artificiality and verbal and rhetorical ingenuities which were the accepted norms, Bārūdī went directly to the early poets and completely immersed himself in reading their great works. (See Shauqī Ḍaif, *al-Bārūdī Rā'id al-Shi'r al-Ḥadīth*, Cairo 1964, pp. 98ff.) In this he is a perfect example in Arabic literature of the application of the well-known Horatian (and subsequently neoclassical) precept on literary formation.

12 Bārūdī's mastery of the technique and form of traditional Arabic verse was recognized at once by his contemporaries and immediate successors. See e.g. Khalīl Muṭrān, *Marāthī al-Shu'arā'*, Maṭba'at al-Jawā'ib al-Miṣriyya (n.d.), p. 25.

13 See e.g. *Dīwān* II, 249 where the use of terms like *ma'qil ashib* at once puts the reader in mind of Abū Tammām's '*Ammūriyya* poem, or even more obviously II, 446, where nearly a whole half line from a *mu'allaqa, fala'yan 'arafta'l dāra ba'da tarassumi*, is quoted. See Zuhair ibn abī Sulmā's *mu'allaqa*, 1.4.

14 For instance the use of *yā nūra 'ainī* and *Shubrā* in I, 168.

15 See Shauqī Ḍaif, *al-Bārūdī*, p. 76.

16 See *Dīwān*, I, 18.

17 See, e.g. *Dīwān* I, 123, 142, 152, 153, and II, 519, 532.

18 *Ibid*, 21, 49, 57, 211.

19 Some of this criticism was quietly suppressed by his editor, as has been shown in a recent study of the poet. See 'Alī Muḥammad al-Ḥadīdī, *Maḥmūd Sāmī al-Bārūdī* (Cairo, 1967).

20 See, e.g. *Dīwān*, I, 184–5, 186 and II, 207–266.

21 See, for instance, *Dīwān*, I, 63.

22 See, for instance, his poem about the railway in *Manāhij al-Albāb al-Misriyya fī Mabāhij al-Ādāb al-'Aṣriyya*, 2nd edn. (Cairo, 1912), pp. 126–8.

23 Yaḥyā Haqqī, 'Marāthī Shauqī', *al-Majalla* (Cairo), no. 144 (Dec., 1968), 64.

24 Aḥmad Shauqī, *al-Shauqiyyāt* II (Cairo, 1948), p. 243.

25 See above, pp. 24f. and M. M. Badawi, '*Al-Hilāl*, Moon or Poet? A Critical Analysis of a Poem by Shauqī', *Journal of Arabic Literature*, II (1971), 127–35.

26 The last two paragraphs are derived from my article 'Convention and Revolt in Modern Arabic Poetry' published in G. E. von Grunebaum, *Arabic Poetry: Theory and Development* (Wiesbaden, 1973), pp. 187ff.

27 S. A. Khulusi, 'Modern Arabic Poetry', *Islamic Quarterly*, XXXII, no. 1 (Jan., 1958), 71.

28 A. J. Arberry, 'Ḥāfiẓ Ibrāhīm and Shauqī, *JRAS* (1937), 58.

29 *Ibid*, p. 54.

30 Muḥammad Ṣabrī, *Al-Shauqiyyāt al-Majhūla* (Cairo, 1961), I, 11.

31 The references between brackets here and in the rest of this section on Shauqī are to *al-Shauqiyyāt* (Cairo), vol. I (1950), vol. II (1948), vol. III (1950), vol. IV (1951).

32 For an intelligent discussion of Shauqī's creative imitation see Shauqī Ḍaif, *Shauqī Shā'ir al-'Aṣr al-Ḥadīth* (Cairo, 1963), pp. 72–84.

33 Ṭāhā Ḥusain, *Ḥāfiẓ wa Shauqī* (Cairo, 1962), p. 8; 'Abbās Maḥmūd al-'Aqqād, *Shu'arā' Miṣr wa Bī'ātuhum fi'l Jīl al-Māḍī* (Cairo, 1950), p. 156.

34 Shauqī Ḍaif, *Shauqī*, pp. 160ff.

35 On the political relevance of Shauqī's poetry see Mounah Khouri, *Poetry and the Making of Modern Egypt 1882–1922* (Leiden, 1971).

36 Shauqī Ḍaif, *Shauqī*, p. 114; H. A. R. Gibb, 'Arab Poet and Arabic Philologist', *Bulletin of the School of Oriental and African Studies*, XII (1947–48), 576ff.

37 For an analysis of this poem see Badawi, 'Al-Hilāl: Moon or Poet?'

38 Ṭāhā Ḥusain, *Ḥāfiẓ wa Shauqī*, p. 13.

39 See, e.g. *al-Shauqiyyāt*, I, 272; II, 3–4.

40 See, e.g. *Riwāyat Fāṣhūda* and *Ḥikāyat al-Sūdān* in Muḥammad Ṣabrī, *Al-Shauqiyyāt al-Majhūla*, vol. I, pp. 121ff. and 131ff. For further examples of the poet's ability as a political satirist see *ibid*, vol. I, pp. 255ff., 271.

41 On the effect of the music of Shauqī's verse See Shauqī Ḍaif, *Shauqī*, pp. 44ff.

42 See, e.g. Aḥmad Maḥfūẓ, *Ḥayāt Ḥāfiẓ Ibrāhīm* (Cairo n.d. [1958–9?]), p. 191; 'Abd al-Ḥamīd Sanad al-Jundī, *Ḥāfiẓ Ibrāhīm Shā'ir al-Nīl* (Cairo 1959), pp. 28, 164ff. and Fatḥī Raḍwān, *'Aṣr wa Rijāl* (Cairo 1967), p. 143. Among those who have recently defended him against the charge of lack of nationalism are Muhammad Harūn al-Hulw, *Ḥāfiẓ Ibrāhīm Shā'ir al-Qaumiyya al-'Arabiyya* (Cairo n.d.), p. 35 and Muhammad Kāmil Jum'a, *Ḥāfiẓ Ibrāhīm mā lahu wa mā'alaihī* (2nd edn. Cairo 1960), pp. 113ff.

43 See Raḍwān, *'Aṣr wa Rijāl*, p. 155 and *Dīwān Ḥāfiẓ Ibrāhīm*, ed. Amīn, al-Zain and Ibyārī (Cairo 1939), vol. II, p. 105.

44 Al-Jundī, *Ḥāfiẓ Ibrāhīm*, p. 17.

45 Maḥfūẓ, *Ḥayāt Ḥāfiẓ Ibrāhīm*, pp. 229–30.

46 See Jum'a, *Ḥāfiẓ Ibrāhīm*, p. 358. For a discussion of echoes of medieval Arabic poets in Ḥāfiẓ's poetry see A. S. al-Jundī, *Ḥāfiẓ Ibrāhīm*, pp. 201ff.

47 The references between brackets here and in the rest of this section on Ḥāfiẓ Ibrāhīm are all to *Dīwān Ḥāfiẓ Ibrāhīm*, edited by A: Amīn, A. Al-Zain and Ibrāhīm al-Ibyārī, vol. I (Cairo, 1948), vol. II (Cairo, 1939).

48 Ṭāhā Ḥusain, *Ḥāfiẓ wa Shauqī*, pp. 152ff.

49 Al-Jundī, *Ḥāfiẓ Ibrāhīm*, p. 13.

50 *Ibid*, p. 135.

51 Jum'a, *Ḥāfiẓ Ibrāhīm*, p. 264; al-Jundī, *Ḥāfiẓ Ibrāhīm*, p. 126 and Maḥfūẓ, *Ḥayāt Ḥāfiz Ibrāhīm*, p. 203.

52 S. K. Jayyusi, 'Trends and Movements in Contemporary Arabic Poetry', unpublished Ph.D. thesis (London University, 1970), vol. I, p. 111.

53 Raḍwān, *'Asr wa Rijāl*, p. 137.

54 See, for instance, the poems on the Messina Earthquake and 'Mit Ghamr Fire', *Dīwān*, I, 204ff; 239ff.

55 Even new poems of a strictly 'contemporary' type are written on the incident. See, e.g. Ṣalāḥ 'Abd al-Ṣabūr's remarkable poem *Shanq Zahrān* (the Hanging of Zahran) in his volume of verse *Al-Nās fī Bilādī* (People in my Country) (Beirut 1957), pp. 48ff.

56 See Māhir Ḥasan Fahmī, *Al-Zahāwī* (Cairo, n.d.), pp. 178ff.

57 Published in the periodical *Al-Kātib al-Miṣrī* (Cairo), IV, 15 (Dec. 1946), p. 459.

58 See his autobiographical preface to his collection *Rubā'iyyāt* (Quatrains) (Beirut, 1924), reprinted in Muḥammad Yūsuf Najm, ed., *Dīwān Jamīl Ṣidqī al-Zahāwī* (Cairo, 1955), vol. I, p. 176.

59 Here are the Arabic titles: *al-Kalim al-Munẓum* (Beirut, 1327 A. H.) *Rubā'iyyāt al-Zahāwī* (Beirut, 1924), *Dīwān al-Zahāwī* (Cairo, 1924), *al-Lubāb* (Baghdad, 1928), *Thaura fī'l Jaḥīm* published in *al-Duhūr* (Beirut 1931), *al-Aushāl* (Baghdad, 1934), *al-Thumāla* (Baghdad, 1939), and *al-Naẓaghāt*, published in Hilāl Nājī, *Al-Zahāwī wa Dīwanuh al-Mafqūd* (Cairo, 1963).

60 Rūfā'īl Buṭṭī, *Al-Adab al-'Aṣrī fī'l 'Iraq al-'Arabī*, 2 vols (Baghdad — Cairo, 1923), vol. I, p. 5; Ibrāhim Sāmarrā'ī, *Lughat al-Shi'r bain Jīlain* (Beirut, n.d.), p. 46.

61 See Nāṣir al-Ḥāni, *Muḥāḍarāt 'an Jamīl al-Zahāwī, Ḥayātuh wa Shi'ruh* (Cairo, 1954), p. 18 and Ibrāhim Sāmarrā'ī, *Lughat al-Shi'r*, p. 47.

62 See his poem *Ilā shaikh al-Ma'arra* in *Dīwān Jamīl Ṣidqī al-Zahāwī* (Dar al-'Auda, Beirut, 1972), vol. I, p. 487.

63 *Ibid*, pp. 671, 673.

64 See e.g. the poem *'Alā'l Qabr* in *Dīwān al-Zahāwī* (Cairo, 1924) (henceforth to be referred to simply as *Dīwān*), p. 171.

65 Hilāl Nājī, *Al-Zahāwī*, pp. 75ff.

66 Ibrahim Sāmarrā'ī, *Lughat al-Shi'r*, pp. 53ff.

67 See e.g. the poem *Ba'da alf 'ām* in J. S. al-Zahāwī, *Al-Lubāb* (Baghdad, 1928), pp. 280ff.

68 Muḥammad Yūsuf Najm ed., *Dīwān Jamīl Ṣidqī al-Zahāwī*, vol. I, (Cairo, 1955), p. 179.

69 See e.g. the poems *al-Ḥayat wa'l ṭabī'a* and *Qird al-ghāb* in *Dīwān J. S. al-Zahāwī* (Beirut, 1972), pp. 497ff. and 506, which show the influence of the ideas of Darwin and Nietzsche. Cf. Hilāl Nājī, *Al-Zahāwī*, pp. 87ff.

70 *Dīwān*, pp. 156ff. and 135ff: *Naẓra fī'l Nujūm, Mashhad al-Samā'*.

71 *Ibid*., pp. 90ff., 83ff., 168ff.

72 See Dawūd Sallūm, *Taṭawwur al-Fikra wa'l Uslūb fī'l Adab al-'Irāqi fī'l Qarnain al-Tāsi' 'Ashar wa'l 'Ishrīn* (Baghdad, 1959), pp. 82ff.; Yūsuf 'Izzil-Dīn, *Al-Zahāwī al-Shā'ir al-Qaliq* (Baghdad, 1962), p. 31; Hilāl Nājī, *Al-Zahāwī*, pp. 34ff; Māhir Ḥasan Fahmī, *Al-Zahāwī*, pp. 136ff. and 'Abd al-Razzāq al-Hilālī, *Al-Zahāwī bain al-Thaura wa'l Sukūn* (Beirut, n.d.).

73 See Zahāwī, *Al-Kalim al-Manẓūm* (Beirut, 1327 A.H.), pp. 121, 139, and *Dīwān*, pp. 68, 90, 93.

74 *'Alā Qabr Ibnatihā* (On her daughter's grave), *Dīwān*, pp. 77ff.

75 See e.g. *Sa'imtu Ḥayātī* (I have grown tired of my life), *Al-Lubāb* (Baghdad, 1928), pp. 328—30.

76 *Dīwān*, p. 122.

77 Hilāl Nājī, *Al-Zahāwī*, pp. 321, 326, 350.

78 Jamīl Sa'īd, *Al-Zahāwī wa Thauratuh fī'l Jaḥīm* (Cairo, 1968), pp. 32—4.

79 See Nāṣīr al-Ḥāni, *Muḥāḍarāt*, pp. 58ff. and Muḥammad Abdul-Ḥai, 'Tradition and English and American Influence in Modern Romantic Arabic Poetry', unpublished D.Phil. thesis (Oxford, 1973), pp. 307ff.

80 Māhir Ḥasan Fahmī, *Al-Zahāwī*, p. 223.

81 Jamīl Sa'īd, *Al-Zahāwī*, pp. 68ff.; 110. Cf. Sallūm, *Taṭawwur al-Fikra*, pp. 85ff.

82 Buṭṭī, *Al-Adab*, p. 67.

83 See Ra'ūf Wā'iz, *Ma'rūf al-Ruṣāfī, Ḥayātuh wa Adabuh al-Siyāsī* (Cairo, n.d.), p. 77.

84 Muṣṭafā 'Alī, *Al-Ruṣāfī, Ṣilati bihi wa Ṣītuh wa Mu'allafātuh* (Baghdad, 1948) vol. I, pp. 27; 185; Ra'ūf al-Wā'iẓ, *Ma'rūf al-Ruṣāfī*, pp. 261ff, and Al-Maghribī's Introduction to *Dīwān al-Ruṣāfī* (Cairo, 1958?), 2 vols.

85 See Muṣṭafā 'Alī, *Al-Ruṣāfī*, p. 88. For a list of Ruṣāfī's complete works see Muṣṭafā 'Ali, *Muḥāḍarāt'an Ma'rūf al-Ruṣāfī* (Cairo, 1954), pp. 10ff.

86 See particularly Muṣṭafā 'Alī, *Adab al-Ruṣāfī* (Baghdad, 1947) and Al-Ḥusaini 'Abdul Majīd Hāshim, *Ma'rūf al-Ruṣāfī, Shā'ir al-Ḥurriyya wa'l 'Urūba* (Cairo, n.d.), p. 73.

87 *Dīwān al-Ruṣāfī*, 6th edn. (Cairo, 1958?), p. 138. All subsequent references between brackets in this section will be to this edition.

88 See Muṣṭafā 'Alī, *Muḥāḍarāt 'an Ma'rūf al-Ruṣāfī*, p. 30 and Badawi Tabāna, *Ma'rūf al-Ruṣāfī Dirāsa Adabiyya li Shā'ir al-'Irāq wa bi'atihi al-Siyāsiyya wa'l Ijtimā'iyya* (Cairo, 1957), pp. 255ff.

89 See Maghribī's introduction to Ruṣāfī's *Dīwān*, 6th edn., Tabāna, *Ma'rūf al-Ruṣāfī* p. 190 and Muṣṭafā 'Ali, *Adab al-Ruṣāfī*, pp. 27ff.

90 See Al-Shaikh Jalāl al-Ḥanafī, *Al-Ruṣāfī fi Aujihi wa Ḥaḍīdihi* (Baghdad, 1962), vol. I, p. 348.

91 See Muṣṭafā 'Alī, *Muḥāḍarāt*, p. 25 for a discussion of Ruṣāfī's attack on Iraqi feudalism in his still unpublished prose work: 'Al-Risāla al-'Irāqiyya'.

92 See Shaikh Jalāl al-Ḥanafī, *'Al-Ruṣāfī'*, vol. I, p. 275.

93 Ra'ūf Wā'iẓ, *Ma'rūf al-Ruṣāfī*, pp. 261ff. The Arabic title is *Junūn al-Zaman au al-Fatra al-Mujrima*. Ruṣāfī's authorship of this poem is not beyond dispute.

94 *Ibid.*, p. 327.

95 For a discussion of traditional language and imagery in Ruṣāfī see Ibrāhīm Sāmarrā'ī, *Lughat al-Shi'r*, pp. 72ff. and for his use of ancient poetic conventions and language see Tabāna, *Ma'rūf al-Ruṣāfī*, pp. 238; 243ff.

96 Jayyusi, Trends and Movements, vol. I, pp. 65ff.

97 *Diwañ al-Ruṣāfī*, p. 277.

98 *Dīwān al-Jawāhirī*, vol. III, (Baghdad, 1953), p. 131.

99 'Abd al-Karīm al-Dujailī, *Al-Jawāhirī Shā'ir al-'Arabiyya* (Nejev, 1972), pp. 20ff.

100 For a detailed list of Jawāhirī's publications see al-Dujailī, *Al-Jawāhirī*, pp. 128ff. The Arabic titles of the collections cited here other than the *Dīwān* are *Barīd al-Ghurba, Barīd al-'Auda* and *Ayyuha'l Araq*. The references between brackets in this section on Jawāhirī are to *Dīwān al-Jawāhirī*, vol. I (Baghdad, 1961) and vol. III (Baghdad, 1953).

101 See, e.g. Sallūm, *Taṭawwur al-Fikra*, p. 100.

102 Al-Sāmarrā'ī, *Lughat al-Shi'r*, pp. 116–17.

103 Al-Dujailī, *Al-Jawāhirī*, p. 35.

104 *Ibid.*, p. 117.

105 See 'Abd al-Karīm al-Dujailī, *Muḥāḍarāt 'an al-Shi'r al-'Irāqī al-Ḥadīth* (Cairo, 1959), pp. 213ff. and 218ff.w

106 *Ibid.*, p. 194.

107 E.g. the repetition of *nāmī* in *'Tanwīmat al-Jiyā''*, of *ata'lamu anna jirāḥa'l shahīd* and *taqaḥḥam* in *'Akhī Ja'far'* and *Aṭbiq* in *'Aṭbiq Dujan'* (*Dīwān*, Baghdad, 1961, vol. I, pp. 41, 139, 149ff. Also cf. *wa kāna lizāman an* (I, 68ff.)

108 Dujaili, *Jawāhirī*, pp. 38–9.

109 See e.g. the poems *Awwal al-'Ahd* (I, 106); *Al-Nazgha* (I, 171) and *Badī'a* (III, 118).

110 Muḥammad Mahdī al-Jawāhirī, *Al-Majmū'a al-Shi'riyya al-Kāmila* (Beirut, 1968), vol. I, p. 121.

111 See Dujailī, *Muḥāḍarāt*, p. 202.

CHAPTER 3: THE PRE-ROMANTICS

1 On the experiments of these poets and the possible influence of Marrāsh on *Mahjari* poets, especially Jibrān, as well as the part played by Arabic translations of English hymns, see S. Moreh, 'Strophic, Blank and Free Verse in Modern Arabic Literature', unpublished Ph.D. dissertation (University of London, 1965).

2 See my book *An Anthology of Modern Arabic Verse* (Oxford, 1970), p. xiii and my article 'Convention and Revolt in Modern Arabic Poetry' in G. E. von Grunebaum, ed., *Arabic Poetry: Theory and Development*, p. 192.

3 See Maḥmūd Ibn al-Sharīf, *Khalīl Muṭrān Shā'ir al-Ḥurriyya* (Cairo, 1967), p. 61.

4 On the part played by Muṭrān in promoting the cause of the Egyptian theatre when he was Director of the National Theatre Company see Jamāl al-Dīn al-Ramādī, *Khalīl Muṭrān, Shā'ir al-Aqṭār al-'Arabiyya* (Cairo, n.d.) pp. 55ff. For a brief assessment of his translation of Shakespeare see my article 'Shakespeare and the Arabs' in *Cairo Studies in English* (Cairo, 1964–5), p. 189.

5 For his unpublished works see Ibn al-Sharīf, *Khalīl Muṭrān*, pp. 120ff.

6 Ramādī, *Khalīl Muṭrān*, p. 300.

7 See M. Musṭafā Badawī, *Dirāsāt fi'l Shi'r wa'l Masraḥ* (Cairo, 1960), p. 21.

8 Jamīl Sidqī al-Zahāwī, *Al-Lubāb* (Baghdad, 1928), p. 6.

9 Muḥammad Mandūr, *Muḥādarāt 'an Khalil Muṭrān* (Cairo, 1954), pp. 32–3.

10 In order to realize the extent to which this concept is new to the Arabic literary tradition see G. E. von Grunebaum, 'The Concept of Plagiarism in Arabic Theory', *Journal of Near Eastern Studies*, III, 1944, 234–53, where he shows 'the precedence accorded to wording over meaning, to form over content' in the Arabic critical tradition, and how 'the concept of form itself is being reduced so as to mean little if anything more than phrasing'. On this point Arabic opinion was 'fairly unanimous': e.g. al-Jāḥiẓ- al-Āmidī, al-'Askarī, and Ibn Rashīq subscribed to this view, the only possible exception being 'Abd al-Qāhir al-Jurjānī. Hence the concentration on words by both critics and poets.

11 Ramādī, *Khalīl Muṭrān*, p. 224.

12 Ibn al-Sharīf, *Khalīl Muṭrān*, p. 93.

13 *Al-Muqtaṭaf* (Cairo), June 1939, p. 87.

14 All the references in this section, including those between brackets are to the four volume edition of *Dīwān al-Khalīl* (Cairo, 1948–9).

15 Ramādī, *Khalīl Muṭrān*, pp. 99ff.

16 See, e.g. the poems on pp. 23, 29, 47, 53, 73.

17 'Abd al-'Azīz al-Dusūqī, *Jamā'at Apollo wa Atharuhā fi'l Shi'r al-Ḥadīth* (Cairo, 1971), p. 83.

18 Ramādi, *Khalīl Muṭrān*, p. 157.

19 See, e.g. the poems on the following pages: I, 20, 25, 31, 111, 112, 259; II, 57; III, 246; IV, 170, 220.

20 Shauqī Ḍaif, *Dirāsāt fi'l Shi'r al-'Arabī al-Mu'āṣir* (Cairo, 1959), pp. 122–41; Maḥmūd Ibn al-Sharīf, *Khalīl Muṭrān*.

21 Mandūr, *Muhādarāt*, p. 13; Ramādī, *op. cit.*, pp. 6, 22 and Mounah A. Khouri, *Poetry and the Making of Modern Egypt* (Leiden, 1971), p. 149.

22 On this point see Ramādī, *Khalīl Muṭrān*, p. 253ff. To realize the extent of Muṭrān's revision of his early poetry, cf. the two versions of a poem, e.g. *Dīwān al-Khalīl* (1st edn.), p. 96 and the second edition (1948–49), vol. I, p. 117.

23 Ramādī, *Khalīl Muṭrān*, p. 301.

24 Ibn al-Sharīf, *Khalīl Muṭrān*, pp. 31ff.

25 Here are the Arabic titles: *Dau' al-Fajr* (1909), *La'ālī' al-Afkār* (1913); *Anāshīd al-Ṣibā* (1915); *Zahr al-Rabī'* (1916); *Al-khaṭarāt* (1916); *Al-Afnān* (1918); *Azhār al-Kharīf* (1919). Volume VIII was added by Nīqūlā Yūsuf in his edition of the Complete Works: *Dīwān 'Abd al-Raḥmān Shukrī* (Alexandria, 1960).

added by Nīqūlā Yūsuf in his edition of the Complete Works: *Dīwān 'Abd al-Raḥmān Shukrī* (Alexandria, 1960).

26 In Arabic: *Dīwān al-'Aqqād; Hadiyyat al-Karawān; 'Ābir Sabīl; Waḥy al-Arba'īn; A'āṣīr Maghrib; Ba'd al-A'āṣīr; Mā Ba'd al-Ba'd.* A selection of his verse was made by the author and published in 1958 under the title *Dīwān min al-Dawāwīn.*

27 'Abbās Maḥmūd al-'Aqqād, *Shu'arā' Miṣr wa bī'atūhum fi'l Jīl al-Maḍī*, 2nd edn. (Cairo, 1950), pp. 191ff.

28 Muḥammad Mandūr, *Muḥāḍarāt fi'l Shi'r al-Miṣrī ba'da Shauqī* (Cairo, 1953), p. 37.

29 The correct date is most probably 1920, as can be inferred from pp. 82–3 of vol. II. The second edition of vol. I (the only edition available to the author) is dated April 1921, while the first edition of vol. II is dated February 1921.

30 Cf. 'Abbās Maḥmūd al-'Aqqād and Ibrāhīm 'Abdul Qādir al-Māzinī, *Al-Dīwān* (Cairo 1921), vol. II, pp. 45–7.

31 'Abdul Raḥmān Shukrī, *Dīwān'Abd al-Raḥmān Shukrī*, ed. Nīqūlā Yūsuf (Alexandria, 1960), p. 366. All references between brackets in the section on Shukri will be to this edition.

32 'Aqqād and Māzinī, *Al-Dīwān*, II, 45ff.

33 *Ibid.*, vol. I, p. 1.

34 Shukrī, *Dīwān*, pp. 364ff.

35 'Aqqād and Māzinī, *Al-Dīwān*, I, 16ff.

36 Quoted by Mandūr, *Muḥāḍarāt fi'l Shi'r al-Miṣri*, p. 39.

37 Mikhā'īl Nu'aima, *Al-Ghirbāl*, 6th edn. (Beirut, 1960), pp. 10–11:

38 See Shukrī, *Dīwān*, p. 16.

39 'Abdul Raḥmān Shukrī, *Kitāb al-I'tirāf* (Alexandria, 1916). The references between brackets preceded by the letter C are to this edition.

40 'Abdul Raḥmān Shukrī, *Kitāb al-Thamarāt* (Alexandria, 1916), p. 6.

41 *Ibid.*, p. 8.

42 Muhammad Abdul-Hai, 'Tradition and English and American Influence in Modern Arabic Romantic Poetry', unpublished D. Phil. thesis (Oxford, 1973), p. 265.

43 *Ibid.*

44 See Maḥmūd 'Imād, ed., *Dīwān al-Māzinī* (Cairo, 1961), pp. 233, 247, 250, and 258. All the references between brackets in this section on Māzinī will be to this edition.

45 See 'Abbas Maḥmūd al-'Aqqād, *Dīwān al-'Aqqād* (Aswan, 1967), p. 41.

46 Shukrī, *Dīwān*, p. 373.

47 Maḥmūd 'Imād, *Dīwān*, pp. 22ff.

48 See, e.g. 'Abbās Maḥmūd al-'Aqqād, *Dīwān al-'Aqqād* (Aswan, 1967), p. 199. All references between brackets in this section on 'Aqqād are to this edition.

49 For instance his use of words such as *Shādin* (gazelle), *ibid.*, p. 75.

50 See Abdul-Hai, 'Tradition and English and American Influence', pp. 97ff.

51 Mārūn 'Abbūd, *'Ala'l Miḥakk* (Beirut, 1970), pp. 173–236.

52 See M. M. Badawi, *Coleridge, Critic of Shakespeare* (Cambridge, 1973), pp. 14ff.

53 Muḥammad Mandūr, *Muḥāḍarāt fi'l Shi'r al-Miṣrī*, pp. 62ff.

54 See 'Abbās Maḥmūd al-'Aqqād, *Sā'āt bain al-Kutub*, 3rd edn. (Cairo, 1950), pp. 257 for his three articles on Hardy.

CHAPTER 4: THE ROMANTICS

1 *Qaṭra min Yarā' fi'l Adab wa'l Ijtimā'*

2 'Abd al-'Azīz al-Dusūqī, *Jamā'at Apollo wa Atharuhā fi'l Shi'r al-Ḥadīth* (Cairo, 1971), p. 160.

3 Kamāl Nash'at, *Abū Shādī wa Ḥarakat al-Tajdīd fi'l Shi'r al-'Arabī al-Hadīth* (Cairo, 1967), p. 174.

4 Here are the Arabic titles: *Andā' al-Fajr; Zainab; Anīn wa Ranīn, al-Shafaq al-Bākī;*

Waḥy al-'Ām; Ashi''a wa Ẓilāl; al-Shu'la; Atyāf al-Rabī'; al-Yanbū'; Fauqa'l 'Ubāb; Audat al-Rā'ī; Minal' Samā'. The prose works cited here are *Dirāsāt Islāmiyya; Dirāsāt Adabiyya, Shu'arā' al-'Arab al-Mu'āṣirūn* and *Qaḍāyā al-Shi'r al-Mu'āṣir.*

5 Kamāl Nash'at, *Abū Shādī*, p. 50.

6 *Ibid.*, p. 52. Cf. *Apollo*, December 1934, p. 417.

7 Kamāl Nash'at, *Abū Shādī*, p. 65.

8 On the extent and variety of Abū Shādī's experimentation in verse forms see S. Moreh, 'Free Verse (al-shi'r al-hurr) in Modern Arabic Literature: Abū Shādī and his school, 1926–46' *BSOAS*, vol. XXXI, part I, 1968.

9 The Arabic titles are: *Nakbat Navarīn; Mafkharat Rashīd; 'Abduh Bey; Mahā; Iḥsān; Ardashīr wa Ḥayāt al-Nufūs; al-Zabbā' Malikat Tadmur; al-Āliha.*

10 Aḥmad Zakī Abū Shādī, *Qaṭra min Yarā'*, vol. II (Cairo, 1910), pp. 10, 40 82. Cf. Nash'at, *Abū Shādī*, pp. 292ff.

11 *Qaṭra min Yarā'*, II, 128.

12 A. Z. Abū Shādī, *Andā' al-Fajr*, pp. 81, 63.

13 Muḥammad Mandūr, *al-Shi'r al-Miṣrī ba'd Shauqī, Jamā'at Apollo* (Cairo, 1957), p. 27.

14 See Nash'at, *Abū Shādī*, pp. 119ff.

15 *Ibid.*, pp. 126ff., 154ff.

16 I. A. Edham, *Abushady the Poet* (Leipzig, 1936), is an example of uncritical adulation while an instance of unfair treatment can be found in Salma Khadra Jayyusi, 'Trends and Movements in Contemporary Arabic Poetry', unpublished Ph.D. thesis (London, 1970), vol. I, pp. 532ff. Some doubt has been cast on the authorship of Edham's book: see Nash'at, *Abū Shādī*, p. 209 and G. H. A. Juynball, 'Ismā'īl Adham, the Atheist', *Journal of Arabic Literature*, III (1972), pp. 58ff.

17 A. Z. Abū Shadī, *Al-Shafaq al-Bākī* (Cairo, 1926), p. 322.

18 Edham, *Abushady the Poet*, pp. 22, 30, 38, 43, 47.

19 Abū Shādī, *Al-Shafaq al-Bākī*, p. 233.

20 Abū Shādī, *Fauqa'l 'Ubāb* (Cairo, 1935), p. 83.

21 Abū Shādī, *Mina'l Samā'* (N.Y., 1949), pp. 30, 15.

22 See Nash'at, *Abū Shādī*, pp. 171, 327.

23 Abū Shādī, *Fauqa'l 'Ubāb*, p. 68.

24 Nash'at, *Abū Shādī*, pp. 329ff.

25 *Ibid.*, pp. 342ff.

26 Edham, *Abushady the Poet*, p. 191.

27 Abū Shādī, *Atyāf al-Rabi'* (Cairo, 1933), p. 191.

28 Edham, *Abushady the Poet*, p. 21.

29 Abū Shādī, *Mina'l Samā'*, p. 22.

30 Muḥammad 'Abd al-Mun'im Khafāja, *Rā'id al-Shi'r al-Ḥadīth* (Cairo, 1955), vol. II, p. 300.

31 *Ibid.*, II, 338.

32 Edham, *Abushady the Poet*, p. 19.

33 See Nash'at, *Abū Shādī*, pp. 389ff.

34 Edham, *Abushady the Poet*, p. 28.

35 Abū Shādī, *Mina'l Samā'*, p. 13.

36 *Ibid.*, p. 27.

37 *Ibid.*, p. 58.

38 *Ibid.*, p. 38.

39 Khafāja, *Rā'id al-Shi'r*, II, 349. Cf. II, 219ff; 267.

40 *Ibid.*, II, 294, 240.

41 Abū Shādī, *Mina'l Samā'*, p. 154; Khafāja, *Rā'id al-Shi'r*, II, 304.

42 Khafāja, *Rā'id al-Shi'r*, II, 302.

43 *Ibid.*, II, 294.

44 Here are the Arabic titles: *al-Mallāḥ al-Tā'ih; Warā' al-Ghamām; al-Aḥlām al-Ḍā'i'a; Anfās Muḥtariqa; al-Zauraq al-Ḥālim; Aḥlām al-Nakhīl; al-Shāṭi' al-Majhūl.* See Muḥammad Mandūr, *al-Shi'r al-Miṣrī*, p. 5.

45 *Ilā Jītā al-Fātina.* See Ṣāliḥ Jaudat, *M. 'A. al-Hamsharī, Ḥayātuh wa Shi'ruh* (Cairo, 1963), p. 20.

46 *Shā ṭi' al-A'rāf.* See *Apollo*, I, 629–45.

47 See Jaudat's biographical introduction to *Dīwān Nājī* (Cairo, 1961), p. 16. This edition will be referred to simply as *Dīwān* and all the references between brackets in this section on Nājī will be to it throughout.

48 The Arabic titles are: *Warā' al-Ghamām; Layālī al-Qāhira; Al-Ṭā'ir al-Jarīḥ.* The prose works cited are *Risālat al-Ḥayāt, Kaifa Tafham al-Nās* and *Taufīq al-Ḥakīm al-Fannān al-Ḥā'ir.*

49 These are the poems on the following pages: 45, 52, 78, 98, 111, 114, 162, 174, 201, 202, 215, 325, 326, 356 (all of which are included in Nash'at's volume *Riyāḥ wa Shumū'* published in Cairo in 1951) and also most probably the poem on p. 137.

50 *Dīwān*, pp. 87, 131, 157, 284, 307.

51 *Ibid.*, pp. 46, 62, 64, 83, 164, 283, 296.

52 *Ibid.*, pp. 49, 130, 133, 170, 179, 239, 252, 303.

53 Ibrāhīm Nājī, *Risālat al-Ḥayat* (Cairo, n.d.), p. 18.

54 See the introduction to his *Dīwān*, pp. 31–2.

55 See, e.g. the poems on pp. 39, 42, 61, 75, 118.

56 See pp. 39, 91, 97, 141, 175, 218 and pp. 55, 56ff., 85, 238.

57 Muḥammad 'Abdul-Ḥai, 'Tradition and English and American Influence in Arabic Romantic Poetry', unpublished D.Phil. thesis (Oxford, 1973). See especially the chapter entitled 'The Night of the Creative Mind', pp. 84–128.

58 See, e.g. *Dīwān*, pp. 56, 65, 148.

59 *Ibid.*, e.g. 57, 218, 248.

60 Ni'māt Fu'ād, *Nājī al-Shā'ir* (Cairo, 1954), pp. 66–7.

61 See *Dīwān*, p. 39 n.

62 Nājī, *Risālat al-Ḥayāt*, p. 25.

63 For an able and penetrating analysis of Ṭāhā's music see Nāzik al-Malā'ika, *Muḥāḍarāt fi Shi'r Alī Maḥmūd Ṭāhā* (Cairo, 1965), pp. 64ff.; 144ff.

64 This is the generally accepted date of his birth, but according to one biographer he was born in 1901. See N. Sayyid Taqiyy al-Dīn al-Sayyid, *'Alī Maḥmūd Ṭāhā: Ḥayātuh wa Shi'ruh* (Cairo, 1964), p. 25.

65 See 'Abdul-Ḥai, 'Tradition and English and American Influence', pp. 23–4.

66 In Arabic: *Al-Mallāḥ al-Tā'ih, Layālī al-Mallāḥ al-Tā'ih; Arwāḥ wa Ashbāḥ; Ughniyyat al-Riyāḥ al-Arba'; Zahr wa Khamr; al-Shauq al-'Ā'id; Sharq wa Gharb.* The Arabic title of the volume of essays cited above is *Arwāḥ Shārida.*

67 'Alī Maḥmūd Ṭāhā, *Dīwān* (Beirut, 1972), p. 149. All the references between brackets in this section on Ṭāhā will be to this edition.

68 See 'Abdul-Ḥai, 'Tradition and English and American Influence', pp. 84ff.

69 Al-Malā'ika, *Muḥādarāt*, p. 27.

70 *Ibid.*, pp.8ff.

71 Jayyusi, 'Trends and Movements', I, pp. 552ff.

72 Muḥammad Mahdī al-Jawāhirī, *Al-Majmū'a al-Shi'riyya al-Kāmila* (Beirut, 1969), vol. II, pp. 63ff.

73 Al-Malā'ika, *Muḥāḍarat*, pp. 81, 365.

74 On Ṭāhā's prosodic skill and originality see part III of al-Malā'ika's book.

75 See Razzūq Faraj Razzūq, *Ilyās Abū Shabaka wa Shi'ruh* (Beirut, 1956), p. 45.

76 *Rawābiṭ al-Fikr wa'l Rūḥ bain al-'Arab wa'l Firinja* (Beirut, 1943).

77 In Arabic: *Al-Qaithāra, al-Marīḍ al-Ṣāmit, Afā'ī al-Firdaus, al-Alḥān, Nidā' al-Qalb, Ilā al-Abad, Ghalwā'* and *Min Ṣa'īd al-Āliha.*

78 See the essay by Buṭrus al-Bustānī in *Ilyās Abū Shabaka, Dirāsāt wa Dhikrayāt* (Beirut, 1970), pp. 18ff. and Razzūq, *Abū Shabaka*, p. 148.
79 Razzūq, *Abū Shabaka*, p. 134.
80 *Ibid.*, p. 149.
81 *Ibid.*, p. 261.
82 Ilyās Abū Shabaka, *Ghalwā'* (Beirut, 1959), p. 130.
83 *Ibid.*, p. 85.
84 *Ibid.*, pp. 70–4.
85 Razzūq, *Abū Shabaka*, p. 175.
86 See *Ilyās Abū Shabaka, Dirāsāt*, etc. . . , p. 225.
87 Mario Praz, *The Romantic Agony* (1933); see particularly the chapter entitled '*La Belle Dame Sans Merci*'.
88 *Ghalwā'*, p. 113.
89 Razzūq, *Abū Shabaka*, pp. 179ff.
90 Abū Shabaka, '*Afā'ī al-Firdaus*, 2nd edn. (Beirut, 1948), p. 45.
91 Abū Shabaka, *Nidā' al-Qalb* (Beirut, 1963), p. 18.
92 In the poem 'Shā'iran', *Nidā' al-Qalb*, p. 20.
93 See Razzūq, *Abū Shabaka*, p. 113. Cf. *Ilyas Abū Shabaka, Dirāsāt*, pp. 158ff.
94 Razzūq, *Abū Shabaka*, p. 106.
95 *Afā'ī*, p. 59.
96 Razzūq, *Abū Shabaka*, pp. 180ff.
97 *Afā'ī*, pp. 50ff.
98 Razzūq, *Abū Shabaka*, p. 106.
99 *Afā'ī*, p. 38.
100 *Ibid.*, p. 30.
101 *Ibid.*, p. 32.
102 *Ibid.*, p. 32.
103 *Ibid.*, p. 47; the Arabic title is *Ḥadīth fi'l Kūkh*.
104 Razzūq, *Abū Shabaka*, p. 64.
105 Abū Shabaka, *Rawābiṭ al-Fikr wa'l Ruḥ*, pp. 87ff.
106 See Jayyusi, 'Trends and Movements', vol. i, pp. 621ff.
107 Abū Shabaka, *Al-Alḥān* (Beirut, 1963), pp. 73–5.
108 *Ibid.*, p. 79.
109 Abū Shabaka, *Nidā' al-Qalb* (Beirut, 1963), p. 61.
110 *Ibid.*, p. 35.
111 *Ibid.*, pp. 37–9.
112 *Ibid.*, p. 53.
113 See Razzūq, *Abū Shabaka*, pp. 248–9.
114 *Nidā'*, pp. 7ff.
115 *Ibid.*, pp. 30, 39, 58.
116 See Abu'l Qāsim Muḥammad Karrū, *Al-Shābbī, Ḥayātuh, Shi'ruh* (Beirut, 1964), pp. 47ff. and Khalīfa Muḥammad al-Tillīsī, *Al-Shābbī wa Jubrān* (Beirut, 1967), pp. 219ff.
117 Muḥammad al-Ḥilaiwī, *Rasā'il al-Shābbī* (Tunis, 1966), pp. 40, 60.
118 Abu'l Qāsim Muḥammad Karru, *Āthar al-Shābbī wa Ṣadāhu fi'l Sharq* (Beirut, 1961), p. 33.
119 Abu'l Qāsim al-Shābbī, *Aghānī al-Ḥayāt* (Tunis, 1955).
120 Abu'l Qāsim al-Shābbī, *Al-Khayāl al-Shi'rī 'inda'l 'Arab* (Tunis, 1961), p. 18. All the references between brackets are to this edition.
121 On the controversies that arose round Shābbī see e.g. Ni'māt Fu'ād, *Sha'b wa Shā'ir: Abu'l Qāsim al-Shābbī* (Cairo, 1958), pp. 114ff. and 'Umar Farrūkh, *Al-Shābbī Shā'ir al-Hubb wa'l Ḥayāt* (Beirut, 1960), p. 128 and the chapter devoted to the subject of controversies. A good bibliography on Shābbī is provided by A. Bernardini –

Mazzini in *Institut des belles lettres Arabes*, Tunis No. 131 (1973–1), pp. 97–117.
122 See 'Abdul-Ḥai, 'Tradition and English and American Influence', pp. 197ff.
123 '*Ṣalawāt fī Haikal al-Ḥubb*', Abu'l Qāsim al-Shābbī, *Aghānī al-Ḥayāt* (Tunis, 1955), p. 121. The references between brackets in this section on Shābbī will be to this edition throughout.
124 *Ibid.*, pp. 33, 35, 87, 127.
125 Cf. *Ibid.*, p. 65.
126 Ni'māt Fu'ād, *Sha'b wa Shā'ir*, p. 45.
127 On this point see e.g. Muṣṭafa al-Ḥabib Baḥrī, *Al-Shābbī al-Nabiyy al-Majhūl* (Damascus, 1960).
128 See Al-Tillīsī, *Al-Shābbī*, pp. 47–59.
129 On this point see Abu'l Qāsim Karrū, *Kifāḥ al-Shābbī* (Tunis, 1957), pp. 52ff.
130 *Ibid.*, p. 55.
131 In the Tunisian magazine *al-Fikr*, April 1966, p. 153 as cited by S. K. Jayyusi.
132 The word *sāḥir* (magician) occurs both in the Tunis edition of *Aghānī al-Ḥayāt* of 1955 and in the Beirut edition of his *Dīwān* of 1972, but Karrū's reading *sākhir* (master of irony) which is followed in his book *Al-Shābbī, Ḥayātuh wa Shi'ruh (Beirut,* 1954, p. 214) is certainly more appropriate to the context. However, in Karrū's later book *Āthar al-Shābbī wa Ṣadāhu fi'l Sharq* (Beirut, 1961, p. 90) the word strangely enough appears again as *sāḥir.*
133 Cf. 'Abd al-Majīd 'Ābidīn, *Al-Tijānī Shā'ir al-Ḥubb wa' al Jamāl* (Cairo, 1962), p. 52.
134 See e.g. Abu'l Qāsim Badrī, *Al-Shā'irān al-Mutashābihān al-Shābbī wa'l Tijānī* (Cairo, 1954).
135 See 'Abd al-Majīd 'Ābidīn's preface to Al-Tijānī's *Ishrāqa*, 3rd edn. (Khartoum, 1956), pp. 7ff.
136 *Ibid.*, p. 10.
137 Al-Tijānī Yūsuf Bashīr, *Ishrāqa*, 3rd edn. (Khartoum, 1956), pp. 38, 53. All references between brackets in this section on Tijānī will be to this edition of his poems.
138 This date of his birth is the one given by Sāmī al-Dahhān, *Al-Shi'r al-Ḥadīth fi'l Iqlīm al-Sūrī* (Cairo, 1960), 241; but it is 1908 according to his friend Aḥmad al-Jundī, *Shu'arā' Sūriyya* (Beirut, 1965), p. 113.
139 The Arabic titles are: *Shi'r* (Aleppo, 1936); *Min 'Umar Abū-Rīsha: Shi'r* (Beirut, 1947); *Mukhtārāt* (Beirut, 1959) and *Dīwān 'Umar Abū Rīsha*, vol. I (Beirut, 1971).
140 For *Dhi Qār* see Dahhān, *Al-Shi'r*, p. 242. *Maḥkamat al-Shu'arā'* was advertised in his volume *Shi'r* while the last two plays were announced in his volume *Min 'Umar Abū Rīsha.*
141 Dahhān, *Al-Shi'r*, pp. 255–57.
142 *Ibid.*, p. 254.
143 *Ibid.*, p. 267.
144 See, e.g. '*Sukūn*' in his volume *Shi'r*, p. 84.
145 *Shi'r*, pp. 133ff.
146 *Ṭūfān* and '*Adhāb* in *Shi'r*, pp. 7–60.
147 See Jundī, *Shu'arā'*, p. 122, Dahhān, *Al-Shi'r*, p. 216 and Shauqī Ḍaif, *Dirāsāt fi'l Shi'r al-'Arabī al-Mu'āṣir* (Cairo, 1959), pp. 235ff.
148 '*Al-Raudat al-Jā'i'a*' in *Min 'Umar Abū Risha*, p. 54.
149 *Ibid.*, p. 252.
150 '*Maṣra' Fannān*' in *Shi'r*, p. 63.
151 *Al-Nūr; Murfīn, Shā'ir al-Ṭabī'a*, in *Shi'r*, pp. 82, 121, 163.
152 *Sukūn; Imra'a* in *Shi'r*, pp. 84, 89.
153 *Ḍajar*, in *Shi'r*, p. 92.
154 '*Āṣifa* in *Shi'r*, p. 115; *Dalīla*, in *Dīwān 'Umar Abū Rīsha*, p. 240; *Shaqiyya* in *Shi'r*, p. 139.

155 *Miṣbāh wa Sarīr*; *Muḥāwala* in *Shi'r*, pp. 99, 101. The former appears as *Ḥirmān* in *Min Shi'r*, p. 222.
156 *Shabaḥ al-Māḍī* in *Shi'r*, p. 111.
157 *'Inād* in *Mukhtārāt*, p. 8; *Nasr* in *Min 'Umar*, p. 193.
158 *Al-Rukūd* in *Shi'r*, p. 138.
159 *Imra'a wa Timthāl* in *Min 'Umar*, p. 17.
160 Dahhān, *Al-Shi'r*, pp. 242–43.
161 *Jān Dārk, Shahīd, Lamḥa* in *Shi'r*, pp. 127, 160, 179.
162 *Min Shi'r 'Umar Abū Rīsha*, pp. 112, 231.
163 *Ḥadīth fi'l Khandaq; Ba'd al-Nakba* in *Mukhtārāt*, pp. 110, 268.
164 *Dīwān 'Umar Abū Rīsha*, p. 21.
165 *'Ām Jadīd* in *Mukhtārāt*, p. 107.
166 *Nasr* in *Min 'Umar*, p. 193. Cf. *Shi'r*, p. 207; *Min 'Umar*, pp. 109, 172.

CHAPTER 5: THE EMIGRANT POETS

1 See e.g. Iḥsān 'Abbās and Muḥammad Yūsuf Najm in *Al-Shi'r al-'Arabī fi'l Mahjar* (Beirut, 1957). This, however, is an excellent and thoughtful book to which the reader is advised to refer for a more detailed study than it has been possible to attempt here.
2 *Ibid.*, p. 19.
3 Muhammad 'Abdul Ghanī Ḥasan, *Al-Shi'r al-'Arabī fi'l Mahjar*, 2nd edn., (Cairo, (1958), p. 24.
4 Khalil S. Hawi, *Khalil Gibran, His Background, Character and Works* (Beirut, 1972), p. 281. Much has been written on the theme of nostalgia and homesickness in *Mahjar* poetry. See e.g. Farīd Jiḥā, *Al-Ḥanīn fī Shi'r al-Mahjar* (Aleppo, n.d.) and *Al-'Urūba fī Shi'r al-Mahjar* (Beirut, 1966); Wadī' Dib, *Al-Shi'r al-'Arabī fi'l Mahjar al-Amrīkī* (Beirut, 1955), pp. 78ff.; Muḥammad Muṣtafa Haddāra, *Al-Tajdīd fī Shi'r al-Mahjar* (Cairo, 1957), pp. 95ff.; 'Īsā al-Nā'ūrī, *Adab al-Mahjar* (Cairo, 1959), pp. 73ff., and Uns Dāwūd, *Al-Tajdīd fī Shi'r al-Mahjar* (Cairo, 1967), pp. 171ff.
5 See M. 'A. Hasan, *Al-Shi'r*, pp. 51ff.; Wadī' Dīb, *Al-Shi'r.*, pp. 158–9 and Nādira Jamīl Sarrāj, *Shu'arā' al-Rābiṭa al-Qalamiyya* (Cairo, 1957), pp. 69ff.
6 Jibrān Khalīl Jibrān, *Al-Majmū'a al-Kāmila li Mu'allafāt Jibrān Khalīl Jibrān* (Beirut, 1959), pp. 278, 307.
7 Mīkhā'īl Nu'aima, *Al-Ghirbāl* (Beirut, 1960), p. 126.
8 Mīkhā'īl Nu'aima, *Jibrān Khalīl Jibrān, Ḥayātuh, Mautuh, Adabuh, Fannuh* (Beirut, 1960), p. 126.
9 Hawi, *Khalil Gibran* p. 283.
10 *Al-Mawākib*: see Jibrān, *Al-majmū'a*, pp. 343ff.
11 The Arabic title is *Ṭalāsim*.
12 Ṭāha Ḥusain, *Ḥadīth al-Arba'ā'*, vol. III (Cairo, 1957), pp. 200ff. For a passionate defence of *Mahjar* poets against this charge, however, see Jūrj Ṣaidaḥ, *Adabunā wa Udabā'unā fi'l Mahājir al-Amrīkiyya* (Beirut, 1957), pp. 575ff.
13 In Arabic *Hams al-Jufūn*.
14 Mīkhā'īl Nu'aima, *Al-Ghirbāl*, pp. 84ff.
15 Mīkhā'īl Nu'aima, *Hams al-Jufūn*, 4th edn. (Beirut, 1962), p. 14.
16 Muḥammad Mandūr, *Fi'l Mīzān al-Jadīd*, 2nd edn. (Cairo, n.d.), p. 50.
17 Mīkhā'īl Nu'aima, *Sab'ūn, Ḥikāyat 'Umr*, vol. I (Beirut, 1959), p. 181.
18 Nu'aima, *Hams*, pp. 64, 96. The Arabic titles are *al-Khair wa'l Sharr, al-'Irāk*.
19 Nu'aima, *Sab'ūn*, vol. II (Beirut, 1960), p. 167.
20 Nu'aima, *Hams*, pp. 47, 10, 26, 40, 35, 52, 55. The titles are *Aurāq al Kharīf, al-Nahr al-Mutajammid, Min Sifr al-Zamān, Ṣada al-Ajrās, Ibtihālāt, al-Tā'ih*, and *Afāqa'l Qalb*.

21 'Abbās and Najm, *Al-Shi'r*, p. 185.
22 Nu'aima, *Hams*, pp. 28, 46, 73: *Lau Tudriku'l Ashwāk, al-Ṭarīq, al-Ṭama'nīna.*
23 Nadeem N. Naimy, *Mikhail Naimy, an Introduction* (Beirut, 1967), pp. 183, 191.
24 Philip Ṭarrāzī, *Tarīkh al-Ṣaḥāfa al-'Arabiyya*, vol. IV, p. 409.
25 Abū Māḍī's volumes of verse are: *Tadhkār al-Māḍī, Dīwān Iliyā Abū Māḍī, al-Jadāwil, al-Khamā'il* and *Tibr wa Turāb.*
26 'Abdul Laṭīf Sharāra, *Iliyā Abū Māḍī* (Beirut, 1961), p. 18.
27 *Iliyā Abū Māḍī, Shi'r wa Dirāsa*, ed. Zuhair Mirzā (Damascus, n.d.), p. 7. The Arabic title is *Falsafaṭ al-Ḥayāt.*
28 Abū Māḍī, *Al-Jadāwil*, 3rd. edn. (Beirut, 1961), pp. 10, 139–78: *Al-'Anqā'*; *al-Ṭalāṣim.*
29 The title is *Ibtasim*: see 'A. L. Sharāra, *Iliyā Abū Māḍī*, p. 124.
30 Abū Māḍī, *al-Jadāwil*, p. 9.
31 *Ibid.*, p. 48. The title is *Fi'l Qafr.*
32 Here are the Arabic titles: *Al-Ghāba al-Mafqūda*; *'Ish li'l Jamāl, Al-Shā'ir fi'l Samā, Ta'ālī, Lail al-Ashwāq, Al-Dam'a al-Kharsā', Al-Ṭīn, Al-Ṭalāsim, Fi'l Qafr*, and *Nār al-Qirā.*
33 Abū Māḍī, *al-Jadāwil*, p. 56.
34 Nasīb 'Arīḍa, *Arwāḥ Ḥā'ira* (New York, 1946). This is now a rare book: where possible references will be given to the much more readily available selection of his poems: *Mukhtārāt min Nasīb 'Arīḍa*, Manāhil al-Adab al-'Arabī series (Beirut, 1950).
35 See Nu'aima, *Sab'ūn*, vol. II, p. 178.
36 The elegy is entitled *Dhikra'l Gharīb.*
37 *Al-Shā'ir*, see 'Arīda, *Arwāḥ*, pp. 39–40.
38 See, e.g. the poem *Limādha* in *Arwāḥ*, p. 44.
39 *Sallat Fawākih* in *Arwāḥ*, pp. 91ff.
40 See *The Song of Solomon*, ii, 13, iv. 3 and vii. 7.
41 See e.g. the poem *Da'nī wa Sha'nī, Arwāḥ*, p. 49.
42 See *al-Nu'āmā* and the conclusion to *Lastu Adrī* in *Arwāḥ*, pp. 53ff., 228.
43 *Mukhtārāt min Nasīb 'Arīḍa*, p. 135.
44 In Arabic *Ishrab Waḥīdan, Da'nī wa Sha'nī, Al-Umm al-Mankūba, Ana fi'l Ḥaḍīḍ, Ṭarīq al-Ḥaīra, Yā Nafsu la Tabkī, Al-Nihāya*, and *Ya Gharīb al-Dār.*
45 *Arwāḥ*, pp. 24, 33: *Al-Ṣamt, Al-Naum wa'l Maniyya.*
46 *Ana fi'l Ḥaḍīḍ, Mukhtārāt*, p. 66.
47 In Arabic *Udnu minnī, Man Naḥnu.*
48 The original titles are *Yā Nafs, Al-Nihāya*. See *Mukhtārāt*, p. 18 and Ḥasan, *Al-Shi'r*, pp. 160–1.
49 Rashīd Ayyūb, *Aghānī al-Darwīsh* (Beirut, 1959), pp. 59, 29: *Al-Rabī', Wa Wallā mā 'Arafnāhū.*
50 In Arabic *Aghāni al-Darwīsh* and *Hiya'l Ḥayat.*
51 Rashīd Ayyūb, *Al-Ayyūbiyyāt* (Beirut, 1959), p. 12.
52 *Ibid.*, p. 68.
53 *Ibid.*, p. 55, 209, 180: *Al-Shaīkh wa'l Fatāh, Ibnat al-Kūkh, Man Anā.*
54 *Al-Āmāl al-Ḍā'i'a, Ma'an'l Ḥayāt, Al-Waraqa al-Murta'isha, Jazīrat al-Nisyān*; *Min Khilāl al-Ḍabāb*, and *Al-Ḍau' al-Ba'īd.*
55 *Rubā'iyyāt Farḥāt*, and *Aḥlām al-Rā'ī*. The 1954 edition of his works contain *al-Rabī', al Ṣayf, al-Kharīf* and *Rubā'iyyāt.*
56 *Yā Rasūl al-Allāh, Ila'l Lāji'īn*, and *Ḥayātu Mashaqqāt*. See Muḥammad 'Abd al-Ghanī Ḥasan, *Al-Shi'r al-'Arabī fi'l Mahjar*, pp. 241, 245, 239. Most of the poems referred to in this section on the Latin American poets are to be found in this excellent anthology and as this is a more easily available book than the complete works of some of these poets, reference will be made to it where possible.

57 See Ilyās Farḥāt, *Dīwān Maṭla' al-Shitā'* (Cairo, 1967), p. 9.
58 Ḥasan, *Al-Shi'r*, pp. 237, 226, 229, 235, 234; *Yā Najmat al-Lail, 'Ijl al-Dhahab, Manābi' al-Shi'r, Yā Naḥla, Ya 'Īd, Mauṭinī*, and *Khayāl al-Waṭan*.
59 Ilyās Farḥāt, *Ahlām al-Rā'ī* (Beirut ,1962), pp. 104, 139.
60 Ḥasan, *Al-Shi'r*, pp. 231, 227, 225: *Khuṣlat al-Sha'r, Al-Rāhiba*, and *Al-Sakra al-Khālida*.
61 Rashīd Salīm al-Khūrī, *Al-A'āṣīr* (Beirut, 1962), pp. 5–17.
62 E.g. *'Īd al-Bariyya* in Ḥasan, *Al-Shi'r*, p. 262 and *'Īd al-Fiṭr* and *Nabiyy* in 'Abdullaṭīf Sharāra, *Al-Shā'ir al-Qarawī* (Beirut, 1960), pp. 188, 212.
63 See Sharāra, *Al-Shā'ir*, p. 56.
64 Ḥasan, *Al-Sh'ir*, p. 249: *Al-Wilāda al-Jadīda*.
65 Sharāra, *Al-Shā'ir*, pp. 124ff.: *Al-Dauḥa al-Sāqita*.
66 Ḥasan, *Al-Sh'ir*, pp. 258, 250, 251, 260: *Baina'l Bashar wa'l Baqar. Al-Fitna al-Kubrā, 'Ināq al-Wujūd*, and *Hiḍn al-Umm*.
67 *'Alā Bisāṭ al-Rīḥ*. See Riaḍ al-Ma'lūf, *Shu'arā' al-Ma'ālifa* (Beirut, 1962), p. 40.
68 Fauzī Ma'lūf, *'Alā Bisāṭ al-Rīh* (Rio De Janeiro, 1929).
69 The Arabic titles are *'Abqar* and *Al-Aḥlām*.
70 Fauzī Ma'lūf, *'Alā Bisāṭ*, pp. 38, 71.
71 See *Dhikrā Fauzī*, a special no. of *Al-Ḍād*, vol. 5, June-August (Aleppo, 1935), p. 103. See also the poem with the significant title 'The Torch of Suffering' in *Dīwān Fauzī al-Ma'lūf* (Beirut, 1957), pp. 121,ff.
72 *Qabr Shā'ir*, *'Ali Maḥmūd Ṭāha, Shi'r wa Dirāsa* ed. Suhail Ayyūb (Damascus, 1962), p. 256.
73 See 'Īsā Yūsuf Bullāṭa, *Al-Rūmanṭīqiyya wa Ma'ālimuhā fi'l Shi'r al-'Arabī al-Hadīth* (Beirut, 1960), pp. 134ff.

CHAPTER 6: THE RECOIL FROM ROMANTICISM

1 See my article 'Convention and Revolt in Modern Arabic Poetry', in G. E. von Grunebaum (ed.), *Arabic Poetry: Theory and Development* (Wiesbaden, 1973), p. 201.
2 Some of the material here and on the question of 'commitment' derives from my article 'Commitment in Contemporary Arabic Literature', *Journal of World History*, XIV, 4 (1972), 858–79. The reader will find a fuller discussion of the question in this article.
3 On the romanticism of young Iraqi poets such as Bayyātī and Buland Ḥaidarī see Iḥsān 'Abbās, *Fann al-Shi'r* (3rd edn., Beirut, n.d.), p. 52.
4 *Ḍajjat al-rabī'*, *al-Risāla* (Cairo), XIII, 1 (1945), 567–8.
5 *'Ilā shā'ir tā'ih, Iṣrār* (Cairo, 1955), no page number.
6 *Al-Adab li'l Sha'b, Maqālāt Mamnū'a*. See a useful translation of Salāma Mūsā's autobiographical work: *The Education of Salama Musa*, tr. L. O. Schuman (Leiden, 1961).
7 On the activities of the Iraqi Communist Party see Iḥsān 'Abbās, *Badr Shākir al-Sayyāb Dirāsa fī Ḥayātih wa Shi'rih* (Beirut, 1969), pp. 91ff. See also Bayyātī's account of his literary 'formation' and that of his generation such as Sayyāb and Buland Ḥaidarī in *Dīwān 'Abd al-Wahhāb al-Bayyātī* (Beirut, 1971), II, 379ff.
8 Muḥammad 'Abdul-Ḥai, 'Tradition and English and American Influence in Arabic Romantic Poetry', unpublished D. Phil. Thesis (Oxford, 1973), pp. 354–5. For a general discussion of *Plutoland and Other Poems* see also Mounah A. Khouri, 'Lewis 'Awad': A Forgotten Pioneer of the Free Verse Movement', *Journal of Arabic Literature*, I (Leiden, 1970), 137–44. .
9 For full details see my article 'Commitment in Contemporary Arabic Literature'.

10 Muḥammad Mufīd al-Shūbāshī, *'Al-Adab al-Ḍāll'*, *al-Thaqāfa* (Cairo), no. 577, 17 Dec. 1951.

11 *Antum al-Shu'arā'*. The influence of French Symbolist poetic theory on 'Aql is obvious in his introduction to *al-Majdaliyya* where he is indebted to Mallarmé, Valéry and Abbé Bremond. His debt to French writers has been amply illustrated by Anṭūn Ghaṭṭās Karam in his book *al-Ramziyya fi'l Shi'r al-'Arabī al-Ḥadith* (Beirut, 1949). 'Aql continued to write, though little. For instance, besides the two verse plays *Bint Yaftāḥ* (1935) and *Cadmus* (1944) he published another volume of verse *Rindalā* (1950). He attained great popularity, especially in the 1940s but he is not much read now, although he had some influence on some Lebanese poets, especially the early Yūsuf al-Khāl.

12 Al-Bayyātī, *Dīwān*, II, 411.

13 *Al-Ādāb* (Beirut), II,8 (August 1954), 24.

14 *Ibid.*, II,6 (June 1954), 56.

15 Bayyātī, *Dīwān*, II, 385.

16 In Arabic: *Fi'l Thaqāfa al-Miṣriyya, Qaḍāya Adabiyya.*

17 See *Ādāb*, III, 5, May 1955.

18 The Arabic titles are: *Malā'ika wa Shayaṭin, Abārīq Muhashshama, al-Majd li'l Atfāl wa'l Zaitūn, Ash'ār fi'l Manfā, 'Ishrūn Qaṣīda min Berlin, Kalimāt la Tamūt, al-Nār wa'l Kalimāt, Qaṣā'id, Sifr al-Faqr wa'l Thaura, Al-ladhī Ya'tī wa lā Ya'tī, al-Maut fi'l Ḥayāt, al-Kitāba 'ala'l Ṭīn. 'Uyūn al-Kilāb al-Mayyita, Qaṣā'id 'alā Bawwābāt al-'Ālam al-Sab'*. Unless otherwise stated the references between brackets in this section will be to Bayyātī's Collected Poems: *Dīwān 'Abd al-Wahhāb al-Bayyātī* (Beirut 1971) in two volumes.

19 The Arabic titles of the poems referred to in this section are: *Aḥlām shā'ir, 'Uzla, Sūq al-Qarya, al-Lail wa'l Madīna wa'l Sull, al-Malja' al-'Ishrūn, Ughniyya ilā Sha'bī, al-Rabī' wa'l Atfāl, 14 Tammūz, Bukā'iyya ilā' Shams Ḥazīrān, al-Fann li'l Ḥayāt. Kābūs al-Lail wa'l Nahār, Marthiyya ila'l Madīna allatī Lam Tūlad,* and *al-Kābūs*. Maḥmūd Ḥasan Ismā'īl's collection is called *Aghāni al-Kūkh.*

20 See Iḥsān 'Abbās, *'al-Ṣūra al-Ukhrā fi Shi'r al-Bayyātī'*, *Ādāb*, XIV, 3 (March 1966), 28ff.

21 'Abd al-Wahhāb al-Bayyātī, *Qaṣā'id Hubb 'alā Bawwābāt al-'Ālam al-Sab'* (Baghdad, 1971), pp. 152–4.

22 The Arabic titles of Ṣalāh 'Abd al-Ṣabūr's volumes are *al-Nās fī Bilādī, Aqūlu Lakum, Aḥlām al-Fāris al-Qadīm,* and *Ta'ammulāt fi Zaman Jarīḥ*. His collected works appeared in Beirut in 1972 in two volumes entitled *Dīwān Ṣalāḥ 'Abd al-Ṣabūr*. The references in this section will be to this edition. The original titles of the poems referred to are *Ughniyya li'l Shitā', Mudhakkirāt al-Ṣūfī Bishr al-Ḥāfī, Ḥadīth fi'l Maqhā* and *Unthā*. His prose work mentioned here is *Ḥayātī fi'l Shi'r*. For an English translation of some of 'Abd al-Ṣabūr's poems see *JAL*, I, (1970), II, (1971).

23 See my article 'Commitment in Modern Arabic Literature', pp. 874–9.

24 Hijāzī's collections are *Madīna bilā Qalb, Lam Yabqa illa'l I'tirāf* and *Marthiyyat al-'Umr al-Jamīl*. His collected works came out in Beirut in 1973 under the title *Dīwān Aḥmad 'Abd al-Mu'ṭī Hijāzī*. The Arabic titles of the poems referred to are: *Ila'l Liqā', Maqtal Ṣabiyy, al-'Ām al-Sādis 'Ashar,* and *al-Riḥla Ibtada'at.*

25 Faitūrī's collections are *Aghānī Ifrīqiya, 'Āshiq min Ifrīqiya, Udhkurīnī yā Ifrīqiya* and *Ma'zūfat li-Darwīsh Mutajawwil*. An edition including these works together with other poems was published in Beirut in 1972 under the title *Dīwān Muḥammad al-Faitūrī*. All references in this section will be to this complete edition. The Arabic titles of the poems referred to are: *Taḥt al-Amṭār, Aḥzān al-Madīna al-Saudā', Māta Ghadan, Ilā Wajh Abyaḍ, Ṣaut Ifrīqiya, Yaumiyyāt Ḥājj ilā Bait al-Allāh al-Ḥarām,* and *Suquṭ Dabshalīm.*

26 Nizār Qabbānī produced his collected works in one volume in 1967: *al-A'māl al-Shi'riyya al-Kāmila*, Manshūrāt Nizār Qabbānī, Beirut. This volume, which covers his works only up to 1967 includes seven collections: *Qālat liya'l Samrā'*, *Ṭufūlat Nahd*, *Antī lī*, *Samba*, *Qaṣā'id*, *Ḥabībatī*, and *Al-Rasm bi'l Kalimāt*. Since then Qabbānī has produced several other volumes. Unless otherwise stated the reference will be to this edition of his Collected Works.

27 '*Īd Milādihā*' from *Qaṣā'id*, p. 47, *Khubz wa Hashīsh wa Qamar*, *Ibid.*, p. 172. An English translation of this poem has appeared in *JAL*, vol. III (1972). For translations of other poems by Qabbānī see vol. I (1970) of the same Journal.

28 Nizār Qabbānī, '*Alā Hāmish Daftar al-Naksa* (Beirut, 1967), pp. 7, 9.

29 Yūsuf al-Khaṭīb, *Dīwān al-Waṭan al-Muḥtall* (Damascus, 1968).

30 E.g. Darwīsh's *F'Intiẓār al-'A'idīn* and Qāsīm's *Khiṭāb min Sūq al-Baṭāla*, *Ibid.*, pp. 180, 323.

31 '*Āshiq min Filasṭīn*, *Qamar al-Shitā'*, *Ibid.*, p. 184. An English translation of 'Lover from Palestine' is available in *JAL*, V (1974). A selection of Darwīsh's poems in English translation has recently been published under the title Mahmoud Darwīsh, *Selected Poems*, edited and translated by Ian Wedde and Fawwaz Tuqan (Cheadle, Cheshire, 1973). The titles of other poems referred to in this section are: *al-Ward wa'l Qāmūs* (p. 216), *Wu'ūd min al-'Aṣifa* (p. 217), *Waṭan* (p. 244).

32 The titles of al-Qāsīm's two volumes mentioned are *Aghānī'l Durūb* (1965?) and *Damī 'alā Kaffī* (1967) and the poems are on pp. 291 and 323 of al-Khaṭib's collection.

33 Mu'āwiya Nūr, *Dirāsāt fi'l Adab wa'l Naqd* (Khartoum, 1970), pp. 207–213. See Abdul-Hai, 'Tradition and English and American Influence', pp. 337ff.

34 Abdul-Hai, 'Tradition and English and American Influence', p. 342.

35 See e.g. M. Muṣṭafā Badawī, *Rasā'il min London* (Alexandria, 1956), p. 8.

36 See e.g. Iḥsān 'Abbās, *Badr Shākir al-Sayyāb*, pp. 251–63; S. K. Jayyusi, 'Trends and Movements in Contemporary Arabic Poetry', unpublished Ph.D. Thesis (London, 1970), pp. 1011–12, 1015–18, 1025, 1027 and Abdul-Hai, 'Tradition and English and American Influence', pp. 269–74. See also S. Moreh, 'Free verse (*al-Shi'r al-Ḥurr*) in Modern Arabic Literature: Abū Shādī and his School 1926–46', *BSOAS*, vol. XXXI, part I (1968) 45ff. and 'The Influence of Western Poetry and Particularly T. S. Eliot on Modern Arabic Poetry (1947–1964)', *Asian and African Studies*, V (1969), 47–9.

37 See *Shi'r*, no. 25 (1963), 143 and *Ādāb* (Beirut), II, 3 (Summer 1963), 8. Cf. *Shi'r*, no. 44 (1969), 5.

38 *Shi'r*, no. 26 (1963), p. 110.

39 Muḥammad al-Faitūrī, *Aghānī Ifrīqiya* (Cairo, 1955), pp. 120ff. and Maḥmūd Darwīsh, '*Āshiq min Filasṭīn* (2nd edn., Beirut, 1969), pp. 47ff.

40 S. Moreh, 'Strophic, Blank and Free Verse in Modern Arabic Literature'. Unpublished Ph.D. thesis (London, 1965) and Jayyūsī, 'Trends and Movements'.

41 See Shmuel Moreh, 'Nāzik al-Malā'ika and al-Shi'r al-Ḥurr in Modern Arabic Literature', *Asian and African Studies*, IV (1968), 66–8, 70ff.

42 For a discussion of the present writer's experiments see Jayyusi, 'Trends and Movements', pp. 905–9 and S. Moreh, 'Blank Verse in Modern Arabic Literature', *BSOAS* vol. XXIX, part 3 (1966), 497 and 'Free Verse in Modern Arabic Literature: Abū Shādī and his School, 1926–46' *Ibid.* vol. XXXI, part 1 (1968) 44–6. For al-Khāl's statement see his magazine *Adab* (Beirut), no. 5 (Winter 1963), 12.

43 *Ādāb*, II, 6 (June 1954), 69. See S. Moreh, 'Nāzik al-Malā'ika', *Ibid.*, 79.

44 See Hijāzī's satire on 'Aqqād prompted by the latter's opposition to the new form in *Dīwān Aḥmad 'Abd al-Mu'ṭī Ḥijāzī*, pp. 433ff.

45 Buland Ḥaidarī in *Shi'r* (Beirut), 42 (Spring 1969), 112. See S. Moreh, 'Poetry in Prose in Modern Arabic Literature', *Middle Eastern Studies* IV, 4 (1968), 330–60.

46 See, e.g. his poem *Rubā'iyyāt* in M. M. Badawi, *An Anthology of Modern Arabic Verse*, pp. 230–6.

47 For an assessment in English of Taufīq Ṣāyigh's poetry see Issa J. Boullata, 'The Beleaguered Unicorn: A Study of Tawfīq Ṣāyigh', *JAL*, IV (1973), 69–94. Here are the Arabic titles of the volumes: *Tammūz fi'l Madīna, al-Madār al-Mughlaq; Thalāthūn Qaṣīda, al-Qaṣīda Kāf, Mu'allaqat Taufīq Ṣāyigh; Ḥuzn fī Ḍau' al-Qamar, Ghurfa bi Malāyīn al-Judrān*, and *al-Faraḥ laysa Mihnatī*.

48 Unsī al-Ḥājj. *Lan* (Beirut, 1960), pp. 6–9; 14–15.

49 *Dīwān Nāzik al-Malā'ika* (Beirut, 1970), 2 vols. This is the edition to which references are made in this section. The Arabic titles of the works discussed are: *Qaḍāyā al-Shi'r al-Mu'āṣir, Ma'sāt al-Ḥayāt, Ughniyya li'l Insān* I, II, *'Āshiqat al-Lail, Shaẓāya wa Ramād, Qarārat al-Maujah*, and *Shajarat al-Qamar*, The poems alluded to are *'Āshiqāt al-Lail, al-Ghurūb, Marra'l Qiṭār, al-Uf'uwān, Nihāyat al-Sullam, al-Hāribūn, al-Zā'ir alladhī lam yaji'*, and *Khams Aghānin li'l Alam*.

50 The Arabic titles are *Dalīla, Qālat al-Arḍ, Qaṣā'id Ūlā, Idhā qultu yā Sūriyya, Aurāq fi'l Rīḥ, Aghānī Mihyār al-Dimashqī, Kitāb al-Taḥawwulāt wa'l Hijra fī Aqālīm al-Nahār wa'l Lail, al-Masraḥ wa'l Marāyā, Waqt bain al-Ramād wa'l Ward, Qabr min ajl New York*. The Complete Works edition to which all references to the poems are made is Adūnīs, *al-Āthār al-Kāmila*, 2 vols. (Beirut, 1971). Adūnīs's collection of critical essays used in this discussion is *Zaman al-Shi'r* (Beirut, 1972). On the unusual and somewhat romantic tale of Adūnīs's education see the Introduction to *The Blood of Adonis*, Transpositions of Selected Poems of Adonis (Ali Ahmed Said) by Samuel Hazo (University of Pittsburgh Press, 1971).

51 See the interview with Adūnīs reported in his periodical *Mawāqif* 13/14 (1971), 5.

52 See *Mawāqif*, 15 (June 1971), 3–7.

53 Maṭar published several volumes, e.g. *Min Daftar al-Ṣamt* (1969), *Kitāb al-Arḍ wa'l Dam* (1971), *al-Jū' wa'l Qamar* (1972).

54 The Arabic titles of poems discussed are: *Ḥudūd al-Ya's, Farāgh, Qultu lakum, Laysa laka Ikhtiyār, al-Zamān al-Saghīr, Waṭan, Shajarat al-Nār, Janāzat Imra'a, Mir'āt al-Ard, Muqaddima li Tarīkh Mulūk al-Ṭawā'if*, and *Hādha huwa Ismī*.

55 Khālida Sa'īd, *al-Baḥth 'an al-Judhūr* (Beirut, 1960), p. 60.

56 The Arabic titles of Khāl's works are *al-Ḥurriyya, Hirūdiyā, Dīwān al-Shi'r al-Amrīkī, al-Bi'r al-Mahjūrā, Qaṣ ā'id fi'l Arba'īn*, and *Qaṣā'id Mukhtāra*.

57 *Qaṣā'id Mukhtāra*, p. 22. The Arabic titles of poems are *al-Shā'ir, al-Ḍayā', al-Dāra al-Saudā', Nidā' al-Baḥr, al-Du'ā', al-Safar, al-'Auda, al-Bi'r al-Mahjūra, Umniyyat Shā'ir, Ṣalāh fi'l Haikal, al-'Umr, al-Raḥīl, al-Qaṣīda al-Ṭawīla*.

58 *Al-'Umr*, from *Qaṣā'id Mukhtāra*, pp. 137ff.

59 *Qaṣā'id fi'l Arab'in*, pp. 54, 65.

60 The Arabic titles of Ḥāwī's collections are *Nahr al-Ramād, al-Nāy wa'l Rīḥ* and *Bayādir al-Jū'*. The references are to the second edition of *Nahr* (1961), but to the first edition of the other two.

61 *Al-Baḥḥār wa'l Darwīsh*. For an English translation see *JAL*, I (1970), 83ff. The Arabic titles of other poems alluded to are: *Layālī Bairūt, Na'sh al-Sukārā, Jahīm Bārid, Bilā 'Unwān, Fī Jauf al-Ḥūt, Ḍaḥikāt al-Ṣighār, Sadūm, al-Majūs fī Ūrubba, Ba'd al-Jalīd, al-Ḥubb wa'l Juljula, 'Auda ila Sadūm, al-Jisr, 'Inda'l Baṣṣām, āl-Nāy wa'l Riḥ, Wujūh al-Sindibād, al-Sindibād fī Rihlatihi al-Thāmina, al-Kahf, Jinniyat al-Shāti', La'āzir 'Ām 1962, Ḥufra bilā Qā'*.

62 *Qasā'id Mukhtāra min al-Shi'r al-'Ālamī al-Ḥadīth* (Baghdad, n.d.). The Arabic titles of Sayyāb's works are: *Azhār Dhābila, Asāṭīr, Unshūdat al-Maṭar, al-Ma'bad al-Gharīq*,

Manzil al-Aqnān, Shanashīl Ibnat al-Jalabī, Iqbāl, Qaithārat al-Rīḥ and *A'āṣīr*. The last three were published posthumously.

63 See Issa J. Boullata, 'The Poetic Technique of Badr Shākir al-Sayyāb', *JAL*, II (1971), 104ff.

64 *Ilā Hasnā' al-Qasr* in *Asaṭīr* (Nejev, 1950), p. 93 n.

65 *Ibid.*, pp. 11, 70–2: *Fi'l Sūq al-Qadīm* and *Ughniyya Qadīma*. For an English translation of *Ughniyya* (An Ancient Song) see *JAL*, III (1972), 118–19.

66 The Arabic titles of the poems are: *Ḥaffār al-Qubūr, al-Mūmis al-'Amyā', al-Asliḥa wa'l Aṭfāl.*

67 On the autobiographical interest of the poem see Iḥsān 'Abbās, *al-Sayyāb*, pp. 163ff.

68 In Arabic: *Gharīb 'alā'l Khalīj, Unshūdat al-Maṭar*. See the English translation 'Hymn to Rain' by Adel Salama in *JAL*, III (1972), 119–22 of which some use is made here.

69 See *Mawāqif*, 15 (May–June 1971), 52. Badr Shākir al-Sayyāb, *Unshūdat al-Maṭar*

70 *Al-Nahr wa'l Maut, ibid.*, pp. 141ff. For an English translation of some of Sayyāb's poems including 'The River and Death' and 'City of Sindbad' see *JAL*, I (1970), 119–28.

71 See Iḥsān 'Abbās, *al-Sayyāb*, chapter 21 where he discusses in some detail Sayyāb's debt to Edith Sitwell and Lorca. The Arabic titles of other poems cited here are *Risāla min Qabr, al-Masīḥ ba'd al-Ṣalb, Madīnat al-Sindbad, Madīnah bilā Maṭar*. They are all from *Unshūdat at-Maṭar*.

72 Issa J. Boullata, 'The Poetic Technique of Sayyab', *JAL*, II (1971), 109–10.

73 *Ibid.*, p. 113.

74 Sayyāb, *Unshūdat al-Maṭar*, pp. 154, 157.

75 *Min Ru'yā Fūkāy, ibid.*, pp. 46–57. For a criticism of the use of allusions in this poem see M. Muṣṭafā Badawī, 'T. S. Eliot wa'l Shi'r al-'arabī al-mu'āṣir', *al-Adab* (Cairo), III, 1 (April, 1958), 13ff.

76 *Badr Shākir al-Sayyāb al-Rajul wa'l Shā'ir*, Manshūrāt Aḍwā' (Paris, 1966), p. 25.

77 Sayyāb, *Manzil al-Aqnān* (Beirut, 1963), p. 36: *Sifr Ayyūb*.

78 Sayyāb, *Shanāshīl Ibnat al-Jalabī* (Beirut, 1964), p. 59: *Ahibbīnī*, p. 98: *Fi'l Mustashfā*, p. 19: *Fi'l Lail*. For examples of his extreme eroticism see p. 68.

79 Sayyāb, *Iqbāl* (Beirut, 1965), p. 36: *Ḥāmid*, p. 46: *Fī Ghābat al-Ẓalām*.

80 Khālida Sa'īd, *al-Baḥth*, p. 18.

81 Jaroslav Stetkevyeh, *The Modern Arabic Literary Language* (Chicago, 1970), p. 78. For a detailed study of some of the daring innovations in the language of the modern Iraqi poets Buland Ḥaidarī, al-Malā'ika, al-Bayyātī and al-Sayyāb see the last six Chapters of Ibrāhīm Sāmarrā'ī's book *Lughat al-Shi'r bain Jīlain* (Beirut, n.d.). However, the even more daring use of the language in the later work of someone like Bayyātī had clearly not appeared when the author wrote his study, but for an enthusiastic discussion of it see Ṣabrī Ḥāfiẓ, *Al-Raḥīl ilā Mudun al-Ḥulm* (a study and selection of Bayyātī) (Damascus, 1973), pp. 39ff.

82 Muḥammad al-Māghūṭ, *Ghurfa bi Malāyīn al-Judrān* (Damascus, 1964), pp. 34, 35, 96; 108, Taufiq Ṣāyigh, *Mu'allaqat Taufīq Ṣāyigh* (Beirut, 1963), section 2.

83 See As'ad Razzūq, *Al-Usṭūra fi'l Shi'r al-Mu'āṣir al-Shu'arā' al-Tammūziyyūn* (Beirut, 1959).

84 See Adūnīs, 'Khawāṭir ḥaula tajribatī al-Shi'riyya', *Ādāb*, XIV, 3 (March 1966), 3.

85 Maḥmūd Muḥammad Shākir, *Abāṭīl wa Asmār* (Cairo, 1964), pp. 237ff. The Arabic words he objected to are *al-Khaṭī'a, al-khalās* and *al-salb*. See also 'Abduh Badawī, 'Shu'arā' al-Rafḍ', *al-Thaqāfa*, no. 74 quoted by Hādi Tu'ma, 'Al-Taf'īla bid'a li tabdīd fanni'l shi'r al-'arabī, *al-Aqlām* (Baghdad), (Sept., 1966), III/i, 114ff., in particular Ṭu'ma's attack on Luwīs 'Awaḍ and Ghālī Shukrī.

CHAPTER 7: EPILOGUE

1 Donald Keene, ed., *Modern Japanese Literature: An Anthology* (London, 1956), pp.19–20.
2 *The Times Literary Supplement*, 30 April 1971, p. 492.
3 Stanley Burnshaw, ed., *The Poem Itself* (London, 1964).
4 See *Al-Ādāb* (Beirut), 12 (Dec., 1970), 8.
5 Keene, *Modern Japanese Literature*, p. 19. See also M. ʿAbdel-Hai, 'Shelley and the Arabs: an Essay in Comparative Literature', *JAL*, III (1972), 72–89.
6 Al-Āmidī, *al-Muwāzana*, ed. A. Ṣaqr (Cairo, 1961), pp. 6,256.
7 On the significance of clarity as the *sine qua non* of good style in the Arabic tradition see M. Muṣṭafā Badawī, *Dirāsāt fi'l Shiʿr wa'l Masraḥ* (Cairo, 1960), pp. 32ff. On the Arab critics' insistence on the exact correspondence between the two elements of a simile – another European Neoclassical feature – see Kamal Abu Deeb, 'al-Jurjānī's Theory of Poetic Imagery and its Background', unpublished D.Phil. dissertation (Oxford, 1970), I, 139, 156.
8 G. E. von Grunebaum, 'The Aesthetic Foundation of Arabic Literature', *Comparative Literature*, IV, 4 (Fall, 1952), 323.
9 *Ibid.*, p. 326.
10 *Akhī*: Mīkhā'īl Nuʿaima, *Hams al-Jufūn* (Beirut, 1962), pp. 14ff.
11 *al-Ṣabāḥ al-Jadīd*: Abu'l Qāsim al-Shābbī, *Aghānī al-Ḥayāt* (Cairo, 1955), pp. 159ff.
12 *al-Masā'*: Iliyā Abū Māḍī, *al-Jadāwil* (Beirut, 1961), pp. 56ff.
13 *Min ru'yā Fūkāy*: Badr Shākir al-Sayyāb, *Unshūdat al-Maṭa* (Beirut, 1960), pp. 46ff.
14 *al-Nahr wa'l Maut*: al-Sayyāb, *Unshūdat*, pp. 141ff.
15 al-Sayyāb, *Manzil al-Aqnān* (Beirut, 1963), pp. 36ff.

INDEX